Clothing the Poor in Nineteenth-Century England

In this pioneering study Vivienne Richmond reveals the importance of dress to the nineteenth-century English poor who valued clothing not only for its practical utility, but also as a central element in the creation and assertion of collective and individual identities. During this period of rapid industrialisation and urbanisation, formal dress codes, corporate and institutional uniforms and the spread of urban fashions replaced the informal dress of agricultural England. This laid the foundations of modern popular dress and generated fears about the visual blurring of social boundaries as new modes of manufacturing and retailing expanded the wardrobes of the majority. But a significant impoverished minority remained outside this process. Clothed by diminishing parish assistance, expanding paternalistic charity and the second-hand trade, they formed a 'sartorial underclass' whose material deprivation and visual distinction was a cause of physical discomfort and psychological trauma.

VIVIENNE RICHMOND is a lecturer in Modern British History at Goldsmiths, University of London.

She spoke of the poor of Beccles, being very careful to allude only to their material position. There was too much beer drank, no doubt, and the young women would have finery. Where did they get the money to buy those wonderful bonnets which appeared every Sunday?

Anthony Trollope, *The Way We Live Now*

Clothing the Poor in Nineteenth-Century England

Vivienne Richmond

CAMBRIDGE
UNIVERSITY PRESS

University Printing House, Cambridge CB2 8BS, United Kingdom

Cambridge University Press is part of the University of Cambridge.

It furthers the University's mission by disseminating knowledge in the pursuit of education, learning and research at the highest international levels of excellence.

www.cambridge.org
Information on this title: www.cambridge.org/9781107645349

© Vivienne Richmond 2013

This publication is in copyright. Subject to statutory exception
and to the provisions of relevant collective licensing agreements,
no reproduction of any part may take place without the written
permission of Cambridge University Press.

First published 2013
First paperback edition 2016

A catalogue record for this publication is available from the British Library

Library of Congress Cataloguing in Publication data
Richmond, Vivienne.
Clothing the poor in nineteenth-century England / Vivienne Richmond.
   pages cm.
Includes bibliographical references and index.
ISBN 978-1-107-04227-8 (hardback)
1. Clothing and dress – England – History – 19th century.   2. Poor – Clothing – England – History – 19th century.   3. England – Economic conditions – 19th century.   4. England – Social conditions – 19th century.
I. Title.
GT737.R54   2013
391.0094209′034–dc23   2013013495

ISBN 978-1-107-04227-8 Hardback
ISBN 978-1-107-64534-9 Paperback

Cambridge University Press has no responsibility for the persistence or accuracy of URLs for external or third-party internet websites referred to in this publication, and does not guarantee that any content on such websites is, or will remain, accurate or appropriate.

For my parents

Contents

	List of illustrations	*page* viii
	List of tables	x
	List of abbreviations	xi
	Acknowledgments	xii
	Introduction: Identifying the poor, locating their clothes	1
1	Setting the standard: working-class dress	20
2	'Frankly, a mystery': budgeting for clothes	52
3	'Poverty busied itself': buying clothes	72
4	'Woman's best weapon': needlework and home-made clothing	93
5	'The struggle for respectability'	121
6	The sense of self	161
7	'The bowels of compassion': clothing and the Poor Law	186
8	'An urgent desire to clothe them': ladies' clothing charities	212
9	'We have nothing but our clothes': charity schools and servants	242
10	'The greatest stigma and disgrace': lunatic asylums, workhouses and prisons	261
	Conclusion: No finery	293
	Bibliography	300
	Index	331

Illustrations

1.1 Ethel Melloy with drawers visible below her skirt. *c.*1910. By kind permission of Mrs Ethel Melloy and Mrs Angela MacFarlane Melloy. *page* 37

3.1 Samuel Coulthurst, Flat Iron Market, 1894. Courtesy of Manchester Libraries, Information and Archives, Manchester City Council. 77

3.2 Whit Walk of St Paul's Sunday School, Blackley, Manchester, *c.*1900. Courtesy of Manchester Libraries, Information and Archives, Manchester City Council. 79

4.1 'Education Under the Government Code – Teaching Needlework by Demonstration', *Graphic*, 1883. © The British Library Board HS.74/1099, 1883, p. 641. 103

5.1 Left: Ellen Grounds in Wigan pit-brow working dress with Arthur Munby, *c.*1873. By kind permission of The Master and Fellows of Trinity College Cambridge. Right: Ellen Grounds in day dress, with skirt and apron down, *c.*1873. By kind permission of The Master and Fellows of Trinity College Cambridge. 124

5.2. Left: Ellen Grounds in Sunday best, *c.*1866. By kind permission of The Master and Fellows of Trinity College Cambridge. Right: Ellen Grounds in Sunday best, *c.*1873. By kind permission of The Master and Fellows of Trinity College Cambridge. 128

8.1 E. F. Brewtnall, 'A Jumble Sale: A New Way of Raising Money for Charitable Purposes', *Graphic* 1892. © The British Library Board HS.74/1099, 1892, p. 619. 232

9.1 Left: Girls from Bluecoat School, Isle of Wight, 1865. By kind permission of The Master and Fellows of Trinity College Cambridge. Right: Uniform of the Blue School, Shifnal, the school Hannah Cullwick attended. By kind permission of The Master and Fellows of Trinity College Cambridge. 245

9.2 A general servant in Marylebone, 1872. By kind
permission of The Master and Fellows of Trinity College
Cambridge. 255

10.1 Top: Dining Hall, St Pancras Workhouse, *c.*1897. Mary
Evans Picture Library. Bottom: Dining Hall, St
Marylebone Workhouse, *c.*1905. Mary Evans Picture
Library. 277

Tables

8.1 Items for maternity boxes and ladies' infants as stipulated in *Instructions for Cutting Out Apparel for the Poor* (1789), *The Lady's Economical Assistant* (1808) and *The Workwoman's Guide* (1838). *page* 215

10.1 Examples of clothing issued to prisoners compiled from data in the prison inspectors' 1842 report. 280

Abbreviations

BAWCA	Burnett Archive of Working Class Autobiographies, Brunel University
COC	Churchwardens and Overseers Committee
DHC	Dorset History Centre
ESRO	East Sussex Record Office
GMCRO	Greater Manchester Country Record Office
HRO	Herefordshire Record Office
LLHAC	Lewisham Local History and Archives Centre
LMA	London Metropolitan Archives
MALS	Manchester Archives and Local Studies
RRB	Rotherfield Request Book
SHL	Senate House Library
TCLC, MUNB	Trinity College Library Cambridge, Papers of A. J. Munby
THLHLA	Tower Hamlets Local History Library and Archive
TWL	The Women's Library

Acknowledgments

I must first thank the Arts and Humanities Research Council for funding the doctoral research from which this book has grown. My thesis was expertly and meticulously supervised by Professor Sally Alexander, subsequently my mentor, colleague and dear friend, who arrived at Goldsmiths shortly after me and whose inspiration, encouragement and advocacy on my behalf have kept me there much longer than I ever anticipated. Thank you. Thanks also to Professor David Killingray, my reserve supervisor, especially for making me think about the little things – like scissors (though I still haven't been able to answer most of the questions you asked about them).

I owe an enormous debt to my two anonymous CUP readers, for their invaluable thoughtful and detailed comments and suggestions. Also to my editor, Michael Watson, for seeing the potential in my project and waiting rather longer than planned while I realised it, and to all the production team.

All academics know how difficult it is to juggle teaching, administrative duties and writing, and I am grateful to Goldsmiths for granting me research leave to complete this volume. Also to my Special Subject students who have taken such an interest in my work and made me think about it in so many new ways.

Numerous librarians and archivists have fetched and carried material for me – many thanks to you all and to those people and institutions who have allowed me to reproduce images in this volume: Ethel Melloy and Angela MacFarlane Melloy, The Master and Fellows of Trinity College Cambridge, Mary Evans Picture Library, The British Library, Greater Manchester County Record Office and Manchester Archives and Local Studies.

On a personal note, inexpressible thanks to my parents for unconditional love, an excellent education (which I didn't value enough at the time), patience during what might be termed my 'circuitous years' while I looked for what I wanted to do with my life, faith that I would eventually get there – it's been quite a wait! – and that brilliant little sewing machine.

To Jack and Charlie, who often did their homework while I did mine and who made sure my feet stayed firmly on the ground during my transformation into an academic. On their account I am sincerely grateful that, while I was often pressed for money as a student, we did not have to live like the people I researched for this book. And finally to Kevin who now knows far more about the dress of the poor in nineteenth-century England than he ever expected (or possibly wanted) to, and who has shopped, cooked, laundered and proofread while reaching acceptance of the gradual, awful, realisation of what it takes for this historian to write a book. I never said it would be easy!

Introduction
Identifying the poor, locating their clothes

> During researches over the last twenty-five years or so in rural history I have gathered pockets of information about the way people dressed... before the First World War. I did not, at first, go after specific details about the clothes they wore: they told me about this aspect of their lives of their own accord; it was important to them. Later I became convinced that dress... is an integral part of the history of any society.[1]

My earliest memory is of a multi-coloured chequerboard-pattern skirt I am wearing while sitting by the cooker in the kitchen, aged about three. Then there is the Fair Isle cardigan with enamelled dachshund brooch (a reward for bravery at the doctor's) which I wear while helping to hang out the washing; the Marks & Spencer's houndstooth, scoop-neck pinafore trimmed with three pairs of black ball buttons (Sunday school); a tartan kilt – I still have the matching scarf – the only one of these outfits preserved in a photograph (Kew Gardens); the white Crimplene shift dress with lace yoke (Windsor Safari Park); the turquoise dress with waterfall cuffs (holiday in Devon). Ask me what I was doing and I can probably tell you what I was wearing – or rather, ask me what I was wearing and I can probably tell you what I was doing, for the clothes lead the way in these memories. 'If fashion is your trade', sings Jarvis Cocker in the Pulp song 'Underwear', 'then when you're naked I guess you must be unemployed.'[2] My clothes and my sense of who I am are so inseparable that, potentially, when I am undressed, I don't exist.

My passion for clothes was fostered by my maternal aunts who worked as professional seamstresses and provided much of my childhood clothing.[3] Auntie Rose was my main supplier. She sewed for the Frank Usher label by day and for private clients in her own time to save enough money to buy a house in which she and her mother lived, together with Rose's sister Lil, also a seamstress. The kilt was made by another Auntie

---

[1] George Ewart Evans, 'Dress and the rural historian', *Costume*, 8 (1974), 38–40; 38.
[2] Pulp, 'Underwear', *Different Class* (Universal/Island, 1999).
[3] They were actually my mother's aunts and cousins, but all known to me as 'Aunties'.

Lil, a pleater for The Scotch House. She wasn't actually a blood relation but the close friend of Auntie Bet, who was, and who made shirts for George VI. There was also my father's twin sister, Auntie Julie, a skilled amateur seamstress who came for extended visits from Australia, during which she bought wonderful fabrics from Liberty's. Back home she made some beautiful garments for me. I still have one dress, full-skirted, pink, with a story-border hem.

My mother, also a good home-dressmaker, taught me, the keenest of pupils, to sew and knit when I was very young. Sewing became my main hobby and as a teenager I spent Saturdays running up outfits to wear the same evening. Later, as a mother myself, I sewed and knitted for my two small boys, conscious that my skills as a needlewoman enabled me to dress my family far better than my limited economic circumstances would otherwise have allowed. Being also fascinated with nineteenth-century social history – the men in my mother's family were East End dockers – I became curious about how people then, with little money and many children, managed their clothing. When the history books proved silent I realised I'd have to write my own. This posed something of a challenge, not least because it necessitated a return to college and I was by then a single mother of two children, but I kept us throughout my studies by working as a freelance dressmaker. Daniel Miller proposes that 'things, such as clothing, come not to represent people, but to actually constitute who they are'.[4] As a dressmaker I didn't just make clothes for my clients, but refashioned their identities through the manipulation of a few yards of cloth.

Why dress?

Dress enters so fully into our notions of individuals, that a particular kind of garment has as much human character about it as even a definite form of countenance.[5]

The nineteenth-century was a period of great sartorial change. As cities expanded the loose smocks and sunbonnets of rural England gave way to the tailored business suits of office workers, and corporate and institutional uniforms answered to the growing taxonomic impulse. Cotton gained ascendancy over wool and linen, while new modes of production, distribution and retailing brought cheap, ready-made clothes to the

---

[4] Daniel Miller, *Stuff* (Cambridge: Polity Press, 2010), p. 23.
[5] Henry Mayhew and John Binny, *The Criminal Prisons of London and Scenes of Prison Life* (London: Frank Cass, 1968 [1862]), p. 483.

masses, diminishing the need for the home manufacture of cloth and clothing and speeding the spread of fashions.

Dress served a multiplicity of functions for rich and poor, but since the latter were more limited in their agency and resources, clothing, which often comprised the largest part of their (literally) material possessions, was of supreme significance. In addition to its practical functions of providing physical comfort and protection from the elements, clothing could indicate – or disguise – the wearer's occupational or regional identity, age, gender, religion and social allegiance. It determined inclusion or exclusion, denoted conformity or differentiation, conferred or withheld respectability, attracted admiration and derision and could be the key to advancement or degradation. Charles Russell noted of the Manchester 'street arabs' in the late nineteenth and early twentieth centuries that lack of education excluded them from certain occupations, but the 'want of decent clothes, too', he said, 'prevents their getting the situations usually given to youngsters fresh from school'.[6] An individual's life chances might, therefore, be determined by the possession or lack of a suit of clothes.

In Renaissance Europe, notes Ulinka Rublack, textiles retained their value better than metal currencies with little gold or silver content 'and could be pawned, rented, or sold'.[7] Similarly, in the 1700s, says Beverly Lemire, '[c]lothing was negotiable, portable and readily converted into cash or kind: it was a type of currency in itself'.[8] This remained true in the nineteenth century and clothing was often bought with an eye to its potential for future liquidation. Lemire's analysis of 800 transactions at a Sheffield pawnbroker in 1816 revealed that at least 90 per cent were for clothing or footwear. A similar analysis in London in the 1830s returned at least 79 per cent.[9] Much of the loaned money would have been used to buy food, but many of the poor, especially women and children, would at some point have gone without food to buy clothing. Ultimately, also, when a choice had to be made, clothing could be more important than shelter – even (especially) the homeless needed clothes. And for the poor a choice was always necessary; there was never enough money to pay for clothes *and* food *and* fuel *and* rent. I wanted to find out why, and under

---

[6] Charles E. B. Russell, *Manchester Boys: Sketches of Manchester Lads at Work and Play*, 2nd edn (Manchester University Press, 1913), p. 45. He gives another example on p. 11.
[7] Ulinka Rublack, *Dressing Up: Cultural Identity in Renaissance Europe* (Oxford University Press, 2010), p. 6.
[8] Beverly Lemire, *Dress, Culture and Commerce: The English Clothing Trade Before the Factory, 1660–1800* (Basingstoke: Macmillan, 1997), p. 127.
[9] Beverly Lemire, *The Business of Everyday Life: Gender, Practice and Social Politics in England, c.1600–1900* (Manchester University Press, 2005), p. 95.

what circumstances they prioritised clothing – to reveal why, as George Ewart Evans discovered, 'it was important to them'.[10]

History and 'non-elite' dress

As Lou Taylor pointed out, until the 1970s dress history was largely relegated to the academic hinterland.[11] Since then it has been gaining scholarly recognition which John Styles attributes to the rise of feminist history, cultural studies and a focus on consumption rather than production, all of which are concerned with subjectivities and identity.[12] Despite this, Margaret Spufford, in her pioneering study of seventeenth-century chapmen, noted the imbalance of scholarly attention to the basic needs of human existence and a tendency, when clothing history has been addressed, to focus on elites even though the 'lower orders' formed by far the largest section of the population.[13] Even when nineteenth-century historians have broached the subject of non-elite dress, some, curiously,

---

[10] See the *epigraph* to this chapter.
[11] Lou Taylor, *The Study of Dress History* (Manchester University Press, 2002), pp. 1–2.
[12] John Styles, 'Dress in history: reflections on a contested terrain', *Fashion Theory*, 2:4 (1998), 383–9; 385, 387.
[13] Margaret Spufford, *The Great Reclothing of Rural England: Petty Chapmen and Their Wares in the Seventeenth Century* (London: Hambledon Press, 1984), pp. 98–9. Elizabeth Ewing makes a similar point. Elizabeth Ewing, *Everyday Dress 1650–1900* (London: Batsford, 1984), p. 7. Among historians of the nineteenth century, clothing occurs in the Hammonds' pioneering three-volume study of labouring life, for example, only in their reproduction of labourers' budgets, such as those recorded by Eden at the close of the eighteenth century. J. L. Hammond and Barbara Hammond, *The Village Labourer 1760–1832: A Study in the Government of England Before the Reform Bill* (London: Longmans, Green, and Co., 1911); J. L. Hammond and Barbara Hammond, *The Town Labourer 1760–1832: The New Civilisation* (London: Longmans, Green, and Co., 1917); J. L. Hammond and Barbara Hammond, *The Skilled Labourer 1760–1832* (London: Longmans, Green, and Co., 1919). John Rule is among the few writers of general histories who have considered clothing, but even he devotes only four pages to it compared with twenty-one on food and twenty-six on housing. John Rule, *The Labouring Classes in Early Industrial England 1750–1850* (Harlow: Longman, 1986). Eric Hopkins has short sections on housing and diet, but not clothing, yet he implies its importance when discussing the difficulties of assessing standards of living by pointing out that: 'The cost of food and clothing varied from place to place and from one year to the next'. Eric Hopkins, *A Social History of the English Working Classes 1815–1945* (London: Edward Arnold, 1979). James Treble's study of urban poverty devotes a chapter to food and housing, but less than two pages to clothing. James. H. Treble, *Urban Poverty in Britain 1830–1914* (London: Batsford, 1979). John Burnett has produced dedicated studies on both housing and diet across all classes from 1815 to *c.*1970, but no parallel study of clothing. He does address the issue in his work on the cost of living, but devotes less space to it than to housing and diet. John Burnett, *A Social History of Housing 1815–1970* (Newton Abbot: David & Charles, 1978); John Burnett, *Plenty and Want: A Social History of Diet in England from 1815 to the Present Day*, 3rd edn (Abingdon: Routledge, 1989); John Burnett, *A History of the Cost of Living* (Harmondsworth: Penguin, 1969).

seem to dismiss its significance as they acknowledge it. G. E. Fussell, for example, noted in 1949 the '[p]eculiarities of costume in different districts', but gave examples from just four southern counties before concluding that this afforded 'a fairly complete picture of the appearance of the people in different parts of the country'.[14] Similarly Pamela Clabburn, in the 1970s, found the minimal interest in working-class dress 'understandable, for the poor generally wear a very watered-down version of the dress of the rich, with only now and again a special garment appropriate to a particular trade'.[15] Yet this was in her introduction to an edition of early-nineteenth-century illustrations whose author had set out to produce seventeen volumes specifically to catalogue the great variety of dress among labourers nationwide.

Happily, the scholarly neglect of English non-elite clothing has begun to change, not least with John Styles's magnificent examination of eighteenth-century plebeian fashions.[16] There has also been sporadic interest in occupational dress, but as the authors range across several centuries, countries and classes – skilled craftsmen and professionals, as well as the semi-skilled, or unskilled – the attention paid to the nineteenth-century English poor is necessarily partial.[17] Also, studies of occupational dress say very little about what clothing meant, how it was obtained, or its place in the hierarchy of domestic priorities. Yet as Negley Harte has long argued, dress history, to be meaningful, must be studied in its economic, cultural and social context.[18] Without this we have, as T. H. Breen says, only 'decontextualized things... that no longer tell us stories about the creative possibilities of possession, about the process of self-fashioning'.[19]

Recent, more nuanced studies, focusing on the dress of specific sections of the population or on the use and meaning of particular fabrics or garments have begun to address this. Beverly Lemire has blazed a trail

---

[14] G. E. Fussell, *The English Rural Labourer, His Home, Furniture, Clothing and Food from Tudor to Victorian Times* (London: Batchworth Press, 1949), pp. 74–6.

[15] Pamela Clabburn (ed.), *Working Class Costume from Sketches of Characters by William Johnstone White, 1818* (London: Costume Society, 1971), Introduction.

[16] John Styles, *The Dress of the People: Everyday Fashion in Eighteenth-Century England* (New Haven and London: Yale University Press, 2007).

[17] See Phillis Cunnington, *Costume of Household Servants From the Middle Ages to 1900* (London: Adam and Charles Black, 1974); Phillis Cunnington and Catherine Lucas, *Occupational Costume in England From the 11th Century to 1914* (London: Adam and Charles Black, 1967); Christobel Williams-Mitchell, *Dressed for the Job: The Story of Occupational Costume* (Poole: Blandford, 1982); Diana de Marly, *Working Dress: A History of Occupational Costume* (London: Batsford, 1986); Madeleine Ginsburg, *Victorian Dress in Photographs* (London: Batsford, 1982).

[18] L. Taylor, *Study of Dress History*, pp. 67–8.

[19] T. H. Breen, 'The meanings of things: interpreting the consumer economy in the eighteenth century', in John Brewer and Roy Porter (eds), *Consumption and the World of Goods* (London: Routledge, 1993), pp. 249–60; 251.

with her extensive and illuminating work on the rise and use of cotton in the eighteenth and early nineteenth centuries.[20] Steven King and Peter Jones have both highlighted the role of the parish as a supplier of clothing under the Poor Law.[21] Christopher Breward's analysis of urban male consumption emphasises the relationships between dress, class, identity and display.[22] And Laura Ugolini's work on menswear between the 1880s and the beginning of the Second World War examines the connection between masculinity and consumption, as does Clare Rose's study of late-Victorian boys' clothes which also considers the role of clothing in the creation of normative modes of 'respectability'.[23] Alison Toplis's thesis on retailing in Herefordshire and Worcestershire illustrates the range of acquisition methods, legal and illicit, independent and assisted, available to provincial non-elite consumers during the first half of the nineteenth century, while Rachel Worth has highlighted the middle-class lament at the perceived demise of an idyllicised rural dress.[24]

While most of these authors have focused on one half of the nineteenth century, this study spans the period from the late eighteenth to early twentieth centuries. My focus is the changes in the dress of the poor resulting from the industrialisation, urbanisation and democratisation that characterised the period, disrupting traditional communities and generating fears about the blurring of social boundaries. Although, as Lemire reminds us, English sumptuary legislation ended in 1604, 'governments and moralists [still] claimed the right to restrain material expression within the lower ranks' in an attempt to maintain separation between classes.[25] In the nineteenth century, under the pervasive

---

[20] See in particular Beverly Lemire, *Fashion's Favourite: The Cotton Trade and the Consumer in Britain, 1660–1800* (Pasold Research Fund and Oxford University Press, 1991).

[21] Steven King, *Poverty and Welfare in England 1700–1850* (Manchester University Press, 2000); Steven King, 'Reclothing the English poor, 1750–1840', *Textile History*, 33:1 (2002), 37–47; Peter Jones, 'Clothing the poor in early-nineteenth-century England', *Textile History*, 37:1 (2006), 17–37; Peter D. Jones, '"I cannot keep my place without being deascent": pauper letters, parish clothing and pragmatism in the south of England, 1750–1830', *Rural History*, 20:1 (2009), 31–49.

[22] Christopher Breward, *The Hidden Consumer: Masculinities, Fashion and City Life 1860–1914* (Manchester University Press, 1999), p. 95.

[23] Laura Ugolini, *Men and Menswear: Sartorial Consumption in Britain 1880–1939* (Aldershot: Ashgate, 2007); Clare Rose, *Making, Selling and Wearing Boys' Clothes in Late-Victorian England* (Farnham: Ashgate, 2010).

[24] Alison E. M. Toplis, 'The non-elite consumer and "wearing apparel" in Herefordshire and Worcestershire, 1800–1850', PhD, University of Wolverhampton (2008). Rachel Worth, 'Rural laboring dress, 1850–1900: some problems of representation', *Fashion Theory*, 3:3 (1999), 323–42; Rachel Worth, 'Rural working-class dress, 1850–1900: a peculiarly English tradition?', in Christopher Breward, Becky Conekin and Caroline Cox (eds), *The Englishness of English Dress* (Oxford: Berg, 2002), pp. 97–112.

[25] Lemire, *Business of Everyday Life*, p. 110.

influence of evangelicalism which regarded social stratification as providential, this was effected directly by supplying only 'useful and necessary' clothing through the Poor Law and charity, and indirectly via a constant stream of didactic literature decrying 'finery', which was perceived to betoken pride, vanity, luxury, idleness and improvidence, especially when worn by the poor. 'Ignota', for example, writing in *The Cottager's Monthly Visitor* in March 1828, warned that dress was dangerous to both sexes and all ranks, but especially to middle- and lower-class women since: 'The present low price of articles of dress naturally tempts persons to an improper fondness for show, and seems to plead an excuse for it.' But this might attract the attention of social superiors, leading many 'once lovely females' to 'perish in vice and infamy' at the hands of those 'who would be but too ready to take liberties with persons who had the slightest appearance of levity and vanity'.[26] The fault for such catastrophe would lie not only with the assailant, but also with the females who tempted them, reflecting what Alan Hunt identifies as 'a moral preoccupation with female modesty that mingled with a concern about the controllability of women'.[27] Borrowing from linguistics Roland Barthes proposes distinguishing between clothing and dress, with clothing being 'the structural, institutional form of what is worn... (that which corresponds to language)', and dress being 'this same form when actualized, individualized, worn... (that which corresponds to speech)'. Within this framework, and during a period of increasing demands for political representation, efforts to restrict the dress of the poor can be read as attempts to silence them.[28]

Identifying 'the poor'...

Many people who talk glibly of 'the poor' as of one homogenous group fail to recognise how sharply divided are the social classes and how immensely various the standards of life.[29]

A 1999 inter-disciplinary conference at Oxford Brookes University, 'The Dress of the Poor 1750–1900: Old and New Perspectives', was the clearest indication of the awakening of academic interest in this

---

[26] *The Cottager's Monthly Visitor*, 8 (1828), 115–16.
[27] Alan Hunt, *Governance of the Consuming Passions: A History of Sumptuary Law* (Basingstoke: Macmillan, 1996), p. 218.
[28] Roland Barthes, *The Fashion System*, trans. Matthew Ward and Richard Howard (Berkeley: University of California Press, 1990 [1967]), p. 18.
[29] Mrs Carl Meyer and Clementina Black, *Makers of Our Clothes: A Case for Trade Boards* (London: Duckworth and Co., 1909), p. 164.

subject.³⁰ Inevitably, as an initial venture into largely uncharted waters, the conference raised more questions than it answered, chief among which were: What constituted poverty? Who were 'the poor'? These questions are still in need of a conclusive answer and to some extent it is perhaps easier to define who, for the purposes of this volume, 'the poor' were not rather than who they were. So, they were not synonymous with the 'lower orders', despite the tendency of wealthier contemporaries, especially in the early part of the century, to treat either group as an homogenous mass. According to François Bédarida, in the latter part of the nineteenth century the 'lower orders' accounted for five-sixths of the population and could be divided into skilled, semi-skilled and unskilled. Fifteen per cent were skilled and could earn around £80–90 per year, 45 per cent were unskilled and could expect to earn around half that amount while the remaining 40 per cent of semi-skilled workers could expect to earn about two-thirds as much as their skilled contemporaries.³¹ Nor, although they formed a part of them, were 'the poor' interchangeable with 'the working, or labouring, class(es)'. These terms mask a complex social stratification in which, as John Burnett underlines, 'there were infinite gradations of skill and an infinite range of earnings, which gave some workers unprecedented standards of comfort while plunging others into unparalleled poverty'.³² For the same reason, in the parlance of modern historiography, 'the poor' does not equate to 'non-elite', although that has been my focus in this introduction so far.

The problem of identifying 'the poor' is exacerbated by the absence of a precise and stable concept of poverty. As Gertrude Himmelfarb shows, from Edmund Burke's 1795 attempt to differentiate 'the labouring people' who earned their own livelihood from those dependent on aid, to the distinction in the 1834 amended Poor Law between poverty and indigence, to the 'discovery' of poverty manifested in Mayhew's mid-century *London Labour and the London Poor*, and the *fin-de-siècle* social surveys of

---

[30] Selected papers were published in *Textile History*, 33:1 (2002). See also Vivienne Richmond, 'Report back: "The dress of the poor 1750–1900"', *History Workshop Journal*, 49 (2000), 271–3.
[31] François Bédarida, trans. A. S. Forster and Jeffrey Hodgkinson, *A Social History of England 1851–1990* (London: Routledge, 1991), pp. 56, 60–1.
[32] Burnett, *History of the Cost of Living*, p. 195. Robert Roberts makes the same point. Robert Roberts, *The Classic Slum: Salford Life in the First Quarter of the Century* (Harmondsworth: Penguin, 1973), Chapter 1. See also Brian Harrison, *Peaceable Kingdom: Stability and Change in Modern Britain* (Oxford: Clarendon Press, 1982), pp. 159–60; Barry Reay, *Microhistories: Demography, Society and Culture in Rural England, 1800–1930* (Cambridge University Press, 2002), pp. 152–3.

Charles Booth and Seebohm Rowntree, 'the mischievous ambiguity of the word "poor"' persisted.[33]

According to Steven King and Christiana Payne, there is 'convincing evidence' to show that in the early nineteenth century:

at least 70 per cent of all people would experience part of their lives in absolute or relative poverty... However, this 'crude' perspective really conflates the *risk of poverty* and the *actuality of poverty*. In practice, only perhaps one-fifth of the 'labouring classes' might be actually 'poverty stricken' (in the sense of being dependent upon community or charity or on the margins of being in such a position) at any point in time.[34]

Nevertheless, in a separate study of English poverty King argues that in the early nineteenth century '[m]ore people became more poor', while according to Bédarida although by the close of the century living standards for skilled workers had improved and industrialisation had restructured occupations and industries, the 'lowest ranks of the proletariat... remained chained to their degradation'.[35] As Eric Hobsbawm emphasised, the transition to wage labour meant that insecurity hung like a pestilence over the lives of nineteenth-century workers.[36] Lady Bell considered that most of the employees at her husband's Middlesbrough ironworks were:

living under conditions in which the slightest lapse from thrift and forethought is necessarily conspicuous, and brings its immediate consequences... any indisposition, any passing bodily ills... assume a more sinister aspect when physical discomfort and suffering are but a small part of the misfortune they entail, when there is not one penny to meet the extra expense by which alleviation would be bought, unless it is taken off something else which up to that moment has seemed essential.[37]

By the end of the 1800s investigators such as Charles Booth and Seebohm Rowntree were seeking to define poverty on an empirical basis with their respective surveys of London and York. Booth set the poverty

---

[33] S. G. and E. O. A. Checkland (eds), *The Poor Law Report of 1834* (Harmondsworth: Penguin, 1974), p. 334. For a full discussion of changing concepts of poverty in nineteenth-century England, see Gertrude Himmelfarb, *The Idea of Poverty: England in the Early Industrial Age* (London: Faber & Faber, 1985); Gertrude Himmelfarb, *Poverty and Compassion: The Moral Imagination of the Late Victorians* (New York: Knopf, 1981).

[34] Steven King and Christiana Payne, 'The dress of the poor', *Textile History*, 33:1 (2002), 3–8; 3.

[35] S. King, *Poverty and Welfare*, p. 105; Bédarida, *Social History of England*, pp. 64–5.

[36] Eric Hobsbawm, *The Age of Capital 1848–1875* (London: Weidenfeld & Nicolson, 1995), pp. 219–20. Bédarida also stresses the insecurity of the workers, living 'ever on the verge of pauperism'. Bédarida, *Social History of England*, pp. 150–1.

[37] Lady Bell, *At the Works: A Study of a Manufacturing Town* (London: Virago, 1985 [1907]), pp. 52–3.

line at an income of less than 18–21s. a week 'for a moderate family' and unexpectedly, the surveys revealed around 30 per cent of the population in receipt of an income inadequate for their support.[38] Rowntree's subsequent rural survey, with May Kendall, published in 1913, adjusted the poverty line to 20s. 6d. for a family of five. The findings revealed that with the exception of five northern counties – where the availability of alternative employments increased the agricultural wage – and despite having calculated 'a poverty line so low as to be open to the criticism of serious inadequacy ... the average earnings in every county of England and Wales are below it'.[39]

Booth distinguished between the 'poor' whom he described 'as living under a struggle to obtain the necessaries of life and make both ends meet', and the 'very poor' who lived 'in a state of chronic want'.[40] Rowntree's pioneering concept of 'primary' and 'secondary' poverty, defined the first as: 'Families whose total earnings are insufficient to obtain the minimum necessaries for the maintenance of merely physical efficiency'; and the second as: 'Families whose total earnings would be sufficient for the maintenance of merely physical efficiency were it not that some portion of it is absorbed by other expenditure, either useful or wasteful.'[41] Rowntree, as Asa Briggs points out, was also unique in identifying alternating cycles of 'want and comparative plenty' through which an individual might pass in the course of a lifetime, with poverty most likely to occur in childhood, as the parent of young children, and in old age.[42] Rowntree's model was based on the two-parent family, but there were also many households which deviated from this, not least the numerous widows and deserted women – and their dependants – unsupported by a male wage, who experienced extended periods of extreme poverty.

Rowntree's conclusion that 10 per cent of the population of York lived in primary, and 18 per cent in secondary, poverty was based solely on

---

[38] Charles Booth, *Life and Labour of the People in London*, 17 vols (London: Macmillan, 1902–3), *First Series: Poverty*, vol. I, p. 33. B. Seebohm Rowntree, *Poverty: A Study of Town Life* (Bristol: Policy Press, 2000 [1901]), pp. 117–18; 299–301. For debate about the reliability of Booth's and Rowntree's empiricism see Carl Chinn, *Poverty Amidst Prosperity: The Urban Poor in England, 1834–1914* (Manchester University Press, 1995), pp. 30–2. Similarly, Lady Bell calculated that the inhabitants of one third of the 900 houses 'carefully investigated' for her study were either 'absolutely poor' or 'so near the poverty-line that they are constantly passing over it', their lives 'an unending struggle... to keep abreast of the most ordinary, the simplest, the essential needs'. Bell, *At the Works*, pp. 50–1.
[39] B. Seebohm Rowntree and May Kendall, *How the Labourer Lives: A Study of the Rural Labour Problem* (London: Thomas Nelson and Sons, 1913), pp. 28–30.
[40] Booth, *Life and Labour*, First Series: Poverty, vol. I, p. 33.
[41] Rowntree, *Poverty*, pp. 86–7.
[42] Asa Briggs, *A Study of the Work of Seebohm Rowntree 1871–1954* (London: Longmans, 1961), pp. 40–1.

an assessment of the income necessary to meet physical needs – food, rent, light, fuel and clothing. He made no allowance for what he termed the 'mental, moral and social sides of human nature'.[43] But his explicit disregard of these factors was implicit recognition that poverty was not simply the absence of the means of subsistence but a complex relative experience rooted in customary ways of life.

Max Hartwell argues that:

three concepts... underline all ideas of poverty: first, *subsistence*, an empirical concept of the real wage necessary to maintain life and economic efficiency; second, *normative*, a value concept of what is reasonable in any given society; third, *relative*, a relative deprivation concept of poverty felt, and experienced, because of inequality.[44]

The difficulty with these three concepts is determination. First, it is often impossible to establish the actual income of any individual or family which varied with, among other things, the trade cycle, health and the number and ages of any children. But even if precise income figures were available, considerations such as who managed the budget, their financial skills and priorities, affected the distribution of income among individual family members. As Lady Bell realised:

There are so many uncertain elements to deal with, such a constant variation of possibility, dependent upon the health, the temperament, the capacity, of both the man and the woman concerned, that though we may attempt to lay down general rules, we shall be constantly misled in our judgment of individual instances. When we say that what for one household is enough is for another absolutely not enough, we are simply restating what may be said of all human beings in any class.[45]

Carl Chinn highlights the problems of both the normative and relative elements of Hartwell's model. In terms of the normative he points out that as far back as 1776 Adam Smith had argued that poverty had to be seen not only in terms of the minimum necessary 'for the support of life, but whatever the custom of the country renders it indecent for creditable people, even of the lowest orders to be without'.[46] According to Lorna Weatherill, even in the seventeenth century goods considered to be necessities were no longer limited simply to those things without

---

[43] Rowntree, *Poverty*, p. 87.
[44] R. M. Hartwell, 'The consequences of the Industrial Revolution in England for the poor', in R. M. Hartwell (ed.), *The Long Debate on Poverty: Eight Essays on Industrialisation and 'The Condition of England'* (London: Institute of Economic Affairs, 1972), pp. 1–22; p. 12.
[45] Bell, *At the Works*, pp. 52–3.
[46] Chinn, *Poverty Amidst Prosperity*, p. 24. Michael Rose made a similar point. Michael E. Rose, *The Relief of Poverty 1834–1914* (Basingstoke: Macmillan, 1972), p. 6.

which physical life could not be maintained.[47] The difficulty lies in identifying a consensus on what those necessities were, which in turn can lead to problems of relativism since persons with high expectations that went unmet might consider themselves poor, while others with lower expectations might perceive them as comfortable.[48]

Inability to precisely define 'the poor' is frustrating but unavoidable, and those who employed, lectured to, educated and assisted them were often equally imprecise in their definition. According to Michel Foucault, '[t]he "Poor Man" was a vague notion', and in many instances the individuated poor man – or woman – scarcely existed, but was subsumed into the homogenised ranks of 'the poor' who, as John Barrell puts it, existed in the collective imaginations of the wealthy, as 'the distant generalised objects of fear and benevolence'.[49] I have adopted a broad definition of 'the poor', incorporating those dependent upon an income derived from earnings, poor relief or charity which, at best, could provide for little more than the minimum quantities of the basic necessities of food, clothing and shelter and, at worst, would not extend even to these. Understanding what, culturally and socially, constituted the minimum quantities of necessary clothing and the form they took is part of my project. And while this book is concerned with the experiences of people living in, or hovering on the brink of poverty, because it was a state through which many people passed at different times in their lives it is concerned not only with those who were born in need and remained there, but also those people who entered poverty from a period of greater prosperity and did so, therefore, with more material resources upon which to draw. Finally, I must emphasise that I place a greater focus on poverty in the family context, rather than with marginal groups such as prostitutes and vagrants.

. . . locating their clothes

The legitimisation of dress history as a scholarly subject has raised questions about the way in which it can and should be studied, evidenced by a 1997 conference at the Gallery of Costume, Manchester, 'Dress in History: Studies and Approaches'. Among the issues that arose were the tensions between object-based and social historians, the latter, says Lorna Weatherill, showing a 'surprising disregard for the physical remains

---

[47] Lorna Weatherill, *Consumer Behaviour and Material Culture in Britain 1660–1760*, 2nd edn (London: Routledge, 1996), p. 15.
[48] Chinn, *Poverty Amidst Prosperity*, p. 24.
[49] Michel Foucault, *Madness and Civilization: A History of Insanity in the Age of Reason*, trans. Richard Howard (London and New York: Routledge, 2001 [1967]), p. 219. John Barrell, *The Dark Side of the Landscape: The Rural Poor in English Paintings 1730–1840* (Cambridge University Press, 1980), p. 3.

of the past' and tending to use them solely 'as illustrative material for their studies'.[50] This is less of a problem among historians of the dress of the poor since, with a few exceptions, the object-based approach is hampered by the paucity of extant garments. As Spufford discovered, 'the clothes of the humble... had a very slim chance of survival indeed', and very few have done so.[51] The poor's clothing was worn until it fell apart, or passed on to other people, salvaged to patch other garments and sold as rags for recycling. 'As garments became worn', wrote waggoner's daughter, Susan Silvester, born in 1878, 'the good parts were cut out and made into new articles. The worn parts became dusters, dish-cloths, and floor-cloths ... the feet of stockings which were past further darning were cut off and new ones knitted on'.[52]

For C. V. Horner born in 1897, the son of a Wensleydale gamekeeper, a favourite winter pastime 'was making hearth rugs from old clothes cut into strips about four inches long' which were poked through a piece of hessian.[53] Silvester and Horner were by no means among the poorest, but they exemplify the culture of recycling that predominated even at the end of the period. Any clothing that might have survived would usually have been worn, faded and patched and so lacking the aesthetic qualities that more generally make clothes appealing to collectors. Worth suggests that middle-class romanticisation of the vanishing picturesque sun bonnet and embroidered agricultural labourer's smock means these were the garments most likely to be preserved and so now found in museum collections, presenting a distorted and partial picture of nineteenth-century proletarian dress.[54] By the time the importance of 'history from below' was recognised in the 1970s, most clothes of the poor from earlier centuries had long since disintegrated. One of the arguments I develop in the following chapters is the continuing reliance of the poor on second-hand garments and, as Madeleine Ginsburg points out, 'the staples of the nineteenth-century second-hand clothing trade are most of the items missing from most museum collections'.[55]

---

[50] Styles, 'Dress in history', 383. See also L. Taylor, *Study of Dress History*, p. 64; Weatherill, *Consumer Behaviour*, p. 21.
[51] Spufford, *Great Reclothing*, p. 130.
[52] Burnett Archive of Working Class Autobiographies (hereafter BAWCA), 1:628, Susan Silvester, 'In a world that has gone', p. 4.
[53] BAWCA, 2:422, C. V. Horner, 'Up and downs. A lifetime spent in the Yorkshire Dales', p. 20. For a discussion of the poetics and symbolism of the rag rug see Carolyn Steedman, *Dust* (Manchester University Press, 2001), pp. 112–41.
[54] R. Worth, 'Rural working-class dress', p. 104. R. Worth, 'Rural laboring dress', 330–2, and 335–7 for a discussion of Thomas Hardy's disappointment at the decline of these garments in both his fiction and non-fiction writing.
[55] Madeleine Ginsburg, 'Rags to riches: the second-hand clothes trade 1700–1978', *Costume*, 14 (1980), 121–35; 128.

Nor can nineteenth-century historians turn to the probate inventories on which Spufford's and Weatherill's studies were based, their compulsory production having ceased in 1782.[56] And sadly there was no English counterpart of Frédéric Le Play, whose systematic collection of data on clothing ownership and cost over six decades allowed Diana Crane to investigate the wardrobes of nineteenth-century French working-class families.[57] But the dress of the poor surfaces repeatedly in a plethora of other sources which, borrowing from New Historicism's 'fascination with the entire range of diverse expressions by which a culture makes itself manifest', form the evidential base for this book: autobiographies and diaries, evidence submitted to Parliamentary Commissions, inspectors' reports, sermons, religious tracts, parish magazines, instruction books for district visitors and domestic servants, accounts of foreign visitors, newspapers, journals, novels and short stories, sewing manuals, school curricula, churchwardens', overseers' and Poor Law Guardians' accounts and relief books, records of charities, schools, prisons, workhouses, asylums, social investigators, shops and advertisements.[58]

Most of these sources have been mined by nineteenth-century historians for a variety of purposes, but rarely for what they reveal about proletarian clothing. For example, so extraordinary was the romance between Arthur Munby and Hannah Cullwick and its detailed recording in their diaries, that scholarly work on them has focused on that relationship, or on the questions they raise about class and gender relations. But as Michael Hiley shows, on his travels around the country in search of working women Munby also often recorded what they were wearing.[59] Mayhew similarly took a keen interest in the sartorial practices of the London poor, but Munby takes the reader beyond the metropolis into the surrounding countryside of Surrey, Kent, Middlesex and Berkshire, south to Devon and Hampshire and northwards to Staffordshire, Lancashire, Cheshire, Shropshire, Derbyshire and Yorkshire.

Munby's eye for detail and his desire to record accurately mean there is little reason to doubt his descriptions of the style of clothes worn by the women he encountered. But any assumption that his views about them were shared by those women is prohibited by his anxiety about the demise of 'rustic dress' and his condemnation of urban fashions.

---

[56] Spufford, *Great Reclothing*; Weatherill, *Consumer Behaviour*, p. 3.
[57] Diana Crane, *Fashion and Its Social Agendas: Class, Gender and Identity in Clothing* (Oxford University Press, 2000).
[58] Catherine Gallagher and Stephen Greenblatt, *Practicing New Historicism* (University of Chicago Press, 2001), p. 13.
[59] Michael Hiley, *Victorian Working Women: Portraits from Life* (London: Gordon Fraser, 1979).

Equally, Mayhew was clearly attracted to the more colourful characters he encountered and his biographer, Anne Humpherys, points out that her subject's 'sincere desire to follow scientific methodology was at times coupled with assertions of blatant prejudice'.[60] But again, there is little to suggest inaccuracy in the costumes he describes even though we must treat his analyses of them with caution.

Also, as Sally Alexander says: 'Every Victorian inquiry into the working classes is steeped in ... improving moralism', with the poor 'seldom allowed to speak for themselves.'[61] And like Munby and Mayhew, the majority of the sources listed above tell us less about how the poor viewed their clothing than what wealthier contemporaries had to say about it, which was often a great deal. Parliamentary Commissioners, philanthropists, employers, clergy, district visitors, teachers, moralists, social investigators and reformers all took an active interest in what the poor were, or were not, wearing and used their extensive involvement in charity and institutional work as a means to try to influence the kind of clothes the poor wore. And the guiding spirit of nineteenth-century philanthropy was evangelicalism with its emphasis on self-help and its condemnation of 'finery'.

Furthermore, as Keith Snell cautions, some of the issues which concerned the poor in the nineteenth century are quite remote and we must try to comprehend and adopt contemporary priorities.[62] Similarly, there is the risk of our own experiences and assumptions influencing our interpretation of the past – Anna Davin gives the example of higher present-day expectations of domestic warmth.[63] And so if we are to understand how the poor viewed their clothes we must seek out their own voices. These do come through in their statements to Munby and Mayhew, as well as to Parliamentary Commissions and Select Committees, but are filtered through socially superior intermediaries and the subjects may have felt intimidated, or tailored their evidence to suit what they believed was required. It is, though, striking how often and how insistently witnesses assert the issues they feel to be important, against the grain of

---

[60] Anne Humpherys, *Travels into the Poor Man's Country: The Work of Henry Mayhew* (Athens: University of Georgia Press, 1977), p. 2.
[61] Sally Alexander, *Becoming a Woman and Other Essays in 19th and 20th Century Feminist History* (New York University Press, 1995), p. 6. As Aileen Ribeiro has shown, the relationship between dress and morality has a long history. Aileen Ribeiro, *Dress and Morality* (London: Batsford, 1986).
[62] K. D. M. Snell, *Annals of the Labouring Poor: Social Change and Agrarian England 1660–1900* (Cambridge University Press, 1985), pp. 3–4. Lorna Weatherill makes a similar point. Weatherill, *Consumer Behaviour*, p. 15.
[63] Anna Davin, *Growing Up Poor: Home, School and Street in London 1870–1914* (London: Rivers Oram Press, 1996), p. 8.

the interrogators' agenda, and how stoutly they defend their skills, customs and culture in the face of official doubt or disapproval. In so doing they help to demonstrate the gulf in understanding between rich and poor.

The other source I have used extensively to access the poor's own views is their autobiographies. They catalogue not only poverty and the want of clothing, but also the joy it could bring, its multiplicity of use and meaning and the mechanisms by which it was acquired – the lived experience of dress. Clare Rose is critical of autobiographies as a source for the history of dress, questioning the 'seemingly unmediated evidence of past practice' they offer.[64] But it is the very fact that they *are* mediated, by the passage of time, the limitations of memory and the necessity of selection when recalling a life's experiences, which makes them so valuable. What impresses is the vividness and frequency of the memories of clothing often after several decades, and in many autobiographies its first mention occurs in the opening pages. The 'earliest recollection' of Jack Goring, for example, a London porter's son born in 1861, was of seeing his mother 'drop her crinoline over her head before putting her dress on over her white petticoat'.[65]

The representative nature of autobiographies is always questionable, but just as George Ewart Evans discovered the importance of clothing from the unsolicited information supplied by his oral history interviewees, so the prevalence of dress in so many written life histories clearly reveals it as a common preoccupation. To accusations of subjectivity I can only say that this is wholly appropriate because clothing is subjective and it is a part of my purpose here to demonstrate that, despite small wardrobes and restricted finances, the dress of the poor engendered a rich variety of experiences and meanings. Additionally, accounts of ostracism due to being inappropriately clothed, for example, or the role of dress in communal celebrations move the discussion outside the author's unique experience to reveal shared standards, expectations and understandings.

Where possible I have tried to corroborate the evidence of one autobiography with others, or with other types of sources. But autobiographies can also be usefully compared with other sources to highlight the disparity between theory and practice. School sewing manuals with rigidly stratified attainment goals contrast sharply with individual accounts of ineptitude. Manuals for employers repeatedly echo the fear that domestic servants waste money dressing above their station, while many servants'

[64] C. Rose, *Making, Selling and Wearing*, p. 227.
[65] BAWCA, 1:274, Jack Goring, 'Untitled'.

autobiographies reveal them to be in receipt of wages barely sufficient to dress decently.

* * *

This book explores four themes beginning with the practicalities of what people wore, and how they budgeted for and obtained clothing when reliant on their own resources. Chapter 1 sets out the sartorial landscape the poor inhabited and against which their clothing was assessed. It examines the changes in English working-class dress during the century as the population and economy changed from largely rural and agricultural to urban and industrial. As part of this process cotton mostly replaced linen and wool, and clothing prices fell as new manufacturing processes increased production of, and access to, cheap ready-made garments, fuelling fears, already well established, that sartorial democracy was blurring the visual distinction between the upper and lower classes.

Chapter 2 demonstrates the very small sums of money available to the poor to buy clothes, women's responsibility for the domestic budget and the place of clothing in it, the familial hierarchy of clothing priorities and the inferior goods the poor were forced to buy. New forms of retailing are examined in Chapter 3, encompassing covered markets, department stores, co-operatives, ready-made-clothing shops and mail order, to show that the poor were largely excluded from them, remaining highly dependent on second-hand clothing when the more affluent working classes were increasingly moving to new clothing. After brief consideration of clothing made by tailors and dressmakers, and alternative sources such as clothing as prizes, borrowing and theft of garments, the chapter concludes by highlighting the crucial role of credit and pawning in the clothing strategies of many poor families.

Chapter 4 examines the continuing practical and ideological importance of home clothing production. It details the emphasis on plain needlework in the curricula of state-funded elementary schools and the simultaneous extra-curricular focus on needlework education for working-class females of all ages. Home-made clothing was a necessary means of providing and maintaining garments for poor families, but it was also a focal site for debates about the relationship between women, paid work and industrialisation. In stressing the perceived intrinsic link between needlework and femininity, this chapter forms a bridge to the book's second theme: the social and cultural significance of dress. In Chapter 5 this is explored through the relationship between dress and respectability, discussing how this could be conferred or withheld by the presence or absence of certain garments, as well as their condition, and the supreme importance of 'Sunday best'. This chapter also questions what, given the limited water supplies available to the poor, constituted cleanliness of bodies and clothing, and examines attitudes toward undress as well as the implications for the condition of clothing of the way menstruation was managed and clothes were stored. Chapter 6 takes a close look at two autobiographies, that of waterman-turned-miller Joseph Terry, born *c.*1816, and dressmaker-turned-domestic servant Louise Jermy, born in 1877. Both aid our understanding of the role clothing plays among children and young adults in the creation of identity, affective relationships, and the sense of self, and help to fill what Lou Taylor identifies as '[o]ne of the great voids of dress history', which is 'its failure to examine emotional responses to clothing and appearance'.[66] The chapter ends by taking Isobel Armstrong's idea of the creation of a vitreous scopic culture to suggest that the full-length mirror, plate glass and photography offered new forms of bodily self-awareness which largely functioned to the disadvantage of the poor.

This understanding of the social and cultural importance of dress, especially its role in self-determination, is necessary to fully appreciate the privation of those to whom it was denied, which is explored in the third theme: parish and charity clothing. Chapter 7 examines the provision of clothing under the Poor Laws. Through case studies of Sussex and Kent, it engages with Steven King's and Peter Jones's claims that parishes clothed their poor well, both before and after 1834, to argue that the abolition of outdoor clothing relief was a central aim of the New Poor Law, and the creation of self-help clothing societies, which supplied only utilitarian garments and fabrics, was not a supplement to, but a replacement for, parish provision. Chapter 8 outlines the vast range of clothing charity provided by middle- and upper-class women which, like the clothing societies, operated under the influence of evangelicalism and supported the dual credos of self-help and 'no finery'. However, it also details the emergence in the 1880s of new forms of clothing charity, such as the Needlework Guilds and jumble sales which, amid widening opportunities for middle- and upper-class women to participate in the public sphere and the rise of liberalism and Christian Socialism, sought more efficient ways to aid the poor and, sometimes, put fewer restrictions on the clothing they supplied.

The fourth and final theme, uniforms, is also concerned with the limitation on sartorial freedom resulting from the imposition of dress. Chapter 9 begins with an examination of uniforms in charity schools to understand their psychological effect on the wearer and the extent to which those worn by girls prepared them for the subservience required in

[66] L. Taylor, *Study of Dress History*, p. 102.

their destined employment as domestic servants. It continues by examining the reasons for the imposition of a uniform for domestic servants and the extent to which employers were successful in limiting the dress, both on and off duty, of female 'domestics'. Finally, Chapter 10 considers the differing uses of uniforms in three major institutions which were transformed during the century: lunatic asylums, workhouses and prisons. Each aimed to effect a psychological reform of the inmates and return them to the community as productive, participatory citizens. Clothing, especially uniforms, played an important – and resisted – role in that process.

As Clare Rose notes, in the nineteenth century, 'changes in production, distribution and retailing practices instigated an era of truly mass consumption'.[67] People with modest incomes were able to own an increasing amount of new clothing which they employed and enjoyed not only for its practical and aesthetic properties, but also as a means of self-definition and a key marker by which others would assess and attribute status. My purpose is to show that there remained a significant section of the population who either continually or during certain periods in their lives were, through poverty, largely excluded from this process. The result was the creation of a 'sartorial underclass' whose material deprivation and visual distinction was a cause of physical discomfort and psychological trauma.

[67] C. Rose, *Making, Selling and Wearing*, pp. 1–2.

1 Setting the standard: working-class dress

Visiting Guildford one Sunday in 1860, Arthur Munby watched a congregation leaving church at midday. 'I saw', he lamented,

> no pretty faces, no rustic pleasant costumes, always excepting the old men, who came out of church in clean white smocks and gaiters. The same thing was to be noticed everywhere: it was sad to see standing at an old timehonoured cottage door a grey old peasant in his Sunday Smock, with his strong hearty wife beside him, in her high cap and old fashioned russet gown, whilst a couple of pert flimsy girls, in worthless garments of a pseudofashionable kind, stood talking to them, gaudy with ribbons and crinoline.

He contrasted the 'old people with their grave solid self respect and their picturesque and honourable class-costume' with the 'young ones, all show from head to foot', condemned the women as 'fifty times more evil than the men', and concluded that it was:

> the darkside, among many blessings, of our railway days; which will ultimately destroy all the refreshing ruggedness, all the valuable folklore, of our rural dialects, and all the charming differention [*sic*] – or what little is still left – of our rustic dress and manners.[1]

For Munby simplicity of dress equated to rural innocence, contented class awareness and the rejection of modernity. Similarly, garden designer Gertrude Jekyll, born in 1843, could sixty years later, 'just remember when' in Surrey, 'both men and women wore a real country dress'. This included the smock and 'ingenious and pretty' sun bonnet, with a curtain of fabric at the back to protect the neck from the sun, often adorned with frills and ruffles, and the making of which showed 'how the older folk took pleasure in doing dainty work'.[2] This sorrow at a vanishing folk culture, the valorising of 'picturesque' 'class-costume' over the 'worthless', 'gaudy' dress of the young – especially women – and the implicit

---

[1] TCLC, GBR/0016/MUNB, Papers of A. J. Munby (hereafter MUNB), 5, 15 July 1860.
[2] Gertrude Jekyll, *Old West Surrey: Some Notes and Memories* (London: Longmans, Green and Co., 1904), pp. 249, 255–6.

moral degradation, are the musings of middle-class sentimentalists. But it is true that in the 1800s urbanisation and industrialisation brought significant changes to proletarian dress. Those changes form the subject of this chapter which highlights significant garments and fabrics, new modes of clothing production and promotion, and considers the repeated claim that the working classes were bent on the imitation of elite dress.

Between 1801 and 1911, the population of England and Wales increased from 9 million to over 40 million.[3] Over the same period urban residents increased from approximately one third to nearly 80 per cent of the English population, with 75 per cent of the total population comprising urban industrial working-class families.[4] In 1815, 40 per cent of those in employment worked in agriculture, but by the outbreak of the First World War, this had fallen to 8 per cent, while in the three decades between 1871 and 1901 employment in the retail, clerical, transport and commercial sectors increased fourfold.[5] New energy industries also offered new employments with, for example, electrical supply workers increasing from around 2,500 to nearly 100,000 in the thirty years to 1911.[6] While male domestic servants were employed only by the very wealthy, female domestic service rapidly expanded, their numbers in England and Wales increasing by 60 per cent, from 750,000 to over 1,200,000 in the twenty-year period from 1851 to 1871.[7] For practical, ideological and aesthetic reasons, the dress styles of the eighteenth century, predominantly suited to rural living and labour, were no longer appropriate in the nineteenth.

Change

In the late eighteenth century the typical dress of non-elite men consisted of a linen shirt, knee breeches of heavy cotton, leather or wool, a smock or a woollen, linen or cotton waistcoat and a woollen coat or jacket. Accessories comprised worsted or cotton stockings, buckled shoes

---

[3] Robert Woods, *The Population of Britain in the Nineteenth Century* (Cambridge University Press, 1995), p. 10. Though separate figures are not given for England and Wales, the numerical supremacy of the former is evident from the fact that by 1900 England accounted for 73 per cent of the total British population, Wales just 5 per cent.
[4] *Ibid.*, pp. 13, 15.
[5] Mark Blaug, 'The myth of the old Poor Law and the making of the new', *The Journal of Economic History*, 23:2 (1963), 151–84; 154; Jose Harris, *Private Lives, Public Spirit: Britain 1870–1914* (London: Penguin, 1994), pp. 41–3, 127.
[6] Woods, *Population of Britain*, p. 14.
[7] John Burnett (ed.), *Useful Toil: Autobiographies of Working People from the 1820s to the 1920s* (London: Routledge, 1994), p. 130.

or boots, a hat and silk or muslin neckcloth or handkerchief and, for a number of trades, an apron, often of leather.[8] When Arthur Young estimated the annual clothing expenses for a Sussex labouring man in 1793, the garments he allowed for were: 'frock' (smock), waistcoat, breeches, shirt, shoes, stockings, hat and handkerchief.[9] By 1901, when Rowntree identified the basic garments for a working man, in his survey of York, the smock and breeches had been replaced by a suit of trousers, waistcoat and jacket or coat, and the fustian suit had become the typical dress of manual labourers, rural and urban.[10] Their growing number of white-collar counterparts were increasingly adopting the tailored woollen suit, although Katrina Honeyman found this did not become 'truly democratic' until the 1920s.[11]

During the eighteenth and early nineteenth centuries trousers were mostly the dress of sailors, being easier than breeches to kneel and crouch in, to put on and off, and not requiring stockings.[12] In George Walker's 1814 *Costume of Yorkshire* the only men depicted in trousers are soldiers, alum workers, the moor guide and whalebone scrapers. In the remaining twenty-four plates where it is possible to discern the men's leg wear, they are wearing breeches.[13] But by about the mid 1820s ankle-length 'trowsers', initially with a fall-down flap fastened with two buttons at the waist, were standard.[14] Diana De Marly attributes this change to the influence of fashion and the *sans-culottes* of the French Revolution, whose name derived from their adoption of the working man's trousers and rejection of elite breeches.[15]

Typical dress for non-elite women in the late eighteenth century comprised a linen shift under boned or leather stays, one or more petticoats of woollen, linen or cotton fabric, perhaps one of which was quilted, and either a jacket, a linen or cotton bedgown, or a cotton, linen or stuff gown. Worsted or cotton stockings, leather or stuff buckled shoes, a linen or cotton apron, linen cap, a straw, silk or chip hat, a linen, silk or cotton handkerchief or shawl and a cloak, usually either of red woollen cloth

---

[8] Styles, *Dress of the People*, pp. 31–45.
[9] Arthur Young, *General View of the Agriculture of the County of Sussex with Observations on the Means of its Improvement* (London, 1793), p. 91.
[10] Rowntree, *Poverty*, pp. 381–2.
[11] Katrina Honeyman, *Well Suited: A History of the Leeds Clothing Industry, 1850–1990* (Oxford University Press, 2000), p. 21.
[12] Dudley Pope, *Life in Nelson's Navy* (London: Allen & Unwin, 1981), p. 163.
[13] George Walker, *The Costume of Yorkshire* (Firle: Caliban, 1978 [1814]).
[14] Vanda Foster, *A Visual History of Costume: The Nineteenth Century* (London: Batsford, 1992), p. 15. See also Clabburn, *Working Class Costume*, pp. 8–9.
[15] de Marly, *Working Dress*, p. 76. See also Aileen Ribeiro, *Fashion in the French Revolution* (New York: Holmes and Meier, 1988), p. 140.

or black silk, completed the outfit.[16] Arthur Young's 1793 estimate of annual expenses for a Sussex labouring woman omits the more expensive items since these would have been replaced only at long intervals, not yearly.[17] Writing in 1797 Frederick Eden estimated, for example, that women's cloaks and hats would last two years and a pair of stays six.[18]

Ben Brierley, born in Lancashire in 1825, could remember when the red woollen cloaks worn by country women meant that 'a funeral procession resembled at a distance a troop of soldiers'. By the time he wrote his autobiography in the 1880s the 'crimson cloaks' had disappeared and Rowntree found the basic clothing for working-class York women, in 1901, to be boots, slippers, dress, aprons, skirt, stockings, underclothing, stays, hat, jacket and shawl.[19] In many instances the 'dress' was probably a two-piece garment of skirt and bodice or blouse. The stays or corset, previously visible, had become invisible undergarments, and the cap had virtually disappeared except, much to their chagrin, for domestic servants.[20] The undergarments would have consisted of shift and petticoat(s), although the latter would probably not be quilted. Drawers, as discussed below, were also a possibility.

Despite the rapidity of industrialisation and urbanisation, the displacement of 'rustic' or 'traditional' dress was drawn out and uneven. Some garments lingered because they formed part of the collective identity of their wearers. Dustmen, for instance, who became central figures in nineteenth-century caricature, appear to have continued wearing breeches until at least mid century as part of their distinctive costume.[21] And while Munby had complained of Guildford in 1860 that smocks were only worn by old men, in another visit to Surrey over a decade later what surprised him was, 'the great number of smockfrocks...here at Ockley, men of all ages wear them, and lads, and little boys...even on Sunday and at Church, worn with corduroys and leggings'.[22] Likewise, Edwin Grey remembered that during his childhood in a Hertfordshire agricultural village during the 1860s and 1870s 'the principle (sic) article

---

[16] Styles, *Dress of the People*, pp. 31–44.
[17] Young, *General View of the Agriculture*, p. 91.
[18] Frederic Morton Eden, *The State of the Poor: or, An History of the Labouring Classes in England, from the Conquest to the Present Period*, 3 vols (London, 1797), vol. III, p. cccxliii.
[19] Ben Brierley, *Home Memories and Out of Work* (Bramhall: Reword, 2002 [1885–6]), p. 33; Rowntree, *Poverty*, pp. 382–4.
[20] For domestic servants, see Chapter 9.
[21] Henry Mayhew, *London Labour and the London Poor*, 4 vols (New York: Dover and London: Constable, 1968 [1861–2]) vol. II, p. 175; Brian Maidment, '101 things to do with a fantail hat: dustmen, dirt and dandyism, 1820–1860', *Textile History*, 33:1 (2002), 79–97; 86.
[22] TCLC, MUNB, 41, 13 April 1873.

of attire of all agricultural labourers', was the round smock.[23] The picturesque, home-made, embroidered smock so appealing to romantics did undoubtedly decline with the shrinking of the agricultural-labouring population.[24] But the plain smock continued as a practical garment for both urban and rural working men. Journalist James Greenwood, observing the 230 navvies excavating a London railway cutting in 1867, noted that while some were bare-chested, others wore 'red smocks, blue smocks, [and] white smocks'.[25] Furthermore, from mid century smocks were mass-produced indicating that there was still a good market for them.[26]

Changes in women's dress were also gradual. Pattens, for example, worn over shoes to keep them out of the mud, became less common as the century progressed, but still in the 1860s and 1870s Edwin Grey remembered seeing them '[h]ere and there' in rural Hertfordshire, 'placed outside and close up to the back door of the cottage' ready for use.[27] And on more than one occasion Munby encountered female 'rustic' dress even as he mourned its passing. In the 1860s, when the crinoline dominated women's fashionable dress, and when Munby had been so condemnatory of their wear by young working women in Surrey, he also saw, near Runcorn in Cheshire, women field-workers all in 'close white caps or cotton bonnets, loose lilac or pink jackets, and short striped lindsey skirts', while another group near Brotherton in North Yorkshire wore belted 'white smocks and rustic bonnets and kerchiefs'. Still further north-east, at Whitby the flax-spreaders caught his attention by their 'short scarlet kirtles & looped up gowns, & red or brown kerchiefs on the head'.[28] Admittedly, this was the women's working attire and they may have had more fashionable clothes for Sunday, but even in the 1910s Christopher Holdenby (the pen-name of agriculturalist Ronald Hatton), was able to comment on female field-workers near Bristol looking 'vastly picturesque in their pink and lilac sun-bonnets'.[29]

Under the *ancien régime*, says Daniel Roche, 'children of the rich were dressed like children, the rest like miniature adults'.[30] This was still

---

[23] Edwin Grey, *Cottage Life in a Hertfordshire Village* (Harpenden: Harpenden and District Local History Society, 1977 [1935]), p. 30.
[24] Toplis, 'The non-elite consumer', p. 39.
[25] James Greenwood, *Unsentimental Journeys, or Byways of the Modern Babylon* (London, 1867), p. 202.
[26] Stanley Chapman, 'The innovating entrepreneurs in the British ready-made clothing industry', *Textile History*, 24:1 (1993), 5–25; 6–7.
[27] Grey, *Cottage Life*, p. 33.
[28] TCLC, MUNB, 6, 28 September 1860; 16, 7 October 1862; 33, 6 March 1865.
[29] Christopher Holdenby, *Folk of the Furrow* (London: Smith, Elder & Co., 1913), p. 143.
[30] Daniel Roche, *The Culture of Clothing: Dress and Fashion in the 'Ancien Régime'*, trans. Jean Birrell (Cambridge University Press, 1996), p. 117.

true at the beginning of the nineteenth century, but by the twentieth distinct clothes for working-class boys had developed, though less so for girls. Infant boys and girls were dressed alike in petticoats, and for most boys the ritual of 'breeching', whereby the petticoats were replaced by breeches, signalled entrance into the masculine world. Frank Marling, whose father was a clerk for a Gloucestershire Canal Company, recalled in the 1860s being jeered at by a group of newly-breeched boys because he was:

still wearing afrock [sic]! Not long afterwards I came out in my first pair of breeches. What a big step up in life it was! I was now able to take my place as a boy and meet other boys on an equal footing.[31]

There was some flexibility about the age at which breeching occurred although it was unlikely to take place until the boy was toilet-trained. Self-styled 'Factory Cripple' William Dodd was breeched around 1809–10 when he was aged between five and six. It would have happened earlier, but his parents had to wait until they were able to borrow sufficient money to buy the clothes.[32] Clare Rose says that in the 1860s and 1870s breeching was sometimes delayed until the age of eight, but by the end of the century virtually all boys had given up 'skirts' by the age of four, although Anna Davin found that in London breeching could occur anywhere between the ages of three and six.[33]

Rose also reveals that by the late-Victorian period breeching was only the first in a multi-stage sartorial transition from infant to adult male. Petticoats were replaced by shorts or knickerbockers worn with a blouse, which in turn were replaced by a jacket and shorts, before giving way to adult suits with long trousers, usually by the age of thirteen. The sailor suit became the most popular boys' outfit, but more crucially Rose found that with the rise of mass production 'boys' clothing became much cheaper in real terms between 1870 and 1900, eliding 'the sharp distinction between clothes for working boys, and clothes for young gentlemen'.[34]

The clothing of working-class girls changed less during the century, mainly comprising a one-piece dress worn under a pinafore, the dress shorter and less closely fitted than that of adult women's and the sleeves

---

[31] BAWCA, 1:492, Frank Marling, 'Reminiscences', pp. 2–3.
[32] William Dodd, *A Narrative of the Experience and Sufferings of WD, Written by Himself* (London, 1841), pp. 6–7.
[33] C. Rose, *Making, Selling and Wearing*, p. 167; Davin, *Growing Up Poor*, p. 18.
[34] C. Rose, *Making, Selling and Wearing*, pp. 130, 158, 167; Clare Rose, *Children's Clothes Since 1750* (London: Batsford, 1989), p. 99.

also possibly shorter.³⁵ There was no equivalent of breeching for girls, but their skirts lengthened to reach ankle- or ground-length at adulthood.³⁶ The pinafore might also be replaced by an apron, although in some areas, such as the textile districts of Lancashire, adult women continued with pinafores. For teenage girls, permission to wear one's hair 'up' was often the first acknowledged step towards womanhood. Holdenby remembered in Bristol 'watching one shy little girl of fifteen go from short skirts to long' and then join the women working in the fields where she was greeted with: 'Wot! Nellie with 'er 'air up a'ready! The men'll soon be looking after thee then.'³⁷

Laurence Fontaine and Margaret Spufford agree that pedlars clothed seventeenth-century England.³⁸ Fontaine says their distribution of fabrics, bought principally in London, and haberdashery from provincial specialists, resulted in a degree of commonality of textiles and clothing across England.³⁹ John Styles also found eighteenth-century regional dress variation to be 'muted', taking the form of modifications of the typical costume, rather than an entirely different dress style. Thus, for instance, he notes men wearing shirts of hempen rather than linen cloth in Suffolk.⁴⁰ But the early nineteenth century saw the production of a number of publications which focused on the variety of British dress. In 1808 W. H. Pyne produced sixty paintings, including many of the labouring poor, in *The Costume of Great Britain*. The commissioning publisher felt that '[i]n a country presenting such an infinite variety of interesting subjects, the only difficulty has been to compress the Volume within moderate bounds', and Pyne continued the theme in an 1827 four-volume work, *England, Scotland, & Ireland*.⁴¹ George Walker believed the county of York alone offered 'a greater variety and peculiarity of manners and dress than any other in the kingdom', and therefore set out, in 1814, to capture it in a series of forty plates.⁴² In 1816 engraver William Johnstone White began work on a proposed seventeen-volume edition. It was to comprise 'an entire work of national costume thro' the various counties of England etc. embracing the habits of mechanics or artificers above or under ground'. In the event, possibly due to his wife's ill health, he produced only one volume covering Norfolk, Cambridgeshire and

---

³⁵ C. Rose, *Children's Clothes*, pp. 36, 89, 97–8.
³⁶ Elizabeth Ewing, *History of Children's Costume* (London: Batsford, 1977), p. 65.
³⁷ Holdenby, *Folk of the Furrow*, p. 145.
³⁸ Laurence Fontaine, *History of Pedlars in Europe*, trans. Vicki Whittaker (Cambridge: Polity, 1996), pp. 186–7. Spufford, *Great Reclothing*, passim.
³⁹ Fontaine, *History of Pedlars*, pp. 87, 186–8.   ⁴⁰ Styles, *Dress of the People*, pp. 35, 55.
⁴¹ W. H. Pyne, *The Costume of Great Britain* (London, 1808), p. ii; W. H. Pyne (ed.), *England, Scotland, and Ireland*, 4 vols (London, 1827).
⁴² Walker, *Costume of Yorkshire*.

Middlesex, but the anticipated scope of the project suggests significant sartorial diversity.[43]

Vanda Foster believes these works 'provide a major source of information on working-class dress', but cautions that they were often produced over several years, or even reproduced images from earlier publications, and so their reliability as sources for the period in which they were produced is variable.[44] Sean Shesgreen and Sam Smiles have also questioned their reliability although Smiles does not 'deny that distinctions existed in reality'.[45] But while the illustrators seem to suggest a great deal of regional variation, their main focus was in fact occupational dress, although the regional specificity of many occupations means the two were intimately connected.[46] And while Jane Tozer and Sarah Levitt correctly point out that dress was not 'exactly matched to status, region and occupation', some dress styles were distinctive enough to indicate their wearers' regional affinity and employment.[47] In 1872, for example, among the 'mere Cockney farrago of shabby old hats and gowns' worn by local women working in the Middlesex market gardens, Munby spotted some young women who, from their distinctive dress, he thought to be Shropshire pit-girls. Each:

wore a pink or buff hood bonnet of cotton, large and serviceable; a bright-coloured kerchief over the shoulders; a short skirt made of an old potato sack, with the dealer's name still visible on it in large letters; and beneath the skirt their stout legs were cased in warm grey stockings that led down to massive ankle boots, heavy with nails... And some had their brown arms bare, and some wore coarse smocks with sleeves.[48]

They came, in fact, not from Shropshire, but neighbouring Staffordshire, but Munby had correctly identified them as pit-brow workers.

On his travels Munby encountered many women whose dress, had he met them elsewhere, would have indicated their home region and occupation. At Filey, North Yorkshire, for example, the bait-gathering

---

[43] Clabburn (ed.), *Working Class Costume*, Introduction.
[44] Foster, *Visual History of Costume*, p. 16.
[45] Sean Shesgreen, *Images of the Outcast: The Urban Poor in the Cries of London* (Manchester University Press, 2002), p. 17; Sam Smiles, 'Defying comprehension: resistance to uniform appearance in depicting the poor, 1770s to 1830s', *Textile History*, 33:1 (2002), 22–36; 27, 35.
[46] The focus on occupational dress leads the illustrators to pay more attention to men than to women who are mostly depicted performing domestic labour such as spinning, or work specific to their location and of novelty interest to more distant readers such as shrimping or gathering cranberries.
[47] Jane Tozer and Sarah Levitt, *Fabric of Society: A Century of People and their Clothes 1770–1870* (Carno, Wales: Laura Ashley, 1983), p. 121.
[48] TCLC, MUNB, 40, 7 June 1872.

'flither' women sported 'red kirtles, white or blue guernseys, red or grey kerchiefs over bonnets'. Scarborough mussel gatherers were clad in 'white jersey sleeves, short skirts, tarpaulin coat on back, strong boots', but at Lympstone in Devon, they wore elements of masculine dress. Munby sketched one who was wearing 'a large black pokebonnet, a cloth coat or rather jacket, buttoned up... whitish fustian trousers' and an apron 'tucked round her waist'. Two more had 'shawls for jackets, and one had wide breeches & bare legs, and the other her petticoats tucked in between her legs and tied', while a fourth, 'wore a pair of loose fishy breeches, tied at the knee'. There was also 'an elderly woman' who, 'except her bonnet was dressed entirely in men's clothes... a thick blue mariner's jersey, reaching to her hips; a pair of patched and stained canvas trousers; no stockings, & thick shoes'.[49]

Trousers and trouser- or breech-like garments were worn by a number of groups of working-class women. Lancashire pit-worker Mary Glover, who worked underground, told the 1842 Children's Employment Commission that she worked in 'a shift and a pair of trousers'. She also indicated their novelty and erotic potential by adding that she had been given 'many a 2d.... by the boatmen on the canal side to show my breeches'.[50] This suggests that outside the workplace the breeches were hidden under a skirt, but such a story would have confirmed the common view that women in bifurcated clothing were morally offensive. Munby, in contrast, greatly admired, and enthusiastically recorded, women who dressed in men's clothing.[51] The most (in)famous and best documented were the Wigan pit-brow girls, who wore:

A hooded bonnet of padded cotton, pink blue or black, a blue striped shirt, open at the breast; a waistcoat of cloth, generally double-breasted, but ragged and patched throughout; fustian or corduroy or sometimes blackcloth trousers, patched with all possible materials except the original one; and stout clog shoon, brass clasped, on their bare feet: round the waist is tucked a petticoat of striped cotton, blue and black, rolled up as a joiner rolls his apron.[52]

The outfit was also worn at the nearby Haigh Moor Brewery where the employees were former pitwomen, taken on when, in 1842, they were

---

[49] TCLC, MUNB, 33, 13 January 1865; 33, 17 February 1865; 9, 19 August 1861. The 'short' skirts would still have reached below the knee.
[50] *Children's Employment Commission. Appendix to First Report of the Commissioners. Mines. Part II*. Parliamentary Papers 1842 XVII, p. 214.
[51] Munby, however, balked at Hannah Cullwick's suggestion that she disguise herself as a man to be able to travel with him. Derek Hudson, *Munby, Man of Two Worlds: The Life and Diaries of Arthur J. Munby 1828–1910* (London: Abacus, 1974), p. 133.
[52] TCLC, MUNB, 3, 19 August 1859. See Chapter 5, Fig. 5.1.

forbidden to work underground and who 'brought their costume with them'.[53]

The adoption of men's clothing by women was a response to the perceived impracticality of female garments for the manual work they performed. Munby noted that at the St Helen's pits, just ten miles from Wigan, the pit-brow women performed the same work but 'mostly' wore skirts instead of trousers, 'and very draggled and torn they get' he said.[54] There were, though, few parallel imperatives for men to adopt women's garments. A London police sergeant told one of Charles Booth's researchers that he had sent out men 'dressed as females to convict the brothels'. But the experiment failed: 'They always know', said the sergeant.[55] Mostly men dressed as women only for fun.[56] Plough Monday celebrations, for example, included 'a ludicrous procession' with 'a huge clown in female attire', and in 1877 John Thomson photographed a Guy Fawkes' procession which included 'the absurd appearance' of a man in woman's clothes accompanying a November 5th effigy.[57] Men dressed as women, it seems, were largely considered ridiculous.

Accessories

Accessories were an important means by which different groups distinguished themselves. Canal men wore unexceptional corduroy or moleskin trousers, waistcoats and jackets, but their shirts, belts and braces were ornamented with a distinctive form of embroidery stitched by the canal women, who also crocheted lace to trim their own clothes and so distinguish them from women 'off the land'.[58] Mayhew noted that the waistcoats of London costers were adorned with buttons of mother-of-pearl, or 'plain brass, or sporting buttons, with raised fox's or stag's heads upon them – or else black bone-buttons, with a flower-pattern'. They also wore a bright silk neckerchief or 'King's-man', without which the coster was 'known to be in desperate circumstances', and costerwomen wore a silk King's-man as a shawl.[59]

---

[53] TCLC, MUNB, 6, 29 September 1860; See also Angela V. John, *By the Sweat of Their Brow: Women Workers at the Victorian Coal Mines* (London: Croom Helm, 1980), p. 114.
[54] TCLC, MUNB, 6, 28 September.1860; See also John, *Sweat of Their Brow*, p. 181.
[55] Jess Steele (ed.), *The Streets of London: The Booth Notebooks – South East* (London: Deptford Forum, 1997), p. 56.
[56] I am not including transvestitism here.
[57] Walker, *Costume of Yorkshire*, p. 38; John Thomson, *Victorian London: Street Life in Historic Photographs* (New York: Dover, 1994), p. 104.
[58] Avril Lansdell, *The Clothes of the Cut: A History of Canal Costume* (London: British Waterways Board, 1976), pp. 13–14, 21–3.
[59] Mayhew, *London Labour*, vol. I, p. 51.

The coster's silk King's-man was a very specific type of kerchief, but more commonly kerchiefs were made of cotton and were versatile and virtually indispensable items, varying in size from a few inches to a few feet square. They were used by both men and women as shawls, scarves and head coverings, makeshift aprons and bags. As a young man in the early 1840s Ben Brierley needed something in which to carry his 'day's sustenance' for a Whitsun outing. 'Suitable baskets were not easily attainable', he explained,

> pockets were limited in their holding capacity; and satchels were unknown. The check napkin, the most useful article in a weaver's household, had generally to be resorted to; and it was not a matter of pride to be seen with one under his arm.[60]

An Oldham woman remembered accompanying her mother to the Co-operative Stores toward the end of the century 'and carrying the flour tied up in a check handkerchief on my head'.[61] Much less common among the masses was the pocket handkerchief.[62] An Oxfordshire schoolgirl recalled that on the occasion of the funeral of her Dame School mistress in 1829, she and her classmates were issued with a white pocket handkerchief, but as they had not been used to them she had to ask 'what it was for'.[63]

Aprons were also used to carry things. Anna Clark cites an observer at the 1842 Preston Plug Plot Riots who said women brought 'stones in the brats and aprons and lay them down in the street for the use of the mob'.[64] Robert Roberts recalled Mrs Carey, a poor customer at his parents' shop in Edwardian Salford, who came in to settle and stock

---

[60] Brierley, *Home Memories*, p. 28.
[61] Margaret Llewelyn Davies (ed.), *Life As We Have Known It by Co-operative Working Women* (London: Virago, 1977 [1931]), pp. 102–3. An excellent example of the handkerchief's versatility and cultural embedment is provided in two of Beatrix Potter's children's tales, set in a romanticised Victorian rural England. In *The Tale of Benjamin Bunny* (1904), the eponymous rabbit finds his cousin, Peter, wrapped 'in a red cotton pocket-handkerchief', having lost his clothes while stealing from Mr McGregor's garden. The pair reclaim Peter's clothes then use the handkerchief to carry home some stolen onions. Peter is last seen with his sister folding up the handkerchief as humans might fold a sheet. In the prequel, *The Tale of Peter Rabbit* (1902), their mother is seen on her way to the baker's wearing a smaller version of the red handkerchief as a head covering. Beatrix Potter, *The Tale of Peter Rabbit* (London: Frederick Warne, 1902); Beatrix Potter, *The Tale of Benjamin Bunny* (London: Frederick Warne, 1904).
[62] Laurence Fontaine similarly documents the ubiquity, variety and versatility of handkerchiefs in the early-modern period, and their rare usage for wiping noses. Fontaine, *History of Pedlars*, pp. 197–201.
[63] Mary Smith, *The Autobiography of Mary Smith Schoolmistress and Nonconformist. A Fragment of a Life with Letters from Jane Welsh Carlyle and Thomas Carlyle* (London: Bemrose and Sons, 1892), p. 19.
[64] Anna Clark, *The Struggle for the Breeches: Gender and the Making of the British Working Class* (London: Rivers Oram, 1995), p. 241.

up every Saturday. 'She left the shop "skint" but happy, with enough basic foodstuffs in an apron (not owning a shopping bag) to see them through the following week.'[65] Some women wore sacking aprons for very dirty jobs, but more usually a long plain or check apron of linen, or increasingly, cotton. Most women's aprons tied round the waist and did not have a bib, but for children and mill workers the pinafore was common. 'A white pinafore served for Sunday, and Monday at school', wrote Daisy Cowper, the daughter of an impoverished Liverpool ship's captain, 'and pretty coloured print ones each for two or three days, for the rest of the week'.[66]

Blacksmiths and carpenters were among the men who wore a leather apron, while those of grocers were white linen or cotton, and butchers were blue.[67] Potters also wore aprons and according to Charles Shaw, in the early Victorian period it was 'usual' for potters 'to wear a white apron ... even during holidays'.[68] Still in twentieth-century Salford, artisans 'worked at lathe or bench, sleeves of their union shirts rolled, in white aprons, overalls as yet being hardly known'.[69] No matter how the aprons of male trades differed, they remained a signifier of manual labour, whereas 'collars and ties or clean, tidy clothes' were the 'visible signs that a man did not have to undertake manual work'.[70] 'In the social classification of the nether world', proclaimed George Gissing in his 1889 novel, 'it will be convenient to distinguish broadly, and with reference to males alone, the two great sections of those who do, and those who do not, wear collars'.[71] Between 1851 and 1911 clerical workers increased from 95,000 to 843,000. The majority of these were male, their number rising from 93,000 to 677,000, but also the number of female clerical workers multiplied by a factor of eighty-three from 2,000 to 166,000, at which point they comprised one-fifth of the 'white-collar' workforce.[72]

'Clerks and shop assistants', writes Sarah Levitt, historian of nineteenth-century patented clothes, 'were among the chief patrons of such devices as shirt fronts, paper, rubber and celluloid collars and

---

[65] Robert Roberts, *A Ragged Schooling: Growing Up in the Classic Slum* (Manchester University Press, 1987 [1976]), p. 67.
[66] BAWCA, 1:182, Daisy Cowper, 'De nobis'.
[67] Jekyll, *Old West Surrey*, p. 262. For more apron variations see Sarah Levitt, 'Cheap mass-produced men's clothing in the nineteenth and early twentieth centuries', *Textile History*, 22:2 (1991), 179–92; 180–1.
[68] Charles Shaw, *When I Was a Child* (Firle: Caliban, 1977 [1903]), p. 92.
[69] R. Roberts, *Classic Slum*, p. 38.   [70] Ugolini, *Men and Menswear*, p. 31.
[71] George Gissing, *The Nether World* (Oxford University Press, 1999 [1889]), p. 69.
[72] Meta Zimmeck, 'Jobs for the girls: the expansion of clerical work for women, 1850–1914', in Angela V. John, *Unequal Opportunities: Women's Employment in England 1800–1918* (Oxford: Basil Blackwell, 1986), pp. 152–77; 154.

cuffs'.[73] She was referring to men, but female clerks also had problems with dirty cuffs. In 1863 Munby met a then rare female clerk who worked in a London mercantile house, 'our sleeves get worn with leaning on the desk, & our white cuffs get dreadfully inked', she told him.[74]

London costers, male and female, wore 'heavy boots', but in general good quality footwear was less of a priority for urban workers than for rural. Indeed, for Munby the costergirls' 'short cotton gowns' and 'thick laced boots' made them 'the most rural looking thing to be seen' on the London streets.[75] Ginsburg points out that in Rowntree's survey of working-class budgets in late-nineteenth-century York the men bought a mixture of new and second-hand boots, whereas in Kendall and Rowntree's 1913 rural survey all the men bought new, which, she says, 'were still regarded as an essential though expensive item of family expenditure'.[76]

In the north, however, metal-tipped, wooden-soled clogs with leather uppers were the characteristic footwear of men, women and children. 'The adult population (I would estimate 90%)', wrote Jack Lanigan of Salford at the turn of the twentieth century, 'wore clogs, and you could hear them half a mile away'.[77] Clogs were cheap, hard-wearing, could be repaired by replacing the wooden soles and metal tips and were deeply culturally embedded. Their sound was exploited in clog dancing, and children adapted them for ice skating and sparked them by striking the metal part against the kerbstone.[78] Men used them for 'up and down' or 'purring' which involved 'kicking each other with their clogs on every part of the body and... squeezing the throat', sometimes with fatal results.[79] In the 1870s a Manchester parish magazine claimed to know of people who could remember when the local newspapers 'used every day to set apart half a column for recording the mighty deeds of men who knew how to use their clogs', but the magistrates had now suppressed this 'custom'.[80] However, according to Robert Roberts, in Salford groups

---

[73] Sarah Levitt, *Victorians Unbuttoned: Registered Designs for Clothing, Their Makers and Wearers, 1839–1900* (London: Allen & Unwin, 1986), p. 10.
[74] TCLC, MUNB, 18, 10 April 1863.
[75] Mayhew, *London Labour*, vol. I, p. 51; TCLC, MUNB, 33, 15 June 1865.
[76] Ginsburg, 'Rags to riches', 127.
[77] BAWCA, 1:421 Jack Lanigan, 'Thy kingdom did come', p. 5.
[78] Brierley, *Home Memories*, pp. 16, 20–1. Similarly one Parliamentary investigator discovered that South Staffordshire miners danced 'the double shuffle, to the music of the fiddle or hurdy-gurdy. The noise of the shoes is the source of delight in this dance, and the hobnails of the colliers afford great advantage'. *Children's Employment Commission. Appendix to First Report of the Commissioners Mines. Part I.* Parliamentary Papers 1842 XVI, p. 63.
[79] Evelyn Vigeon, 'Clogs or wooden soled shoes', *Costume*, 11 (1977), 1–27; 11.
[80] MALS, L135/1/11/1, *St. Clement Urmston Parish Magazine*, January 1875.

of young men known as scuttlers 'sought escape from tedium in bloody battles with belt and clog – street against street... until the early days of the first world war'.[81]

Head coverings were universal; as Asa Briggs pointed out, '[e]ven beggars wore hats'.[82] The common hat of the male agricultural labourer was the low-crowned, broad-brimmed wideawake, while in 1867 James Greenwood was dazzled by the 'fantastic costumes' of the London railway navvies who, atop their coloured smocks, wore:

> caps of the woollen 'night' sort – green, pink, and yellow, or elaborately barred and spotted with these colours and some others; hair caps, made of the hide of the cow, the bear, and the badger; tarpaulin and shiny oilskin caps and caps of cloth, worn peak astern invariably – all these various shapes and colours.[83]

In 1892 Keir Hardie shocked Parliament by making his first appearance in a tweed suit and deerstalker hat instead of the customary black coat and tall silk hat. Journalists mistook the deerstalker for a workman's cloth cap, which Hardie then obtained, and the cloth cap has endured as a potent class symbol.[84] Jose Harris, however, questions the ubiquity of the working-man's cloth cap, claiming that it was far less common than the 'democratic bowler'.[85] But according to Arthur Harding, in the 1900s a bowler hat 'was unusual for the working class' in his East London neighbourhood.[86] A photograph of residents on the balcony of a York tenement in Rowntree's 1901 publication includes three men. One wears a cap, another a bowler and the third, much older, is bare-headed.[87] Breward notes Arthur Morrison's suggestion that age and status were a factor, the wearing of bowler hats by apprentices with fewer than four years' service being pretentious, but among older men it may simply have been a matter of personal preference and local practice.[88]

Women's head coverings varied from the mob caps of the early 1800s through the sun bonnet and the 'coal-scuttle' poke bonnet of the 1840s to the straw boater at the close of the century. But northern women were again distinctive, wearing a shawl or kerchief over their head and shoulders, rather than the hat or bonnet and jacket favoured in the south. Brierley noted this tendency in the 1830s, and the organiser of a Leeds

---

[81] R. Roberts, *Classic Slum*, pp. 155–6.
[82] Asa Briggs, *Victorian Things* (Stroud: Sutton, 2003), p. 346.
[83] Greenwood, *Unsentimental Journeys*, p. 202.
[84] Fred Reid, *Keir Hardie: The Making of a Socialist* (London: Croom Helm, 1978), pp. 140–1.
[85] Harris, *Private Lives, Public Spirit*, pp. 9–10.
[86] Raphael Samuel, *East End Underworld: Chapters in the Life of Arthur Harding* (London: Routledge & Kegan Paul, 1981), p. 103.
[87] Rowntree, *Poverty*, p. 157.   [88] Breward, *Hidden Consumer*, p. 211.

sewing school for factory girls in the 1860s commented that on entering the pupils would 'throw off the red handkerchiefs which in the north are the useful and becoming substitutes for bonnets'.[89]

Drawers

From at least the seventeenth century, men's breeches were commonly lined, the (possibly detachable) lining serving as integral drawers.[90] According to the dress historians Willett and Phillis Cunnington, by the nineteenth century drawers were standard wear among men of the elite and middling classes, but the extent to which they were worn by labouring men after the transfer from breeches to trousers is less clear.[91] However Harriet Martineau, visiting a Birmingham glass factory in 1852, commented that some of the workers wore 'no clothing but drawers and a blue shirt'.[92] And in 1870 the prison inspectorate recommended that at Exeter prison 'some cheap form of drawers should be issued to prisoners in lieu of their own', which suggests it had become commonplace for inmates to be wearing drawers on admission.[93]

Some women were also wearing drawers, 'an English fashion', according to one mid-century French author.[94] They were standard wear for elite girls and young women and dress historians agree that some older elite women were also wearing them by the early 1800s and that they were common wear among middle-class women by the 1840s.[95] There is, though, little to suggest that drawers were worn by poorer women before the last quarter of the century.[96] When women did wear drawers they were voluminous garments, gathered onto a waistband, and 'open' – that

---

[89] Brierley, *Home Memories*, p. 33; Mrs Hyde, *How to Win Our Workers: A Short Account of the Leeds Sewing School for Factory Girls* (Cambridge, 1862), pp. 36–7.
[90] Spufford, *Great Reclothing*, p. 121; C. Willett and Phillis Cunnington, *The History of Underclothes* (New York: Dover, 1992 [1951]), p. 78.
[91] C. W. and P. Cunnington, *History of Underclothes*, p. 27.
[92] Isobel Armstrong, *Victorian Glassworlds: Glass Culture and the Imagination 1830–1880* (Oxford University Press, 2008), pp. 20, 33.
[93] *Thirty-fourth Report of the Inspectors Appointed, under the Provisions of the Act 5 & 6 Will. IV. c.38, to Visit the Different Prisons of Great Britain. I. Southern District*. Parliamentary Papers 1870 XXXVII, p. 46.
[94] Philippe Perrot, *Fashioning the Bourgeoisie: A History of Clothing in the Nineteenth Century* (Princeton, NJ: Princeton University Press, 1994), p. 146.
[95] Jill Fields, *An Intimate Affair: Women, Lingerie, and Sexuality* (Berkeley and London: University of California Press, 2007), pp. 24, 296 n. 2. Alia Al-Khalidi, 'Emergent technologies in menstrual paraphernalia in mid-nineteenth-century Britain', *Journal of Design History*, 14:4 (2001), 257–73; 259–6.
[96] Shelley Tobin, *Inside Out: A Brief History of Underwear* (London: The National Trust, 2001), p. 12; C. W. and P. Cunnington, *History of Underclothes*, p. 112; Joan Nunn, *Fashion in Costume 1200–2000* (London: Herbert, 2000), p. 117.

is, without a crotch seam.[97] Suffragette Selina Cooper worked in a Lancashire textile mill in the 1890s where, she said, the women 'wore sort of drawers, and they were just legs up to here and all open at the –'.[98] This differentiated women's drawers from male bifurcated garments and the potential 'immodesty' of the garment was reduced by the shift, which reached to the knees and was tucked into the drawers.

School sewing manuals gave instructions and patterns for a variety of garments, including shifts and aprons, but not until the 1870s are there specific, but sporadic, references to drawers and these are to children's drawers.[99] And as Anna Davin suggests, it is difficult to know whether they were included because they were commonly being worn by the poor or because genteel authors hoped to encourage their use.[100] Minnie Frisby born in 1877, the daughter of West Midlands nail makers, remembered that as a child:

> One of the things which upset me was that I used to wear white drawers 2 or 3 inches below my frock... and the boys called my briches (*sic*) (some people called drawers, briches) were coming down; Oh, the shame, and they was'nt (*sic*).[101]

Elite girls, earlier in the century, displayed a few lace-trimmed inches of drawers below their skirts, and it is not clear from Frisby's account whether the visibility of her drawers was intentional or whether they were simply too long.[102] If the latter, this would account for the boys' teasing, but the reference to them as 'briches' (breeches) suggests they perhaps viewed drawers as a novel and masculinised garment for a working-class girl.

Another account, however, suggests that by the early twentieth century in south London, at least, drawers were commonly worn and were expected to be a concealed garment. Ethel Melloy ('Gran'), who grew up in Deptford in the 1900s and 1910s, was the daughter of a clerk and

---

[97] For the significance of open vs closed drawers, see Fields, *Intimate Affair*, p. 24. For an example and analysis of a pair of working-class women's late-nineteenth-century open drawers, see Vivienne Richmond, 'Stitching the self: Eliza Kenniff's drawers and the materialization of identity in late-nineteenth-century London', in Maureen Daly Goggin and Beth Fowkes Tobin (eds), *Women and Things: Gendered Material Practices, 1750–1950* (Farnham: Ashgate, 2009), pp. 43–54.
[98] Jill Liddington, *The Life and Times of a Respectable Rebel: Selina Cooper (1864–1946)* (London: Virago, 1984), p. 52.
[99] See, for example, M. E. Bailey, *School Needlework and Cutting Out: A Scheme of Instruction to Suit the New Government Code, Adopted by the Liverpool School Board* (Liverpool: George Gill & Co., 1875), p. 14.
[100] Davin, *Growing Up Poor*, p. 148.
[101] BAWCA, 1:250, Minnie Frisby, 'Memories', p. 2.
[102] See Foster, *Visual History of Costume*, p. 66 plate 60, and p. 55 plate 47; C. Rose, *Children's Clothes*, p. 41.

domestic servant. She told her daughter-in-law that in the years leading up to the First World War,

> her mother and grandmother made their own drawers. They wore a chemise and open drawers that didn't need to be opened or taken down so had easy access! The drawers buttoned around the waist. Gran's drawers were much the same and had buttons around the waist. She wore a bodice that buttoned down the front and... it had holes or buttons on each side so that the drawers buttoned on to it.

Ethel also recalled:

> that all of her contemporaries had drawers like hers and knows that all of the women must have had drawers along the same lines as those of her mother and grandmother as she saw them hanging on washing lines. Most of them were pink flannelette! All buttoned around the waist and were home-made.

One Saturday, when Ethel and her brother were doing domestic chores, an uncle arrived unexpectedly, having just been 'paid off his ship'. He took them to a studio to be photographed as a surprise for their mother, but gave them no time to change out of their working clothes. One of the buttons to attach Ethel's drawers to her bodice was missing, and so, to Ethel's shame, the drawers were visible in the photograph, hanging below her skirt (Fig. 1.1).[103]

Cotton

At least as significant as the changing style of clothes were the fabrics from which they were made. Although cotton garments had become 'conventional commodities in the clothing of the working population' by the end of the eighteenth century, in the following decades expansion of the Manchester cotton industry, mass production of clothing and improved transportation to ease distribution, meant that among the working classes cotton virtually obliterated woollen and linen clothing.[104] In 1828, a 'Mr. Hall of Sneed park, near Bristol', felt the English wool trade to be in such decline, and 'the unfortunate grower' in such 'deep distress' that he sent some woollen cloth to the King with a request that he wear it as a coat 'conceiving that this would set an illustrious example to the nobility

---

[103] A. McFarlane-Melloy, email to V. Richmond, 25 April 2004. Diana Gittins noted that female patients at Severalls Hospital in Essex were still wearing open drawers in the late 1950s. Diana Gittins, *Madness in its Place: Narratives of Severall's Hospital, 1913–1997* (London: Routledge, 1998), p. 135.

[104] For cotton consumption among the 'working population' in eighteenth-century Britain see Lemire, *Fashion's Favourite*, pp. 96–108 and Styles, *Dress of the People*, Chapter 7.

Fig. 1.1. Ethel Melloy with drawers visible below her skirt. c.1910.

and kingdom, and lead them to encourage a manufacture, which he conceived to be of great importance to the public good'. The King expressed 'the real satisfaction' he would 'feel in wearing so beautiful a specimen of the cloth', but the wool trade could not compete with cotton.[105]

Cotton fabrics came in a variety of weights and qualities, from the heaviest fustian to the finest cambric, but calico became the ubiquitous fabric for working-class underclothes and many women's and children's

[105] *The Cottager's Monthly Visitor*, 8 (1828), 83–5.

garments.[106] Stiff and often scratchy when new, though softening with wear and washing, it was used for numerous garments, including shirts, shifts, baby clothing, caps and aprons. Spufford and Fontaine both document chapmen and pedlars selling cotton as well as linen for non-elite underclothing in the seventeenth century, although linen still predominated.[107] John Styles identified linen as the usual cloth for men's shirts in the 1700s, and Beverly Lemire argues that by the third quarter of the eighteenth century linen shirts 'were plentiful even in the most humble communities'.[108] But both Styles and Lemire also note the use of cotton in the closing decades of the century, and in the 1800s, according to Vanda Foster, 'Fine white linen shirts were a status symbol' among the elite.[109] Styles, however, questions how rapidly cotton assumed ascendancy as *the* fabric for plebeian underclothes, arguing that it began 'to gain a foothold in the markets for plain shirting and shifting' only in the 1820s.[110] But that it did so from at least that point is certain and a Sussex curate, who established a local clothing charity, remembered that in the 1820s, '[t]he lower classes did not wear linen underclothes, but calico'.[111]

Styles found that in the late eighteenth century the dress of the different classes was distinguished not by the type of clothing but by the quality and costliness of the fabrics from which it was made.[112] In the nineteenth century both the style and the fabrics would denote class differences. As a child in the 1830s, Warwickshire agricultural labourer Joseph Arch, who later founded the National Union of Agricultural Labourers, was regularly involved in 'pitched battles' between the children of agricultural labourers, like himself, and the sons of wheelwrights, master tailors and

---

[106] According to *The Draper's Dictionary*, the first all-cotton calico appeared in 1773, calicos until then having been made with a linen warp and cotton weft. S. William Beck, *The Draper's Dictionary. A Manual of Textile Fabrics: Their History and Applications* (London: The Warehousemen & Drapers' Journal Office, 1844), p. 43.
[107] Spufford, *Great Reclothing*, pp. 90, 144–5; Fontaine, *History of Pedlars*, p. 188.
[108] Lemire, *Business of Everyday Life*, pp. 118–19.
[109] Lemire, *Fashion's Favourite*, p. 103; Beverly Lemire, '"A good stock of cloaths": the changing market for cotton clothing in Britain, 1750–1800', *Textile History*, 22:2 (1991), 311–28; 311–8; John Styles, 'Manufacturing, consumption and design in eighteenth-century England', in John Brewer and Roy Porter (eds), *Consumption and the World of Goods* (London: Routledge, 1993), pp. 527–54; 538; Styles, *Dress of the People*, pp. 109–32, though here Styles warns against assuming too widespread use of cotton; Foster, *Visual History of Costume*, p. 15.
[110] Styles, *Dress of the People*, p. 129.
[111] Edward Boys Ellman, *Recollections of a Sussex Parson* (London: Skeffington & Son, 1912), pp. 21, 23.
[112] Styles, *Dress of the People*, p. 32.

tradesmen who 'were just becoming genteel'. These he said were the battles 'of smock-frock against cloth-coat'.[113]

Fustian, the typical fabric of nineteenth-century labouring men's trousers and other outer garments, was the generic term for a variety of cloths, including moleskin, jean and corduroy. Originally a linen fabric, then a linen-cotton mix and by the nineteenth century increasingly cotton only, fustian, long associated with the working man, became a metaphor for him.[114] In 1845 Friedrich Engels declared that fustian had 'become the proverbial costume of the working men, who are called "fustian jackets"... in contrast to the gentlemen who wear broad cloth'.[115] At mid century it was a common journalistic device to indicate the extremes of the social hierarchy by claiming that a man was a man whether in 'velvet or fustian' or 'ermine or fustian'.[116] With the growth of class consciousness the difference in fabrics assumed political connotations. 'Place *Fustian* in the dock, let *Silk Gown* charge the culprit with being a "physical force Chartist"... and forthwith *Broad Cloth* in the jury box will bellow out 'GUILTY', claimed Julian Harney during the trials of Chartist activists in 1848.[117] By this time, as Paul Pickering demonstrates, fustian had become the 'symbolic lingua franca' of Chartism, not least because of Feargus O'Connor's appearance in a suit of fustian, specially manufactured in Manchester, for his staged release from prison in 1841.[118]

The use of cotton also challenges J. C. Flugel's theory that in the nineteenth century men put aside colourful and decorative dress in favour of sober plain clothing in dark colours.[119] This has been questioned by Christopher Breward and even, in the case of working-class men's dress, John Harvey, who otherwise vigorously supports it.[120] As Sarah Levitt

---

[113] Joseph Arch, *From Ploughtail to Parliament: An Autobiography* (London: Cresset Library, 1986 [1898]), p. 31.
[114] S. F. A. Caulfeild and Blanche C. Saward, *The Dictionary of Needlework* (London: L. Upcott Gill, 1882), p. 218; Lemire, *Fashion's Favourite*, p. 90.
[115] Friedrich Engels, *The Condition of the Working Class in England* (London: Penguin, 1987 [1845]), pp. 102–3.
[116] *The Family Economist*, 1 (1854), p. 22; *The Quarterly Magazine of the Independent Order of Odd-Fellows, Manchester Unity Friendly Society*, 3 (1861), 94, 113.
[117] John Belchem, *Popular Radicalism in Nineteenth-Century Britain* (Basingstoke: Macmillan, 1996), pp. 93–4. See also Lemire, *Business of Everyday Life*, pp. 132–3.
[118] Paul Pickering, 'Class without words: symbolic communication in the Chartist movement', *Past and Present*, 112 (1986), 144–62.
[119] J. C. Flugel, *The Psychology of Clothes* (London: Hogarth Press and Institute of Psychoanalysis, 1940 [1930]), pp. 110–11.
[120] Breward, *Hidden Consumer*, pp. 24–5; Christopher Breward, *The Culture of Fashion: A New History of Fashionable Dress* (Manchester University Press, 1995), pp. 170–6; John Harvey, *Men in Black* (London: Reaktion, 1997), p. 196.

points out, the fustian clothes of the majority 'made a strong contrast with the dark woollens of tailored suits. They were cut loosely without padding ... and their colours ranged from white buff and yellow to brown and blue'.[121]

Ready-made clothing

In tandem with changes in dress style and the rise of cotton was the eclipse – though not the obliteration – of home-made, bespoke and second-hand clothing by ready-made. It has been well established that ready-made clothing was available from at least the eighteenth century, but it was with the slop dealers, originally suppliers of clothing to the navy and army, that from the 1830s the ready-made trade began to expand most rapidly.[122] Hyam and Co., for example, with a manufacturing base in Colchester and shops in London, Birmingham, Liverpool and Manchester, had some 8,000 employees by 1852.[123] Jewish companies dominated the trade, many entrepreneurs transferring from the declining used-clothing trade, but they were criticised for their use of sweated – including prison – labour to keep prices low.[124] Mayhew recorded that prisoners at Brixton supplied Moses and Son, the largest clothing firm in England by mid century, with shirts, while inmates at Holloway House of Correction made men's outerwear 'for different mercantile firms in the Metropolis'.[125] There was also criticism of the poor quality of ready-made goods.[126] The 'staple' fabric of the industry, says Ginsburg, was 'shoddy', made from old materials, shredded, respun and rewoven.[127] This was Engels's 'so-called "Devil's-dust" cloth, manufactured for sale and not for use'.[128]

Nevertheless, comparatively low prices made ready-made clothing popular. Moses boasted: 'Ready-made Suits that a Beau Brummel would

---

[121] Levitt, 'Cheap mass-produced men's clothing', 179–80.
[122] John Styles, 'Clothing the north: the supply of non-elite clothing in the eighteenth-century north of England', *Textile History*, 25:2 (1994), 139–66; 156–7; Beverly Lemire, 'Developing consumerism and the ready-made clothing trade in Britain, 1750–1800', *Textile History*, 15:1 (1984), 21–44; 30–3; Levitt, 'Cheap mass-produced men's clothing', 184. Spufford also cites the availability of ready-made clothing in the seventeenth century. Spufford, *Great Reclothing*, p. 125; Lemire, *Dress, Culture and Commerce*, Chapter 1.
[123] Clare Rose and Vivienne Richmond (eds), *Clothing, Society and Culture in Nineteenth-Century England*, 3 vols (London: Pickering & Chatto, 2011), vol. I, pp. liv, 1.
[124] Ginsburg, 'Rags to riches', 125; Ugolini, *Men and Menswear*, pp. 137–40. For the role of Jews in the seventeenth- and eighteenth-century clothing trades see, Lemire, *Dress, Culture and Commerce*, Chapter 3.
[125] Mayhew and Binny, *Criminal Prisons*, pp. 195, 563.
[126] Ugolini, *Men and Menswear*, pp. 137–9.   [127] Ginsburg, 'Rags to riches', 128.
[128] Engels, *Condition of the Working Class*, p. 103.

have been proud to wear, at prices that a mechanic could afford to pay.'[129] In 1846, for example, they were advertising ten different types of men's trousers, ranging from fustians at 1s. 10d. a pair to 'Plain and Fancy Gambroon' at 5s., plus: 'An endless variety of Plain and Fancy Winter and Summer Trousers, which defy description.'[130]

The early expansion of the ready-made industry was mostly, but not exclusively, focused on male clothing. But the development of standardised sizing opened the way for mass production of ready-made women's clothes, beginning in the 1870s, at the same time as improvements in commercial sewing machines. The trade increased in the 1880s with the use of jersey fabrics, which allowed a more 'flexible fit', and took off in the 1890s with the move away from dresses to skirt and blouse or tailored coat. These, says Clare Rose, 'were turned out in their thousands by factories in Manchester and Bradford'.[131]

Sales of ready-made clothing were promoted, from at least the 1840s, by aggressive advertising.[132] The abolition of advertisement and newspaper stamp duties in the 1850s, and the rising disposable incomes of the working classes encouraged the great expansion of the advertising industry in the second half of the nineteenth century and estimates suggest that by 1907 annual corporate expenditure on advertising in press, posters and transport stood around £12m.[133] Breward, Ugolini and Rose all demonstrate the extensive use of advertising by clothing manufacturers and retailers.[134] And borrowing from Rob Schorman's work on clothes' retailing in late-nineteenth-century America, Rose suggests that the abundance of images in advertising material helped to shape normative ideas and expectations about clothing styles, whether or not people could afford to buy them.[135]

---

[129] E. Moses & Son, *The Universal Passport* (London, 1858), p. 18; E. Moses & Son, *The Growth of an Important Branch of British Industry. (The Ready-made Clothing System)* (London, 1860), p. 6.

[130] E. Moses & Son, *The Past, The Present, and the Future, A Public Address on the Opening of the New Establishment of E. Moses & Son* (London, 1846), p. 15.

[131] C. Rose and Richmond, *Clothing, Society and Culture*, vol. I, p. lvii; Andrew Godley, 'The development of the UK clothing industry, 1850–1950: output and productivity growth', *Business History*, 37:4 (1995), 46–63; 56–9; Andrew Godley, 'Singer in Britain: the diffusion of sewing machine technology and its impact on the clothing industry in the United Kingdom, 1860–1905', *Textile History*, 27:1 (1996), 59–76; 62–3.

[132] C. Rose and Richmond, *Clothing, Society and Culture*, vol. I, p. liv.

[133] T. R. Nevett, *Advertising in Britain: A History* (London: Heinemann, 1982), pp. 67–8, 71.

[134] C. Rose and Richmond, *Clothing, Society and Culture*, vol. I, p. lix; C. Rose, *Making, Selling and Wearing*, Chapter 3; Ugolini, *Men and Menswear*, pp. 221–2; Breward, *Hidden Consumer*, pp. 166–70.

[135] C. Rose, *Making, Selling and Wearing*, p. 109.

Occupational uniforms

Styles notes the relative paucity of eighteenth-century civilian occupational uniforms, but they spread exponentially during the nineteenth.[136] As new occupations were created and some older ones expanded or professionalised, and as employers sought to create corporate identities and impose a visual order on the swiftly industrialising and often confusingly anonymous urban sprawl, uniforms, previously the distinctive attire of the few, became the working dress of many.[137] Legislation between 1829 and 1856 to establish police forces nationwide, for example, made uniformed policemen a familiar sight.[138] From the 1880s canal companies began issuing uniforms to employees, but more noticeable were the railway workers who, between 1850 and 1905 increased tenfold to some 600,000, most of whom wore a uniform.[139]

Railways also spawned a host of related service industries such as restaurants and hotels whose staff were often liveried. An obvious benefit to employees of a corporate uniform was that it saved wear and tear of their own clothes, but additionally, while those at the bottom of their company or institution hierarchy could be as economically hard pressed as many of their non-uniformed and unskilled peers, more senior employees received higher wages and salaries and some positions came with other benefits. Railway workers, says Trevor May, were provided with 'cheap coal, free clothing, company housing, relative security, and the prospect of a pension'. There was also the possibility of promotion. Engine-drivers, for example, who on the London & North Western railway earned at least 33s. a week at mid century, usually began as engine-cleaners.[140] Combined with the other benefits this lifted such workers well out of the ranks of 'the poor'.

Fashion and emulation

A common complaint in nineteenth-century England was the impossibility of distinguishing the different classes, due to the similarity of their

---

[136] Styles, *Dress of the People*, p. 51.
[137] Elizabeth Wilson, *Adorned in Dreams: Fashion and Modernity*, revd edn (London: I. B. Tauris, 2003), p. 36.
[138] David Philips, 'Crime, law and punishment in the Industrial Revolution', in Patrick O'Brien and Roland Quinault (eds), *The Industrial Revolution and British Society* (Cambridge University Press, 1993), pp. 156–82; pp. 159–60; Carolyn Steedman, *The Radical Soldier's Tale* (London: Routledge, 1988), p. 53.
[139] Lansdell, *Clothes of the Cut*, p. 19. Trevor May, *The Victorian Railway Worker* (Princes Risborough: Shire, 2003), p. 3.
[140] May, *Victorian Railway Worker*, pp. 5, 15, 23–4, 29.

dress.¹⁴¹ As many foreign visitors commented, there was no national peasant dress and the invention of a 'traditional' costume for Scotland and Wales had no English parallel.¹⁴² German Max Schlesinger found his co-passengers on a mid-century Thames pleasure steamer to be 'of a mixed description', but noted that in England:

a 'mixed society' does not by any means present so striking an appearance as in Germany or France... The French blouse, or the German 'kittel', have no existence in this country.¹⁴³

While visitors may have taken longer to discern the differences in appearance between the different classes, they existed nevertheless. Arthur Munby, walking through the city on a Saturday afternoon, could easily distinguish between different types of metropolitan female worker. He saw:

elegant milliners and shopwomen, earning good wages & affecting the dress and style of ladies; & needlewomen & prentice girls, whose clothes are of fashionable cut but worn and poor... Below them both are the common work-girls, shabby & lean & careless of appearance.¹⁴⁴

Beverly Lemire notes that by the end of the eighteenth century comparatively cheap fashionable clothing was available in all corners of the country, and Munby had such a keen eye for women's modes of dress because he feared the encroachment of fashion was having a deleterious effect on 'rustic' clothing.¹⁴⁵ In 1868 a Parliamentary Assistant Commissioner considered Cumberland and Westmoreland 'probably the last counties of England to receive the impulse of advancing civilization', yet even here, he asserted, the female farm servants displayed:

A passion for dress... a girl whose ordinary costume is a coarse petticoat, pinned close round her body, and wooden clogs, will appear at a dance in a white muslin

---

¹⁴¹ Neil McKendrick, 'The commercialization of fashion', in Neil McKendrick, John Brewer and J. H. Plumb (eds), *The Birth of a Consumer Society: The Commercialization of Eighteenth-century England* (London: Europa, 1982), pp. 34–99; pp. 53–4; Beverly Lemire, 'Peddling fashion: salesmen, pawnbrokers, taylors, thieves and the second-hand clothes trade in England, c.1700–1800', *Textile History*, 22:1 (1991), 67–82; 69.
¹⁴² For the creation of 'traditional' Scottish and Welsh costume see Hugh Trevor-Roper, 'The invention of tradition: the Highland tradition of Scotland', and Prys Morgan, 'From a death to a view: the hunt for the Welsh past in the Romantic period', in Eric Hobsbawm and Terence Ranger (eds), *The Invention of Tradition* (Cambridge University Press, 2002), pp. 15–41 and 43–100.
¹⁴³ Max Schlesinger, *Saunterings In and About London* (London, 1853), p. 140. The 'kittel' was a kind of smock.
¹⁴⁴ TCLC, MUNB, 12, 22 February 1862. ¹⁴⁵ Lemire, *Fashion's Favourite*, pp. 187–9.

dress, white kid boots and gloves, and with a wreath of artificial flowers on her head.[146]

Eighteenth-century commentators complained about the spread of London fashions occasioned by the improved road system, and in the succeeding century what the roads had started the railways hastened, further lessening the isolation of those who remained in rural areas.[147] But even more than new forms of transport, domestic servants have been credited with the spread of fashionable dress down the social scale in provincial and rural areas.[148] Flora Thompson claimed that in her Oxfordshire hamlet in the 1880s, girls in domestic service, returning for holidays, 'helped to set the standard of what was worn'.[149] Most servants originated in the country and moved to the towns and cities with, as John Burnett points out, London – the fashion centre of Britain – 'the strongest magnet'.[150] In the city, they had access to a greater variety of shops, and drapers were the first to introduce plate-glass windows and to dress them with dazzling displays.[151] At eight o'clock in the morning, wrote journalist George Sala, the West End's 'magnificent linendrapery establishments' took down their shutters to reveal, 'the rich piled velvet mantles... the *moire* and *glacé* silks arranged in artful folds, the laces and

---

[146] *Commission on the Employment of Children, Young Persons, and Women in Agriculture (1867). Appendix Part I, To Second Report.* Parliamentary Papers 1868–69 XIII, pp. 134, 141.
[147] Breward, *Culture of Fashion*, p. 129.
[148] McKendrick, 'The commercialization of fashion', pp. 59–60.
[149] Flora Thompson, *Lark Rise to Candleford: A Trilogy* (London: Penguin, 1973 [1939–45]), p. 102. Barbara English's assessment of the reliability of *Lark Rise* asserts that 'some sections... can be shown to be true, some doubtful or suspect, others untrue'. She reaches this conclusion by comparing it with other sources and assuming, when they differ, that the inaccuracy lies in *Lark Rise*. This may often be the case, but English does not question the reliability of those other sources which include, for example, 'decennial census enumerators' returns' which are known to often contain errors. In using *Lark Rise* I acknowledge its romanticisation of rural poverty, and treat Thompson's dates with caution, seeing her descriptions as relevant to the general period rather than a specific year. I have also tried to apply a 'common sense' approach to its usage, questioning what Thompson would have achieved by falsification or invention, which would be tedious to discuss in each instance, but also bearing in mind that for some purposes impressions are as important as 'truth'. Where possible I have supported or contrasted Thompson's evidence with other sources. Where this is not possible readers must make their own decision about reliability. Barbara English, 'Lark Rise and Juniper Hill: a Victorian community in literature and history', *Victorian Studies*, 29:1 (1985), 7–34; 19.
[150] Burnett, *Useful Toil*, p. 129. See also Theresa M. McBride, *The Domestic Revolution: The Modernisation of Household Service in England and France, 1820–1920* (London: Croom Helm, 1976), Chapter 2.
[151] David Alexander, *Retailing in England During the Industrial Revolution* (London: Athlone Press, 1970), p. 136.

gauzes, the innumerable whim-whams and fribble-frabble of fashion'.[152] Even if the servants could not afford to buy the goods they could pass on, in letters and visits home, what they had seen.

Living in their employers' homes and caring for their clothes may also have led servants to assimilate the sartorial practices they observed – such as the wearing of drawers by women. Although the initial adoption of an unfamiliar garment would be a learned process, regular wearing would soon make it, for them, an unconscious practice – a form of habitus. Returning home could lead to a sense of alienation. Thirteen-year-old Edward Humphries' first post in service was as page-boy at a bridge club in London's West End. 'Here was I', he wrote,

a raw Devonshire dumpling suddenly brought into contact, however remote, with the aristocracy of Britain. Smartly dressed for the part, too... page's uniform, plus box calf leather boots, black raincoat and a silk top-hat with a cockade.

This was a boy who had previously shared a bedsitter with his mother, and when he returned to visit her he 'had a feeling of not belonging any more'.[153] Humphries eventually 'drifted away', but others retained contact and would surely have disseminated to younger siblings the habits they had absorbed and, later, instilled them in their own children.[154]

Katrina Honeyman offered the 'powerful force of emulation' as a reason why, in the early decades of the twentieth century, working-class men adopted the tailored woollen suit, previously worn only by elite men, when for many it 'was neither a comfortable nor a practical garment'.[155] But Beverly Lemire is one of several historians who caution against presupposing 'a slavish and uncritical interpretation of high fashion by non-elites'.[156] Weatherill and Fontaine both note that in the early-modern period those at the top of the social hierarchy often owned less of the new consumer goods than those lower down, indicating a differentiated culture of fashionable consumption.[157] In the eighteenth century, says Styles, emulation and social aspiration – roundly condemned in the nineteenth century – could be interpreted positively as a desirable spur to economic and social improvement. But he also points out that the

---

[152] George Augustus Sala, *Twice Round the Clock, or the Hours of the Day and Night in London* (London: Richard Marsh, 1862), pp. 75, 77.
[153] BAWCA, 1:361, Edward S. Humphries, 'Childhood. An autobiography of a boy from 1889–1906'.
[154] Lucy Delap found this to be the case among Edwardian servants. Lucy Delap, *Knowing Their Place: Domestic Service in Twentieth-century Britain* (Oxford University Press, 2011), p. 28.
[155] Honeyman, *Well Suited*, p. 3. [156] Lemire, *Business of Everyday Life*, p. 111.
[157] Weatherill, *Consumer Behaviour*, p. 195. Fontaine, *History of Pedlars*, p. 188.

wealthy adopted elements of plebeian dress.[158] This also sometimes happened in the nineteenth century; Anne Buck, for example, documented the fashion among middle-class girls in the 1870s and 1880s for a costume based on that of Newhaven fishwives. Described by one wearer as 'striped cotton skirts, turned up tunics of blue serge, striped cotton collar and cuffs and little aprons with pockets', it became, she said, 'a passion – *not* to be like a Newhaven fishwife was tragedy'.[159]

Among the working classes peer pressure, rather than elite emulation, was more often the sartorial driver. In 1816, William Lloyd, Secretary of the Sunday School Union, gave evidence to a Select Committee on education in London. Sunday school attendance, he said, made the pupils 'clean in their persons and respectful in their behaviour', and instead of 'dirty, ill-behaved children' they became 'decent and creditable'. The reason he gave was that:

When they see other children better clothed than themselves, they apply to their parents for clothes, and generally succeed and get better clothes... [Parents] are very desirous for the creditable appearance of their children, and they often deny themselves many gratifications to procure clothing for them.[160]

The Sunday schools were attended exclusively by working-class children and it was, therefore, peer conformity not socially superior emulation that the children and their parents strove for.

Autobiographical accounts also negate the emulation theory and stress that although working-class people were often concerned to dress in fashion, that fashion had little or nothing to do with the changing dress styles of elite circles, but was a peer-group and locally determined mode of dress. Brierley commented that the influence of Parisian fashions in the 1820s 'was confined to the aristocracy. The working classes did not share it.'[161] Revisiting the Haigh Moor Brewery in 1873, Munby was dismayed to find the women in the barrel-washing house 'actually in petticoats' rather than trousers. Asking one of them what she had done with her 'breeches', she replied: 'Left 'em off!... Ah thowt Ah'd be i't fashion, yo see!', but her 'fashion' was simply standard local 'kirtles and clogs.'[162] The clothes sent home to relatives by domestic servants were often cast-off garments from their employers and, as discarded garments,

---

[158] Styles, *Dress of the People*, pp. 188–93.
[159] Anne Buck, *Clothes and the Child: A Handbook of Children's Dress in England 1500–1900* (Bedford: Ruth Bean, 1996), p. 234.
[160] *First Report. Minutes of Evidence Taken Before the Select Committee Appointed to Inquire into the Education of the Lower Orders of the Metropolis. 1816*, Parliamentary Papers 1816 IV, p. 77.
[161] Brierley, *Home Memories*, p. 33.   [162] TCLC, MUNB, 41, 11 September 1873.

would not have been in the latest fashion. Nevertheless, according to Flora Thompson, the women in her 1880s Oxfordshire hamlet, despite their mantra of 'Better be out of the world than out of the fashion', considered them rather avant-garde, the hamlet fashion being 'a year or two behind outside standards, and strictly limited as to style and colour'. The garments might, therefore, be cut down for children's clothes, only to be later regretted when the hamlet fashion caught up.[163]

The middle- and upper-class fashion for white weddings, following Queen Victoria's marriage in 1840, was rarely copied by the working classes. When, in 1904, Gertrude Jekyll saw the wedding photograph of a Surrey labouring couple, the bride with 'a veil and orange blossoms, a shower bouquet, and *pages!*' and the bridegroom in a cheap suit, billycock hat and '*white cotton gloves!*', she concluded that 'Every sort of folly or absurdity', was being committed by their class in their 'insane striving to be what they think is "fashionable"'.[164] But the fact that she thought it worthy of (indignant) comment indicates its novelty. Hannah Mitchell was explicit that her marriage, in 1895, was 'no white satin and orange-blossom wedding'. This is not to deny the influence of elite fashion on her wedding-dress choices, but it was an inspiration rather than a model for simple imitation. Styles acknowledges that elite fashions trickled down the social scale, but he points out that as they did so the fabrics changed, as did the way they were worn, the garments they were worn with, and the occasions on which they were worn, the lives of ordinary people being greatly different from those of the wealthy.[165]

As a workshop dressmaker in the 1880s, Mitchell was daily surrounded by 'rich brocades, gleaming satins and velvets, with a bloom like ripe fruit' and on one occasion was chosen to be the mannequin for a customer's wedding dress. It was 'heavy white satin embroidered with silver', and the ten bridesmaids' frocks were 'a lovely shade called 'vieux rose', neither pink nor mauve, but like the sunrise itself, and the dress for the bride's mother 'French grey', pale grey with a pink flush over it'. Given Mitchell's obvious appreciation it is perhaps inevitable that this wedding influenced her own. She had three bridesmaids – 'a novelty for working-class folk... [and] thought rather swank' – two of whom she dressed in pink. Her own dress was a 'simple grey frock and grey velvet hat', and the third, adult, bridesmaid, also 'looked like a bride herself in grey, trimmed with lace'.[166] Rather than the client's bridal dress, Mitchell echoed the

---

[163] F. Thompson, *Lark Rise*, p. 102.   [164] Jekyll, *Old West Surrey*, p. 264.
[165] Styles, *Dress of the People*, pp. 323–4.
[166] Geoffrey Mitchell (ed.), *The Hard Way Up: The Autobiography of Hannah Mitchell, Suffragette and Rebel* (London: Virago, 1977), pp. 74, 90.

pinks and greys of the bridesmaids and the bride's mother, even with her own dress, and seemingly harboured little desire to differentiate herself from her third bridesmaid. Mabel Nicholls from Southsea, the daughter of a docker turned tobacconist, and Susan Silvester, who worked in a West Midlands bakery, also both wore grey when they married around the turn of the twentieth century.[167] And while most brides strove to be married in a new gown, it was usually obtained with subsequent use in mind, not as a garment to be worn solely on the wedding day.

The same year that Hannah Mitchell married, Alice and Ruby Chase, Portsmouth carpenter's daughters, acted as bridesmaids at their brother's wedding in outfits very different from those worn by Mitchell's bridesmaids. The sisters proudly sported, 'blue corduroy dresses, blue moire sashes, blue velvet hats, blue hair ribbons, black stockings and court shoes, and white gloves'. Later that year they wore the outfits to the Church Anniversary Sunday. 'That summer', wrote Alice,

everyone wore blue. The popular song of the day was 'Two Little Girls in Blue' and we led the fashion by being the first two sisters to go out in our blue, dressed exactly alike. It made us very happy to lead the fashion instead of following it.[168]

The sartorial reference, then, was not elite fashion, but a music-hall story of lost love, written in 1892 and popularised by 'Lovely Lively Lily Burnand' who had begun life in the East End of London.[169] Breward similarly charts the relationship between music hall and menswear, tracing the transition from 'swell magnificence' with its celebration of fashionable opulence, to the 'masher' who disdained elite fashionable emulation in favour of 'novelty'. The latter's accessible image 'generally cemented its popularity' and was embraced by ready-made tailoring firms as an advertising ploy.[170]

For both men and women, any emulation of elite fashions could only be partial, because the working classes could not afford clothes of the same quality or quantity, nor the array of accessories and accoutrements necessary to achieve the complete 'look'; because elite fashions were

---

[167] BAWCA, 1:532, Dora Nicholls, 'My story'; BAWCA, 1:628, Susan Silvester, p. 21.
[168] BAWCA, 1:141, Alice Maud Chase, 'The memoirs of Alice Maud Chase', p. 31.
[169] 'Two Little Girls in Blue', *Folksongs Around the World*: ingeb.org/songs/twolittg.html; 'Lily Burnand': freepages.genealogy.rootsweb.ancestry.com/~jgar/lily burnand music hall artist.htm; Michael Kilgarriff, *Sing Us One of the Old Songs: A Guide to Popular Song 1860–1920* (Oxford University Press, 1998), pp. 94, 138–9. (Kilgarriff gives 1892 as the date of the song, *Folksongs* as 1893.) For female music-hall performers see also Judith Walkowitz, *City of Dreadful Delight: Narratives of Sexual Danger in Late-Victorian London* (London: Virago, 1992), pp. 45–6.
[170] Breward, *Hidden Consumer*, pp. 222–36. See also Walkowitz, *City of Dreadful Delight*, pp. 43–4.

designed for people who lived an elite lifestyle and so, for instance, travelled in a carriage rather than walked dirty streets; and because their bodies bore the irremovable marks of their labour. Munby, visiting a Wigan pit-brow girl one Sunday morning, noticed that her face, neck and arms 'were comparatively clean, though the traces of coaldust were visible in every fold of the skin'. She had been house-cleaning, 'and hadn't yet got smartened up for the day', but the coal dust would still be there where she had.[171]

And beside the impossibility of the working classes being able to pull off a faithful imitation of the sartorial practices of the wealthy, there is also the question of how much they wished to. The elite's conviction of their own desirable superiority led them to assume others aspired to imitate them, but there was a great deal of class and community pride among the working classes and Breward detects 'the potential of social and work relations for producing a clearly defined, almost subcultural series of working-class "looks"'.[172] This is clearly demonstrated in Charles Shaw's description of the group of young men for whom two pews were reserved at the annual celebration at his Staffordshire Primitive Methodist chapel in the 1840s. They wore distinctive 'neckerchiefs... about three inches deep, with the ends tied in little bows in front... they were all made of dark blue silk, with small white spots'. The young men were 'well-known prize-fighters or celebrated footracers and their abetters', and their distinctive dress clearly advertised their allegiance and virility. 'You saw no other class but the class these men represented with these neckties on', said Shaw.[173]

As Lemire says, changes in dress style 'arose from a host of intersecting factors rooted in personal, local and regional influences'.[174] The 'union shirt, bell-bottomed trousers, the heavy leather belt, pricked out in fancy designs with the large steel buckle and the thick, iron-shod clogs' of Manchester scuttlers owed nothing to elite fashions.[175] And although, as an aspiring young poet, Ben Brierley 'went so far as to adopt the "Byron tie," and try to look melancholy', it was the cultural resonance that attracted; he was aiming to look like a poet rather than an aristocrat.[176] Indeed, men who adopted elements of socially superior dress risked assaults on their masculinity. Umbrellas appear to have been especially suspect; Francis Place recalled that at the end of the eighteenth century his father would wear a large canvas hat in wet weather,

---

[171] TCLC, MUNB, 6, 30 September 1860.   [172] Breward, *Hidden Consumer*, p. 95.
[173] Shaw, *When I Was a Child*, p. 214.   [174] Lemire, *Business of Everyday Life*, p. 111.
[175] R. Roberts, *Classic Slum*, p. 155. See also Breward, *Hidden Consumer*, p. 94.
[176] Brierley, *Home Memories*, p. 31.

50   Setting the standard: working-class dress

but refused to use an umbrella as 'he scorned the effeminacy'.[177] Breward similarly highlights the presumed connection, a century later, between sartorial display and homosexuality, and Robert Roberts detailed how, in Edwardian Salford:

> The proletariat knew and marked what they considered to be sure signs of homosexuality, though the term was unknown. Any evidence of dandyism in the young was severely frowned on. One 'mother bound' youth among us... strolled out on Sundays wearing of all things gloves, 'low quarters' and carrying an umbrella! The virile damned him at once – an incipient 'nancy' beyond all doubt.[178]

Peer pressure could also act to regulate women's dress that was perceived to be inappropriately aspirational. Robert Roberts remembered a family who moved out to the new suburbs where to be seen in the characteristic northern 'clogs and shawl would have meant instant social demotion for the whole family'. The daughter was therefore 'sent to the weaving shed wearing coat and shoes and thereby shocked a whole establishment. Here was a "forward little bitch", getting above herself'.[179] Anita Hughes who began work in a Leyland cotton mill in 1904, objected to wearing the shawl instead of a coat because, 'it seemed stupid to me wearing it 6 days a week when we had coats that wanted wearing up. I plucked up courage and went to work one day in a coat and head shawl.' But 'It was all eyes on deck', and although she claimed to have started a new fashion and 'it wasn't long before others were doing the same', she also said her sisters 'hesitated for weeks before they followed suit'.[180] According to Roberts, not until the First World War did shoes and coat, rather than clogs and shawl become acceptable in the mills.[181]

* * *

Changes in nineteenth-century working-class dress were closely related to the urbanisation and industrialisation that characterised the period. New or expanding occupations brought new or more widespread forms of proletarian dress, such as the corporate uniform, or the collars, cuffs and ties of clerical workers which visually differentiated them from manual labourers. While the demise of traditional rural dress was gradual

---

[177] Mary Thale (ed.), *The Autobiography of Francis Place, 1771–1854* (London: Cambridge University Press, 1972), p. 62.
[178] Breward, *Hidden Consumer*, pp. 246–8; R. Roberts, *Classic Slum*, pp. 54–5; 'low quarters' were essentially shoes as opposed to boots. Keith Snell notes that in some areas the low status of rural labourers in a world of increasing urbanisation and industrialisation was exacerbated by 'their smocks [which] were seen to add feminine contours to such denigration'. K. D. M. Snell, *Parish and Belonging: Community, Identity and Welfare in England and Wales, 1700–1950* (Cambridge University Press, 2009), p. 487.
[179] R. Roberts, *Classic Slum*, pp. 20–1.
[180] BAWCA, 1:357, Anita Elizabeth Hughes, 'Untitled', pp. 7–8.
[181] R. Roberts, *Classic Slum*, pp. 20–1.

and regional differences persisted, such as the northern clogs and shawl, cotton became the staple fabric of the working classes. Although the middle and upper classes feared the erosion of visual distinctions between ranks, peer pressure, lack of funds, the practical demands of labouring lifestyles, and the availability of alternative sartorial models which reflected working-class culture, acted as a brake on anything beyond partial imitation of elite dress styles. But more importantly, for the first time, large-scale production and promotion brought new, comparatively cheap, ready-made clothing to the masses, reshaping normative ideas about the kind and quantity of clothing owned. This set the standard for the poor, and the next chapter considers the extent to which they were able to keep pace with the changes.

2   'Frankly, a mystery': budgeting for clothes

> Those labourers who can rent a cottage and a garden, can generally keep poultry and fatten a hog – and all have frequent and great help from the charitable and considerable farmers, such as milk, broth, and inferior meat, which must make up the deficiencies of earnings.[1]
>
> (Arthur Young, 1793)

> Here, and subsequently in the accounts of the weekly expenditure of labourers, I shall not insert rent or clothing, as I find that these are generally not paid for weekly, but are reserved to be paid for at harvest, or at odd times when more than the usual wages are earned.[2]
>
> (Edward Carleton Tufnell, 1841)

> Clothing is, frankly, a mystery... A patient visitor may extract information, perhaps, that the father gets overtime pay at Christmas, and applies some of it to the children's clothes... But in the great number of cases there is no extra money at Christmas, or at any other time, to depend upon.[3]
>
> (Maud Pember Reeves, 1913)

In his analysis of the family budgets collected at the end of the eighteenth century by the Revd David Davies and Sir Frederick Morton Eden, John Styles noted their difficulty in both obtaining accurate information on clothing expenditure and understanding 'how many of the families they studied could afford any clothing whatsoever, given that a large majority of the budgets revealed an excess of spending over income'.[4] Their contemporary, the agriculturalist Arthur Young, faced precisely the same problems, as did Edward Tufnell, researching the living conditions of south-eastern rural labourers in the mid-nineteenth century and Maud

---

[1] Young, *General View of the Agriculture*, p. 91.
[2] Edward Carleton Tufnell, *On the Dwellings and General Economy of the Labouring Classes in Kent and Sussex* (London: W. Clowes & Sons, 1841), p. 4.
[3] Maud Pember Reeves, *Round About a Pound A Week* (London: Virago, 1979 [1913]), pp. 61–2.
[4] Styles, *Dress of the People*, p. 214. Peter Jones made the same point. P. D. Jones, 'I cannot keep my place', 35–6.

Pember Reeves investigating urban poverty in the early twentieth century. Each found that even the most basic living costs generally outstripped labourers' incomes. Young presented the annual budgets of six families in the Sussex parish of Glynd (*sic*) in 1793. In each case the 'expences' of basic clothing for the man and woman – rent, fuel, food, washing materials, candles and haberdashery – exceeded the family's combined income. The shortfall in earnings, which in one instance amounted to £14 2s. 2d., was in most cases greater than the entire cost of the man's and woman's clothing, which he estimated to be £3 11s., and Young had included no allowance for children's clothes. The reality could be still more frugal: Young's figures included an adjustment of £1 12s. for decreased earnings during periods of 'Lying-in, sickness and loss of time', but extended sickness, crop failure and the death or desertion of the main breadwinner further depleted scanty incomes. While Young assumed the farmers' benevolence bolstered inadequate food supplies, he offered no suggestions about how the labourers obtained their clothing.[5]

Five decades later, Assistant Poor Law Commissioner Tufnell also found a negative disparity between incomes and expenses among Kent and Sussex labourers. He recorded, for example, a family of nine all dependent on the husband's regular earnings of 12s. a week. After deducting food, soap, candles and haberdashery the family were left with 2½d. a week, but they were drinking 'tea made with burnt crusts', and 'have no meat except on a Sunday, when a meat pudding is made'. Tufnell argued that the family's distress arose 'from the "unusual" circumstances that the children', all below working age, 'are nearly all girls, and hence can earn nothing'. But a number of children (of whichever sex) unable to contribute to the family income was common in most labouring families for many years after marriage; indeed, it was one of the life-cycle points that Rowntree identified as likely to be spent in poverty. And although Tufnell added that the man was able sometimes to earn an extra three shillings a week from piecework, he made no allowance for periods of sickness, nor did he include rent, fuel or clothes in the expenses. Faggots were bought from the man's employer, the cost stopped out of his wages, and Tufnell said that 'generally' rent and clothing expenses were met out of exceptional earnings, such as harvest, but he gave no evidence that these earnings were sufficient and no suggestions about what

---

[5] Young, *General View of the Agriculture*, p. 91. Young allowed the man one smock, waistcoat, breeches, pair of shoes and stockings, hat, handkerchief and two shirts, and the woman one gown, petticoat, and pair of shoes, two shifts, aprons, and pairs of stockings and an unspecified number of handkerchiefs and caps. He also included an unspecified 'etc.' for both the man and the woman.

happened when they were not.⁶ In 1850, for example, the *Morning Chronicle* reported that Kent women usually contributed around £7 to the family's annual income by hop-picking, which financed a number of 'extra expenses', including 'shoes, change of raiment', but the past year had seen 'the almost universal of the failure of the hops', throwing many people into 'deep distress'.⁷ Still, on the eve of the First World War, Rowntree and Kendall pointed out that in rural areas it was commonly assumed that clothing was paid for with overtime or Michaelmas money:

> But, except in the case of those definitely engaged for six months or a year, overtime money is often more than counterbalanced by the amount of 'standing off' in bad weather. And where 30s. or even £2 Michaelmas money is received, it is sometimes required for rent; but even if the cottage is free, such a sum cannot cover clothing for a family for a year.⁸

Some of the rural poor, as Young suggested, kept a pig or two. A Sussex woman recalled that as a child in the 1850s and 1860s, her father, when possible, 'bought two little pigs every spring'. After fattening, one was kept for home eating and the other sold, some of the money used 'to buy clothing for us all'.⁹ John Benson also highlights the importance of pig-keeping in the domestic economy, and Robert Malcolmson and Stephanos Mastoris estimate that between a quarter and a half 'of cottagers, small-holders and rural labourers probably kept a pig'. But this leaves between half and three-quarters who did not. Pig-keeping was more difficult, though not impossible, in urban areas, but even in rural areas was not evenly distributed across the country, being 'particularly prevalent' in Lincolnshire, but 'exceptional' in Norfolk. The reasons are unclear, but some employers forbad pig-keeping fearing that workers would steal their grain to feed the pig. Also, according to Rowntree and Kendall, labourers who worked with horses or cattle were rarely allowed to keep pigs, presumably for fear of spreading diseases. And while one of the attractions of pigs was that they could be fed on waste food, and neighbours would sometimes contribute in return for a share of the meat, the very poorest homes would have produced little waste and by the early twentieth century the rising price of pigmeal was forcing former pig-keepers to give up. Finally – or rather initially – the necessary capital to buy a pig was an 'insuperable obstacle' for the poorest.¹⁰

---

⁶ Tufnell, *Dwellings and General Economy*, pp. 3–4.   ⁷ Reay, *Microhistories*, p. 110.
⁸ Rowntree and Kendall, *How the Labourer Lives*, pp. 40–1.
⁹ Alice Catherine Day, *Glimpses of Rural Life in Sussex During the Last Hundred Years* (Oxford: The Countryman, 1927), p. 22.
¹⁰ John Benson, *The Penny Capitalists: A Study of Nineteenth-century Working-class Entrepreneurs* (Dublin: Gill & Macmillan, 1983), pp. 20, 22–3, 28–9; Robert Malcolmson

In Edwardian Lambeth, where there were no benevolent farmers, no harvest, no chance of keeping a pig, and only the possibility of Christmas overtime for a few, Pember Reeves examined clothing expenditure over fifteen months. She found that 'extra careful women, or women with more money for housekeeping' subscribed 6*d.* a week to clothing or calico clubs, or 1*s.* to a boot club, but '[i]n the poorer budgets items for clothes appear at extraordinarily distant intervals, when, it is to be supposed, they can no longer be done without', or were bought only 'when summer comes and less is needed for fuel'. Apart from the club subscriptions, virtually the only expenditure on clothing in Pember Reeves's budgets was the occasional 3*d.* on cotton and tapes necessary for repairs.[11]

In the first half of the nineteenth century, and in contrast with Young's and Tufnell's findings were the budgets of northern industrial workers presented to the 1833 Factory Inquiries Commission and the 1842 Children's Employment Commission. Dr Mitchell, reporting on the South Durham coal field, told the latter that in terms of earnings, colliers had 'the advantage over the agricultural labourers', and the 1833 Commission had heard the same about cotton-factory workers.[12] Mrs B—, for example, was the wife of a fine spinner who, to his wife's knowledge, earned about 20*s.* a week. The couple had five children, only the eldest of whom was working, contributing another 5*s.* to the family budget to give a weekly total of 25*s.* After deducting food, coals, rent, candles and soap, the family were left with almost 7*s.* for other expenses including clothing. In fact, another operative considered the family 'somewhat below the average of comforts possessed by working families' thereabouts. He was also certain that as a fine spinner 'the husband must earn at least 1*l.* 8*s.* . . . instead of 1*l.*, as his wife states'.[13] If that is so, in similar families where the husband contributed a greater portion of his income to the family budget the surplus would have been even greater.

---

and Stephanos Mastoris, *The English Pig, a History* (London: Hambledon Press, 1998), pp. 63–4, 47; Rowntree and Kendall, *How the Labourer Lives*, p. 333; Anthony S. Wohl, *Endangered Lives: Public Health in Victorian Britain* (London: Dent, 1983), p. 83.

[11] Pember Reeves, *Round About a Pound*, pp. 61–3, 83–4, 86.

[12] *Children's Employment Commission. Appendix . . . Mines. Part I.* Parliamentary Papers 1842 XVI, p. 145.

[13] *Factories Inquiries Commission. First Report of the Central Board of His Majesty's Commissioners Appointed to Collect Information in the Manufacturing Districts, as to the Employment of Children in Factories, and as to the Propriety and Means of Curtailing the Hours of their Labour: with Minutes of Evidence, and Reports by District Commissioners. D.1. Lancashire District.* Parliamentary Papers 1833 XX, pp. 39–40.

The overall impression is that, whether or not women's and children's earning were included, northern factory workers, and miners, enjoyed a higher standard of living than their agricultural counterparts. But this is not to say very much since agricultural earnings were often pitifully low. And poverty was certainly not confined to the rural south-east and parts of London. Dr Mitchell claimed that colliers not only enjoyed better earnings than agricultural labourers, but 'compared with the hand-loom weavers and greater part of the population engaged in the making of cotton, linen, woollen, and silk goods' were 'highly paid'. But he also noted that 'compared with the earnings of the highly-skilled artisans in large towns, those of the collier population are decidedly inferior'.[14]

Furthermore, even if workers in northern textile factories were relatively well paid, textile towns harboured more than textile workers. Factory hands accounted for only 7 per cent of those relieved from the £26,000 raised by the Manchester and Salford District Provident Society during the severe winter of 1878–9, the majority of the remaining 93 per cent were in the building trade. When Fred Scott investigated Mancunian living standards in 1889, using the criteria employed by Booth in London, he concluded that half of the Ancoats sample, and over 60 per cent of the Salford sample were 'very poor', and he claimed the survey was conducted at a time of 'exceptionally full employment'.[15] Even among those earning comparatively high wages, growing numbers of children below working age could stretch family finances, and sickness and trade depression drastically reduced the domestic budget. John Rule noted that, 'at the bottom of the pile the farm labourers of the south and east could often afford no change of clothing at all', while the mule-spinners of the cotton towns 'gave an appearance of unostentatious comfort', but this was only 'in times of full employment'.[16]

The historian who tries to assess the quality, quantity and suitability of the poor's clothing based on income and the retail price of new cloth and clothing, or to identify a general minimum clothing budget for any given point in the century is likely to be as baffled as Young, Tufnell and Pember Reeves, and the findings would be as inconclusive.[17] In the first instance, lack of information on wage rates, hours of work and continuity

---

[14] *Children's Employment Commission. Appendix... Mines. Part I.* Parliamentary Papers 1842 XVI, p. 145.
[15] Alan J. Kidd and K. W. Roberts (eds), *City, Class and Culture: Studies of Social Policy and Cultural Production in Victorian Manchester* (Manchester University Press, 1985), pp. 50–1; Andrew Davies, *Leisure, Gender and Poverty: Working-Class Culture in Salford and Manchester, 1900–1939* (Buckingham: Open University Press, 1992), pp. 16–17.
[16] Rule, *Labouring Classes*, p. 68.
[17] Burnett and Breward also highlight the difficulty of generalising about expenditure on clothing. Burnett, *History of the Cost of Living*, p. 214; Breward, *Hidden Consumer*, p. 92.

of employment prohibits accurate income assessments. But also, as Craig Muldrew and Stephen King point out, wages must be considered in the context of 'the total value of all sources of income available to the family through what has been termed an economy of makeshifts'.[18] Hence, in addition to wages, vital resources could be obtained from, for example, home production, perquisites, gleaning, charitable gifts, crime and credit.

On the other hand, the wages of workers subjected to the truck system which, despite prohibitive legislation, persisted in some metal, mining and construction trades until at least the end of the 1880s, were likely to be worth less, in real terms, than those of workers paid in cash and free to shop where they chose. In the 1830s, prices of foodstuffs sold to workers in the handmade nail, chain and rivet trades, forced to buy from truck shops, were estimated to be between 20 and 25 per cent higher than in independent shops and, in the 1880s, up to double the cost. Similarly, South Staffordshire miners, in the 1830s, were estimated to be losing five shillings in the pound through buying at truck shops. Clearly, this left less money for other purchases. Also, says George Hilton, some masters refused to stock clothing in their truck shops, despite the potential profits, because they thought it would be pawned, or because they believed it would encourage parents to spend money on their own clothing at the expense of food for their children.[19]

Additionally, different occupations demanded different types and quantities of clothing. To be adequately equipped, the agricultural labourer working outside in cold weather, for example, required warmer clothing – and stronger boots – than the factory employee in a hot building. There was also a range of jobs which had a detrimental effect on the operatives' clothing. Munby, for example, met a young London woman who earned between two and three shillings a week scraping pigs' trotters and steeping them in lime. 'We makes a place in the lime for ourselves to sit down in', she said, 'it do burn one's clothes so (this is lime on my frock).'[20]

---

[18] Craig Muldrew and Steven King, 'Cash, wages and the economy of makeshifts in England, 1650–1800', in Peter Scholliers and Leonard Schwarz (eds), *Experiencing Wages: Social and Cultural Aspects of Wage Forms in Europe since 1500* (New York and Oxford: Berghahn, 2003), pp. 155–80; p. 155. See also, Alannah Tomkins and Steven King, 'Introduction', in Steven King and Alannah Tomkins (eds), *The Poor in England 1700–1850: An Economy of Makeshifts* (Manchester University Press, 2003), pp. 1–38; p. 13.

[19] George W. Hilton, *The Truck System* (Westport, CT: Greenwood Press, 1975), pp. 17, 30.

[20] TCLC, MUNB, 24, 27 May 1864.

As the occupational landscape changed, increasing numbers of clerks and shop assistants were required to maintain a high standard of dress on a low wage. As Lady Bell noted:

The man who is in receipt of £2 and upwards a week... and does not need to dress other than as a workman, does not need to be what the workmen call a 'collar-and-tie man,' is obviously much better off than many a clerk with the same amount.[21]

In fact, anyone earning £2 a week was 'better off than many a clerk', but Bell's main point was valid – maintaining the formal wear required for clerical and shop work was a costly business. Mrs Layton, who grew up in the East End of London during the 1860s, described her father as 'a well-educated man... employed in a government situation'. This, she explained,

compelled him to keep up an appearance which an ordinary workman, earning the same wages, would not have had to do. He always went to business in nice black clothes and a silk hat. His appearance was quite out of keeping with the neighbourhood we lived in.[22]

Female office workers often faced the same problem. A 1906 survey found that female typists earned, on average, 25–30s. a week. This was good money for a young single woman living with her parents, but Bank of England clerk Janet Courtney said that for those living independently, 30s. a week was a 'bare subsistence' since 'partial board' at a boarding house was likely to consume at least 25s. a week, which meant that '[n]othing to speak of was left for clothes'.[23] Similarly, shop assistants, male and female, had to maintain an appearance superior to their salaries.[24] 'We have to dress nicely for the shop, of course', a young draper's shopwoman told Munby, though not 'too smart'.[25] They were not to rival the customers, but even if they wished to most simply did not have the means.

Budgeting skills varied from one individual to another and the same amount of money in the hands of people with time and skill to make, repair and re-make garments went further than in the hands of those without. Moreover, the clothing needs of family members were assigned different priority according to gender and age, with working men often taking precedence. And clothing costs differed from place to place. For example, while Young gave 6s. as the price of a waistcoat and breeches

---

[21] Bell, *At the Works*, p. 52.
[22] Llewelyn Davies (ed.), *Life as We Have Known It*, pp. 6–7.
[23] Christopher Keep, 'The cultural work of the type-writer girl', *Victorian Studies*, 40:3 (1997), 401–26; 410–11.
[24] de Marly, *Working Dress*, p. 116.   [25] Hudson, *Munby*, p. 99.

in Glynd in 1793, the draper and shoemaker contracted to supply the St Paul's, Deptford, workhouse in London, which would have been looking to buy as cheaply as possible, was quoting 8s. 6d. for these items in the same year. And while Young estimated men's stockings and shoes at 4s. and 9s. respectively, the St Paul's contractor was quoting 1s. 2d. for men's stockings, and between 4s. 6d. and 5s. 11d. for men's shoes, depending on size.[26]

The figures quoted by Young and the St Paul's contractor were for new garments, but the poor could rarely afford new clothes. At the end of the century, Rowntree asked the York poor to calculate the minimum necessary annual cost of clothing for a working man and his wife. The average estimate was 26s. each, a reduction of 19s. on Young's estimate over a century earlier. But this had nothing to do with the availability of cheap ready-made clothing; it was because the vast majority of the clothing in the estimates was second-hand.[27] Clare Rose shows that ready-made boys' clothes became 'much cheaper in real terms between 1870 and 1900', but she also acknowledges that they remained beyond the reach of the poorest.[28] And when the poor did buy new clothes, it was often on credit, the interest adding to the cost.

The remainder of this chapter, then, examines the strategies employed by the poor to budget for clothing, and the prioritisation of clothing needs. It finishes with a discussion of 'flannelette', to illustrate how the spread of cotton fabrics, though cheap and washable, could impact negatively on the poor, and how economic disadvantage could force them to choose between clothing children in potentially lethal garments or not clothing them at all.

Budgeting

Mothers of families sometimes said in despair that they supposed they would have to black their own backsides and go naked. They never quite came to that; but it was difficult to keep decently covered.[29]

The various 'shifts and contrivances' required of the poor to clothe themselves and their families required ingenuity, work and careful financial management. One agricultural labourer, for example, earned the 7s. 11d. necessary for a new pair of boots by catching moles and selling the skins

---

[26] Young, *General View of the Agriculture*, p. 91; LLHAC SPD/4/2, Churchwardens and Overseers Committee (hereafter COC) Minutes 1785–1793.
[27] Rowntree, *Poverty*, pp. 381–4.
[28] C. Rose, *Making, Selling and Wearing*, pp. 124–5, 130.
[29] F. Thompson, *Lark Rise*, p. 32.

for a penny each: ninety-five moles caught and skinned and ninety-five pennies carefully stored away.[30] '[E]ven farthings had their value', said Robert Roberts. 'The smallest coin could still buy a little candle, a paper of pins, a "Dolly blue" for washing day, a good box of matches, cloth buttons or an ounce of toffee', three of his six listed items being clothing-related.[31]

Single men and women, young and in employment, often had the most money to spare for clothing, and many used it to prepare for marriage. Young men were generally charged with providing and furnishing a home, while young women built up a stock of clothing and household linen to provide for the first few years after marriage. In 1888 the Girls' Friendly Society, publishing a suggested trousseau for a working-man's wife, exhorted young women to begin preparing the items 'as soon as ever they have any thought at all of being married'.[32] But even if they did, as the family grew, the husband's wages remained static, fell or rose only minimally, and garments wore out, clothing could become a chronic problem. Munby recorded in his diary two collier girls he had seen near Shifnal, one in a straw bonnet spectacularly trimmed with 'glowing' crimson ribbon, but the dress of the other 'worn and shabby', he said, 'for she was married'.[33] As an adult, Flora Thompson recalled childhood walks in the 1880s with 'Mother in her pretty maize-coloured gown with the rows and rows of narrow brown velvet sewn round the long skirt, which stuck out like a bell, and her second-best hat with the honeysuckle'. But as the 'family grew larger and troubles crowded upon her... and the last of the pre-marriage wardrobe had worn out, the walks were given up'.[34]

Doubtless the 'troubles' that concerned Thompson's mother included the family finances. Lady Bell – yet another who found it 'somewhat difficult to obtain much information about the important item of expenditure on clothing' – stressed the need for a 'careful manager' to oversee the domestic budget.[35] Barry Reay argues that budgeting was so important that it deserves as much attention in labour history 'as the male wage and organized labour'.[36] He is also among the many who highlight the role of women as domestic-budget managers. As Jose Harris says: 'the management and expenditure of a working-class family's collective resources fell universally upon the wife. It was she who paid the bills,

---

[30] Rowntree and Kendall, *How the Labourer Lives*, pp. 55, 115–16.
[31] Roberts, *Ragged Schooling*, p. 15.
[32] TWL 5GFS/10/012, *Friendly Leaves*, February 1888.
[33] TCLC, MUNB, 40, 28 June 1872. [34] F. Thompson, *Lark Rise*, pp. 36–7.
[35] Bell, *At the Works*, pp. 69–70. [36] Reay, *Microhistories*, p. 120.

planned the menus, negotiated credit, traded with pawnbrokers, saved for clubs and holidays'.[37] Beverly Lemire identified the establishment, during the eighteenth century, of a 'culture of accounting' which required middle-class housewives to keep household accounts. By the close of the nineteenth century the same was expected of working-class women, but some lacked the necessary skills, and in any case they thought differently about money. Lemire illustrates the point with the Edwardian Lambeth housewives requested to keep accounts by Pember Reeves and her fellow Fabians. While the latter were 'steeped in the tenets of statistical evaluation' and 'the rationale of stark numeric tabulations', the housewives still 'conceived of their interactions in terms of relational narratives, explaining the context of decisions, valuing the adjudication of each purchase'.[38] And aside from periods of exceptional earnings, like harvest, many of the poor grappled with the question of how to obtain new or replacement garments only when need or opportunity arose. 'Perhaps the most necessary mental acquirement for the poor', suggested district nurse Martha Loane, was 'the ability to spread out unequal earnings equally over the entire year.'[39]

Akihito Suzuki found that a common source of anxiety among male working-class patients at Hanwell Asylum in the 1840s was an 'intemperate and extravagant wife'.[40] But the responsibility of financial management also caused women a great deal of distress. Mrs Leigh, an agricultural labourer's wife who participated in Rowntree and Kendall's 1913 survey, was more than £10 in debt, the family having, of necessity, lived for years 'a trifle above their annual income' of approximately £34. She had had no new clothes since marriage and on the day of the interview had a child away from school for want of shoes. 'I sleep all right till about twelve', she said, 'and then I wake and begin worrying about what I owe, and how to get things. Last night I lay and cried for a couple of hours.' Mrs Leigh could not sleep, but she lived, said Rowntree and Kendall, 'in a nightmare'.[41]

---

[37] Harris, *Private Lives, Public Spirit*, p. 73. See also Melanie Tebbutt, *Making Ends Meet: Pawnbroking and Working-Class Credit* (Leicester University Press, 1983), p. 38; Davies, *Leisure, Gender and Poverty*, p. 56; Ellen Ross, *Love and Toil: Motherhood in Outcast London, 1870–1918* (Oxford University Press, 1993), p. 22.
[38] Lemire, *Business of Everyday Life*, pp. 213–14.
[39] M. Loane, *From Their Point of View* (London: E. Arnold, 1908), p. 215.
[40] Akihito Suzuki, 'Lunacy and labouring men: narratives of male vulnerability in mid-Victorian London', in Roberta Bivins and John V. Pickstone (eds), *Medicine, Madness and Social History: Essays in Honour of Roy Porter* (Basingstoke: Palgrave Macmillan, 2007), pp. 118–28; p. 125.
[41] Rowntree and Kendall, *How the Labourer Lives*, pp. 59–61.

In the early 1900s Martha Loane found the 'custom of leaving the management of money to the wife is so deeply rooted, that children always speak of the family income as belonging entirely to her'.[42] But each woman's budget depended on the number of her family in work and how much of their income she received. In 1833 a Leeds overseer, for example, claimed that it was common in his township for girls, from about the age of fifteen, to keep more of their earnings for clothes, and to leave home and live independently if their parents objected.[43] Michael Anderson disputes the extent of this practice, but it nevertheless seems to have been much less common for the children of agricultural labourers to retain part of their earnings.[44] Barry Reay says it is 'clear' that even at the end of the century, among the children of agricultural labourers, 'the little money they earned was not seen as their own'.[45] However, this should not be taken as an indication of the relative prosperity of rural women; the extremely low wages of agricultural labourers meant all the children's income was required.

Ironically, wives themselves frequently enjoyed the least part of the family income since, as Ellen Ross has shown, men took priority as the primary breadwinners.[46] 'If there's anythink extra to buy, such as a pair of boots for one of the children', a poor woman told one of Rowntree's investigators, 'me and the children goes without dinner', but her husband always got his.[47] It was also common for husbands to retain a varying portion of their wages to buy alcohol, tobacco, and their own clothes.[48] Anna Clark, citing Chartist T. B. Smith's denunciation of this 'destructive selfishness', says low wages meant that frequently even 'very moderate drinking and smoking could deprive wives and children of food'. But Smith's appeal to husbands focused less on the detrimental effect of their habits on the family's food supplies, than on its clothing. 'Look at the tattered gowns of your wives', he commanded the men,

---

[42] M. Loane, *The Queen's Poor: Life as they Find it in Town and Country* (London: Middlesex University Press, 1998 [1905]), p. 12.
[43] *Factories Inquiries Commission. First Report... Employment of Children in Factories... C.2. North-eastern District.* Parliamentary Papers 1833 XX, p. 59.
[44] Michael Anderson, *Family Structure in Nineteenth-Century Lancashire* (Cambridge University Press, 1971), pp. 53–6.
[45] Reay, *Microhistories*, p. 114.
[46] Ross, *Love and Toil*, pp. 32–6; Ellen Ross, 'Survival networks: women's neighbourhood sharing in London before World War I', *History Workshop Journal*, 15:1 (1983), 4–28; 7. See also, Harris, *Private Lives, Public Spirit*, p. 73; Joanna Bourke, *Working-Class Cultures in Britain 1890–1960: Gender, Class and Ethnicity* (London: Routledge, 1994), p. 67.
[47] Rowntree, *Poverty*, p. 55.
[48] Clark, *Struggle for the Breeches*, p. 258; Harris, *Private Lives, Public Spirit*, p. 73; Ross, 'Survival networks', 7.

at the frockless and shoeless children who are crawling on the floor, at the almost coalless grate, and the nearly breadless cupboard, and then look at the well-filled tobacco pouch, and the flowing pint, and blush for your own delinquencies.

Smith refers to the 'almost coalless', rather than the empty grate, the 'nearly breadless', rather than the bare cupboard. And while the wife has a 'tattered' gown rather than none at all, the children are absolutely 'frockless and shoeless'.

Similarly, Smith put food and fuel secondary to clothes in the advantages to be gained by a man's surrender of his nightly pint and tobacco. He could buy his wife 'two gowns, a bonnet, shoes, shawl, stockings, and petticoat, and same for children as well as a pig and extra coals'.[49] Smith's promise of a pig – not bread – and *extra* coals suggests that, in his view, moderate smoking and drinking still allowed the purchase of basic fuel and foodstuffs. The real sacrifice was clothing.

Wives and mothers frequently had to choose between buying food and clothing. '"Boots mended" in the weekly budget means less food for that week', noted Pember Reeves.[50] Or, as one rural housewife put it: 'When it comes to the come to, we have to go short to buy shoes.'[51] But the women's own clothing needs claimed very low priority. Rowntree and Kendall interviewed several women who had not had new clothes for years. Mrs Shaw, for example, was a skilled needlewoman who earned a little money by 'smocking' and had made a suit for her six-year-old son from an old pair of her husband's trousers. But: 'She herself has never had a new dress since her marriage, though she has been married thirteen years.'[52]

When, in his attempt to establish the poverty line, Rowntree asked his interviewees to calculate the minimum necessary annual cost of clothing for working people, he stipulated that a man's clothing 'should not be so shabby as to injure his chances of obtaining respectable employment'. The estimates each gave the cost of boots, socks, coat, vest, trousers, shirts, cap and scarf, averaging 26*s.* a year. Fourteen of the fifteen estimates quoted for second-hand coats and vests, with the prices in the fifteenth suggesting the same probability. Eight of the fifteen also quoted for second-hand trousers and boots. The clear implication is that, among the poor, second-hand clothing was both normal and acceptable. But this should not be taken to mean that it was good quality. Indeed, Rowntree's need to caution against the clothing being too shabby implies that a certain degree of shabbiness was customary.

[49] Clark, *Struggle for the Breeches*, p. 249.
[50] Pember Reeves, *Round About a Pound*, p. 62.
[51] Rowntree and Kendall, *How the Labourer Lives*, p. 95. [52] *Ibid.*, pp. 43–4.

Except for socks, shirts and second-hand boots, the estimates allowed for only one of each garment, but there seems to have been no question that each of these items should be replaced every year. The same exercise for women's clothing produced the identical annual average cost of 26s., the listed clothes being boots, slippers, dress, aprons, skirt, stockings, underclothing, stays, hat, jacket and shawl. Again, much of the clothing was second-hand, but the cost for hats, shawls and jackets was for new garments. However, this was not because it was considered necessary for the women, like the men, to buy annual replacements since it is explicit that each of these items 'would last several years'. Furthermore, in twelve of the thirteen estimates, a skirt was to be either done without or made from an old dress.[53] And even when women did get new clothes they never, as Leonora Eyles commented, got the different garments 'at the same time; if she buys a new coat and skirt, she has to have a much washed blouse and trimmed up last year's hat; she never experiences the delicious thrill of looking at herself in the mirror and feeling how nice she looks'.[54]

Rowntree's estimates also included the cost of new boots for women, but it is not clear whether they expected to have a new pair each year, or, like the hats, jackets and shawls, the cost was included simply to indicate how much money would be required should they need replacing. Other evidence suggests the latter and for Lady Bell the 'question of boots' was 'one of the most serious' the poor had to face –

and the miserable foot-gear of the women and children especially – the men are obliged to have more or less good boots to go to work in... One reason why so many of the poor women go about with skirts which drag about in the mud is that they do not want to display what they have on their feet by holding their skirts up.[55]

As Clare Rose says, school clothes were not officially prescribed, but the inculcation of habits of clean and tidy dress was part of the schools' civilising mission and together with the desire of many parents to send their children adequately clad put further pressure on the family budget.[56] Ellen Ross points out that schools judged children's 'neatness and manners' as well as their academic performance.[57] Martha Loane wrote of the distress of a mother who, on being told by 'the School Board man' that it was time for her two small daughters to attend, 'did not even know

---

[53] Rowntree, *Poverty*, pp. 107–8, 381–4.
[54] Standish Meacham, *A Life Apart: The English Working Class 1890–1914* (London: Thames & Hudson, 1977), p. 84.
[55] Bell, *At the Works*, p. 69. [56] C. Rose, *Making, Wearing and Selling*, p. 26.
[57] Ross, 'Survival networks', p. 20.

how she could get decent pinafores to cover their shabby little frocks'.[58] Again, it was often women who went without. Like Lady Bell in Middlesbrough, Maud Pember Reeves found that boots formed 'by far the larger part of clothing expenses in a family of poor children' in Edwardian Lambeth and the women often were entirely without them, forcing them into the isolation of appearing only after dark:

> The men go to work and must be supplied, the children must be decent at school, but the mother has no need to appear in the light of day. If very badly equipped, she can shop in the evening... and no one will notice under her jacket and rather long skirt what she is wearing on her feet.[59]

But even this sacrifice did not solve the boot problem. Jack Lanigan recalled that in Salford in the 1890s: 'Shoes on your feet were the last thing you could expect... Many were the days during winter we went to school with sacking round our feet.'[60] Around the same time Kate Taylor, in rural Suffolk, took over her sister's job working before school hours as day girl at a farmhouse for 9*d*. a week. This 'didn't pay for the amount of shoe leather we wore out as the roads then were rough, muddy and stony, and we frequently had our feet bound in rags which would flap in the mud'.[61] In the autobiographies generally, however, references to bare feet among the agricultural poor are much less common than among their urban counterparts. Although by 1913 Charles Russell was claiming it to be 'rare to see a child under twelve years of age barefooted in winter in the streets of the City of Manchester', Robert Roberts, born in 1905, remembered seeing 'a quarter of a class sixty "strong" come to school barefoot'.[62]

Children were often particularly ill served in terms of the quality, quantity and fit of their clothing, commonly wearing the cast-offs of older siblings and adult cut-downs. Daisy Cowper born in 1890, remembered that she and her siblings:

> all had very limited wardrobes, and what we had, had to be worn and passed down in the family till the last possible moment. Of course, in my case, hems were deep and tucks abounded, and after that, there were false hems![63]

In Cowper's case it seems there was at least some attempt to modify the cast-offs to fit her, but many children had to make do with garments that

---

[58] Loane, *Queen's Poor*, p. 56.   [59] Pember Reeves, *Round About a Pound*, pp. 63–4.
[60] BAWCA, 1:421, Jack Lanigan, p. 5.
[61] John Burnett (ed.), *Destiny Obscure: Autobiographies of Childhood, Education and Family from the 1820s to the 1920s* (London: Routledge, 1994), p. 304.
[62] Russell, *Manchester Boys*, p. 158. R. Roberts, *Classic Slum*, p. 79. See also Davin, *Growing Up Poor*, pp. 136–7.
[63] BAWCA, 1:182, Daisy Cowper.

were too small or too large. In the rare event of new clothes being purchased, longevity was particularly important. Four-year-old Ben Brierley's breeching outfit in 1829 would, he said, 'have fitted a boy of ten. But I had to grow prodigiously, and the clothes had to do for my brother when I cast them off'.[64] 'All clothes, of course, were made to last', said Robert Roberts of the 1900s, 'and many were designed to allow adaptation later to meet the needs of successive younger members in a family.'[65]

In an 1893 Society for the Prevention of Cruelty to Children survey of fifty-two Birmingham pawnbrokers, over half said they thought pawning children's clothes caused the children suffering (although only two refused to accept children's clothes), and one quarter identified the parents' desire for alcohol as the reason for the clothes being pawned.[66] In 1901 Rowntree identified alcohol as the major cause of secondary poverty, but A. E. Dingle found that in fact the peak of alcohol consumption had occurred in the 1870s, after which it fell considerably by the early 1880s and sharply from 1900 to 1914.[67] But throughout, the catastrophic effect of alcohol consumption on family living standards, including clothing, was a recurrent theme in temperance literature. *The Romance of a Rag*, for example, published in 1876, tells of a daughter's dress torn apart by her drunken father, sold for rags and turned into a temperance pledge card signed by the reformed father.[68] While the plot is improbable, the story is correct in making a direct connection between excessive alcohol consumption and the absence of clothing.

Dingle attributed the 1870s increase in alcohol consumption to the 'relatively skilled, higher-income wage-earner', since the unskilled would not have been left with any surplus income to spend on alcohol once basic needs had been met.[69] However, this assumes that the unskilled breadwinner did not consider alcohol a basic need or did not prioritise his desire for alcohol above basic needs. This, as many wives knew, was not always the case. Mrs L. was the wife of a labourer earning 24s. a week and with only one child the family was able to live in relative comfort. Except, Rowntree heard, when Mr L. had one of his 'drinking bouts'. These, 'entailing...loss of time from work, in addition to the cost of the drink, hamper her very much'. During one 'bout', for instance, when

---

[64] Brierley, *Home Memories*, p. 3.   [65] R. Roberts, *Classic Slum*, p. 38.
[66] 'The pawning of children's clothing', *Birmingham Daily Post*, 19 June 1893, p. 4.
[67] Rowntree, *Poverty*, pp. 141–3; A. E. Dingle, 'Drink and working-class living standards in Britain, 1870–1914', *The Economic History Review*, 25:4 (1972), 608–22; 611. See also Ross, *Love and Toil*, pp. 42–4.
[68] M. A. Paull, *The Romance of a Rag, and Other Tales* (London, 1876).
[69] Dingle, 'Drink', p. 618.

Mr L. failed to go to work for two days, he was suspended for the remainder of the week with the consequent loss of pay.[70]

Excessive drinking appears to have been a predominantly male problem. In 1910, for example, 82 per cent of drunken offences were committed by men, but women also drank.[71] Albert Goodwin heard how, in the 1880s, his father, a Stoke china presser, had to keep his Sunday suit at a friend's or relative's house and go there to change into it because:

> if he took anything home on which a few shillings could be obtained his Mother would have pawned them, sold the ticket and had a most glorious orgy of drinking. It had happened so many times before... [that the] expression used by my father's family of 'I've got what I stand up in' was simply the truth and nothing but.[72]

From flannel to flannelette

The replacement of linen, woollen and leather clothing by cotton was not only one of the most significant changes in nineteenth-century working-class clothing, but also one of the most contentious.[73] Cotton, unlike many woollen fabrics, could be washed and Francis Place considered cotton's widespread use to be doing 'wonders in respect to the cleanliness and healthiness of women', liberating them from their previous 'linsey woolsey petticoats "standing alone with dirt"'.[74]

However, since cotton was not as hardwearing as linen and did not provide the warmth of wool, its professed benefits were hotly contested. According to Spufford, in the 1600s calico had been considered 'healthy to wear', but one 1825 author, commenting on the great usage of calico for sheets and 'body linen', argued that although it might initially be warm, it soon became threadbare, giving no warmth at all, and

---

[70] Rowntree, *Poverty*, p. 279.
[71] G. Hunt, J. Mellor and J. Turner, 'Wretched, hatless and miserably clad: women and the inebriate reformatories from 1900–1913', *British Journal of Sociology*, 40:2 (1989), 244–70; 246.
[72] Burnett, *Destiny Obscure*, p. 298. For women drinking see also Bell, *At the Works*, p. 248; Davies, *Leisure, Gender and Poverty*, pp. 61–4.
[73] There were exceptions. The 1842 Children's Employment Commission heard, for example, that the working dress of many colliers was still woollen flannel. *Children's Employment Commission. Appendix... Mines. Part I.* Parliamentary Papers 1842 XVI, p. 746.
[74] Thale (ed.), *Autobiography of Francis Place*, pp. 2, 14. Giorgio Riello comments on the 'dramatic drop' of vermin in early-modern bedding when linen and then cotton replaced woollen bed hangings. Giorgio Riello, 'Fabricating the domestic: the material culture of textiles and the social life of the home in early modern Europe', in Beverly Lemire (ed.), *The Force of Fashion in Politics and Society: Global Perspectives from Early Modern to Contemporary Times* (Farnham: Ashgate, 2010), pp. 41–65; p. 63.

was 'not half so wholesome as linen'.[75] This was not the pretty Asian calico, printed or painted at source or in Britain, which incited early-eighteenth-century protectionist wool-trade vigilantes to tear the gowns from women's backs and produced a (partially successful) temporary ban on the importation and wearing of decorated calicoes.[76] This was plain, sometimes unbleached, Manchester calico which, when new, was coarse and stiff, though as Flora Thompson said, it 'improved', that is to say, softened, 'with washing' and with wear.[77]

Styles points out that more costly but durable fabrics might be better value, but the poor had to buy what they could immediately afford and cotton was cheap.[78] In 1822 a Northamptonshire charity was buying 'Strong Calico' at 6*d.* per yard, but shirt linen at 1*s.*[79] Similarly, in 1862, Uckfield Union was buying calicoes at 5*d.* a yard, but flannel at 10½*d.* per yard, and it was the substitution of calico for woollen flannel in the making of undergarments that became a particularly controversial issue.[80] Flannel was perceived to have decided health benefits. The surgeon at Millbank prison, for example, was permitted to order flannel waistcoats, drawers and shifts for infirmary patients.[81] And for Engels, the injurious displacement of woollen flannel by cotton was a further element in the degradation of the industrial proletariat. England's damp air, he said,

with its sudden changes of temperature, more calculated than any other to give rise to colds, obliges almost the whole middle class to wear flannel next to the skin, about the body, and flannel scarves and shirts are in almost universal use... the working class [is] deprived of this precaution, it is scarcely ever in a position to use a thread of woollen clothing.[82]

---

[75] Spufford, *Great Reclothing*, p. 121; Esther Copley, *Cottage Comforts, with Hints for Promoting Them, Gleaned from Experience* (London: Simpkin and Marshall, 1834 [1825]), p. 36.
[76] Lemire, *Business of Everyday Life*, pp. 117–18; Lemire, *Fashion's Favourite*, pp. 34–42; Styles, *Dress of the Poor*, pp. 109–10.
[77] F. Thompson, *Lark Rise*, p. 32.   [78] Styles, *Dress of the Poor*, p. 130.
[79] Thomas Jones, *Clothing Societies Upon a Good Plan and Well Managed, Would, of All Institutions, Prove the Most Beneficial to the Poor, and Ought to be Established in All Parts of the Kingdom. A Specimen of One Tried for Years, is Here Exhibited, by the Rev. Thomas Jones, Curate of Creaton, Northamptonshire* (Northampton, c.1822), p. 17.
[80] ESRO, G/11/1a/8, Uckfield Union Minute Book.
[81] *Seventh Report of the Inspectors Appointed Under the Provisions of the Act 5 & 6 Will. IV. c.38, to Visit the Different Prisons of Great Britain. I. Home District.* Parliamentary Papers 1842 XX, p. 151. For the perceived health benefits of flannel in the Georgian navy, see Pope, *Life in Nelson's Navy*, p. 136.
[82] Engels, *Condition of the Working Class*, pp. 102–3. Pinchbeck notes the claims of Arthur Young and other contemporaries that rural cottagers grew flax which was spun by their wives who, after it had been woven, used it to make clothing and household linen. Perhaps Engels' dislike of cotton was also bound up with his belief that industrialisation was causing women to neglect their traditional domestic work. Ivy Pinchbeck,

Engels, of course, had a political axe to grind, but woollen underclothes would have been much warmer than cotton, especially in the poorly heated and often damp homes of the poor.

Lady Bell also thought cotton detrimental to health. For men at the ironworks she considered a 'good quality' flannel shirt 'absolutely necessary', not simply to prevent chills but also because the gas and fumes were believed to destroy cotton fabrics. For this reason, she said, 'when working trousers are bought they are often turned inside-out and the seams sewn with wool before they are worn at the works'. According to Bell, one worker who bought a 'so-called flannel shirt, ready made, for 2s. 11d.' found that it disintegrated within three days. His preference was to buy an old army shirt from the pawnbrokers, which cost between 2s. 6d. and 3s. 9d. Two of these lasted him a year, and Bell considered them 'the most satisfactory things that the workman can buy'.[83] But the poor could not afford so much on one shirt. Rowntree's York interviewees gave the cost of new shirts at between 1s. 11d. and 2s. 3d. each, but there was no guarantee that they would be able to afford even these.[84]

In her *Homely Hints for District Visitors*, Florence Stacpoole opined that: 'The value of woollen clothing for working people and for *infants* and young children cannot be too widely inculcated'. It offered protection from colds and rheumatism and she advocated recycling old woollen stockings to make a variety of garments for the poor including gaiters, vests, petticoats and chest preservers:

cut off the foot and slit the stocking up the back; cut a slit in the middle of the strip thus obtained; through this slit the child's head will easily pass, and thus a capital woollen preserver will be obtained which will protect throat and chest in front, and lungs and spine behind. If the edges be overcast with coloured wool an acceptable present *(and a useful object lesson on thrift)* can thus be made for a poor mother. Two stockings thus joined will make a capital chest preserver for an adult.[85]

I do not think it is just my twenty-first-century sensibility that recoils at the thought of the cast-off stockings of the wealthy being refashioned into underwear for the poor, and I am certain that old woollen garments, matted and scratchy from wear and washing, were as irritating to the skin in the nineteenth century as they are today.

Women Workers and the Industrial Revolution 1750–1850 (London: Virago, 1981 [1930]), pp. 23–4.

[83] Bell, *At the Works*, pp. 71–2.   [84] Rowntree, *Poverty*, pp. 381–2.

[85] Florence Stacpoole, *Homely Hints for District Visitors* (London: National Health Society, 1897), pp. 3–5.

Stacpoole also believed some people refused woollen underwear because it was difficult to wash, becoming 'thick, hard, and shrunken' if left too long in the water or washed in overly hot water.[86] But according to Robert Roberts it was neither laundry difficulties, nor a preference for cotton, but simply poverty that inhibited the use of flannel which was, he said:

> much valued... among the working class. Most men tried to come by at least one flannel vest, and women a petticoat of the same material... Often enough, though, one made do with cheap, all-purpose 'flannelette', a cotton substitute.[87]

An 1882 *Dictionary of Needlework*, defines flannelette as 'a very soft warm Flannel', the implication being that it was a woollen fabric'.[88] There seems, however, to have been no mention of flannelette before 1882 and in 1888 *The Glasgow Herald* reported that a 'new substance made of cotton, with only the semblance of wool', which 'the Manchester people call cotton flannelette', was, due to its low price, having a deleterious effect on the wool trade.[89] In their January 1895 Great Winter Sale, Rackstraws of Islington offered 'Good Shirting Flannelettes' from 1¾d. a yard, while their cheapest flannel was 4¾d. a yard.[90] We do not have to believe Rackstraws' claims about the quality of their flannelette, but it was extremely cheap.

The *Glasgow Herald* was convinced that flannelette's popularity would be short-lived, not only because it returned such a low profit, but also

---

[86] *Ibid.*, p. 12; Anon., *Every Woman's Encyclopaedia* (London: Amalgamated Press, 1910–11), p. 17.
[87] R. Roberts, *Classic Slum*, p. 41. Clare Rose's study of late-Victorian boys' clothes showed a preference for woollen cloth rather than cheaper cotton suits when parents could afford them. C. Rose, *Making, Selling and Wearing*, pp. 152–4.
[88] Caulfeild and Saward, *Dictionary of Needlework*, p. 209.
[89] *Glasgow Herald*, 6 March 1888, p. 5. The *Oxford English Dictionary* gives the 1882 *Dictionary of Needlework* entry as the first citation of 'flannelette' and a keyword search of the online 19th Century British Library Newspapers archive also returned 1882 as the first date of usage. In 1895, department-store owner William Whiteley was prosecuted 'for infringing the Merchandise Marks Act, by selling as flannelette an article made wholly of cotton'. Witnesses for the defence, including a former Vice-Chairman of the Manchester Chamber of Commerce, claimed that the name had been invented by 'a gentleman recently deceased', and the magistrate found in Whiteley's favour on the basis that 'flannelette' was protected by the Act since it 'had been sold as such for 13 years', that is, since 1882. It therefore seems clear that cotton flannelette first appeared at that date, and in the absence of further evidence to suggest there had also been a woollen fabric of the same name it seems the authors of the *Dictionary of Needlework* had simply assumed flannelette was made of wool. *The Standard* [London], 2 January 1895, p. 4. *Liverpool Mercury*, 16 January 1895, p. 4.
[90] *M. H. Rackstraw's Great Winter Sale* (Letterpress Works, 1895), Oxford, Bodeleian Library, John Johnson Collection of Printed Ephemera, Bazaars and Sales 1 (71), in *The John Johnson Collection: An Archive of Printed Ephemera*, johnjohnson.chadwyck.com.

because of its 'comparatively inferior quality'.[91] But in Edwardian Lambeth, Maud Pember Reeves discovered that it was used for children's clothes by all the mothers, even though its flammability made it a 'vexed question': 'It is inflammable the mothers know that, but they hope to escape accident... Better, they think, a garment of flannelette than no garment at all!' Enough fabric to make a child's dress could be bought for 6*d*. she said, and a woman who could find that sixpence would do so rather than let the child go without a dress: 'It is what we should all do in her place.'[92]

* * *

Social investigators often assumed the poor financed their clothing from extra earnings, but frequently there were no such earnings or they were insufficient. And although some of the new and expanding occupations of industrialisation paid higher wages than agricultural labour, they could also require increased expenditure on clothing, or be offset by higher urban living expenses, reducing the money available for clothing. For the poor, the decision to buy clothing always involved a parallel decision about which other basic necessity to do without, whether that was food, fuel, light or rent money.

Even when new clothing could be obtained it was likely to have been made of cotton and the hygiene benefits offered by its low cost and washability were countered by its lack of warmth and durability compared with the woollen and linen clothing it replaced, and the risk posed by the flammability of some fabrics. Apart from Russell's perception that bare-footed children had become less common, it is difficult to detect any improvement in the poor's dress, or the money available for it, by the outbreak of the First World War. And while the shortfall in funds affected the whole family, women bore the brunt, emotionally and physically, shouldering the responsibility for managing the domestic budget, and putting their own needs last. The psychological damage they, especially, experienced, distressed by debt, forced into isolation by the inadequacy of their clothing, and fearful for their scantily-clad children's welfare cannot be measured.

[91] *Glasgow Herald*, 6 March 1888, p. 5.
[92] Pember Reeves, *Round About a Pound*, pp. 64–5.

3 'Poverty busied itself': buying clothes

That the urban poor in the 1910s should be as hard-pressed for clothing as their agricultural counterparts over a century earlier is initially, perhaps, perplexing. Not only is it generally agreed that living standards rose after 1840, but also there was something of a revolution in clothing production and retailing during the nineteenth century, which both reduced the price of new clothes and made physical access to them much easier. This chapter examines those developments, their relevance to the poor and the strategies available to them to obtain and retain clothing without recourse to the parish or charity, in particular the use of credit and pawning.

Changes in retailing

By mid century the long-standing importance of fairs as centres of wholesale and retail exchange had greatly diminished.[1] Held only at long intervals, they fell foul of the more professional sales strategies demanded by increased and continuous levels of industrial output. Markets, on the other hand, improved, with over one hundred local and private market improvement acts relating to English and Welsh towns outside the metropolis being passed between 1785 and 1850. The most advanced market facilities were found in the Midlands and industrial north, particularly Lancashire, the West Riding of Yorkshire and Staffordshire. In the late 1880s, with 10 per cent of the national total, markets in Lancashire were more numerous than in any other county. It was, besides, the 'national stronghold' of 'the undercover, daily-operating municipal market', where the new halls of the second half of the century

---

[1] Christina Fowler, 'Changes in provincial retail practice during the eighteenth century, with particular reference to central-southern England', in Nicholas Alexander and Gary Akehurst, *The Emergence of Modern Retailing, 1750–1950* (London: Frank Cass, 1999), pp. 37–54; pp. 42–3.

provided gas-lighting for after-work shoppers and protection from rain and snow.²

David Alexander argues that by mid century shops rather than markets dominated the retail clothing trade.³ But while markets in southern agricultural counties were relatively few in number and concentrated on perishable foodstuffs and farming supplies, northern markets remained important outlets for working-class clothing and drapery.⁴ Arthur Munby passing through the Scholes market, near Wigan, one Saturday in 1860 enthused about the goods on sale which included:

> neat warm clothing materials for workdays... mobcaps and cotton bonnets, clogshoon, fustian trousers, knitted stockings, strong check aprons, coarse warm petticoats, flannel or lindsey.

But while the customers were 'all working men and women and no mistake', they were also 'comfortable looking', an adjective rarely applied to the poor.⁵

The department store is perhaps the best-known retail development of the nineteenth century, but it was of limited relevance to the working classes. Some, such as Lewis's, which opened in Manchester in the 1880s, directly targeted a less affluent clientele, but department stores usually aimed at a more prosperous market. Nearby Kendal Milne's, for example, was 'the antidote to cheapness'.⁶ In contrast were initiatives established and owned by the working classes. Consumer-owned community bread and flour societies had operated in England from at least 1759, and Thomas Brown, a cotton mill superintendent in Otley, told the Factory Commissioners in 1833 that several of his workers had

> shares in two shops, which they established in the village for the sale of provisions and clothes... One of them is one of the principal shops in the village... It was established in 1815 by the workpeople. They complained of the extortion of the neighbouring shops.⁷

---

² D. Alexander, *Retailing in England*, pp. 31–6, 51–2; Deborah Hodson, ' "The municipal store": adaptation and development in the retail markets of nineteenth-century urban Lancashire', in Nicholas Alexander and Gary Akehurst, *The Emergence of Modern Retailing, 1750–1950* (London: Frank Cass, 1999), pp. 94–114; pp. 95–6, 101.
³ D. Alexander, *Retailing in England*, p. 44.
⁴ Hodson, 'The municipal store', pp. 96, 104.
⁵ TCLC, MUNB, 6, 29 September 1860.
⁶ Alan J. Kidd, *Manchester* (Edinburgh University Press, 2002), pp. 107–8.
⁷ Joshua Bamfield, 'Consumer-owned community flour and bread societies in the eighteenth and early nineteenth centuries', in Nicholas Alexander and Gary Akehurst, *The Emergence of Modern Retailing, 1750–1950* (London: Frank Cass, 1999), pp. 16–36; p. 16. *Factories Inquiries Commission. First Report... Employment of Children in Factories... C.1. North-eastern District.* Parliamentary Papers 1833 XX, p. 111.

When, in 1830, sixty weavers formed the Rochdale Friendly Co-operative Society, established a flannel manufactory and then opened a small retail store, they began a movement which would bring the benefits of mutuality and a larger range of goods to a wider constituency. Although the venture failed within two years, it was followed, in 1844, by the Rochdale Society of Equitable Pioneers which, by 1850, had 600 members buying shares in weekly 3$d.$ instalments, and a store selling foodstuffs, drapery, tailoring and footwear. By 1851 there were at least 130 co-operative societies of varying size, predominantly in Lancashire and the West Riding, and in 1863 the north of England wholesale branch of the enterprise was established.

By 1915 the co-operative movement had 1,385 stores and over three million members, although the peak had been achieved in 1903, with 1,455 stores. Its strength, however, remained in the industrial north and port towns and by 1914 there were still 'co-operative deserts', mainly in the agricultural south and west. Even in London less than one per cent of the population were co-op members in 1911, compared with over 13 per cent in Durham.[8] Furthermore, co-op members belonged chiefly to the more prosperous portion of the working classes.[9]

Ready-made clothing shops were similarly more numerous in urban than in rural areas. Hart & Levy, established in Leicester in 1852 and one of the most successful provincial clothing factories, opened its shops in northern centres such as Leicester, Liverpool, Nottingham, Sheffield, Wakefield and Preston.[10] Although Hyams manufacturing base was in Colchester, where by the 1840s it was employing between 1,000 and 1,500 local women, including many wives of agricultural workers who were willing to take poorly paid outwork, its main shops were in London, the industrial north and the port towns.[11]

Ugolini say that for those who could afford them men's bespoke suits 'were considered vastly preferable' to ready-made, but by the 1880s tailors were becoming increasingly concerned about the growing popularity of ready-mades among working-class men.[12] And early in the twentieth century enterprising manufacturers in the rapidly expanding Leeds

---

[8] Arnold Bonner, *British Co-operation: The History, Principles, and Organisation of the British Co-operative Movement* (Manchester: Co-operative Union, 1970), pp. 42–4, 49, 51, 59–60, 69, 74, 96–9, 103.
[9] Harrison, *Peaceable Kingdom*, p. 180.
[10] Chapman, 'The innovating entrepreneurs', 22.
[11] Pamela Sharpe, '"Cheapness and economy": manufacturing and retailing ready-made clothing in London and Essex 1830–50', *Textile History*, 26:2 (1995), 203–13; 203–4, 205, 207.
[12] Ugolini, *Men and Menswear*, p. 147. See also Breward, *Hidden Consumer*, p. 104.

menswear industry introduced two novel marketing strategies. One was direct selling through manufacturers' own retail outlets, rather than via a wholesaler. The other was wholesale bespoke production, by which a retail outlet sent a customer's measurements and cloth choices to the factory of a wholesale company which manufactured a suit for him.[13] Customers at a distance could also make use of the burgeoning mail-order businesses which, facilitated by Britain's extensive rail network, were operating from at least 1860, but really took off following the introduction of postal orders in 1881 and the Royal Mail parcel delivery service in 1883. Among the major beneficiaries of these new opportunities were a 'cluster of downmarket mail order retailers supplying goods mainly to working-class customers'.[14]

However, the simple fact was that the poor could rarely afford to buy new clothes, even relatively cheap ready-mades. For Kate Taylor, born in 1891, one of fifteen children of a Suffolk agricultural labourer, new clothes 'were an unheard-of luxury'. They were such a novelty that hearing that her sister Nelly, a domestic servant, 'had had a new dress made', Taylor walked to meet Nelly on her afternoon off specifically to see the new dress as soon as possible.[15]

The poor, therefore, remained greatly reliant on second-hand garments. This had been a flourishing trade in the eighteenth century, clothing 'millions of lesser folk', says Lemire.[16] But when industrialised production lowered the cost of new clothes in the nineteenth century, the second-hand trade declined and became associated with poverty.[17] The heart of the trade was in London's wholesale Old Clothes Exchange where dealers from other large towns came to buy.[18] But whereas in 1825 there had been around one thousand, predominantly Jewish, used-clothes dealer in London, by mid century their number had almost halved and they were mainly Irish dealers shipping second-hand clothes to Ireland.[19]

Second-hand clothing varied in quality, the better and more expensive items sometimes being favoured instead of new ready-mades. Around mid-century, when Moses & Son were offering ready-made cloth trousers at 6s. 6d. a London second-hand dealer told Mayhew that his prices for

---

[13] Honeyman, *Well Suited*, pp. 42–7.
[14] Richard Coopey, Sean O'Connell and Dilwyn Porter, *Mail Order Retailing in Britain: A Business and Social History* (Oxford University Press, 2005), pp. 15–16.
[15] Burnett, *Destiny Obscure*, p. 305.   [16] Lemire, *Fashion's Favourite*, p. 62.
[17] See Lemire for the used clothing trade in the late eighteenth century. Lemire, 'Peddling fashion'; Lemire, 'Developing consumerism', 28–30.
[18] Mayhew, *London Labour*, vol. II, p. 28.
[19] Chapman, 'The innovating entrepreneurs', p. 10.

cloth trousers ranged from 6*d*. for a very inferior pair, to 4*s*. at the top of the range.[20] Watts Philips, in his 1855 account of the east London slums, commented on the competitive relationship between the used clothing dealers and the glittering retail warehouses and aggressive advertising of the cheap ready-made trade, claiming that:

> The Wild Tribes of London find in Petticoat-lane and Ragfair outfitters in plenty, who, without the show or shameless puff of their great competitor and his worthy son [Moses], whose Mart is the 'feature of the neighbourhood,' rival that illustrious family in the cheapness of their prices, and surpass them in the quality of their goods.[21]

The poor, however, could rarely afford the better-quality second-hand items. The shops and stalls of Rag Fair formed the centre of the retail trade and here, in the 1860s and 1870s, said City Missionary James Dunn, the poor:

> gathered in hundreds on Sunday mornings. A man could buy a pair of boots for ninepence, another a coat for fifteen pence, another could get a clean-starched shirt for sixpence, another could be seen buying some clean undergarments for a few pence, as those he had on must be burnt; a group of women would select dresses, skirts, shawls, or any other article that could be had for a few pence, and mothers would try all sorts of garments on their children.[22]

Prices in pence, old garments fit only for burning and children subject to whatever could be afforded, rather than what suited them best, paint a grim picture. A little further off were Monmouth Street, the main retail market for used clothes in the eighteenth and early-nineteenth century, but much reduced in size and quality by the mid 1800s, and Rosemary Lane which was shabbier still, having more clothes displayed on the ground.[23]

There was seemingly no item of old clothing for which a use could not be found. Some were resold as they were, others cut up and made into new garments with the very worst sold as rags for the paper mill or to make shoddy.[24] Some items, especially boots and shoes, were 'translated', superficially renovated so that they appeared to be in better condition than they were and rapidly fell apart.[25]

---

[20] *Ibid.*, p. 41; Moses, *Universal Passport*, p. 18.
[21] Watts Phillips, *The Wild Tribes of London* (London, 1855), p. 60.
[22] James Dunn, *From Coal Mine Upwards, or Seventy Years of an Eventful Life* (London: W. Green, 1910), p. 99.
[23] Thomas Carlyle, *Sartor Resartus* (Oxford University Press, 1999 [1833–4]), p. 183. See also Charles Dickens, *Sketches By Boz* (London: Penguin, 1995 [1839]), pp. 96–104; Mayhew, *London Labour*, vol. II, pp. 25–6, 39.
[24] Mayhew, *London Labour*, vol. I, p. 369. [25] Dunn, *From Coal Mine Upwards*, p. 99.

Bespoke clothing 77

Fig. 3.1. Samuel Coulthurst, Flat Iron Market, 1894.

Used clothing predominates in Samuel Coulthurst's 1894 photographs of Manchester's Flat Iron Market, with garments suspended on rails, piled on trestles and barrows or simply heaped on the floor (Fig. 3.1). This, said Robert Roberts, was where '[t]hose in greatest need' bought their clothes. 'Some writers', he continued, 'found a certain romance about the place', but Roberts found this difficult to comprehend. Abutting the railway, the market lay under a pall of smoke which added to the atmosphere of sleaze and grime. 'In such places', he said, 'poverty busied itself.'[26]

Bespoke clothing

Unlike many of the new retailing opportunities which predominated in urban and industrial areas, tailors and dressmakers were found in both town and country. In her study of the 1811–15 sales book of Hampshire tailor Robert Mansbridge, Christina Fowler notes that his bespoke customers ranged from canal workers and labourers on the local estate to the petty gentry, and questions 'the generally accepted view that low

[26] R. Roberts, *Classic Slum*, p. 39.

income levels equated with small wardrobes'. In support she presents the clothing purchases of ten workers on a local estate and the proportion of each man's wages they consumed, which ranged from 3.5 to 40 per cent. However, as Fowler points outs, the occupations, wages, living and marital arrangements of these men varied greatly; six of the ten were earning between £23 and £37 per annum, and some were living in and provided with livery. Given the sharp rise in poor relief spending in southern rural counties between 1795 and 1818, Fowler's conclusion that Mansbridge's customers were probably 'fairly representative of their gender in rural and semi-urban areas of Southern England at that time', and that her findings give the lie to assertions that the rural poor generally had only one suit of clothes each, seems premature.[27]

Nevertheless, Fowler's work does demonstrate the purchase by non-elite customers of bespoke garments and Alison Toplis and Laura Ugolini both record the continuing working-class use of bespoke tailors and dressmakers, despite the growing availability of ready-made clothing.[28] Edwin Grey recalled the women in his Harpenden village during the 1860s and 1870s whose 'everyday frock' was plain, but who also had:

as a matter of course, the best, and if possible a second-best, dress... these special frocks being often nicely braided and tucked, these being, as a rule, made by the cottage dressmakers.[29]

While it is unlikely that tailors and dressmakers numbered many of 'the poor' among their customers, it should not be assumed that poverty prevented all use of bespoke services. Charles Shaw described Charity Sunday, the annual celebration for the children of the Primitive Methodist Sunday school in Tunstall during the 1840s. It was 'the maddest, merriest day' of the year, a time of excitement for children, 'the poorest in the town', because it 'meant new clothes' and, most significantly, a Sunday-morning street procession to show them off. These parades, with the children scrubbed and the girls adorned in a profusion of white, were replicated in the 'Whit Walks' of other congregations, both conformist and dissenting, and the processions of organisations like the Band of Hope (see Fig. 3.2).

For parents, the approach of Charity Sunday was a time of anxiety because the clothes had to be provided 'out of scant resources'. It also appears to have been customary for these clothes to have been bought from tailors and dressmakers with many of the children not seeing them

---

[27] Blaug, 'The myth of the old Poor Law', 163, 178–9; Christina Fowler, 'Robert Mansbridge, a rural tailor and his customers 1811–1815', *Textile History*, 28:1 (1997), 29–38.
[28] Toplis, 'The non-elite consumer', p. 65; Ugolini, *Men and Menswear*, p. 147.
[29] Grey, *Cottage Life*, p. 37.

Alternative strategies 79

Fig. 3.2. Whit Walk of St Paul's Sunday School, Blackley, Manchester, c.1900.

until the actual day of the procession because they 'had to be fetched by fathers and mothers, after a late wage had been paid, from the dressmakers or milliners, or tailors, or boot and shoemakers'. As the children processed their parents, 'the poorest', looked on proudly. Shaw thought memories of their own childhood Charity Sundays placed these parents 'under a gracious and compelling motive to get their children the best they could'. But there was also a lot at stake in terms of loss of social status for those who did not participate, and Shaw notes that some parents had to buy on credit and so as one Charity Sunday approached 'had only just wiped off obligations incurred by clothes for the last'.[30] This was an extraordinary occasion, and patronage of the tailors and dressmakers by the poor more generally must have been exceptional. As a London dressmaker explained, 'in slack times [people] don't have clothes made'.[31]

Alternative strategies

The value of clothing and the difficulty of obtaining it was recognised in the regularity with which garments or fabric were offered as prizes at

---

[30] Shaw, *When I Was a Child,* pp. 208–12. Similarly Mrs Yearn, who grew up in Oldham in the 1880s, recalled that 'when Whitsuntide came round, we were the first out showing our new clothes. So proud were we of them. They were the first we had made by a dressmaker.' Llewelyn Davies (ed.), *Life as We Have Known It,* pp. 102–3.
[31] Benson, *Penny Capitalists,* pp. 47–8.

local, particularly rural, events. At Pinner Fair in 1839, for example, the boy who crossed the line first in the race run backwards was rewarded with a waistcoat. A flannel jacket and a smock went to the winners in the blindfold barrow-wheeling events, and a new hat was awarded to the best at '[e]ating rolls and treacle at the Red Lion'.[32] Clearly, though, these were occasional, limited and unreliable sources of clothing.

Often, as Engels noted, assistance came from the poor themselves, sometimes as insurance against future need on the part of the donors.[33] Ellen Ross found that in London, poor women shared 'extensively and unsentimentally', passing back and forth small amounts of money, washing equipment and clothing, sometimes to pawn. Those who refused to participate could find themselves refused in times of need, and saving could be viewed as meanness when others required help.[34] When his mother's mental illness left the young Joseph Terry to fend for himself in Yorkshire in the 1820s, his clothing, he said, 'was often the gift of some kind-hearted mother which she contrived to spare from the not too plentiful wardrobe of her son or sons'.[35] Similarly, Mrs Layton, in East London, recalled that when, in the 1860s, some local children were found to have nothing to wear but a piece of sacking, 'the people who saw them began to look around to see if they had got something from their own scanty store that they could part with for their less fortunate neighbour'.[36] And when Alice Foley's father lost his job, having recently moved to Dukinfield in the 1890s, her mother wished simply to return to Bolton 'where they might find temporary aid from friends or neighbours'.[37] As with the prizes, this was welcome assistance, but the acknowledgment of the scarce resources from which gifts were made demonstrates their limited nature.

Beverly Lemire has called attention to the high level of clothing theft in the eighteenth century, and stealing garments or materials, or buying stolen goods, continued in the 1800s.[38] Barry Godfrey, for example, recorded the work of the Worsted Committee, established in 1777 as an 'employers' private police force', to limit theft by employees in the

---

[32] *The History of Pinner, Middlesex* [A scrapbook of cuttings from the *Pinner Parish Magazine*, 1887–1908, compiled by the Revd C. E. Grenside]. See also Grey, *Cottage Life*, pp. 196–7 for examples in Hertfordshire, and Robert W. Malcolmson, *Popular Recreations in English Society 1700–1850* (Cambridge University Press, 1973), pp. 19, 21, 31, 60.
[33] Engels, *Condition of the Working Class*, p. 277.
[34] Ross, 'Survival networks', pp. 6, 14, 18–19. See also Reay, *Microhistories*, p. 130.
[35] BAWCA, 1:693, Joseph Terry, 'Recollections of my life', p. 9.
[36] Llewelyn Davies, *Life as We Have Known It*, p. 3.   [37] Burnett, *Destiny Obscure*, p. 91.
[38] Lemire, 'Peddling fashion', 77; Lemire, *Dress, Culture and Commerce*, Chapter 5 *passim*. For theft of food, in particular, as a survival strategy, see Reay, *Microhistories*, p. 100.

domestic textile trade of Yorkshire, Lancashire and Cheshire. With the decline of home-based production the Committee transferred its operations to the burgeoning factories, where, in the West Riding alone, it prosecuted 2,321 textile workers between 1844 and 1876 for embezzling workplace goods.[39] Alison Toplis's work on Hereford and Worcester in the first half of the nineteenth century also confirms the continuation of clothing theft, by both amateur – often opportunistic – and professional thieves.[40]

Some clothing was stolen for the thief's own use. Niblo Clark told co-prisoner George Bidwell how his raid on a London tailor's shop had led to his incarceration in 1873. While putting together a bundle of goods to take away from the shop he noticed 'two nice coats hanging on a nail', and put them on. Out in the street he saw two policemen, panicked, ran and was caught, still wearing both coats. When Bidwell asked why he had not tried to get rid of them, Clark explained 'that they were the best he had ever "owned," and fitted him so nicely he could not bear to part with them'. With two previous convictions, this small pleasure cost Clark fifteen years' imprisonment.[41]

Toplis, however, found that most stolen clothing was sold or exchanged for other goods, rather than retained by the thief.[42] The accomplice of a professional thief told a fellow prisoner in Dartmoor how the woman he worked with had her own clothing modified to steal fabrics. 'She'd smug a whole piece of silk', he said, passing it through an opening in her skirt to 'stow it under her petticoats' where she wore a custom-made steel crinoline with hooks attached, on which she hung the fabric.[43] It is tempting to wonder what happened to her trade when the crinoline fashion passed.

The woman's ability to steal the fabric rested on her not arousing suspicion. But simply getting close enough to steal from wealthier victims could be a problem for the poor. One of Mayhew's interviewees claimed to have stolen only a very few purses 'because I've never been well dressed. If I went near a lady, she would say "Tush, tush, you ragged fellow" and would shrink away'.[44] But the poor were also victims, as well as perpetrators of clothing theft; indeed Toplis found peer theft to be most

---

[39] Barry Godfrey, 'Law, factory discipline and "theft": the impact of the factory on workplace appropriation in mid to late nineteenth century Yorkshire', *British Journal of Criminology*, 39:1 (1999), 56–71; 56–7, 61, 63–4.
[40] Toplis, 'The non-elite consumer', Chapter 6.
[41] George Bidwell, *Forging His Chains. The Autobiography of George Bidwell* (London: H. C. Mott, 1888), pp. 450–4.
[42] Toplis, 'The non-elite consumer', p. 187.
[43] Anon. [Edward Callow], *Five Years' Penal Servitude. By One Who Has Endured It* (London: Richard Bentley and Son, 1877), pp. 246–7.
[44] Mayhew, *London Labour*, vol. I, p. 411.

common.⁴⁵ Mayhew, for example, described child-stripping, whereby 'tidily dressed' children were lured 'away to a low or quiet neighbourhood' with the promise of a treat and then stripped of their clothing.⁴⁶ Between them, Agnes Cowper and her brother were 'thus victimised' four times. 'I remember clearly', wrote Agnes,

> a young woman spoke to me saying, 'What a pretty coat you have. My little girl wants one like that; will you come into the entry and show it to her?' . . . She then said, 'I will take its pattern; I shan't be long away and I'll bring you back some sweets, but don't move away from here until I come back'.

Of course she never returned.⁴⁷

Toplis found a willingness to buy stolen goods with little concern for their provenance. As she says, people with low incomes could not afford to be too scrupulous if the price was right.⁴⁸ Some goods were stolen with the specific intention of pawning them to raise ready money. Although one pawnbroker claimed these constituted only a very small proportion of pawned items, it could be difficult for pawnbrokers to discern whether a customer was the legitimate owner of the goods he or she wished to pledge.⁴⁹ Also, stolen goods often made their way to the pawnbroker and second-hand dealer through indirect routes.⁵⁰ Customers might therefore unknowingly buy stolen clothes from them. And since we cannot know how much clothing theft went unreported and unprosecuted, it is impossible to be more precise about the importance of stolen goods in the poor's clothing strategies.

Credit and pawning

In 1827 W. H. Pyne claimed the proliferation of small shopkeepers was responsible for the declining role of pedlars as clothing and haberdashery suppliers, and retail historians have similarly noted the marked increase in the number of small retail units.⁵¹ Also, from the late eighteenth century legislation protected shopkeepers by restricting the goods pedlars could sell without a licence. Pedlars of foodstuffs did not require a licence, those

---

⁴⁵ Toplis, 'The non-elite consumer', p. 190.
⁴⁶ Mayhew, *London Labour*, vol. IV, pp. 281–2.
⁴⁷ BAWCA, 1:181, Agnes Cowper, 'A backward glance on Merseyside', pp. 33–4.
⁴⁸ Toplis, 'The non-elite consumer', p. 191.
⁴⁹ Anon., *A Few Words on Pawnbroking* (London: Jackson and Keeson, 1866), pp. 3–6.
⁵⁰ Toplis, 'The non-elite consumer', p. 195.
⁵¹ Pyne, *England*, vol. II, pp. 224–5; D. Alexander, *Retailing in England*, p. 102; Alison Adburgham, *Shops and Shopping 1800–1914: Where and in What Manner the Well-Dressed Englishwoman Bought Her Clothes*, 2nd edn (London: Allen & Unwin, 1981), p. 11.

of clothes did, although an indeterminable number operated illegally.[52] Laurence Fontaine also links the independent pedlar's demise with the expansion of retail outlets, but additionally cites better distribution networks, the opening-up of country areas, the success of mail order, the rise of the travelling salesman attached to a shop and, above all, changes in attitudes toward credit.[53]

Pedlars had traditionally bought and sold on a system of ongoing credit that forged strong social as well as economic relationships and ensured the continuation of business. When the new urban capitalist ethos demanded the clearance of all debts, the pedlar, with no way to pay them, went under.[54] The pedlar was replaced by the tallyman, also selling on credit, but working for a shop and carrying samples of the goods for sale (and so not requiring a licence), for which he took orders and then returned at regular intervals for payment by instalment. And whereas in the eighteenth century most itinerant trade was carried out in rural areas, by the early nineteenth century the urban itinerant trade was growing, especially around London and the industrial north.[55] Densely populated urban areas offered plentiful sales opportunities, despite competition from fixed retailers, and could be easily reached by train, although in the early twentieth century Rowntree and Kendall also found many of their rural interviewees buying 'on the instalment system' from an 'outrider' from a local market town.[56]

Credit was essential: 'labouring families would not have survived without it', says Barry Reay.[57] And women, as the domestic budget-holders, were also largely responsible for obtaining it.[58] An increasing number of commercial schemes emerged to meet the need. Check trading, for example, was pioneered and monopolised by the Provident Clothing and Supply Company Ltd, formed in 1881. In return for small weekly

---

[52] D. Alexander, *Retailing in England*, p. 63.
[53] Fontaine, *History of Pedlars*, pp. 136–8, 163.   [54] *Ibid.*, pp. 138–9.
[55] D. Alexander, *Retailing in England*, pp. 63–4; David Brown, '"Persons of infamous character" or "an honest industrious and useful description of people"? The textile pedlars of Alstonfield and the role of peddling in industrialization', *Textile History*, 31:1 (2000), 1–26; 19.
[56] Paul Johnson, *Saving and Spending: The Working-Class Economy in Britain 1870–1939* (Oxford: Clarendon, 1985), p. 154; Rowntree and Kendall, *How the Labourer Lives*, p. 15.
[57] Reay, *Microhistories*, p. 125. See also Lemire, *Business of Everyday Life*, p. 16; Tebbutt, *Making Ends Meet*, p. 1; Gareth Stedman Jones, *Outcast London: A Study in the Relationship Between Classes in Victorian Society*, new edn (London: Penguin, 1984), p. 87.
[58] Lemire, *Business of Everyday Life*, pp. 16–17; Margot C. Finn, *The Character of Credit: Personal Debt in English Culture, 1740–1914* (Cambridge University Press, 2003), p. 78.

instalments customers received a credit cheque, typically £1, which could be redeemed at participating retailers, and on which interest of a shilling in the pound was charged. By 1920 the Provident employed 5,000 agents in 115 branches, with check trading most popular in London and the urban centres of northern England.

According to Sean O'Connell, check trading evolved from credit rotation societies in which customers placed small weekly deposits, with the total collected each week being given to the contributors in turn, the order decided by a lottery.[59] In the 1880s, ill health forced Harry Gosling to abandon his career as a Thames waterman and he found alternative employment with a tailor where he ran the clothing club. Members each paid a weekly instalment and received, in rotation, a suit. They cost about 50s. and were, said Gosling, 'quite a good article for those days'.[60] Mail-order retailers encouraged the formation of purchase clubs on the same lines, originally for the sale of watches but, by the 1890s, extended to footwear, clothing and dressmaking materials. As Richard Coopey *et al.* point out, the clubs increased working-class purchasing power at the same time as they provided the retailer with a profit, but without the risks associated with selling on credit. Nevertheless, most mail-order retailers moved to selling on credit with payment by instalments, organised by part-time agents who earned commission.[61]

Pawnbroking also expanded rapidly in the nineteenth century. It became a primary means of managing the domestic budget and, says Margot Finn, played 'a significant role in displacing barter as a common means of acquiring goods'.[62] Melanie Tebbutt's analysis of the distribution of licence returns in 1870 revealed London as the city with the largest pawnbroking trade, followed by Manchester and Liverpool, with Warwickshire, and especially Birmingham having the highest proportion of licensed pledge shops per head of population. There was also a thriving trade in Yorkshire, particularly in the coastal towns, but as with co-operatives there were pawnbroking 'deserts'. Rutland and Huntingdonshire had no licensed pawnshops at all, with another twenty-two rural counties collectively accounting for less than one per cent of the English total. Even in the predominantly rural counties where licensed pawnshops did exist, such as Devon and Somerset, they were situated mainly in the coastal towns, such as Plymouth and Bristol, where they

---

[59] Tebbutt, *Making Ends Meet*, pp. 186–9; Johnson, *Saving and Spending*, Chapter 6; Sean O'Connell, *Credit and Community: Working-Class Debt in the UK Since 1880* (Oxford University Press, 2009), pp. 55–69; Coopey *et al.*, *Mail Order*, pp. 81–2.
[60] Harry Gosling, *Up and Down Stream* (London: Methuen and Co., 1927), pp. 48–9.
[61] Coopey *et al.*, *Mail Order*, pp. 17–20, 85–6.   [62] Finn, *Character of Credit*, p. 78.

were frequented by sailors and the prostitutes they patronised, who stole their clothes to pledge.[63]

In addition, as John Benson shows, there was an extensive unlicensed trade. Although its very nature makes it hard to be precise about the number and location of unlicensed pawnbrokers, they also appear to have been predominantly urban, or suburban, rather than rural. Benson suggests these pawnbrokers 'filled the gaps left by the licensed trade' by, for example, opening later and on Sundays, and accepting stolen property and perishable items, and Lemire posits that they were used by the 'unreliable or desperately poor'.[64] It is also possible that unlicensed brokers were willing to take less valuable items that the licensed trade would reject, making them of particular service to the very poor. Mrs Layton remembered her first job, in the 1860s, in a small East London general shop where she minded the owner's baby and observed how business was conducted:

Articles of clothing and household goods were brought and left, something like a pawnshop, only food was given instead of money in return for the goods, which would be redeemed when the poor things were able to pay the money... I have seen a pair of children's boots left in pawn for a loaf of bread and a small quantity of butter. Babies' pinafores, frocks, saucepans, candlesticks and all kinds of articles have been brought to hold for food. The practice was illegal, so all articles had to be brought in when no one was about, and I was trained to help to smuggle things in.[65]

Robert Roberts's mother acted as an agent for a local pawnbroker whose shop shut earlier than hers. On Saturdays she would take in bundles of clothes which wives, still waiting for their husbands to return with their wages, had not been able to redeem before the pawnshop shut and which they would then be able to recover in the evening or on Sunday.[66]

The weekday deposit and Saturday redemption of 'Sunday best' was, for many, a vital strategy which regularly provided them with the money to get through the week until payday. Ellen Ross found that London housewives often pawned clothes, including their husbands' Sunday best, without their husbands' knowledge; that pawning could be a collective activity, with one woman taking the pledges of several others to the pawnshop; and that women lent items to friends and neighbours to pawn, although this could lead to accusations of theft if the beneficiary was unable to redeem the pledge.[67]

[63] Tebbutt, *Making Ends Meet*, pp. 2–3.
[64] Benson, *Penny Capitalists*, pp. 94–7; Lemire, *Business of Everyday Life*, p. 44.
[65] Llewelyn Davies, *Life as We Have Known It*, p. 21.
[66] R. Roberts, *Ragged Schooling*, p. 95.   [67] Ross, 'Survival networks', 7, 15.

Pawning also allowed the purchase of garments which were needed immediately, but temporarily, since some of the cost could be recovered by pledging the items until, and if, they were needed again. When Jack Lanigan's father died, in 1897, he was buried in a pauper's grave. Despite the family's evident poverty, Lanigan's mother bought her two sons blue serge suits for the funeral. The following Sunday they joined the promenade along the banks of the River Irwell, the boys in their new clothes 'feeling like King of the Kids'. As the pleasure steamers passed, they pulled the water with them exposing the stones underneath and children ran out onto them and back again as the water returned. One boy fell in, and Lanigan's brother, still wearing his new suit, dived in to rescue him:

Did he get a medal? He got the biggest tanning from mother for spoiling his suit. We never saw those suits again. Mother washed and pressed that suit, and into the pawnshop they both went.

Lanigan's mother was able to buy the suits, not only because she intended to pawn them, but because she bought them 'on tick', doubtless paying some of the credit instalments with money from the pawnbroker.[68] But while credit offered one of the few opportunities for the poor to buy new clothing, it added to the cost. Rowntree and Kendall found that 'buying on the instalment system... inevitably means an unduly high price, and shortage in food'. Debt, they said, acted 'as a leveller of the dietary throughout the year'.[69]

Credit could also be difficult to obtain. When asked how she managed to become over £10 in debt, one interviewee told Rowntree and Kendall, 'They won't let it run here in the village – I go miles sometimes. And when they worry, we have to pay a bit off and go short'. Another thought an individual trader would allow a debt of £2 or £3, but no more. Also, she said: 'One shop tells another – I've heard them doing it – about other people. They tell us such as we *must* pay ready money, for if we can't pay this week, it isn't likely we can pay next.'[70] When Alice Foley's father lost his job in the 1890s, the family, having recently moved from Bolton to Dukinfield, was left 'in dire distress, poor relief being denied them and cautious shop-keepers reluctant to extend credit to strangers'.[71]

Equally, where the poor were known, the very things that made them poor and in need of credit – unemployment, low wages and irregular earnings – could prevent them getting it. Beverly Lemire delineates the alternative credit facilities for the labouring classes that were introduced in

---

[68] BAWCA, 1:421, Jack Lanigan, p. 3.
[69] Rowntree and Kendall, *How the Labourer Lives*, p. 41.
[70] *Ibid.*, pp. 60, 245.   [71] Burnett, *Destiny Obscure*, p. 91.

the nineteenth century, such as philanthropic loan societies, but stresses that these were not available to the very poor.[72] Commercial credit systems demanding regular weekly payments were aimed at families with a regular weekly income and mail-order companies appointed agents with local knowledge specifically so that they could assess the creditworthiness of potential customers. Thus, the family with no regular breadwinner, or one known to have dissolute habits was unlikely to be trusted with credit. The Kays mail-order business, at the beginning of the twentieth century, noted that its customers belonged mainly to 'the artisan classes'.[73]

At the same time, the million-plus cases brought to the county courts between 1910 and 1913 to recover small debts indicates that a considerable amount of credit was extended to people who could not, or would not, repay it. According to Coopey *et al.*, this was largely attributable to tallymen, since mail-order retailers, to avoid bad publicity, tended not to pursue debtors through the courts.[74] Also, John Benson has recorded the elusive, but evidently widespread practice of money-lending for profit, especially by women, among friends, relatives and neighbours. The lenders required no security making their services available to the poorest, but interest rates were extortionate and defaulters could meet with severe violence.[75]

Coopey *et al.* also say that because so much was carried out through small local operators, the true extent of working-class credit usage is unlikely to be known.[76] And while it could be difficult for customers to obtain credit, it could also be difficult for traders to refuse it since to do so could result in loss of trade or cessation of payment for credit already extended.[77] One rural Oxfordshire woman who owed at least £10 to local traders said they 'had never worried her, knowing quite well that they would all be paid when two or three of the children began to earn'.[78] If so, then it seems credit could be viewed by both lenders and borrowers as an extremely long-term arrangement and one for which repayment was a collective responsibility.

---

[72] Lemire, *Business of Everyday Life*, p. 38.
[73] Coopey *et al.*, *Mail Order*, pp. 20–1, 81, 87–8.
[74] *Ibid.*, pp. 83, 90; Margot C. Finn, 'Scotch drapers and the politics of modernity: gender, class and national identity in the Victorian tally trade', in Martin Daunton and Matthew Hilton (eds), *The Politics of Consumption: Material Culture and Citizenship in Europe and America* (Oxford: Berg, 2001), pp. 89–107; pp. 96–100.
[75] Benson, *Penny Capitalists*, pp. 90–93.   [76] Coopey *et al.*, *Mail Order*, p. 79.
[77] Reay, *Microhistories*, p. 125; Christopher P. Hosgood, 'The "pigmies of commerce" and the working-class community: small shopkeepers in England, 1870–1914', *Journal of Social History*, 22:3 (1989), 439–60; 442. See also, Benson, *Penny Capitalists*, p. 124.
[78] Rowntree and Kendall, *How the Labourer Lives*, p. 264.

According to Maud Pember Reeves, Lambeth housewives liked to buy the same things each week, because it helped them to budget, and, she said:

> Payment by instalment fascinates the poor for the same reason. It is a regular amount which they can understand and grasp, and the awful risk, if misfortune occurs of losing the precious article, together with such payments as have already been made, does not inflame their imaginations.[79]

The fact that the housewives did not dwell on the possibility of loss, or did not confide their worries to Pember Reeves and her investigators, did not necessarily mean they were not aware of it, but as with the flammability of flannelette, the alternative of going without was still more bleak.

Bell and Pember Reeves understood, even if they did not condone, the poor's reliance on pawnbroking and credit, but their sympathy was by no means universal. Lemire says that in early-modern England it was believed 'that credit offered at modest interest rates engendered industry and discipline among the working poor'. But in the early nineteenth century there was concern about working-class budgeting practices. Pawning, for long used by both rich and poor to raise ready money, 'gradually assumed a more discreditable taint' as alternative forms of credit became available to the upper and middle classes, so that in the nineteenth century 'it became seen as the practice of the desperate, the indigent or the profligate'.[80] And Fontaine argues that with the debt crisis that prompted the demise of peddling, credit, which had for centuries been a normal and acceptable means of conducting business, lost its respectability.[81] A shortage of coinage had also encouraged both the use of credit and payment in kind.[82] As this situation eased during the nineteenth century, and the regular payment of cash wages increased, there seems to have arisen a belief that, regardless of the adequacy of the wages paid, the fact that they *were* paid should have obviated the workers' need for credit. They simply had to lay out their earnings more prudently, and moralists and reformers railed against the want of thrift and the money wasted on interest.

---

[79] Pember Reeves, *Round About a Pound*, p. 63. Lady Bell claimed the same 'eagerness' to 'embrace any system by which they are enabled to buy in small instalments', among the Middlesbrough housewives. Bell, *At the Works*, p. 70.

[80] Lemire, *Business of Everyday Life*, pp. 37, 57, 96.

[81] Fontaine, *History of Pedlars*, pp. 137–9; Lemire, *Business of Everyday Life*, p. 37. The previous normality of credit trading is emphasised by Tammy Whitlock's comment that one of the aspects of the new commercial bazaars that appeared from the 1810s was their specific avoidance of credit sales. Tammy C. Whitlock, *Crime, Gender, and Consumer Culture in Nineteenth-Century England* (Aldershot: Ashgate, 2005), p. 53.

[82] Muldrew and King, 'Cash, wages and the economy', 158–61; Lemire, *Business of Everyday Life*, pp. 86–8.

It would be naive to suggest that pawning was only used by prudent housewives selflessly eking out small budgets for the familial good, as the discussion of pawning children's clothes in Chapter 2 indicates. But measures to limit pawning could be counter-productive. Martha Loane, for example, visited a town where the principal landlord forbad pawnbroking and no alternative had been introduced in its stead. Therefore, pawnbrokers' agents travelled in from outlying towns and made house calls to solicit business, or women clubbed together to fund a neighbour to take their pledges to a pawnbroker elsewhere. The result, said Loane, was that they ended up 'paying about fifty per cent. instead of the seventeen to twenty-four that it usually works out at'.[83]

A pawnbroker of thirty years' standing felt confident that the trade promoted 'that spirit of independence which it is so desirable to cultivate among the poorer classes; and... may truly be said to afford relief to "Each variety of wretchedness."'[84] We would not expect him to say otherwise, but while his view was far from objective it was not an isolated one and there is some evidence to suggest that pawning could help to avoid parish relief or charity. In 1833, for example, the wife of a cotton-mill operative told the Factories Inquiry Commission that her family had 'never had parish help, but stood greatly in need of it last summer. My husband was six weeks ill... we pledged almost all our things to live; we got through without help.'[85]

Nevertheless, a slew of evangelical tracts spelled out the evils that would surely befall women who fell prey to the pawnbroker or the tallyman. In *Phœbe's Marriage, or, The Perils of Dress*, published by the Society for the Promotion of Christian Knowledge (c.1872), newly-wed Phoebe, a former domestic servant, is persuaded to buy a length of overpriced silk from the tallyman who supplies the enviable clothes of her neighbour. She hides the purchase from her trusting, reliable husband, George (who has his sights set on buying a pig), until one day he tells her that the tallyman has taken the neighbour to the County Court for failing to pay what she owes him. Guilt-stricken, Phoebe confesses. George, realising his legal liability for the debt as Phoebe's husband, instructs her to repay the entire sum with the remainder of the week's housekeeping and the money he has been saving for badly needed new boots. This done, and Phoebe repentant, the couple are reunited and continue with a happy marriage, while the neighbour eventually dies in the workhouse.[86]

---

[83] Loane, *From Their Point of View*, pp. 194–6.
[84] W. A. H. Hows, *A History of Pawnbroking, Past and Present* (London, 1847), p. 101.
[85] *Factories Inquiries Commission. First Report... Employment of Children in Factories... C.2. North-eastern District*. Parliamentary Papers 1833 XX, p. 20.
[86] Anon., *Phœbe's Marriage. Or, The Perils of Dress* (London: Christian Knowledge Society, 1872).

In 'Crooked lives, and how they come so', published in the Congregationalist *Stepney Meeting Magazine* in 1885, alcohol joins pawning and credit to form an unholy alliance of unrelieved catastrophe. Young husband Richard is prevented from attending a friend's midweek club dinner because unbeknown to him, his wife Alice has pawned his Sunday coat, intending to redeem it on Saturday, to pay the tallyman for a dress. Richard, until this point a sober man, goes to walk off his anger but is diverted into a public house. As Alice's 'love of finery' increases her debt to the tallyman and more of their possessions have to be pawned, she neglects her home, driving Richard repeatedly to the alehouse where, despite Alice's faults, he is killed in a fight to defend her honour.[87]

As in *Phoebe's Marriage* and 'Crooked lives', it is almost invariably young wives in these stories who, secretly and to satisfy their own vanity, buy from the tallyman and – without swift intervention from a responsible husband – bring disaster on the family.[88] And so, in addition to highlighting the perceived intrinsic evils of pawning and credit, the stories fuelled the notion that working-class women harboured an almost irresistible love of finery which posed a fatal threat to domestic harmony. They also emphasised the responsibilities women assumed on marriage in their role as family treasurers and the duty of care thereby vested in them, and that to fail in that duty, through love of dress, could result in a neglected home, a drunken husband – or none at all.

In reality, many families and communities accepted the use of credit as a fact of life. Alice Foley recalled her emerging consciousness:

of accompanying mother on her weekly visits to the near-by pawnbroker's. Each Monday morning, after brushing and sorting out the Sunday clothes, such as they were, a big parcel was made up; mother carried this whilst I, clutching her skirt, trotted along quite joyfully.[89]

There certainly seems to be nothing furtive or shameful about her mother's weekly visits.

Also, the Foleys had returned to Bolton where they were known, and where Alice's mother had been a regular customer at the pawnshop. In contrast with their experience in Dukinfield where, as strangers, they were denied credit, the Bolton pawnbroker 'never opened her parcel, but placed it in one of the cubicles just above his head, and then slipped some silver coins to her under the grill'.[90] Being trusted with credit

---

[87] THLHLA, W/SMH/A/29/1/[3], Mrs G. S. Reaney, 'Crooked lives, and how they come so', *The Stepney Meeting Magazine* (August 1885), pp. 195–200.
[88] Alan Hunt makes a similar point. A. Hunt, *Governance of the Consuming Passions*, p. 218.
[89] Burnet, *Destiny Obscure*, p. 95.   [90] *Ibid.*, p. 95.

could endow a degree of status and make it easier to obtain elsewhere.[91] Johnson has suggested that, for the working classes themselves, the key issue was not whether a person used credit, but what they used it for, 'luxuries' being disapproved of, but necessary food and clothing acceptable.[92] Indeed, pawning and credit could be used to ensure other forms of respectability. While social superiors condemned the poor's funeral extravagances, among the working classes a decent send-off was widely acknowledged as a legitimate expense. Had Jack Lanigan's mother not used the combined strategies of pawning and credit to buy her sons' suits for their father's funeral, she risked compromising her respectability by violating the social codes governing funerary rites.

* * *

In the nineteenth century, then, a range of new or improved retailing methods, including covered markets, more shops, co-operatives and mail order, brought new, cheaper, ready-made clothing to the masses, although many of these developments favoured the urban north. Clare Rose says that the falling cost of ready-made boys' clothes at the end of the century 'gave poorer families access to a wider choice of garments from a wider range of retailers',[93] but the true poor remained largely reliant on second-hand, and often poor quality, garments, the effect of which was to create a wider separation between them and their working-class peers above the poverty line. Lilian Westall, for example, recalled schooldays, in the early 1900s:

> when one of the 'rich' girls would bring threepence for the other children. The teacher would ask those who were in need to raise their hands, and she would hand out six halfpennies to be used in the soup kitchen. I rarely raised my hand because pride held me back from admitting poverty, although it must have been plain enough to anyone, as I clumped about in my mother's cast-off lace-up boots, a skirt and blouse from the second-hand-clothes stall, and a boy's peaked cap on my head.[94]

Alternatively there was recourse to strategies such as prizes, sharing or stealing clothes, but apart from any dislike of illegality, these were insufficient and unreliable means by which to clothe a family. Many households were able to retain spare garments only by placing them, weekly, in the pawnshop, and to buy the new clothes social convention demanded for certain occasions by making use of credit, both placing further strain on inadequate budgets. Wealthier contemporaries were condemnatory, especially of the tallyman who replaced the traditional

---

[91] Coopey *et al.*, *Mail Order*, p. 80; Roberts, *Ragged Schooling*, p. 22.
[92] Coopey *et al.*, *Mail Order*, p. 85.   [93] C. Rose, *Making, Wearing and Selling*, p. 130.
[94] Burnett, *Useful Toil*, p. 216.

pedlar and was believed to nurture women's perceived love of finery bringing disaster on her family. The poor, in contrast, generally accepted pawning and credit, if necessary travelling some distance to obtain it, and planning their choice of outlet around the likelihood of its being granted. Credit could be used to buy fabric, as well as ready-made garments. Indeed, a dress length for a woman's gown was among the most common items bought from the tallyman in the didactic literature, and it is to the home production of clothing that I now turn.

4 'Woman's best weapon': needlework and home-made clothing

> take the case of a young female who gains 9s. a week: the hours which she works... give her no chance at all of doing her own washing, getting up her own linen, mending her own clothes... if she knew how to do these things, and had time for them, would she not be much more comfortable herself, make a much better wife and a mother?
>
> (Titus Rowbotham, Manchester machine-maker, 1833)

> I know many girls who acquire thrifty and useful domestic habits in mills, and many who do not... I see girls bring their work to mills, and sew and stitch during the time allowed for dinner and breakfast; I conceive a great deal depends upon the example that their parents set them.[1]
>
> ('L.S.', overlooker in a cotton factory, 1833)

These witnesses, giving evidence to the 1833 Parliamentary Inquiry into the employment of children in factories, differed about the effect of paid work on domestic skills. The Commission to examine children's employment in mines, the following decade, also heard conflicting evidence. While the father of one female miner claimed that 'some girls will learn to be better managers of families that go into pits than many who don't go, and who work elsewhere, because they have time to learn sewing in the evening', a male collier declared there to be 'not one in ten of them that know how to cut a shirt out or make one, and they learn neither to knit or sew'.[2] Likewise, Assistant Commissioner Austin, reporting the following year on the employment of women in agriculture, claimed them to be:

in a state of ignorance affecting the daily welfare and comforts of their families... When a woman is much employed out of doors, many things in the

---

[1] *Factories Inquiries Commission. First Report... Employment of Children in Factories... D.1. Lancashire District.* Parliamentary Papers 1833 XX, pp. 50, 53.
[2] *Children's Employment Commission. Appendix... Mines. Part I.* Parliamentary Papers 1842 XVI, pp. 251, 277.

domestic economy are neglected... Her own clothes, and those of her husband and family, are rarely in such cases properly attended to.[3]

But what is striking about this evidence is that all – inspectors and inspected, male and female, those who thought paid employment detrimental to domestic skills and those who did not – agreed that whether or not women *did* sew, they should be able to.[4]

It was generally accepted that the outer clothing of labouring men and boys would be professionally made since the heavy materials from which it was constructed required skills and equipment seldom found in the labouring home.[5] But it was expected that their underclothing and virtually all garments for the women and girls would be home sewn by wives and daughters. Even as the increasing availability of cheap, ready-made clothing provided a time-saving alternative for greater numbers of women, sewing and femininity were so essentially intertwined that a woman who bought ready-made clothing was still likely to assert her ability to sew even if it was rarely put into practice.

Few women cited the time constrictions and financial rewards of paid employment as a reason to absolve them from domestic duties and many fiercely defended their own and other women's skills. Mary Isherwood, for twenty-eight years a stretcher in a mill, was ablaze with indignation when the Commissioners queried her capabilities:

Can you sew? – Yes.
And wash? – Yes; and we can brew, and we can bake. You think we can do nought but work at factories, neither brew, nor bake, nor sew.
Are the factory operatives as willing to take wives from factories as from any other trades? – They would rather do it; I am certain of that. You think we factory women can do nothing at all; they marry none else, they are so over neater.[6]

And although a Yorkshire pitwoman who had taught her daughters all she could of sewing admitted 'that's not much', mostly women took pride in their needlework.[7]

---

[3] *Reports of Special Assistant Poor Law Commissioners on the Employment of Women and Children in Agriculture*. Parliamentary Papers 1843 XII, pp. 25, 27.
[4] Seth Koven noted a similar attitude toward bread baking among Victorian south London housewives. Seth Koven, *Slumming: Sexual and Social Politics in Victorian London* (Princeton, NJ: Princeton University Press, 2004), p. 191.
[5] Ugolini, *Men and Menswear*, p. 209; C. Rose, *Making, Wearing and Selling*, p. 215.
[6] *Factories Inquiries Commission. First Report... Employment of Children in Factories... D.2. Lancashire District*. Parliamentary Papers 1833 XX, p. 111.
[7] *Children's Employment Commission. Appendix... Mines. Part I*. Parliamentary Papers 1842 XVI, p. 276.

While inspectors, clergymen, teachers and local worthies criticised their domestic skills, the women concentrated on what they could do, or believed they could, rather than what they could not. Manchester power-loom weaver, Jane L., who the Commissioner thought 'remarkably elegant in her appearance, manners, dress and language', earned 13s. per week, plus an extra 25–30s. a year from the sale of caps she made. She admitted that she could not have made a gown such as the one she was wearing '(It was of beautiful silk, and well made.)', but claimed the ability to 'cut out and make a shirt: knows she could, though she never tried'.[8]

Anna Clark argues that from the 1820s the new industrial employment opportunities for women left men feeling emasculated. Women's paid work, they claimed, undercut men's wages, reduced their pay or even threw them out of employment, deskilled them, robbed them of their authority over women and, crucially, rendered women unfit for their domestic chores. Working-class men therefore began calling for the exclusion of women from the workforce and their return to the home, together with the payment of a male-breadwinner wage to facilitate this. In the 1830s and 1840s, while some female Chartists argued that the remedy for the exploitation of women workers was a fair wage, male Chartists advocated women's confinement in the home where they would be protected by their menfolk.[9]

This cult of domesticity became one the tenets of working-class respectability, but while, says Clark, many working people doubtless welcomed its promise of male self-respect and female security, in practice male wages were generally too low for its realisation and the result was marital antagonism, rather than the expected conjugal harmony.[10] In this context of attempted male dominance and women's protection of their financial independence we should not be surprised that women defended their domestic skills so stoutly. If women workers admitted that paid work interfered with their domestic duties they were open to the accusation that they worked simply to pay others to do what they could do themselves if they stayed at home. But nor should we simply assume they are all speaking the truth. Veracity, however, is not the issue; what matters is the shared acceptance that women should be able to make and mend the family clothing.

Some husbands and fathers also spoke proudly of their wives' and daughters' skills. Factory operative Mr Maynes declared that his daughter

---

[8] *Factories Inquiries Commission. First Report... Employment of Children in Factories... D.1. Lancashire District.* Parliamentary Papers 1833 XX, p. 35.
[9] Clark, *Struggle for the Breeches*, Chapters 11, 12 and 13.   [10] *Ibid.*, pp. 248–9.

'began to work between nine and ten; is now married; nineteen; can make her own clothes'. He also claimed that the women in his family even made much of the men's clothing so that 'missing my coat, every thing else is made for myself, and the young men and young women, by my wife and daughters; the clothes I have on are so made'.[11] In addition to the genuine pride men could feel in their wives' and daughters' skills, they also potentially had a lot to lose. They knew the possibility of restricting the work done by women and children was being investigated and that to do so, with no welfare system or increased adult male wages to replace the inevitable shortfall, inadequate domestic budgets would be further stretched. It was, therefore, in their interests to insist that women, even if they were in paid employment, were able to perform their expected domestic duties. Men were also aware that women's needlework could make an important contribution to the domestic budget. In 1849 Joseph Terry, a miller supporting his wife, father, niece and seven children, had 'plenty to do out of our small income'. But he had

a wife against the world. She was never fast with anything belonging to household affairs... From the cutting out and making small clothes for the Twins to the making of my own garments, she was never fast.[12]

Not only in the opening, but also the closing decades of the century, the labouring woman who could not make basic garments and mend her family's clothing was perceived as inadequate by both rich and poor. In the 1880s, in Flora Thompson's rural Oxfordshire community, 'plain sewing was still looked upon as an important part of a girl's education... for it was expected that for the rest of her life any ordinary girl would have at least to make her own underclothes'.[13] Sewing likewise formed an important part of the work for the housewives in Pember Reeves's study of Edwardian Lambeth. She gave the daily timetables of five women with between one and eight children each. All spent some part of the day sewing, principally an hour or more in the evening mending, especially their husbands' clothes. For others, needlework, which could be picked up and left off as other demands permitted, punctuated the day. Mrs O., for example, was making a frock for her small daughter by squeezing three short bouts of sewing into her busy day of cooking, cleaning, shopping, husband- and childcare.[14]

[11] *Factories Inquiries Commission. First Report... Employment of Children in Factories... D.1. Lancashire District.* Parliamentary Papers 1833 XX, p. 97.
[12] BAWCA 1:693, Joseph Terry, p. 78. Here 'fast' means extravagant.
[13] F. Thompson, *Lark Rise*, p. 334.
[14] Pember Reeves, *Round About a Pound*, pp. 159–71.

This chapter traces the ways in which women learned to sew and the reasons why, as the century progressed, it gained greater prominence in school curricula. It also considers the impact of the sewing machine on hand sewing and the relationship between men and needlework, to reveal the pervasiveness and endurance of the notion that needlework formed the very core of working-class femininity.

Learning to sew

Informal and voluntary arrangements

Competence with a needle depended on the amount and quality of instruction, the time available for practice and individual aptitude and inclination. A mid-century survey of the female inmates in London's Tothill Fields prison showed that on admission 72 per cent had some sewing ability, although half of these 'were able to accomplish merely the most simple work in the crudest manner'. (A further 18.5 per cent had learned to sew while in the prison.)[15] But however rudimentary their skills, the figure suggests that most females possessed some ability with a needle, and since this was before the introduction of compulsory education the inference is that they had acquired their knowledge informally.

Many girls learned from their mothers or other female relatives and friends. A Sussex girl, for instance, whose mother died when she was seven, was taught by 'a good, kind neighbour who knew how to cut out and make all manner of things'.[16] In contrast, Assistant Commissioner Austin maintained, in 1843, that in the rural West Country, any sewing ability a woman possessed was, 'generally to be traced to the circumstance of her having, before marriage, lived as a servant in a farmhouse or elsewhere'.[17] However, it is not clear whether the instruction came from the mistress or other servants and many women who had learned or improved their skills in service passed them on. Manchester mill-worker 'W. W.' said she could 'hem a little', cut out a pocket handkerchief, bag, shirt, brat, under petticoat and pinafore, but not a cap, and had learned from her mother, a servant before marriage, the implication being that her mother had learned her skills in service.[18]

---

[15] Figures rounded up to the nearest whole number. Mayhew and Binny, *Criminal Prisons*, p. 393.
[16] Day, *Glimpses of Rural Life*, p. 23.
[17] *Reports... Women and Children in Agriculture*. Parliamentary Papers 1843 XII, p. 25.
[18] *Factories Inquiries Commission. First Report... Employment of Children in Factories... D.1. Lancashire District*. Parliamentary Papers 1833 XX, pp. 75–8.

Sewing was routinely taught to girls who attended school. At the close of the eighteenth century it was Mrs Trimmer's opinion that 'no *Charity Girl* can be deemed properly educated who has not attained to a tolerable proficiency at her needle'.[19] Maid-of-all-work Hannah Cullwick, herself a 'charity girl', ruefully measured her brief school career by the needlework completed, leaving in 1841 'after she'd done her yellow sampler, her mother meaning her to do a white one for framing at a better school, but what her never could afford'.[20] However, until the introduction of universal elementary education, effectively in 1870, regular attendance at day school over an extended period was the privilege of a minority, and Sabbath observance precluded needlework instruction in most Sunday schools.[21] Some of the gaps in day-school provision were, though, plugged by voluntarily-run evening classes. Deptford Ragged School, established in 1844, for example, boasted a nightly attendance of over 140 at its sewing classes.[22]

The quality of tuition varied between institutions and as the number of schools grew, following the introduction of state grants in 1833, increasingly structured courses of instruction were published, recommending the best way of responding to the challenge of teaching needlework simultaneously to large numbers of pupils. *The Sampler*, by 1855 in its second edition, proposed a regimented scheme of instruction on the pupil–teacher system.[23] In Class III, for example, the students were to learn running, hemming and sewing stitches and how to turn down a hem, first on paper, and then on canvas. *The Sampler* also emphasised the importance of every child's work being individually marked 'that she may always have her own'.[24] The point was pursued in *Hints from an Inspector of Schools* which complained of the demoralising effect of the common practice of randomly distributing among the pupils part-finished work. A girl, it said,

---

[19] Sarah Trimmer, *Reflections Upon the Education of Children in Charity Schools. With the Outlines of a Plan of Appropriate Instruction for the Children of the Poor* (London, 1792), p. 22.
[20] Liz Stanley (ed.), *The Diaries of Hannah Cullwick, Victorian Maidservant* (London: Virago, 1984), p. 35. See also June Purvis for sewing at charity schools. June Purvis, *Hard Lessons: The Lives and Education of Working-Class Women in Nineteenth-century England* (London: Polity Press, 1989), pp. 85–6.
[21] Purvis, *Hard Lessons*, pp. 72–9.
[22] George Maslin, 'The Deptford Ragged School', *Lewisham History Journal*, 4 (1996), 1–14; 11.
[23] In the pupil-teacher system, the mistress taught the older most advanced girls who then taught the remaining pupils.
[24] E. Finch, *The Sampler. A System of Teaching Plain Needlework in Schools*, 2nd edn (London, 1855), pp. v, x, 2, 6, 209–10.

works away...sedulously at its puckered production to-day...But tomorrow...chance will give some one else a turn at it, or it will be ruthlessly torn across in some new direction for the reasonable purpose of being sewn together again...it becomes a matter of heartless speculation to the little work-woman, why she was ever employed on it at all, except in accordance with the capricious whim of the mistress.

The author applauded *The Sampler* for advocating '*a* connected system', but considered it 'far too elaborate and tedious for the...National schools', and recommended another in which not only did the girls retain the same item on which to work, but having learned the basics completed entire garments.[25]

Many schools took in sewing which helped with the institution's upkeep and demonstrated to the pupils the potential pecuniary value of their labours, although they did not receive any money themselves. At the Manesty-Lane Charity School in Liverpool, for instance, the seventy-six female pupils in 1820 completed a total of 353 items, including 65 shirts and 52 shifts which raised £14 8s. 1d.[26] In some schools the mistress was allowed a percentage of the profits which one manual feared encouraged concentration on the more able children, who would produce acceptable work, at the expense of the less able. Also, there was a tendency to employ each girl only on the work at which she was most proficient, one doing all the gathering, for example, and another all the buttonholes.[27] All-round proficiency was encouraged not only for the girls' personal benefit, but also to better equip them for domestic service where they were commonly expected to maintain their employer's clothing. In 1808 *The Lady's Economical Assistant* had complained of the inconvenience caused by servants' slovenly work, and over fifty years later instruction manuals were still claiming it to be 'a constant source of complaint that servants know not how to work well at their needle'.[28]

The elementary school system

The perceived importance of needlework for working-class girls, and fears that mothers lacked the skills and time to teach their daughters, ensured

---

[25] John D. Glennie, *Hints from an Inspector of Schools. School Needlework Made Useful and School Reading Made Intelligent* (London, 1858), pp. 4–5.
[26] *Annual Report of the Manesty-Lane Charity School March 14, 1821* (Liverpool: 1821).
[27] A Lady [M. E. B.], *Method for Teaching Plain Needlework in Schools* (London, 1861), p. 5.
[28] A Lady, *The Lady's Economical Assistant. Or, the Art of Cutting Out, and Making, the Most Useful Articles of Wearing Apparel* (London, 1808), p. ix; A Lady, *Method for Teaching Plain Needlework*, p. 4.

it formed a central element in the curriculum when, in 1862, the government introduced payment by results in its grant-aided schools. The amount awarded to each school depended on the pupils' attendance and their performance in reading, writing and arithmetic. Needlework was not to be examined, but the grant was to be 'withheld altogether... If the girls in the school be not taught plain needlework as part of the ordinary course of instruction', a status not afforded any other subject.[29] This was amended in 1875 when, in addition to the grants for reading, writing and arithmetic, 4s. per scholar was to be granted to classes which passed an examination in any two subjects from a list comprising grammar, history, elementary geography and plain needlework. This elevation of the status of needlework confirmed its centrality in the construction of working-class femininity. And its perceived supremacy over other domestic skills is demonstrated by the fact that 'Domestic Economy' – food preparation, laundry, cleaning and sick-room nursing – did not enter the schools' Education Code until 1875, some thirteen years after grants became needlework-dependent, and did not become compulsory until 1878.[30]

The emphasis on hand sewing also led to greater standardisation of instruction with needlework being 'taught according to a system previously approved by the inspector'.[31] The focus was very firmly on *plain* needlework, the Education Department's *New Code of Regulations* in 1876 explaining that 'darning, mending, marking, and knitting', could be taught, 'but no fancy work of any kind may be done in school hours'.[32] As one manual explained, the items made were 'supposed to be "elementary garments," suited to the wants of the girls attending "elementary" schools'.[33] Embroidery served no practical purpose, and when practised

---

[29] *Education. Minute of the Committee of the Privy Council on Education Establishing A Revised Code of Regulations.* Parliamentary Papers 1861 XLVIII, pp. 9–10.

[30] *Education Department. 1875. New Code of Regulations (As Modified by Minute of 5th April 1875) with an Appendix of New Articles and of All Articles Modified, by the Right Honourable the Lords of the Committee of the Privy Council on Education.* Parliamentary Papers 1875 LVIII, p. 24; *Education Department. 1879. New Code of Regulations with an Appendix of New Articles and of All Articles Modified, by the Right Honourable the Lords of the Committee of the Privy Council on Education.* Parliamentary Papers 1878–79 LVII, p. 10; Jane Martin, *Women and the Politics of Schooling in Victorian and Edwardian England* (London: Leicester University Press, 1999), p. 81.

[31] *Education Department. 1875. New Code of Regulations.* Parliamentary Papers 1875 LVIII, p. 7.

[32] *Education Department. 1876. New Code of Regulations with an Appendix of New Articles and of All Articles Modified, by the Right Honourable the Lords of the Committee of the Privy Council on Education.* Parliamentary Papers 1876 LIX, p. 6.

[33] Anon. [L. S. Floyer], *Plain Cutting Out for Standards V., VI., and VII., as Now Required by the Government Education Department, 1885, Adapted to the Principles of Elementary Geometry, Containing Also a Copy of What is Required in Other Subjects (Schedules I, II,*

by the poor was, as Rozsika Parker says, 'regarded as sinful laziness – redolent of aristocratic decadence'.[34]

Although needlework now attracted a grant, it was dependent upon success in other subjects and in 1877 a petition to the Education Department from school managers and teachers, protested that this prevented needlework assuming 'its proper and important position in girls' education'. The signatories urged 'the strong desirableness, if not absolute necessity, of making the grant to girls' schools for needlework a wholly separate grant, and the subject of needlework a wholly separate subject of education, unlinked to any other'.[35] The petition had no immediate effect, but in 1882 grants for needlework did become independent of other subjects.[36]

The veto on embroidery continued. Garments submitted for examination were to be 'of plain simple appearance, showing intelligence and good workmanship, but without elaborate detail'.[37] Printed schedules detailed the pedestrian nature of school sewing, the cheap materials to be used, the utilitarian skills to be acquired and suitable items to be made. Dusters and towels were appropriate in Standard I, work bags and iron holders in Standard II with shirts and repairing stockings in Standard VI.[38] Still, in 1912, the government Code of Regulations stated that the aim of school needlework education was 'a practical knowledge of sewing, cutting-out and making ordinary garments, together with mending and darning'.[39]

At much the same time as payment by results had been introduced, Needlework Prize Associations were established around the country to achieve 'more uniformity, both in the requirements and in the standard of needlework'. At their exhibitions prizes were awarded in various categories, the majority of which were aimed at girls attending public

---

III) *and a Copy of the Instructions to Her Majesty's Inspectors*(London: Griffith, Farran, Okeden & Welsh, 1885), p. 13.

[34] Rozsika Parker, *The Subversive Stitch: Embroidery and the Making of the Feminine* (London: The Women's Press, 1984), p. 154.

[35] *Elementary Education (Needlework). Copy of a Memorial on the Subject of Needlework in Elementary Schools from Managers and Teachers of Schools and Persons otherwise interested in the Education of Girls, presented to the Education Department in July 1877*. Parliamentary Papers 1877 LXVII.

[36] *Education Department. Minute of 6th March 1882, Establishing a New Code of Regulations, by the Right Honourable the Lords of the Committee of the Privy Council on Education.* Parliamentary Papers 1882 L, pp. 15–16.

[37] Ibid., p. 29.   [38] Bailey, *School Needlework*, pp. 13–14.

[39] *Board of Education. 1912. Code of Regulations for Public Elementary Schools in England (Excluding Wales and Monmouthshire), with Schedules*. Parliamentary Papers 1912–13 LXV, p. 4.

elementary schools and the same emphasis was placed on plain needlework, 'elaborate detail' to be avoided. Needlework was considered 'an essential point in the teaching of thrift' and good housewifery, but it was also perceived to inculcate the feminine virtues of modesty, obedience and self-discipline.[40] According to the Prize Associations' organisers, if working-class girls learned needlework the 'familiar' but 'lamentable sight... of ragged slip-shod women gossiping at their doors, their untidy appearance testifying to the neglected state of their husband's and children's clothing', would be a thing of the past.[41]

Knitting was an optional component of school needlework instruction, but according to the author of (the enervating) *Plain Knitting and Mending in Six Standards* it was to be encouraged since it too cultivated:

Cleanliness in personal appearance... because a child cannot so well play in the gutter or knock her playfellows about, if she have knitting in her hands... moreover it helps to give a sober staidness of deportment that may bear fruit in after life.[42]

At the same time, in the Schedules of the revised Education Codes, the disciplinary aims of needlework education reached a Foucauldian pitch of regimentation through the introduction of drill, which from the 1870s preceded each tiny preparatory process from donning a thimble to threading a needle (Fig. 4.1).[43] A typical needle-threading drill for three- and four-year-old children began with picking up the cotton, then passed through a further five stages before the seventh when the pupils were to: 'Hold up needle in right hand with ends hanging.'[44] According to the Principle of the London Institute for the Advancement of Plain Needlework:

All persons whose aim is education rather than mere cram, realize one great fact, – that the first element of success is obedience. This is aided by discipline, and both

---

[40] June Purvis also notes the perceived 'symbolic', as well as practical, value of needlework. Purvis, *Hard Lessons*, p. 148.
[41] Anon., *Hand-Book for Needlework Prize Associations Containing Schedules and Suggestions Adapted to the Various Classes and Districts in Great Britain and Ireland* (London: Griffith, Farran, Okeden & Welsh: 1884), Preface, Introduction, pp. 9, 32; Anon., *Plain Cutting Out*, pp. 85–6.
[42] Anon. [L. S. Floyer], *Plain Knitting and Mending in Six Standards Illustrated with Diagrams* (London, 1876), pp. iv, 15–16.
[43] See the discussions of handwriting and drill in Michel Foucault, *Discipline and Punish: The Birth of the Prison*, trans. Alan Sheridan (Harmondsworth: Penguin, 1991 [1975]), pp. 149, 152–3, 169; Anna Davin also notes the introduction of drills. Davin, *Growing Up Poor*, p. 116.
[44] Amy K. Smith, *Needlework for Student Teachers*, 4th edn (London: City of London Book Depôt, 1897), p. 12.

Fig. 4.1. 'Education Under the Government Code – Teaching Needlework by Demonstration', *Graphic*, 1883.

can only be attained, when large numbers have to be dealt with, by 'Drill.' This fact has already been acknowledged in the Army and Navy, and among those who have had to deal with boys, and though it may be comparatively a new idea among Infants and Girls Schools, experience is giving daily proof of its utility.[45]

For a labouring woman to boast a full complement of domestic knowledge she had also to be able to clean, launder and cook, but sewing required more skill, more patience and more discipline. Also, while cleaning, cooking and laundry all required substantial physical activity, needlework was to be done while sitting quietly, that is to say during time that might be used as simple relaxation. Sewing, then, made potential leisure time – so easily perceived as idleness – productive, as long as the work resulted in useful and not merely decorative items. As Elizabeth Rosevear summarised, needlework, 'develops the thrifty disposition, encourages habits of neatness, cleanliness, order, management, and industry; and may truly be considered a moral and refining influence'.[46]

The emphasis on needlework in elementary school curricula, along with compulsory training for girls in other domestic skills, was also linked to the concern about 'national efficiency' which emerged in the closing decades of the century. The poor physical health of young men revealed by recruitment for the Boer War, coupled with high infant mortality rates led both eugenists and environmentalist anti-eugenists to argue that domesticity and maternity were the primary roles of working-class women. Both believed they had to be trained for the task even though, as Felicity Hunt points out, eugenists insisted that women were biologically and instinctively programmed for it.[47] As the parlous condition of their own children seemingly proved that many mothers were incapable of training their daughters in the domestic arts, the task fell to the schools.

However, the extent to which increased emphasis on needlework education improved sewing skills is unclear. As Alice Morrow, author of a turn-of-the-century drill manual pointed out, drills were introduced specifically to cope with large classes.[48] As such, school instruction made

---

[45] L. S. Floyer, *Needle Drill, Position Drill, Knitting Pin Drill, To Which is Added 'Thimble Drill' as Required by Mundella's Code, Educational Department. Needlework Drill, 1881 'Girls' and Infants' Departments, Boys and Girls Below Standard I* (London: Griffith and Farran, 1881), p. 3. See also, Martin, *Women and the Politics of Schooling*, p. 90.

[46] Elizabeth Rosevear, *A Text-Book of Needlework, Knitting and Cutting Out with Methods of Teaching* (London: Macmillan, 1893), p. 2.

[47] Felicity Hunt, 'Divided aims: the educational implications of opposing ideologies in girls' secondary schooling, 1850–1940', in Felicity Hunt (ed.), *Lessons for Life: The Schooling of Girls and Women 1850–1950* (Oxford: Basil Blackwell, 1987), pp. 3–21; pp. 9–11.

[48] Alice Morrow, *Needlework and Knitting Drills for Infants with Music in Both Notations* (London: T. Nelson and Sons, 1900), pp. viii–ix.

no provision for individual need and lacked the personal element of one-to-one instruction when a girl was taught by a relative or friend. Proficiency depended also on the time devoted to needlework. In schools this could be as much as ten hours per week until a maximum four hours weekly was specified in 1904. Adequate and appropriate materials were also required, but not necessarily forthcoming.[49] In 1879 a Berkshire schoolmistress applying to the Vicar's wife 'received 1 Shirt 1 Shift [and] a few pieces of old calico' which, she said:

> will not do for the Infants it is too closely woven for their little fingers. Have drawn up a needlework scheme and sent it to the Vicarage just to give some idea of what is required.[50]

The outcome is not recorded.

Ultimately no amount of instruction could overcome a lack of individual aptitude or interest. Flora Thompson was educated under the revised Codes, but derived little benefit. 'However hard she tried', she said, 'her cotton would knot and her material pucker.' Coming across an unfinished garment thirty years later with 'the needle rusted into the material half-way up a seam', she 'remembered then the happy evening when her mother told her to put it aside and get on with her knitting.'[51]

Adult and post-school instruction

The need for evening classes after the introduction of compulsory needlework education in schools also suggests the latter were failing, or at least struggling, in their mission. The most challenging task on the syllabus at the evening continuation classes established in 1882 by the School Board for London was construction of 'a simple dress', which scarcely suggests an advanced course of instruction for girls who had already completed several years of needlework education at elementary school.[52]

And evening continuation classes were neither the only nor the earliest indication of a persistent belief that adult working-class females could not, or did not, sew. Mechanics' Institutes began admitting women in the 1830s as did Working Men's Colleges in the 1850s. Both offered

---

[49] Anon., *Plain Cutting Out*, p. 67; Annemarie Turnbull, 'Learning her womanly work: the elementary school curriculum, 1870–1914', in Felicity Hunt (ed.), *Lessons for Life: The Schooling of Girls and Women 1850–1950* (Oxford: Basil Blackwell, 1987), pp. 83–100; p. 90.
[50] 'Education in Langford and Little Faringdon', *Berkshire Family Historian*, www.berksfhs.org.uk/journal/Jun2000/Jun2000EducationLangfordAndLittleFaringdon.htm.
[51] F. Thompson, *Lark Rise*, pp. 333–4.
[52] Elizabeth Rosevear, *Manual of Needlework, Knitting and Cutting Out for Evening Continuation Schools* (London: Macmillan, 1894), Frontispiece.

classes for working-class women in plain needlework as well as reading, writing and arithmetic, paralleling the girls' school curricula. June Purvis emphasises that these programmes of study were narrower, less varied and less intellectually stimulating than those for both male and middle-class female students, reinforcing the ideology that equated working-class women with utilitarian domesticity.[53] Needlework Prize Associations and horticultural societies ran competitions in plain needlework for 'wives or housekeepers of labourers and artisans'.[54] At the 1872 Cottage Garden Show in North Mymms, Hertfordshire, for example, twenty-one cash prizes, between 1s. and 5s., were offered in categories such as best made men's white shirt, children's frock and best patched shift or shirt.[55]

The North Mymms vicar praised the cottagers' wives who stayed at home rather than taking up field work. But unmarried working-class women were expected to work and as a 'natural' female occupation needlework was seen as the obvious solution when they were thrown out of other employments. From 1861 to 1865, thousands of Lancashire textile operatives were made unemployed by the 'cotton famine', a result of cyclical trade downturn combined with a dearth of raw cotton from America, owing to the Civil War.[56] Sewing schools were established to teach them how to make and repair clothing for themselves, their families and other poor people in the neighbourhood. The sewing schools were largely funded by local and national relief committees but in 1862, the *Blackburn Standard* reported an anonymous gift of £100 to be divided between Church of England, Roman Catholic and Nonconformist classes. The donor supported denominational classes because he thought the superintendent 'ladies' would be more active in their support, and some of the time could be devoted to religious instruction. He also believed that inadequate domestic skills made female textile factory workers bad housewives, driving their husbands to the beershop. The donor therefore also proposed that each lady superintendent should give the students, in turn, the run of her own home for a few days, to learn 'household duties and domestic economy' so that on return to their own homes 'their whole domestic circle would be improved'.[57] The sewing schools were, then, to be not only a medium for needlework instruction and paid employment, but a conduit through which wealthy women could effect the domestic and moral reform of the lower classes.

[53] Purvis, *Hard Lessons*, pp. 141, 146, 199.
[54] Anon, *Hand-Book for Needlework*, pp. 36–7.
[55] Peter Kingsford, *Victorian Lives in North Mymms*, Chapter 4, www.brookmans.com/history/kingsford4/ch4.shtml.
[56] See W. O. Henderson, *The Lancashire Cotton Famine 1861–5* (Manchester University Press, 1969 [1934]).
[57] 'Handsome donation to the sewing classes', *Blackburn Standard*, 17 September 1862.

Mrs Hyde, the manager of an evening sewing school for Leeds factory workers, established in the 1850s to counter their assumed lack of domestic skills, similarly anticipated moral improvements. Sewing instruction, she claimed, provided 'opportunity for much other indirect teaching'. Looking back, in 1862, over the ten years since the school's commencement, she thought

> the improvements in the manners, appearance, and conduct of the girls... marvellous... now they almost all dress for school, in a style of neatness and propriety which contrasts strongly with the dirty finery we used to see.

She attributed the change to the influence of 'educated ladies and gentlemen', but the part played by both needlework and the moral inspiration of the middle classes in any transformation is debatable. Mrs Hyde went on to defend the much-maligned sexual morality of factory girls, but in so doing she implied that they operated their own regulatory policies, independent of external influence. When, infrequently, one of the sewing school pupils lapsed, she was 'heartily resented by the rest, and so strongly on one occasion, that they insisted on the expulsion of the offender, her conduct being felt to be a disgrace to the whole school'.[58]

Middle- and upper-class organisers saw the sewing classes as a means of bridging the social divide. In the fictionalised account of a cotton-famine sewing school – probably the one at Blackley, near Manchester – the author commented that: 'A new bond was being formed', between one of the organisers, the vicar's daughter, and the students, 'a bond of lasting interest, which the return "of good times" will be far from dissolving'. But they were still careful to maintain a degree of separation. While the students' preference for certain fabrics and garment styles was 'studied and attended to', at the same time 'care was required not to... make the people too fastidious, – forgetting that they had cause for thankfulness in being enabled to purchase at so low a price'.[59]

In the last quarter of the century, the sexual maturity of adolescence came to be seen as a discrete and potentially dangerous period during which girls required guidance and protection. Although after 1870 many children continued in paid employment before, during and after school hours, the introduction of compulsory education and the establishment of a minimum school leaving age of eleven in 1893, rising to twelve in 1899, created a clearer division between the childhood world of school and the adult world of work and marriage. The social purity movement's campaign against prostitution and the sexual double standard exposed

---

[58] Hyde, *How to Win Our Workers*, pp. 24, 26, 36, 66.
[59] A. E. G., *Lancashire Needles and Thread. Or, the History of the Birtley Sewing Class* (London, 1864), pp. 68–9. For the probability that this is the Blackley class see C. Rose and Richmond, *Clothing, Society and Culture*, vol. III, p. 430 n. 2.

the vulnerability of ignorant or unprotected young women, cheap entertainments such as music halls and day excursions offered ungodly temptations, the growth of socialism threatened the established order, and concern about working-class women's physical and moral capacity for motherhood raised questions about the prospects for the future of nation and empire.

In response, from 1880, girls' clubs were established, in particular by Maude Stanley and Flora Freeman, to keep young women off the streets after work and to offer them wholesome, instructive pursuits and moral guidance.[60] For Stanley the clubs were an 'educational advantage' to the girls, but she also claimed 'great improvement in their manners, in the higher aims their lives are directed to, and in the contentment they acquire'.[61] For both Stanley and Freeman needlework instruction was an unquestioned part of the clubs' activities, even though Freeman had apparently loathed needlework as a child.[62] As ever, the emphasis was on plain sewing. Freeman said that the girls 'should be encouraged to ask for instruction in patching and mending their own garments, also to put on buttons, hooks and eyes', believing the 'rougher girls' to 'have scarcely any notion of neatness'.[63] Stanley similarly advocated 'a mending class ... where patches would be put on or skirts turned or stockings darned'. In schools, she said, girls were taught patching and darning 'but the application to practical life is not always carried out, for we can see many a pinafore or frock which need mending, gaping holes that call for patches or darnings'.[64]

In tandem with the emphasis on needlework in the elementary school curriculum, the philanthropic craft revival movement sought to revivify craftwork as a solution to poverty, rural isolation and the advance of industrial production through instruction and employment of the poor. It began with the Donegal Industrial Fund, followed by the Cottage Arts Association, which soon became the Home Arts and Industries Association, among whose vice-presidents was Maude Stanley's mother.[65]

---

[60] Valerie Bonham, 'Stanley, Maude Alethea (1833–1915)', *Oxford Dictionary of National Biography* (Oxford University Press, 2004), www.oxforddnb.com; Mary Clare Martin, 'Freeman, Flora Lucy (*bap.* 1869, *d.* 1960)', *Oxford Dictionary of National Biography* (Oxford University Press, 2004), www.oxforddnb.com.

[61] Maude Stanley, 'Clubs for working girls', in The Baroness Burdett-Coutts (ed.), *Woman's Mission. A Series of Congress Papers on the Philanthropic Work of Women by Eminent Writers* (London: Sampson Low, Marston & Co., 1893), pp. 49–55; p. 55.

[62] Martin, 'Freeman, Flora Lucy', *Oxford Dictionary of National Biography*.

[63] Flora Lucy Freeman, *Religious and Social Work Amongst Girls* (London, Skeffington & Son, 1901), p. 56.

[64] Maude Stanley, *Clubs for Working Girls* (London: Macmillan, 1890), p. 60.

[65] Anne Anderson, 'Victorian high society and social duty: the promotion of "recreative learning and voluntary teaching"', *History of Education*, 31:4 (2002), 311–34; 334.

The movement incorporated a variety of crafts, including wood- and metalwork, but handmade textile goods produced by women were the focus. In a period of political reform, the organisations, under royal and aristocratic patronage, promoted the production of artistic and tasteful craftwork as a civilising and stabilising influence.[66]

The textile products of the craft revival, which included both household goods and clothing, were destined for elite urban markets and so needed to be decorative and fashionable. Yet, as part of the civilising plan, producers were encouraged to use the skills they acquired to beautify their own homes.[67] In this the movement formed a striking contrast with the emphasis on plain needlework in elementary schools, girls' clubs and evening classes, but the focus on the home, rather than the person, makes the two approaches complementary rather than contradictory.[68] According to Martin Daunton, in the last quarter of the nineteenth century, improvements in working-class housing and changes in the workplace, which provided more stable employment and income but reduced worker autonomy, resulted in a shift of focus from workplace to family and home.[69] Giorgio Riello stresses the position of women as 'the nexus between ideas, expectations and anticipations of familial life and the actual physical forms that these assume'.[70] Although Riello was referring to an earlier period, this remained true in the late nineteenth century and girls were given training to prepare them for the role. As part of its domestic economy programme, for example, the London School Board established centres with cooking and laundry facilities and, in some instances rooms in the style of 'model' artisan dwellings in which, according to the Domestic Economy Superintendent, in 1900, the 'careful arrangement of colours' taught girls 'that usefulness and art may be combined and comfortable substitutes for cheap stuffed furniture are placed before their eyes'.[71] Time and money expended on personal 'finery' was perceived as selfish, thriftless and class-inappropriate, and the teaching of plain sewing focused primarily on the making and mending of clothes. But the creation of an attractive and comfortable home – if

---

[66] Janice Helland, *British and Irish Home Arts and Industries 1880–1914: Marketing Craft, Making Fashion* (Dublin: Irish Academic Press, 2007), pp. 1–4; A. Anderson, 'Victorian high society', *passim*.
[67] Helland, *British and Irish Home Arts*, pp. 4–8.
[68] The embroidered smock, valorised as an emblem of a vanishing folk culture, appears to have been an exception.
[69] M. J. Daunton, *House and Home in the Victorian City: Working-Class Housing 1850–1914* (London: Edward Arnold, 1983), p. 266.
[70] Riello, 'Fabricating the domestic', p. 59.
[71] Carol Dyhouse, *Girls Growing Up in Late-Victorian and Edwardian England* (London: Routledge & Kegan Paul, 1981), p. 90.

not carried to excess – was the sign of a good housewife, a demonstration of selfless care and affection for the family which would provide her husband with a welcome retreat at the end of the working day and prevent him seeking comfort in the alehouse.

Cutting out

When, in 1871, the revised Code of Regulations added cutting out to the mandatory instruction to be provided by grant-maintained elementary schools, it addressed a long-standing criticism of the poor's sewing skills.[72] In 1808 *The Lady's Economical Assistant* had bemoaned the 'great waste occasioned by the usual mode of cutting out linen, &c. for all articles of clothing', and claimed that '[t]here must be a considerable saving where the mistress of a family cuts out, or, at least, superintends the cutting out, those articles which require calculation and exactness'.[73] Thirty years later *The Workwoman's Guide* insisted that,

No one who has not been a frequent visitor in the homes of the poor, is aware of the extravagance and waste usual among women of a humble class, arising from their total ignorance in matters of cutting out and needle-work, nor how much instruction they want on those points.[74]

Mayhew, at mid century, seeing a prisoner 'cutting out a dress for one of the matrons' concluded that 'evidently' she had 'belonged to a better class than her fellow-prisoners'.[75]

The ability to cut out was of vital importance not only to avoid wastage, but also to achieve a finished garment of good quality. No matter how skilled the stitching, if it was badly cut in the first place the garment would always be second-rate. But the requisite equipment and facilities, such as light, working space, a large flat surface on which to cut out and sharp scissors or shears, might be difficult to come by in poor homes. Also, successful cutting out was a highly skilled process which, among professional tailors, was performed by the masters.[76] John Styles records

---

[72] *Education. 1871. Minute of the Right Honourable the Lords of the Committee of the Privy Council on Education Establishing a New Code of Regulations*. Parliamentary Papers 1871 LV, p. 6.

[73] A Lady, *Lady's Economical Assistant*, p. vii.

[74] A Lady, *The Workwoman's Guide Containing Instructions to the Inexperienced in Cutting Out and Completing Those Articles of Wearing Apparel, &c., Which are Usually Made at Home* (London: Simpkin, Marshall and Co. and Birmingham: Thomas Evans, 1838), p. v.

[75] Mayhew and Binny, *Criminal Prisons*, p. 195.

[76] Winifred Aldrich, 'Tailors' cutting manuals and the growing provision of popular clothing 1770–1870', *Textile History*, 31:2 (2000), 163–210; 165.

two eighteenth-century Leeds women who, in possession of ten yards of stolen linen and the skills to sew it into bedgowns, required a third woman to cut it out for them, her services being so valuable that she was rewarded with four of the ten yards of linen.[77]

'Cutting out' referred, in fact, to two related processes: the physical or mental construction of a pattern, and the actual division of a piece of fabric into a garment's constituent parts. Patterns, either full-size, scaled down or simply reduced were included in several early sewing manuals, such as *Instructions for Cutting out Apparel for the Poor* and *The Workwoman's Guide*. The former, for example, gave full-size patterns for a range of garments, including bonnets, caps, bodices and sleeves, as well as a variety of 'Child-bed linen for the poor'.[78] Alternatively, Mrs Howell would supply readers of her *Essay on Corsetry* the 'designed measures in a portfolio . . . for 5s. 6d. the set'. She also offered, at £1 1s., 'the Portfolio of Monthly Fashions, supplied to her direct from Paris', including 'full-size Morning and Evening Sleeves, Bodies, and Trimmings'.[79] But aside from considerations of literacy and the utility to the poor of Parisian fashions, both the manuals and the patterns were far beyond their budgets. Cheap commercial paper patterns appeared in the 1860s, first in America and only later in Europe, and until they became widespread a pattern had to be contrived in a different manner. Joy Spanabel Emery suggests that the later tissue paper patterns may have been inspired by a system of 'fitting thin paper over the body to pin in fitting darts and scribe arm and neck holes', but again, except for those who had received some professional training, the relevance of such a system to the poor is doubtful.[80]

Patterns were often taken from existing garments. Ideally the garment would be unpicked and the pieces used to cut around, but this assumed the availability of other clothing to wear while the new garment was being constructed which many of the poor simply did not possess. Alternatively, the intact garment could be used as a mental guide and a pattern cut freehand. For fitted garments in particular, this required excellent gifts

---

[77] Styles, 'Clothing the north', p. 156.
[78] Anon., *Instructions for Cutting Out Apparel for the Poor. Principally Intended for the Assistance of the Patronesses of Sunday Schools, and other Charitable Institutions, but Useful in all Families* (London, 1789); A Lady, *The Workwoman's Guide*.
[79] M. J. Howell, *The Hand-Book of Millinery. Comprised in a Series of Lessons for the Formation of Bonnets, Capotes, Turbans, Caps, Bows, etc.: to which is Appended a Treatise on Taste and the Blending of Colours; also an essay on Corset Making* (London: Simpkin, Marshall & Co., 1847), pp. 119, 128; M. J. Howell, *The Hand-Book of Dress-Making: Including Correct Rules for the Pursuit of the Above Art, and Concisely Illustrating the Mode of Fitting at Sight* (London: Simpkin, Marshall and Co., 1845), opposite title page.
[80] Joy Spanabel Emery, 'Dreams on paper: a story of the commercial pattern industry', in Barbara Burman (ed.), *The Culture of Sewing: Gender, Consumption and Home Dressmaking* (Oxford: Berg, 1999), pp. 235–53; pp. 235–6.

of visualisation and subsequent transmission through hand and scissor. A third option was to take measurements from the intact garment to construct a replica. The author of a fictionalised account of a Lancashire cotton-famine sewing class described how '[m]any brought their own patterns', and the organiser

was often grieved to see the state of the old garments; torn, and ragged, it seemed doubtful sometimes whether it would last its owner a week longer; when the measure had been taken, and duly entered in the order book, the request might be heard, 'And you'll get it done as soon as ye can, will ye? For he hasn't no other to don.'[81]

The actual cutting-up of the fabric needed a large, flat, clean area – surely a problem in overcrowded homes with little furniture. A good, sharp, pair of scissors or shears might be prohibitively expensive, and where a poor family did own a pair they were precisely the kind of item likely to be placed in the pawnshop. Equally, however, they might have been among the items that women who owned them shared with neighbours. Skill was required to obtain from the fabric all the necessary pieces for a garment and to do so with the minimum wastage. Finally, an understanding of fabric grain and bias was needed as the pieces might otherwise not fit together properly or there could be elasticity in the wrong place.

Here, then, was an opportunity for schools to make a significant contribution, but a cluster of corrective manuals complained of the 'physical impossibility for one teacher... to teach Cutting Out simultaneously to eighty girls at once', and the incompetence of some teachers. One author claimed to know of a school where 'pinafores were cut out with one arm-hole in the middle in front, the other arm-hole divided, half cut out of each back'.[82] Although pupil teachers were supposed to have proven themselves competent needlewomen to be accepted for training, and although sewing instruction continued throughout the training period, the former head of a teacher training school agreed that, 'numbers of young teachers at present engaged in public Elementary Schools have no more notion of cutting out a garment than the children whom they are required to instruct'.[83] In the 1890s Louise Jermy, who trained as a dressmaker but transferred to domestic service, passed on her needlework knowledge to her fellow servants, teaching them in particular how

---

[81] G., *Lancashire Needles and Thread*, pp. 20–1.
[82] Anon., *Plain Cutting Out*, Preface, p. 69.
[83] E. A. Curtis, *Needlework. Schedule III. Exemplified and Illustrated. Intended for the Use of Young Teachers, and for the Upper Standards in Public Elementary Schools* (London: Griffith and Farran, 1879), p. 3.

'to cut out clothes' suggesting that their education in this respect had been incomplete.⁸⁴

Being able to cut out eliminated the need to rely on other people and their ability or willingness to interpret and comply with the wishes of those they were assisting. Initially, the 'ladies' at the Leeds Sewing School used their own patterns to cut out garments for the factory girls to make up. However, they soon discovered themselves to be 'as ignorant of what was best suited to [the girls'] purposes' as the girls were 'of the principles and practice of needlework'. Having listened to one irate mother, disgusted with the slip her daughter had made, it became clear that:

the principles on which these pinafores required to be fitted ... [was] a point of no small importance, as the least over-fulness in the sleeves or waist may cause them to catch in the whirling machinery, and entail terrible consequences on their wearers.⁸⁵

Leeds mill operative Elizabeth Strother, for example, told the Factories Inquiries Commission how:

I was passing the shaft ... it caught hold of my apron first, and afterwards my petticoats, and whirled me round three or four times, when my clothes tore and gave way, and I was thrown to the ground ... very much injured.⁸⁶

The other benefit of learning to cut out – although this was by no means the intention of the teachers – was that it enabled the pupils to make use of the sixpenny (later threepenny) monthly publications such as *Myra's* and *Weldon's*, which from the 1870s brought cheap patterns for the latest fashions to a mass market.⁸⁷ They also continued the educative process by giving instruction and advice on new or difficult techniques. In 1888, for example, because 'striped and chequered materials are so much the rage', *Weldon's Home Dressmaker for Striped Materials* provided diagrams 'showing how the various parts of a bodice must be placed [during cutting out] to bring all the stripes nicely together at the seams and shoulders', an accomplishment still taxing many amateur dressmakers today.⁸⁸

---

⁸⁴ Louise Jermy, *The Memories of a Working Woman* (Norwich: Goose and Son, 1934), p. 112.
⁸⁵ Hyde, *How to Win Our Workers*, pp. 41–2; June Purvis also suggests the use of inappropriate patterns as a reason for poor attendance at some Mechanics' Institute sewing classes. Purvis, *Hard Lessons*, p. 148.
⁸⁶ *Factories Inquiries Commission. First Report... Employment of Children in Factories... C.2. North-eastern District*. Parliamentary Papers 1833 XX, p. 60.
⁸⁷ Christopher Breward, 'Patterns of respectability: publishing, home sewing and the dynamics of class and gender 1870–1914', in Burman (ed.), *The Culture of Sewing*, pp. 21–31; p. 24.
⁸⁸ Anon., *Weldon's Home Dressmaker for Striped Materials* (London: Weldon and Co., 1888).

Felicity Hunt outlines the late-nineteenth century debate about girls' need of, and capacity for, training in mathematics and science which in the early 1900s resulted in some girls being allowed to replace science with domestic science and, except for arithmetic, to abandon mathematics. But domestic science, says Hunt, 'had a dubious reputation in educative terms' and teachers and sewing manual authors argued for the academic as well as practical value of their subject.[89] In the preface to their *Teachers' Manual of Elementary Laundry Work* F. L. Calder and E. E. Mann announced their intention to do something never previously contemplated – to teach 'laundry work scientifically as an educational subject'. To do this properly, they said, teachers needed to be 'as proficient in the chemistry' as the practical aspects of the subject.[90] Similarly, Elizabeth Rosevear, lecturer on Needlework at the Stockwell Training College, explained in her 1893 manual that cutting out could be 'the means of developing some of the intellectual faculties' because: 'When mathematical calculations, exact measurements, true proportions, and correct diagrams are employed, cutting out ranks as a science.'[91]

Rosevear was on the defensive, and it is ironic that, when science was being presented as beyond girls' intellectual capabilities and anyway irrelevant since they were fitted and destined for domesticity, teachers of needlework and domestic economy felt they had to justify their subject by presenting it as a science. But she had a point, nevertheless: without a working knowledge of, at the very least, arithmetic and geometry, girls would not be able to draw or scale up patterns to make a correctly fitting garment, calculate yardages, or make economical use of fabric.[92]

Hand sewing and the sewing machine

Flora Freeman commented that in some of her clubs, 'the girls are allowed the use of a sewing machine', which must surely have enhanced the clubs' attraction.[93] Sales of the domestic sewing machine, which (in a form we might recognise today) appeared around mid century, began to take off at the end of the 1850s, just as the Education Department was preparing to identify plain sewing as a necessary part of the instruction

---

[89] F. Hunt, 'Divided aims', p. 13.
[90] F. L. Calder and E. E. Mann, *A Teachers' Manual of Elementary Laundry Work*, 3rd edn (London: Longmans, Green and Co., 1894), p. ix.
[91] Rosevear, *Text-Book of Needlework*, p. 1. As early as 1845 Mrs Howells was speaking of the 'science' of millinery and dressmaking, insisting that both required 'scientific skill, to be well and effectually accomplished'. Howells, *Hand-Book of Dress-Making*, p. ii.
[92] The relationship between 'science' and laundry is discussed in Chapter 5.
[93] Freeman, *Religious and Social Work*, p. 57.

for girls in grant-maintained schools. In the early 1860s around 5,000 domestic machines were sold each year in Britain. By the 1890s, Singer, which had a virtual monopoly of the UK sewing machine market, was selling about 150,000 machines per annum.[94]

Tim Putnam argues that the 'sewing machine was introduced precisely at a point where the culture of home sewing was being eroded by commercialization', suggesting that the sewing machine rescued home clothing production from obliteration.[95] But sewing machines were expensive. London supplier S. Davis offered the 'Period' machine at £5 10s., for example, and even though he accepted payment in weekly instalments this was still far beyond the means of many.[96] And so, despite the growth in sales, even by the turn of the century owners of domestic machines were in the minority. Robert Roberts listed sewing machines among the '[l]uxury items most longed for' in Edwardian Salford.[97] Only two of the forty-two housewives interviewed by Rowntree and Kendall in 1913 owned a sewing machine. One had bought it in 'the early years of her married life', when the expenses of feeding and clothing the family would have been lower than in subsequent years, and the other had bought hers before marriage.[98] When Maud Pember Reeves recorded a young mother in Edwardian Lambeth who owned 'a large sewing-machine', she described her as being 'intolerably proud' of it, suggesting that she owned something most around her did not.[99]

As Andrew Godley has shown, until at least the early 1890s the majority of domestic sewing machines were bought for professional use by homeworkers, although they would also use them to make clothing for their families.[100] Jane Coombe, mother of suffragette Selina Cooper, bought a sewing machine to facilitate her work as a tailoress and after marriage 'still kept a small sewing machine by her' to 'make clothes for her fast-growing family'. When widowed, impoverished, rheumatic and bed-ridden, a board fixed to the bed held her sewing machine and enabled her to continue making clothes for the relatives she lived with, allowing her the dignity of making a contribution rather than being totally dependent.[101]

---

[94] Andrew Godley, 'Homeworking and the sewing machine in the British clothing industry 1850–1905', in Burman (ed.), *The Culture of Sewing*, pp. 255–68; pp. 258–9.
[95] Tim Putnam, 'The sewing machine comes home', in Burman (ed.), *The Culture of Sewing*, pp. 269–83, p. 279.
[96] Chatterton Keats, *Without a Penny in the World. A Story of the 'Period.' A Christmas Annual* (London, 1870), p. 10.
[97] R. Roberts, *Classic Slum*, p. 32.
[98] Rowntree and Kendall, *How the Labourer Lives*, pp. 231, 263.
[99] Pember Reeves, *Round About a Pound*, p. 160.
[100] Godley, 'Homeworking', p. 262.
[101] Liddington, *Life and Times*, pp. 3, 14, 17, 22, 24.

It was to the domestic home-worker market that much sewing-machine advertising was directed. *Without a Penny in the World, A Story of the 'Period'*, for example, a tale in the style of romantic penny fiction was distributed by S. Davis to promote the Period lock-stitch machine. It follows the fortunes of Rosalie Thornton, an orphan of 'transcendant beauty' who, dismissed from her position of governess, resolves to seek her fortune 'at the point of woman's best weapon, the needle... which Science has brought to such great uses in the sewing machine'. Unfortunately, Rosalie buys a chain-stitch machine, which produces an ugly finish, and is therefore unable to find work. She contemplates suicide, but is rescued by a woman who reveals to her '*the secret of success* in the world of female labour' – the 'Period' lock-stitch sewing machine, which produces a much more attractive finish. This enables Rosalie to find work and eventually results in her marriage to 'handsome, high-souled' Captain Darrell, after which the sewing machine becomes an ornamental treasure in their 'magnificent and luxurious' home.[102] But while Rosalie's machine ultimately became a sentimental reminder of her path to everlasting romantic happiness, it began as her means of subsistence and Davis's focus on its pecuniary possibilities was confirmed in a closing acrostic which positioned the lock-stitch sewing machine as the key to avoiding the workhouse.[103]

For those able to access one, the sewing machine was undoubtedly a boon to home clothing production. It reduced the time needed to make a garment and removed some of the potentially most tedious work, such as the long straight seams of women's skirts. But it could not totally replace hand-sewing skills. Indeed, the machine's utility, to some extent, depended on them since the capabilities of nineteenth-century sewing machines were limited and they could not perform many of the finishing processes in garment production, such as buttonholes.[104] In her 1893 needlework text book, Elizabeth Rosevear argued that sewing machines were 'really necessary in making up some articles of wearing apparel'. But she warned against cheap models which produced inferior stitches and left needle holes in the fabric and pointed out that 'the cutting out and fixing of the garments, as well as the fastening on and off of the stitches, must be done by hand'.[105]

---

[102] Keats, *Without a Penny*, pp. 1–10.
[103] For the aesthetics of the domestic sewing machine see Nicholas Oddy, 'A beautiful ornament in the parlour or boudoir: the domestication of the sewing machine', in Burman (ed.), *The Culture of Sewing*, pp. 285–301.
[104] H. P. T., *The Standard Needlework Book, A System of Graduated Instruction in Plain Needlework In Which Arithmetic is Brought to Bear Practically* (London, 1871), Preface.
[105] Rosevear, *Text-Book of Needlework*, pp. 3–4.

Furthermore, while sewing machines were to a limited extent incorporated into school sewing instruction, the belief that a woman unable to perform hand sewing had 'deliberately neglected one side of her development' ensured its continued instruction.[106] The deep-seated conviction of the fundamental connection between needlework and femininity was hard to shift. Rosevear even went so far as to tell readers tempted not to properly finish off a piece of machined work that: 'God makes everything perfect to its last little atom, to show us how carefully we should work.'[107] So for those both with and without a machine, hand sewing remained important for practical, ideological and even spiritual reasons.

Men's needlework

It is remarkable that the first prize for 'needlework' was awarded to a sturdy young man, a drummer in the Grenadier Guards.[108]

Although needlework was an intrinsic component of nineteenth-century womanhood it was by no means an exclusively female occupation. Many boys and men, not only professional tailors, also learned to sew and knit. George Walker's *Costume of Yorkshire* included the Wensleydale knitters, shepherds and cattle drovers who knitted while they worked and were 'thus industriously and doubly employed'.[109] With few women on board, sailors also needed to sew, and Sunday afternoons were frequently devoted to 'make and mend'. Furthermore, a Georgian midshipman recalled that in the quieter parts of a voyage the captain issued slops 'of duck frocks and trousers which the sailors altered to a kind of uniform, which the captain chose to establish for the ship'. This suggests the men possessed considerable proficiency with a needle and they spent two-and-a-half hours a day on the work. They were, though, seemingly less adept at cutting out since, according to Dudley Pope, the sailor who could cut 'a shirt or a pair of trousers from a piece of cloth could be sure of several tots in return for a few minutes use of his skill'.[110]

Some men – like some women – acquired their skills at Her Majesty's pleasure, their abilities ranging from rudimentary repairs to the construction of entire garments. From the outset of her work at Great Yarmouth in the 1820s, prison visitor Sarah Martin set the young male inmates

---

[106] Turnbull, 'Learning her womanly work', p. 88.
[107] Rosevear, *Text-Book of Needlework*, p. 4.
[108] 'Windsor Royal Association for Improving the Condition of Labourers', *Daily News*, 14 October 1851, p. 6.
[109] Walker, *Costume of Yorkshire*, p. 81.
[110] Pope, *Life in Nelson's Navy*, p. 163. The point is a good one, although Pope's allusion to 'a few minutes' undermines the skill involved.

to patchwork, claiming they valued the occupation 'because it teaches them to sew, so that they may be able to mend or make their clothes'.[111] Similarly, when asked whether, when free, he made and repaired his own clothes, a Tothill Fields' prisoner told Mayhew 'that he liked to be able to do something for his-self'.[112]

The kinship networks through which girls learned to sew could also operate for boys. Alfred Ireson wrote warmly of his mother, an excellent needlewoman, who in her sole desire 'to train the infant mind in all good things' taught all her children 'to sew, and knit, and net'.[113] But needlework never entered the Education Department's Schedules for the instruction of boys, although in the mixed infant classes boys as well as girls participated in the needlework drills. Some voluntary organisations also provided needlework tuition for boys, such as London's Clare Market Mission which ran 'A Lads' Industrial Class' where 'Knitting, Sewing, & c., are taught to poor boys'.[114]

It seems, therefore, to have been acceptable for males to sew when they were children, when they lived in (virtually) all-male communities, or when they did so as a profession. But in other circumstances it could be perceived as emasculating, and for Engels it was the world turned upside-down. Hearing the story of an unemployed man found, by his friend, mending his wife's stockings while she worked at the factory he could not 'imagine a more insane state of things'.[115] Although the mid-century prize-winning Grenadier Guard was clearly keen to display his skill with the needle, Edwardian Martha Loane found that while some soldiers would 'even make clothes for their girl children', which accounted for the look of pride on their faces when taking them for a walk, they did so only 'in the seclusion of the married quarters'. Loane believed all boys should be taught to sew 'when they are too young to imagine that it is an indignity', as it would enable them to repair their own clothes 'in the years when they have lost a mother's care and not yet gained a wife's'. But this was rather a singular view and while she thought many working-class men were happy to help with the heavier housework, most 'draw the line at using a needle and cotton'. She had, though, 'known many expert with a sewing-machine', the implication being that the use of machinery countered any suggestion of effeminacy.[116]

* * *

[111] Anon. [Sarah Martin/George Mogridge], *Sarah Martin, The Prison-Visitor of Great Yarmouth. A Story of A Useful Life* (London: Religious Tract Society, 1872), pp. 55–6.
[112] Mayhew and Binny, *Criminal Prisons*, p. 427.
[113] BAWCA 1:371, Alfred Ireson, 'Reminiscences', p. 10.
[114] *St. Clement Danes Parish Magazine*, June 1870.
[115] Engels, *Condition of the Working Class*, pp. 167–8.
[116] Loane, *From Their Point of View*, pp. 147–8, 267–8.

The labouring woman who admitted she could not sew was considered, by all classes, deficient – as a daughter, a wife and a mother. It was expected that girls would learn to sew, and that to do so was to equip themselves for womanhood. Flora Thompson remembered that while she 'was still struggling with her first hemming strip', the girls about her were 'putting in tiny stitches and biting off their cotton like *grown women*'.[117] For working-class females who internalised the ideology that needlework was a significant part of what determined them as good women, wives and mothers, it became a crucial element of their identity. With five children, Thompson's mother 'was hard-pressed', but maintained her standard of 'seemliness' by 'sewing till midnight and ris[ing] before daybreak to wash clothes'.[118]

The campaign to sustain needlework instruction was buttressed on all fronts – at school, in adult education, the community, the family and by philanthropists. And at its heart lay anxieties about women's relationship with industrialisation, their controllability and the challenge to gender roles posed by women's paid work outside the home. Anna Clark states that: 'The Chartist ideal of marriage had promised intellectual companionship and romance, but working men actually rated housewifery more highly.' She cites tailor Thomas Carter who discovered that his 'domestic happiness' depended on choosing a wife 'of plain good sense and thoroughly domestic habits', rather than 'a "bookish" woman',[119] and needlework was taught and performed at the expense of other intellectual pursuits. Lady Bell's survey of the reading habits among Middlesbrough ironworkers revealed that women read less than their husbands because:

They have no definite intervals of leisure, and not so many of them care to read... And they nearly all of them seem to have a feeling that it is wrong to sit down with a book.[120]

Joseph Terry's 'beloved little wife' managed to read only by combining it with childcare and needlework. In the evening, said Terry, she would:

sit down to her worktable with one child on her knee, one in the cradle, and some interesting book for she always contrived to do some reading, propped up before her on the table, when she would nurse, rock, read and knit, all at the same time, while I sat by her side reading.[121]

But this must have required an extraordinary level of versatility, determination and stamina. Others listened to their husbands read aloud while

---

[117] F. Thompson, *Lark Rise*, p. 184 (emphasis added).
[118] *Ibid.*, pp. 379–80. [119] Clark, *Struggle for the Breeches*, p. 258.
[120] Bell, *At the Works*, pp. 166–7. [121] BAWCA, 1:693, Joseph Terry, p. 78.

they sewed, but the very fact that, like Joseph Terry, the men had the leisure to read highlighted the difference between them and their wives.[122]

The belief in the intrinsic connection between needlework and femininity undoubtedly relegated women to the domestic sphere, and left many dissatisfied, because they were not good needlewomen or because it prevented them pursuing other interests. It is, then, understandable that feminist historians' have focused on the undeniably limiting effects of women's domestic role. But in so doing needlework has itself become devalued. I cannot close this chapter without also emphasising that it is skilled work and by suggesting that some women sewed and knitted because (like me) they enjoyed it, finding satisfaction in the rhythm of stitching, taking pride in the production of clothing and household textiles, and finding it a powerful means of self-expression.

Nevertheless, we must also remember that poor women also sewed for very practical reasons. Annmarie Turnbull points out that amid the emphasis on needlework in school curricula, 'the possibility that the poor might buy ready-made clothing was generally ignored'.[123] But as the preceding chapters have shown, even by the end of the period the poor could rarely afford ready-made clothing. It was common for all classes to have their clothes mended, but the poor also remained greatly dependent on the needle skills of the female members of the family to make whatever new clothes they possessed. Except in the case of the most adept of needlewomen able to work to a professional standard, this, like their continued dependence on second-hand garments, served to separate the poor from the mass of the working-classes increasingly able to dress in shop-bought, professionally manufactured, ready-made clothes.

[122] Bell, *At the Works*, pp. 157, 160.
[123] Turnbull, 'Learning her womanly work', p. 88.

5 'The struggle for respectability'

> Beccles people were born respectable, lived respectable, and died and were buried respectable, leaving their children to follow in a respectable way.[1]
>
> (Arthur Goffin, b. 1879)

> No term is harder to analyse than 'respectability' in the mid-nineteenth-century working class.[2]

Clothing was a fundamental pillar of 'respectability', a term as ubiquitous but often as vaguely defined as 'the poor', and sometimes recognised more in its absence than its achievement. Respectability, says J. F. C. Harrison, 'was maintaining a steady income, preserving the respect of the local community, and avoiding the workhouse and a pauper funeral'.[3] Preserving community respect meant constant attention to the minutiae of everyday life; the company you kept, the amount you drank – and the clothes you wore. 'One had to assimilate the word and adapt oneself to its full significance', said Arthur Goffin, the son of a Beccles printer's reader. For Goffin:

> Being respectable meant cleanliness, morally and physically; paying one's way; living up to one's income, and not over it... accepting things as they were... While money was always forthcoming on pay-day, there were many mouths to feed and boots and clothes to buy.[4]

Respectability, as Standish Meacham points out, was 'a family enterprise', requiring the cooperation of all members and the sacrifice of personal desire to collective reputation.[5] According to Charles Shaw, the importance of new clothes for children to participate in the public display

---

[1] BAWCA, 1:271, Arthur Frederick Goffin, 'A grey life'.
[2] Hobsbawm, *Age of Capital*, p. 224.
[3] J. F. C. Harrison, *The Common People: A History from the Norman Conquest to the Present* (London: Fontana, 1984), p. 302.
[4] BAWCA, 1:271, Arthur Goffin.   [5] Meacham, *A Life Apart*, p. 27.

of the Charity Sunday procession was enough to keep men out of the beershop for weeks beforehand. But women's responsibility for the domestic budget, housework and childcare meant they bore a greater share of the responsibility for maintaining a family's respectability.[6] 'The housewife', said Goffin, 'diligently and heroically did her part, and brought up her family respectably.'[7] Similarly, stonemason's son Alfred Ireson recalled that in Northamptonshire during the 1860s, the low pay of agricultural workers meant that:

> The condition of the children in many cases was pitiable. Rough food and clothes, everything depended on the skill and character of the mother. Nothing ready-made could be purchased, not even a shirt. The struggle for respectability![8]

This chapter is concerned with the role of appearance in the creation and maintenance of respectability. It begins with a discussion of clothing's condition, the significance of particular garments – specifically aprons, hats, silk stockings and stays – and the relationship between respectability and the sartorial conventions surrounding death and the Sabbath. It continues with an examination of bodily cleanliness, to question what constituted 'clean' in the absence of adequate water supplies, and differing attitudes to nudity and menstruation. Cleanliness is explored further in relation to laundry and the chapter ends by considering how storage of the poor's clothing affected its appearance.

For respectability, clothing didn't have to be new, but it did usually have to be clean, in good repair and appropriate for the occasion. 'One wore shining boots and clogs', said Roberts, 'as a blazon of family respectability.'[9] Patches and darns were common as were worn and faded clothes – shabbiness was no disgrace, raggedness was. The point is illustrated in Carl Chinn's citation of Mary Carpenter, 'a leading supporter of reformatory schools', who in 1852 identified 'a very strong dividing line "between the labouring and the 'ragged' class, a line of demarcation not drawn by actual poverty"'.[10] A professional beggar told Mayhew that he had tried numerous 'lurks' but considered 'the clean dodge' and the 'clean family dodge' the most productive. For these, he said, it was imperative that there were 'no rags, but plenty of darns'.[11] However, Clare Rose argues, persuasively, that in the 1890s signs of 'raggedness'

---

[6] Beverly Lemire similarly emphasises 'the active intervention of the housewife' in a family's drive for respectability. Lemire, *Business of Everyday Life*, p. 169.
[7] BAWCA, 1:271, Arthur Goffin.
[8] BAWCA, 1:371, Alfred Ireson, pp. 9–10. When Ireson says 'Nothing ready-made could be purchased', it is not clear whether he means ready-made clothing was not available in his locality, or whether it was too expensive.
[9] R. Roberts, *Classic Slum*, p. 39.   [10] Chinn, *Poverty Amidst Prosperity*, p. 118.
[11] Mayhew, *London Labour*, vol. I, pp. 415–16. A lurk was a method of fraud.

on boys' clothes, such as holes and missing buttons, could be countered by simultaneously wearing a white collar which signified awareness of and the attempt to achieve 'respectability'.[12]

The working clothes of manual labourers were largely excepted from the requirement that clothing be clean and in good repair. As Lady Bell pointed out, employment at the ironworks was:

of course, ruinous to almost any sort of clothing, and it is not surprising that the man as he appears going to his work should wear the very worst clothes he can find... [H]e goes off to his work in the morning, clad almost in rags, as, unwashed, unshaven... he strides along in a greasy, torn old coat with holes in it, patched trousers, frayed at the edge, tied tightly below the knee.

But it was expected that when the day's work was finished he would wash and change 'to turn himself out like an entirely respectable citizen'.[13] A change of outfit not only preserved good clothes, it also prevented the dirt of work being transferred to home. But in his report on the South Staffordshire mines, Sub-Commissioner Mitchell claimed a change of clothes effected a psychological as well as physical transformation. The coarseness of the clothing worn by girls employed in loading coal onto the barges, he said, rendered it unsuitable for wear outside of working hours which was 'an advantage' since 'the girl, when she has changed her dress, feels her taste revived for the rest of the day'.[14]

For working women, a change of dress might differentiate not between work and leisure, but between paid and unpaid labour. After Wigan pit-brow girl Ellen Grounds had been photographed for Munby in her pit dress, in 1873, she went into the photographer's kitchen to rearrange her clothing ready to go home. When she emerged she had 'let down her pitskirt', covering her trousers, 'put on a patched petticoat overall, and then a large white apron'. Munby (typically) thought her 'so picturesque' in her everyday dress that he insisted on having another picture taken of her, this time, much to Grounds' amusement, holding a broom. 'It favvers [looks]', she said, 'as Ah were sweeping t'hahse!' (Fig. 5.1).[15]

Grounds' white apron, which hid her 'patched petticoat', would have been a key factor in her respectability rating. 'Anything did for everyday wear', claimed Flora Thompson, 'as long as it was clean and whole and could be covered with a decent white apron.'[16] A Fenland contemporary remembered seeing her mother 'wearing her outdoor bonnet and a clean white apron, which was "respectable" wear in them days', a hessian

---

[12] C. Rose, *Making, Selling and Wearing*, p. 29.   [13] Bell, *At the Works*, p. 71.
[14] *Children's Employment Commission. First Report of the Commissioners. Mines.* Parliamentary Papers 1842 XV, p. 12.
[15] TCLC, MUNB, 41, 11 September 1873.   [16] F. Thompson, *Lark Rise*, p. 102.

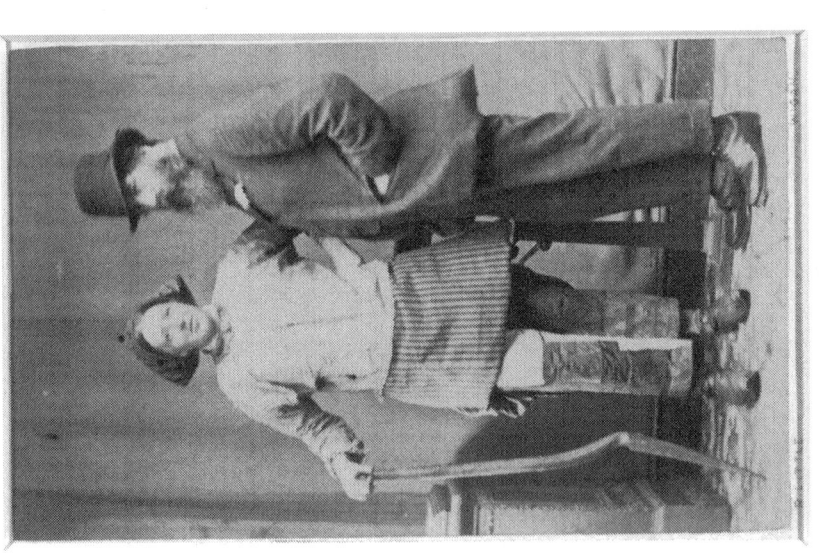

Fig. 5.1. Left: Ellen Grounds in Wigan pit-brow working dress with Arthur Munby, c.1873. Right: Ellen Grounds in day dress, with skirt and apron down, c.1873.

apron being her normal wear for housework.[17] Dresses and petticoats were expensive items and despite Thompson's claim of cleanliness, when a woman owned few changes of clothes they were likely to be washed only at extended intervals. But aprons were relatively cheap and easy to launder. A large clean apron extending almost to the ground could go a long way towards conveying an impression of overall cleanliness, even if the garments underneath were less than pristine. A dirty apron, on the other hand, could be read as a mark of slovenliness. Rowntree and Kendall interviewed a Mrs Smith, who by 'struggling hard and pluckily' just about managed to retain her respectability. But her 'apron might be cleaner' and her neighbours deemed her 'quite inadequate in the sphere of patching and mending and remaking'.[18]

Not simply the condition but the presence or absence of certain garments could be read as immediate indicators of respectability. Mayhew, finding two young women asleep among the empty costers' barrows in a London yard assumed they were prostitutes. 'Their bare heads', he said, 'told their mode of life.'[19] Still, half a century later, Robert Roberts noted that in Salford a woman who appeared in public without a shawl over her head 'was said to be "in her figure", and to be seen that way too often caused comment'. It seems, therefore, that for women the exposed head could be read as a sign of the exposed and available body. But both men and women 'walking the streets hatless', said Roberts, 'struck one as either "low", wretchedly poor, just plain eccentric or even faintly obscene'.[20] When, in 1900, charwoman Kate Elisabeth Dutch was admitted as the first inmate of the Farmfield reformatory for female inebriates, in Surrey, her degraded condition was succinctly summarised as: 'Wretched, hatless and miserably clad.'[21]

In the 1830s Dickens identified a prostitute among a pawnbroker's customers by her 'miserably poor, but extremely gaudy', attire, comprising a 'rich satin gown with the faded trimmings, the worn-out thin shoes, and pink silk stockings'.[22] Thirty years later, early one January morning, Munby 'passed between twenty and thirty strolling prostitutes' near Leicester Square, 'all were in gaudy bonnets and velvet mantles and thin boots and pink silk stockings visible to the calf'.[23] The showiness of the prostitutes' 'gaudy' dress and pink silk stockings were indications of a lack of feminine propriety. Stockings, as Philippe Perrot says, revealing

---

[17] Sybil Marshall, *Fenland Chronicle* (London: Penguin, 1998 [1967]), p. 175.
[18] Rowntree and Kendall, *How the Labourer Lives*, p. 155.
[19] Mayhew, *London Labour*, vol. III, p. 312.   [20] R. Roberts, *Classic Slum*, pp. 39–41.
[21] G. Hunt et al., 'Wretched, hatless and miserably clad', 259.
[22] Dickens, *Sketches by Boz*, p. 228.   [23] TCLC, MUNB, 23, 19 January 1864.

the shape of the calf by their close fit and veiling the skin but suggesting it, 'often ignited strong eroticism'.[24]

While, as Valerie Steele argues, the perception that Victorian women were to keep their legs entirely covered has been greatly exaggerated, there were accepted rules governing how much leg could be exposed and under what circumstances.[25] When Munby spotted the prostitutes in Leicester Square the walking dresses of elite women were beginning to be worn a little shorter exposing stockinged ankles, but the practice was considered 'fast' and evening dress still kept them covered.[26] For working-class women, ankle-length skirts were not only acceptable but actively encouraged by women such as health adviser Florence Stacpoole, since they did not trail in the mud.[27] But while, from the 1860s, coloured stockings were fashionable from time to time among elite women, the stockings of virtuous poor women were in neutral tones. A 'glimpse of an ankle was the utmost one ever got, and that was always encased in a black stocking, as no self-respecting girl wore coloured stockings', wrote autobiographer Edward Brown of the close of the century.[28] The 'virtuous' stockings of the lower orders were also made of cotton or worsted. In the case of the prostitute it was the combination of the silk fabric, the colour and the deliberate exposure up to the calf that was provocative and, as Munby acknowledged, exciting:

As to the pink stockings... I could not but think as I saw them how great is the power of purity and the influence of motive, in such matters. The harlot lifts her dress to the calf to excite your passions; and they *are* excited.

He contrasted this with French fishwomen who, like some of their English counterparts, in the course of their employment walked 'in broad daylight along the crowded quay, barefoot, and barelegged to the very thigh', but of whom, he claimed no one even thought of 'indecency'.[29] Munby was off the mark – in denial even – in his assessment of the erotic potential of the fisherwoman's exposed thighs. Not only was he himself attracted by the muscular limbs of working women but, as Michael Hiley points out, the French fishwomen's bare legs were something of a tourist attraction for elite young Englishmen.[30] Nevertheless, Munby was correct that a fishwoman's uncalculated exposure was not

---

[24] Perrot, *Fashioning the Bourgeoisie*, p. 160.
[25] Valerie Steele, *Fashion and Eroticism: Ideals of Feminine Beauty from the Victorian Era to the Jazz Age* (Oxford University Press, 1985), p. 114.
[26] C. Willett and Phillis Cunnington, *Handbook of English Costume in the 19th Century*, 3rd edn (London: Faber, 1970), pp. 468–9.
[27] Stacpoole, *Homely Hints*, p. 4.   [28] BAWCA, 1:93, Edward Brown, 'Untitled'.
[29] TCLC, MUNB, 23, 19 January 1864.   [30] Hiley, *Victorian Working Women*, pp. 36–7.

the same as the prostitute's deliberate revelation of a pink silk-stockinged ankle.³¹

The respectable woman also had to pay attention to her corsetry. Leather or boned stays, worn over the shift, were the foundation garment of working-class women, although they were not universally worn. '[W]aist she had none for she wore no stays', Munby happily declared of a well-built Staffordshire farm servant.³² However, the general expectation that poor women should wear stays is evidenced by their provision in workhouses, asylums and prisons.³³ Tightly-laced corsetry inhibited movement and so distinguished the leisured woman – or woman at leisure – who did not need to move so freely from her labouring counterpart who did. Photographs of the Wigan pit-brow girls in their working dress mostly show that they are not wearing stays, but they are clearly wearing them under their Sunday crinoline dresses (Figs 5.1 and 5.2).³⁴ But, as Leigh Summers says, corsetry's control of 'unruly female flesh' was, by extension, also read as a means of controlling, or assessing, female sexuality.³⁵ Then, as now, 'loose' behaviour was contrasted with 'straitlaced' prudery and the perceived connection between unseemly behaviour and loose clothing was encapsulated in the word 'slammerkin', meaning both a 'loose gown or dress' and a 'slovenly female' or 'slattern'.

The woman who went without corsetry therefore risked censure, but as Carolyn Steedman points out, 'if you can lace a corset tight, you can also lace it loose'.³⁶ Through illness, dressmaker's apprentice Louise

---

[31] Lynda Nead highlights the groups of figures who 'represent the wild, illicit Cremorne' in Phoebus Levin's 1864 painting, *The Dancing Platform at Cremorne Gardens*. One group features a woman who 'gestures with her fan to a man who whispers behind his hand to a companion' and, as she does so, exposes her pink ankle. Lynda Nead, *Victorian Babylon: People, Streets and Images in Nineteenth-Century London* (New Haven and London: Yale University Press, 2000), p. 129.

[32] TCLC, MUNB, 3, 19 August 1859.

[33] Leigh Summers, *Bound to Please: A History of the Victorian Corset* (Oxford: Berg, 2001), pp. 15–16.

[34] An exception appears in Michael Hiley's *Victorian Working Women*, which contains one picture of a Wigan pit-brow girl who seems to be wearing a corset under her working clothes. However, while most of the photographs in the volume were commissioned by Munby, this one seems unlikely to have been and the girl is much smarter and cleaner generally than the pit-brow girls in the Munby portraits. The sanitized image is likely, therefore, to have been taken by a commercial photographer for sale as a souvenir item and the girl corseted for the sake of propriety and aesthetics. Munby would have been dismayed if a girl he had arranged to have photographed donned a corset under her pit clothes for the occasion. Hiley, *Victorian Working Women*, p. 10.

[35] L. Summers, *Bound to Please*, p. 5.

[36] Carolyn Steedman, 'Englishness, clothes and little things', in Christopher Breward, Becky Conekin and Caroline Cox (eds), *The Englishness of English Dress* (Oxford: Berg, 2002), pp. 29–44; p. 37. For a longer discussion of eighteenth-century stays see Carolyn

Fig. 5.2. Left: Ellen Grounds in Sunday best, c.1866. Right: Ellen Grounds in Sunday best, c.1873.

Jermy was required to wear a back splint during her adolescence. At sixteen, although she no longer wore it, her skin remained sensitive and her corsets, she explained, 'could never be done up properly because the bones rubbed my back sore, so they always had to be left open at the back and the laces loose, so that the bones did not rub me'.[37] Summers notes that institutional corsets 'do not appear to have been designed to allow tight lacing' and so provided 'enough mobility to work', and there is no reason why working women could not likewise have adjusted their lacing according to the activity they were performing.[38] A few of the young female hurriers employed in Yorkshire mines before the prohibition on women and children working underground stated that they wore stays for work. Given that their work required them to pull the loaded trucks of coal, frequently doubled over on hands and feet, it seems improbable that the stays were tightly laced.[39]

Respectability had to be maintained even – perhaps especially – in death, and one of the greatest anxieties of the poor was the prospect of a pauper burial, especially when the New Poor Law reduced expenditure on items such as coffins and grave clothes. 'The desire to secure respectful interment of themselves and their relations', claimed Edwin Chadwick in 1843, 'is perhaps the strongest and most widely diffused feeling among the labouring classes of the population.'[40] Ruth Richardson found that 'shrouds were often lacking altogether, and the poor person buried naked, wrapped only in paper, or with a strip of calico stretched over the body'.[41] Penny burial clubs spread rapidly in the attempt to avoid such indignities.

The bereaved were expected to make some attempt at mourning dress, but this could be expensive and the sums expended on it by the poor attracted criticism from wealthier observers. Lady Bell, for example, commented on the 'wild outbursts of expenditure' a death might provoke, illustrating her point with the story of a Middlesbrough woman who went to nurse her husband in a London hospital. After her husband's death the woman was sent some money to 'tide her over' for a few weeks, but returned home:

Steedman, *Labours Lost: Domestic Service and the Making of Modern England* (Cambridge University Press, 2009), pp. 332–41, where she also makes the point about tight and loose lacing.

[37] Jermy, *Memories*, p. 54. [38] L. Summers, *Bound to Please*, p. 16.

[39] *Children's Employment Commission. Appendix... Mines. Part I.* Parliamentary Papers 1842 XVI, pp. 280–1; *Children's Employment Commission. Appendix... Mines. Part II.* Parliamentary Papers 1842 XVII, p. 123.

[40] See also Pember Reeves for early-twentieth-century burial. Pember Reeves, *Round About a Pound*, pp. 66–72.

[41] Ruth Richardson, *Death, Dissection and the Destitute*, 2nd edn (London: Phoenix Press, 2001), pp. 274–81.

clad in the mourning weeds of the stage, including a long black skirt, a deep crape flounce, and everything complete. The mourning, and what she called a 'proper' funeral had absorbed nearly all the margin which should have kept her for a month, and in a few days she was again in straits, with a piteous request for more help.[42]

Lady Bell's purely fiscal approach failed to acknowledge the cultural significance of mourning dress, even though this was paramount in the complex (if often imperfectly observed) code which governed the mourning garb of her own class.[43] For the poor as much as the rich, mourning clothes instilled in the wearer and conveyed to peers a sense of personal and familial dignity and of having done 'the right thing' by the deceased. As Edwin Grey pointed out, even though 'in many cases the excess of mourning garb could be but ill afforded', the more crape a widow wore, 'the more grief and respect for the departed was supposed to be shown'.[44] So important was mourning dress that various working-class institutions kept it to lend out. The Dockers' Union, for example, in the late nineteenth and early twentieth centuries lent 'a very simple black woollen dress, shawl and bonnet' to widows for wear at their husbands' funerals.[45] But according to Martha Loane, not everyone would have approved such an arrangement since it was the 'element of *sacrifice*' that counted, and which was to be demonstrated by the purchase of new mourning for each bereavement, however short the interval between them.[46]

Above all, however, the sartorial barometer of respectability for both sexes and all ages was Sunday best, worn not only on the Sabbath but on any holiday. The most striking difference in Ellen Grounds's appearance was not between her working and her everyday clothes, but between those and her Sunday dress of crinoline, lace collar and jewellery (Fig. 5.2). Sunday best was equally important for men. 'No man can remember', wrote journeyman engineer Thomas Wright, in 1867:

a time when working men did not take a pride in having, and look upon as necessary to the proper enjoyment of the Sunday, that outward and visible sign of working class respectability and prosperity, a Sunday suit.[47]

Mary Triggle's father was a mid-century Derbyshire coal miner. On leaving the pub one Sunday he went to the market to get some rotten fruit

---

[42] Bell, *At the Works*, pp. 76–8.
[43] See Lou Taylor, *Mourning Dress: A Costume and Social History* (London: Allen & Unwin, 1983), Chapter 6.
[44] Grey, *Cottage Life*, p. 168.   [45] L. Taylor, *Mourning Dress*, p. 39.
[46] Loane, *The Queen's Poor*, pp. 120–1.
[47] Anon. [Thomas Wright], *Some Habits and Customs of the Working Classes. By a Journeyman Engineer* (London, 1867), p. 206.

to throw around and disturb a Primitive Methodist service, but instead was converted. '[F]rom that day', wrote Triggle', my father knew he wanted to live a Christian life . . . So he bought a best suit & a pair of best boots.'[48]

Thorstein Veblen argued that fine clothes should 'make plain to all observers that the wearer is not engaged in any kind of productive labour', but among the working classes the possession and display of Sunday best – surplus clothing – were the visible emblems of industry and thrift.[49] By implication, therefore, its absence suggested, even if it did not prove, idleness and improvidence. Even when contemporaries spoke sympathetically about those without Sunday best there was often an undertone of disapproval. Charles Shaw, for example, described the social hierarchy among the potteries' workmen. At the top were hollow-ware pressers, throwers, turners and printers among whom: 'Even those who did not regularly attend places of worship would be seen on the Sabbath "in their Sunday best".' At the bottom were the plate- and slip-makers and even though Shaw acknowledges that they were 'the hardest worked and the worst paid', there is a clear moral judgement in his comment that on the Sabbath these men 'would be seen, if at all, furtively running from their wretched homes, when the beer shops were open, in their working clothes', and he concluded that: 'There was a want of economical discipline in their work and life.'[50]

Those who could manage a separate Sunday outfit took great care of it. Francis Heath, writing of the west of England in 1880, stated it to be a 'fact that one good black suit, worn only on Sundays, and occasionally on holidays, will sometimes last a farm labourer nearly a lifetime'.[51] Nail-makers' daughter Minnie Frisby, recalled that 'what we had we had to take care of, and keep Sunday clothes for Sunday, and generally had to take our best clothes off when back from Chapel and Sunday school'.[52] Even those who could not afford a separate set of clothes, but sought respectability, strove to make a better appearance on Sundays. Ben Brierley's mother prepared him for his first Sunday school by sewing a frill onto his jacket and polishing his clogs.[53] In Edwin Grey's Hertfordshire village many agricultural labourers kept one smock for everyday wear and one 'for Sundays and special occasions'. Those with only one 'would at these special times turn it inside out so it appeared then

---

[48] BAWCA, 1:719, Mary Laura Triggle, 'Untitled'.
[49] Thorstein Veblen, *The Theory of the Leisure Class* (New York: Dover Publications, 1994 [1899]), p. 105.
[50] Shaw, *When I Was a Child*, pp. 194, 196.
[51] Francis George Heath, *Peasant Life in the West of England* (London: Sampson Low & Co., 1880), p. 296.
[52] BAWCA, 1:250, *Minnie Frisby*, p. 13. [53] Brierley, *Home Memories*, p. 10.

quite fresh and clean'.⁵⁴ Further north, Robert Roberts commented that, day to day, the poor wore 'whatever would hide indecency', but even they made some concession to the Sabbath wearing, for example, 'about the neck a muffler – white, if possible, for the Lord's day'.⁵⁵ And while Ben Brierley remembered that his Lancashire Sunday school in the 1830s was almost universally 'clogged', by the early twentieth century, according to Roberts, wearing clogs on Sundays was considered 'both vulgar and a sure sign of the wearer's poverty'.⁵⁶

As Joanne Entwistle says, 'bodies which flout the conventions of their culture and go without the appropriate clothes are subversive of the most basic social codes and risk exclusion, scorn or ridicule'.⁵⁷ Hence the shame of not being able to dress respectably was powerful enough to keep people hidden from public view. Charles Shaw's conversion to Methodism, with its exuberant Charity Sunday procession, was occasioned by his own sartorial humiliation. In 1842 Shaw was admitted to the Chell workhouse where his clothes were replaced with workhouse dress of 'moleskin breeches...and...a grey "brat" or pinafore, which served as waistcoat and jacket'. When Shaw was later released from the workhouse his own clothes were too dilapidated to resume and he was told to keep the trousers and brat and given another brat for Sundays. Shaw's chief ambition was to return to his Anglican Sunday school, but when he did so:

the scholars in the class looked at me askance, and whispered to each other. I saw their eyes travelling, sometimes furtively, and sometimes boldly over my clothes. They also kept apart from me...I had not yet the consciousness that the workhouse clothes, and my having been to the workhouse, had made such a difference. But I found it out during the afternoon...My clothes were mockingly pointed at, I was laughed at, jeered at, and I saw that I was clothed with contempt in their eyes.

He knew, he said, that 'he was not as other children', but 'tainted with a social leprosy' and for weeks was 'too shamefaced to venture out on a Sunday'. Eventually he 'broke through all shame and fear', making his way to the end of the street where he loitered by the Methodist chapel. He was taken in by the sympathetic Sunday school teacher, George Kirkham, from whom he drew strength: 'I don't know what became of the "brat," but as it made no difference to George Kirkham, I never cared what

---

⁵⁴ Grey, *Cottage Life*, p. 30. ⁵⁵ R. Roberts, *Classic Slum*, p. 39.
⁵⁶ Brierley, *Home Memories*, p. 17; R. Roberts, *Classic Slum*, p. 38.
⁵⁷ Joanne Entwistle, 'The dressed body', in Joanne Entwistle and Elizabeth Wilson (eds), *Body Dressing* (Oxford: Berg, 2001), pp. 33–58; p. 33.

others thought about it.'⁵⁸ Other children, or their parents, were less courageous. 'Sundays were long and weary days when we were kept in for want of decent clothes', remembered Londoner John Shinn in the 1840s:

> My mother who was a good pious woman... would sometimes (after dark) when our clothing was shabby... take us to some chapel a distance from home, where we were not known, which made a little change for us children.⁵⁹

In the reports of Parliamentary Commissioners inquiring into the employment of women and children in factories, potteries, mines and agriculture from 1833 through to 1867, witnesses from all areas and in all occupations repeatedly stated the lack of decent clothing as the reason for absence from Sunday school. 'I do not go to Sunday-school, my clothes are not very clean, else I should', said a fourteen-year-old North Staffordshire miner, while a Leeds mill-worker stated that: 'A great prevention of children going to Sunday school is the want of sufficiently good clothes. That is a well-known fact.'⁶⁰ We cannot, of course, test the truth of these claims and perhaps some children simply stated the lack of clothes because they did not want to go to Sunday school. But the fact that it was understood as a valid excuse to stay away is testimony to the significance of Sunday clothing. Jack Lanigan, in Salford, claimed that in the 1890s he and his brother:

> never went to Sunday School because we never had any decent clothes to go in. You were considered posh if you could attend Sunday School, but we went to Gravel Lane Ragged School on a Sunday evening. You never saw such a bunch of scruffy kids in all your life. If we had been bunched together you could not have made a suit from the lot.⁶¹

The Gravel Lane children were accustomed to poverty, which is not to suggest they were oblivious to it, but it was probably all that most had ever known. For others it was the shame of a decline in fortunes that was hard to bear. 'Some parents', according to Robert Roberts,

> once affluent enough to provide 'best' clothes for the family, then falling on hard times, would on no account allow their children to go out on Sunday in their

---

⁵⁸ Shaw, *When I Was a Child*, pp. 134–9. Although the clothes were ridiculed, the fact that he was given clothing for wear out of the workhouse was contrary to the wishes of the Poor Law Commissioners – see Chapter 7. For Charity Sunday see Chapter 3, and Chapter 10 for Shaw's description of his workhouse clothing.
⁵⁹ BAWCA, 1:622, John Shinn, 'A sketch of my life and times'.
⁶⁰ *Children's Employment Commission. Appendix... Mines. Part II.* Parliamentary Papers 1842 XVII, p. 147; *Factories Inquiries Commission. First Report... Employment of Children in Factories... C.2. North-eastern District.* Parliamentary Papers 1833 XX, p. 33.
⁶¹ Burnett, *Destiny Obscure*, p. 88.

weekday wear. No matter how fine the weather, they were kept cooped up all day in kitchen or bedroom so that face might be maintained before the neighbours.[62]

The lack of Sunday clothes in adolescence, the period when working-class people were most likely to have spare money for clothing, could be especially painful. Charles Russell described the Sunday-evening promenade of young unmarried men and women in early-twentieth-century Manchester. The 'lads', he said, were rarely seen in their weekday clothes on this occasion, and:

> the poor lad out of work, or one whose home is stricken with all the dire accompaniments of poverty will stay indoors on a Sunday, rather than let any of his many acquaintances see that he has lost temporarily the use of his better clothes.[63]

Wesht

> Everyone knows how after a bad night, for instance, or even after a good one, what an extraordinary effect a bath and all the accompanying processes of rubbing, etc., produce in the way of reviving and stimulating. Short of this, the mere fact of a change of clothes, of taking down the hair and brushing it and putting it up again, the possibility of changing shoes and stockings when the feet are cold or damp... all these make more difference than the heroic might be willing to admit. They are nearly all of them luxuries beyond the reach of the worker.[64]

Washing and dressing are so closely associated, psychologically as well as physically, that Mancunians combined them in a single word: 'wesht'.[65] But as Lady Bell recognised, unlike her own class, 'the worker' was largely denied the transformative sensations of either bathing or dressing in a set of clean, dry garments. Shifts and shirts commonly doubled as nightwear and the very poorest (and not just vagrants) with no change of clothing, wore the same garments day after day. Margaret Maynard records that although emigrants claiming a free passage to Australia were required to provide themselves with a sufficient changes of linen to last the voyage, many owned so little clothing that some women reportedly ended up having to stay in bed until they were given clothes on arrival.[66]

As Laura Ugolini says, 'it was the sign of relative comfort to be able to change from one set of working clothes into another if the first was soiled or wet'.[67] In 1843, Special Assistant Poor Law Commissioner Alfred Austin found that for women field-workers in the West Country

---

[62] R. Roberts, *Classic Slum*, pp. 38–9. [63] Russell, *Manchester Boys*, pp. 102–5.
[64] Bell, *At the Works*, p. 227. [65] Brierley, *Home Memories*, p. 33.
[66] Margaret Maynard, *Fashioned From Penury: Dress as Cultural Practice in Colonial Australia* (Oakleigh, Vic. and New York: Cambridge University Press, 1994), p. 144.
[67] Ugolini, *Men and Menswear*, p. 29.

a change of clothing seemed 'to be out of the question'. Yet perspiration and wet weather meant their clothes, 'even their stays', quickly became 'wet through', and 'not unfrequently... a woman, on returning home from work, is obliged to go to bed for an hour or two to allow her clothes to be dried'. Austin therefore felt a change of clothes was, 'necessary not only for cleanliness but for convenience and saving of time'. If the woman did not put her clothes to dry, it was, said Austin, 'by no means uncommon for her... to put them on again the next morning nearly as wet as when she took them off'.[68]

Even if she did take them off, there is no guarantee, especially in winter, that they would have been dry by the time she had to put them back on again, because she would also have required sufficient fuel to build and maintain a fire. Town-dwellers faced the same challenge; according to Robert Roberts, in Salford the 'low class' and the 'no class' rarely bought coal, but 'stole it from spoil heap and wharf, or in bad times, dragged the canals for droppings from barges'.[69] Many people, male and female, rural and urban, must have been used to putting, or just keeping on, damp clammy clothing which chilled and chafed their skin and injured their health. Even when the clothes did dry, they would have been stained and stiffened from sweat and dirt. Yet, as Arthur Goffin stressed, physical cleanliness was an essential component of respectability. Cleanliness, however, is a changing and culturally specific concept, which begs the question of what, in houses with no running water and inhabitants with few changes of clothing, constituted 'clean'?

The question of cleanliness exercised Engels in Manchester. How, he asked:

could the people be clean with no proper opportunity for satisfying the most natural and ordinary wants?... How can people wash when they have only the dirty Irk water at hand, while pumps and water pipes can be found in decent parts of the city alone?[70]

For Engels, bodily cleanliness was an innate desire satisfied by washing with water. But in the 1840s, as Georges Vigarello's and Daniel Roche's studies of France have shown, this was a relatively new (or revived) concept. Early-modern Europeans considered bodily immersion in water potentially dangerous, and in the eighteenth century bodily cleanliness was achieved and expressed through the wearing and display of linen which absorbed sweat and, through its whiteness, symbolised care of

---

[68] *Reports... Women and Children in Agriculture*. Parliamentary Papers 1843 XII, p. 22.
[69] R. Roberts, *Classic Slum*, pp. 75–6.
[70] Engels, *Condition of the Working Class*, pp. 90–1.

the body beneath.[71] Vigarello detects, in hospitals, a previously absent emphasis on the provision of clean underclothing, greater even in England than in France.[72] But the continual display of snowy linen depended on possession of the necessary resources to buy and maintain a good supply of garments. Initially, therefore, it was an elite practice, and although it did become more widespread, the 'true poor' were, as Roche points out, left behind.[73]

By the beginning of the nineteenth century changing ideas about health and hygiene meant it had become normal for the wealthy to wash their face and hands, and to use soap to do so.[74] By mid century, the perceived link between visible and invisible cleanliness had created the belief that 'slovenly dress increasingly revealed moral perversion'.[75] Vigarello links this to the rapid urbanisation which crammed the poor into crowded homes where disease and, it was believed, vice, proliferated, posing a threat to both the moral and the social order.[76] As I discuss further in Chapter 6, Isobel Armstrong identifies a nineteenth-century vitreous culture in which, through the use of windows, mirrors, chandeliers, glasshouses and conservatories, elite spaces became ever brighter, lighter and airier.[77] But its foundation lay in eighteenth-century street-widening schemes, behind which, Emily Cockayne reminds us, lay the 'increasingly fetid and close environments' of 'urban infill'. The very light and air of elite spaces meant that, in contrast, 'the mean alleys and festering courts' of the poor appeared ever darker, dirtier, airless and claustrophobic, and this became a common motif in social commentaries.[78] Alain Corbin argues that the 'hygiene police' intervened to improve sanitary conditions in English slums earlier and more effectively than in France, where a 'law on unhealthy habitations' was not introduced until 1850 and then 'very rarely enforced'.[79] But in Liverpool, in the 1840s, according to Engels, one fifth of the population lived 'in narrow, dark, damp, badly-ventilated cellar dwellings', and in Manchester the closely-packed houses were 'black, smoky, crumbling,

---

[71] Roche, *Culture of Clothing*, pp. 178–9; Georges Vigarello, *Concepts of Cleanliness: Changing Attitudes in France Since the Middle Ages*, trans. Jean Birrell (Cambridge University Press, 1988), pp. 62–3.
[72] Vigarello, *Concepts of Cleanliness*, p. 150.   [73] Roche, *Culture of Clothing*, p 179.
[74] Vigarello, *Concepts of Cleanliness*, pp. 163, 169.
[75] *Ibid.*, p. 192; Roche, *Culture of Clothing*, p. 180.
[76] Vigarello, *Concepts of Cleanliness*, p. 193.   [77] Armstrong, *Victorian Glassworlds*.
[78] Emily Cockayne, *Hubbub: Filth, Noise and Stench in England 1600–1770* (New Haven and London: Yale University Press, 2007), p. 229. Alain Corbin notes a similar contrast in nineteenth-century France. Alain Corbin, *The Foul and the Fragrant: Odor and the French Social Imagination* (Leamington Spa: Berg 1986), p. 148.
[79] Alain Corbin, *The Foul and the Fragrant*, pp. 159–60.

ancient, with broken panes and window frames'.[80] Half a century later, in York, Rowntree found 'typical slum dwellings... in confined courts' with 'too little sunlight and air', and 'separated from the main street by dark covered passages... They have dirty windows, broken panes are frequently stuffed with rags or pasted over with brown paper', and inside the rooms were 'dark and damp, and almost always dirty'.[81]

Seth Koven suggests 'the dirtiness of the poor and their homes' were perceived to be 'symptomatic of a moral indecency so fundamental to their nature that even the hottest bath could not cleanse them'.[82] To avoid censure, says Roche, poverty now 'had to show itself to be clean'.[83] The poor were to learn to be ashamed of dirt and Koven, discussing philanthropic slum workers, points out that: 'It was the prerogative of elite women to define what dirt was – and was not – and to dictate how, where, and when their social inferiors should remove it.'[84] Mrs Layton, growing up in poverty in East London in the 1850s and 1860s, identified herself as 'rather a lazy little girl' and so 'often went out in the morning without washing my face'. She remembered being approached in the park by 'a lady' who asked about her schooling and ability to read:

Then she asked me if I had washed myself before I came out that morning. I felt so ashamed when I had to admit that I had not done so. Then she gave me the nice little Testament I had read from, and made me promise that I would never neglect to wash myself before leaving home either for school or play, and never to miss an opportunity of improving myself if only I had more time to give to educating myself.[85]

Journalist George Sims similarly connected cleanliness and education. The latter, he believed, planted and nurtured the seed of ambition and separated the present and the previous generations. He singled out one bright pupil in a class who would 'do well, whatever she undertakes', not least, because she had 'learnt to be ashamed of dirt'.[86]

But for the poor, bodily cleanliness was a challenge since simply obtaining water could be very arduous. Edwin Grey recalled that his Hertfordshire village was 'supplied with a number of wells', but some had to serve over a dozen cottages and the water had to be drawn, transported and stored in large, heavy earthenware pots.[87] Flora Thompson similarly described 'weary journeys' to the wells in rural Oxfordshire, 'in all weathers, drawing up the buckets with a windlass and carting them home

---

[80] Engels, *Condition of the Working Class*, pp. 78, 89.   [81] Rowntree, *Poverty*, pp. 153–4.
[82] Koven, *Slumming*, p. 193.   [83] Roche, *Culture of Clothing*, p. 180.
[84] Koven, *Slumming*, p. 192.   [85] Llewelyn Davies, *Life as We Have Known It*, p. 5.
[86] George R. Sims, *How the Poor Live* (Gloucester: Dodo Press, 2009 [1883]) p. 60.
[87] Grey, *Cottage Life*, pp. 47–8.

on a yoke... In dry summers, when the hamlet wells failed, water had to be fetched from a pump at some farm buildings half a mile distant.[88] In urban areas water was supplied from communal facilities in the street and had to be carried back to lodgings and often up several flights of stairs.[89]

The introduction of piped water was gradual and uneven. In the 1840s 30,000 Londoners were without local access to a communal street tap. In other places, such as Wolverhampton and the Potteries, the water supply was turned off for hours, days or weeks at a time.[90] In such cases, the poor were reliant on the water collected in communal butts or tubs, open to the elements and sometimes containing stagnant water. In 1883, George Sims, looking for a suitable example to demonstrate the difficulties of the London poor in 'attaining that cleanliness which we are told is next to godliness', was favoured by the arrival, in a courtyard, of a baked-potato seller who had come to wash the dirt from his potatoes in the communal water tub.[91]

Even at the close of the century unlimited access to clean water in the home was far from universal. Arthur Harding recalled moving to a new home in East London in 1902 where: 'For the first time, we had two rooms... And we had our own water tap.' In their previous accommodation they had 'shared the one on the landing'.[92] T. R. Marr, in a 1904 survey of Manchester and Salford housing conditions declared the water supply to be clean and plentiful, but inaccessible with one tap frequently serving a whole street and some tenants therefore having to carry the water 'a considerable distance'.[93] Charles Russell, Secretary of a Manchester Lads Club in the 1900s, received a letter from a fifteen-year-old office worker who shared one poorly furnished room with two friends. Their washing facilities consisted of 'an old lading-can, placed under the tap on the slopstone'. The tap was shared with the tenants of the front room in return for use of their room as a short-cut to the street.[94] Rowntree in 1908 reported that less than half of the 1,642 houses in one poor district of York could 'boast a private water-tap' and sometimes one

---

[88] F. Thompson, *Lark Rise*, pp. 22–3.
[89] Elizabeth Wilson, *The Sphinx in the City: Urban Life, the Control of Disorder, and Women* (London: Virago, 1991), pp. 36–7.
[90] Wohl, *Endangered Lives*, p. 62.   [91] Sims, *How the Poor Live*, p. 78.
[92] Samuel, *East End Underworld*, p. 63.
[93] T. R. Marr, *Housing Conditions in Manchester and Salford* (Manchester University Press, 1904), p. 43.
[94] Russell, *Manchester Boys*, pp. 134–5. Similarly, Ellen Ross found that in London neighbours 'might have to walk through each other's rooms routinely to reach the shared facilities'. Ross, 'Survival networks', p. 10.

tap was shared by more than twenty houses.[95] In rural areas the problem could be even worse with still no access to piped water and continued reliance on wells.[96]

Whether from a well or a tap the water was cold and, as with drying damp clothes, warm water required money for fuel. Soap demanded a further outlay. According to Jan de Vries, use of soap was linked to the spread of piped water and did not reach a mass market in Britain until the 1880s. At this point annual consumption stood at 14 lbs per capita, compared with just over 3 lbs in 1791.[97] Averages, however, conceal great extremes. According to Pember Reeves, Edwardian housewives in Lambeth would ideally have spent 5*d.* a week on soap, but often had to make do with 2*d.* worth:

> to wash the clothes, scrub the floors, and wash the people of a family, for a week. It is difficult to realise the soap famine in such a household. Soda, being cheap, is made to do a great deal. It sometimes appears in the children's weekly bath; it often washes their hair.[98]

At 3*d.* a pound, 2*d.* a week bought just under 35 lbs of soap a year – or enough for two-and-a-half people based on the average of 14 lbs per person.[99] But most families were much larger. Rowntree and Kendall's budgets for forty-two rural families at the same period showed weekly expenditure on washing materials, including soap, soda, starch and blue, varying from nothing, in two instances, to 6*d.* in the case of one family, although this also included black lead, laces and an unspecified 'etc.'. The average for the remaining thirty-nine families was just over 3*d.*, but again this sometimes included other items such as hearthstone, blacking and matches.[100] Robert Roberts described the public scolding meted out by teachers to dirty pupils, but as he observed: 'It was difficult for a child to keep himself clean in a house where soap came low on the list of necessaries.'[101]

Abundant evidence testifies to the inadequacy of washing facilities throughout the period, and yet the 1846 Baths and Washhouses Act

---

[95] Rowntree, *Poverty*, p. 201; See also Wohl, *Endangered Lives*, pp. 62–3, for continuing inadequate water supplies elsewhere in Edwardian England.
[96] Rowntree and Kendall, *How the Labourer Lives*, p. 330.
[97] Jan de Vries, *The Industrious Revolution: Consumer Behavior and the Household Economy, 1650 to the Present* (Cambridge University Press, 2008), p. 197.
[98] Pember Reeves, *Round About a Pound*, pp. 60–1.
[99] The report of the 1871 Truck Commission found that nailers paid in truck were charged 5*d.* for a cake of soap sold at 3*d.* in independent shops. G. W. Hilton, *Truck System*, p. 15.
[100] Rowntree and Kendall, *How the Labourer Lives*, Chapter 3.
[101] R. Roberts, *Classic Slum*, p. 138.

allowed local authorities to levy rates to fund the erection of public amenities. The Act set maximum charges of 1d. for a cold, and 2d. for a warm individual bath, and 2d. and 4d. respectively for a cold and a warm bath shared by up to four children.[102] But while some towns and cities, including London, Birmingham and Liverpool adopted the Act, Anthony Wohl reports that even twenty years after its introduction many others, including Leeds, Manchester and York were still without public baths and washhouses. Nevertheless, by 1912 there were over five million visits to British public baths, with more than three million of these in London and Wohl, therefore, concludes that 'a visit to the public baths became a regular part' of the lives of 'thousands of men and women'. But London's population was numbered in millions not thousands – over seven million in 1911 – and three million visits to the public baths meant only a very small proportion having a weekly bath or a much larger proportion having a bath very irregularly.[103]

As Pember Reeves found in Lambeth, even the seemingly small cost of the public baths was beyond many families. 'The mother', she wrote of one family, 'manages to bathe herself once a fortnight in the daytime when the five elder children are at school, and the father goes to public baths when he can find time and afford twopence.' Another woman, she noted, 'generally has a bath herself on Sunday evening when her husband is out. All the water has to be carried upstairs, heated in her kettle, and carried down again when dirty. Her husband bathes, when he can afford two pence, at the public baths.' Similarly, a third woman bathed 'when the two elder children are at school. The father, who can never afford a twopenny bath, gets a "wash-down" sometimes after the children have gone to sleep at night.'[104]

Katherine Ashenburg claims that public baths were under-used because 'the majority of the poor did not crave baths', fearing chills and infections.[105] But when collieries introduced pithead baths they were widely welcomed, not only by the men who used them but also (particularly) by their wives who no longer had to prepare baths for their husbands and clean up after them. When, in 1930, a Lancashire miner's wife wrote to the Women's Co-operative Guild extolling the virtues of the baths at her husband's colliery, which he had been using for fifteen

---

[102] *A Bill (as amended by the Committee) for promoting the voluntary Establishment, in Boroughs and Parishes in England and Wales, of Public Baths and Washhouses.* Parliamentary Papers 1846 I, p. 13. (Passed 7 August 1846, Hansard).
[103] Wohl, *Endangered Lives*, pp. 74–5.
[104] Pember Reeves, *Round About a Pound*, pp. 55–6.
[105] Katherine Ashenburg, *Clean: An Unsanitised History of Washing* (London: Profile Books, 2008), p. 176.

years, her assurance that he had done so 'without being afflicted with any cold or rheumatism or illness', would seem to confirm Ashenburg's assertion that this had been a prevalent fear. But according to her husband's testimony this was easily overcome, since the baths were used by some 90 per cent of both 'miners and officials at our colliery... so you see they are all in favour of baths'. Indeed, he believed the baths actively promoted health, 'because, going to and from the colliery, [the men] always have a change of fresh clothes when it is raining, from wet clothes to dry ones'.[106]

Ashenburg also says that public baths were used more by men than women and suggests three reasons for this: men's work made them dirtier; men had fewer domestic responsibilities and therefore more time at the end of the day; and women did not consider public bathhouses respectable.[107] Yet she says nothing about cost, and this would seem to be yet another instance of men's needs taking priority. If there were insufficient funds for poor men to have baths, there would certainly not have been any money for their wives to do so. But the frequent references to snatched washes while children were at school are testimony to their determination to achieve a level of bodily cleanliness despite the lack of desired privacy for bathing. Perhaps poor women would also have welcomed the opportunity to visit the public baths, given the money to do so.

For the vast majority of the poor bodily cleanliness lay not in frequent bathing, but in the observation of such toilet practices as the available resources allowed. On a day-to-day basis the emphasis was on the removal of visible dirt and grime from visible areas. Washing away bodily fluids and odours from covered parts of the body was performed at longer intervals. Child potter Charles Shaw described his pre-Sunday-school ablution, in the 1840s, when he 'got a washing... such as I had not time to get on other mornings'.[108] Edwin Grey remarked that in mid-Victorian Hertfordshire, the well water 'having to be obtained at considerable trouble, care was taken to use no more than was really necessary at one time'. Clothes were washed in large wooden troughs which 'were also used for the children's Saturday night bath, and by the adults also when required for the same purpose'. Although the latter 'was but occasionally', he also said that in summer 'many of the young men, and also most of the lads and boys, bathed frequently in the nearby little river Lea', suggesting they may have bathed more often at home given the right facilities.[109]

---

[106] Llewelyn Davies, *Life as We Have Known It*, pp. 136–7.
[107] Ashenburg, *Clean*, p. 176.   [108] Shaw, *When I Was a Child*, p. 7.
[109] Grey, *Cottage Life*, pp. 48–50.

When Christopher Holdenby set out to get to know English agricultural labourers by working and living among them, in the early twentieth century, he at one point lodged in 'a very good modern "estate cottage"', but even here he abandoned his 'morning tub' on discovering that the only water supply was 'one small rainwater tank' and that he was drinking his soapsuds at supper.[110] Pember Reeves noted that in Lambeth the 'daily ablutions' were generally:

> confined to face and hands when each person comes downstairs, with the exception of the little baby, who generally has some sort of wash over every day. Once a week, however, most of the children get a bath.[111]

Alain Corbin detects in the early decades of nineteenth-century France a new 'bourgeois emphasis on the stench of the poor' and an 'image of the masses... constructed in terms of filth'.[112] Anthony Wohl and Katherine Ashenburg similarly identify bodily odour as a new form of class division in nineteenth-century England, exemplified in the introduction of the epithet for the masses of the 'Great Unwashed'.[113] But this was an intra- as well an inter-class division. 'Some men working in the many offensive trades of the day', said Robert Roberts, 'smelled abominably, and people would avoid the public houses where they forgathered.'[114] 'Whole worlds of meaning', wrote Jose Harris, 'were conveyed by microscopic household practices, such as whether one washed in the morning or the evening, in the bathroom, in the bedroom, or at the kitchen sink.'[115] This was private practice made public knowledge and Arthur Harding's account of his family's move to a new home illustrates how an assertion of status could be made through a display of the apparatus of cleanliness. The new accommodation was 'a wee bit higher in the social ladder' than their previous home and Harding's mother was anxious 'to look a bit more respectable'. This was achieved by the purchase of new pieces of furniture, which neighbours would see as they were taken into the building, including 'a wash hand-stand' which held a basin, water-jug stand and chamber pot.[116]

According to Virginia Smith, the development of germ theory in the second half of the century meant that by the 1890s 'the public's

---

[110] Holdenby, *Folk of the Furrow*, p. 59.
[111] Pember Reeves, *Round About a Pound*, p. 55.
[112] Corbin, *The Foul and the Fragrant*, p. 144.
[113] Wohl, *Endangered Lives*, p. 64. Ashenburg, *Clean*, p. 170. Ashenburg credits William Makepeace Thackeray with coining the term which appears in *Pendennis* (1848–50), but it had been used by Edward Bulwer-Lytton in the 'Dedicatory Epistle' of *Paul Clifford* in 1830. Edward Bulwer-Lytton, *Paul Clifford*, 2 vols (New York, 1830), vol. I, p. xiii.
[114] R. Roberts, *Classic Slum*, p. 38.   [115] Harris, *Private Lives, Public Spirit*, p. 8.
[116] Samuel, *East End Underworld*, pp. 63–4, 98–9.

belief in the existence of "germs" was strong and unstoppable'; they were 'the invisible enemy, fought at every turn'.[117] The new 'scientific' approach to laundry work in elementary schools considered the relative merits of carbolic acid, eucalyptus and running cold water (some chance!) for '[d]isinfecting... to destroy the germs of disease'.[118] But as Smith subsequently acknowledges, 'the very poorest were still completely powerless'.[119] They were also quite possibly ignorant, and Wohl proposes that the welcome given to local authority distribution of free disinfectant probably rested less on a close acquaintance with bacteriology than the fear of compulsory house fumigation and the potential destruction of property without compensation. Visible vermin were a more pressing and stigmatic issue than invisible germs.[120] According to Robert Roberts, for example, children with severe lice infestations would be isolated at school and 'later be kept at home, their heads shaven, reeking of some rubbed-in disinfectant', their status intact because 'they had already reached rock bottom'.[121]

Hair, as a natural and free accessory, could be a source of great pride and make a significant contribution to respectable appearance. Charles Shaw recalled that as part of his Sunday school preparations 'my hair got brushed and combed and oiled (with scented oil), so that I always carried a fragrance with me'.[122] When Alice and Ruby Chase, the daughters of a Portsmouth carpenter, were bridesmaids in 1895 their 'mother washed and brushed our lovely hair till it shone like silk and it hung down our backs in deep waves'.[123] The cultural value of beautiful hair heightened the humiliation of its absence. In 1864 Arthur Munby found a homeless young woman in St James's Park. She was a 'mass of broken hoops and frowsy crape and napless velvet' and her head, he realised, though covered by a bonnet, *was shaven*. A shaved head commonly indicated recent release from prison and so, 'for all her rags and desolation, she had tried to conceal in part the loss of her hair', not only with the bonnet, but also 'by wearing the usual netbag behind her neck, and stuffing it with horsehair'. The woman claimed her head had been shaved because she had been ill with fever, but Munby was not convinced.[124]

---

[117] Virginia Smith, *Clean: A History of Personal Hygiene and Purity* (Oxford University Press, 2007), p. 299.
[118] Calder and Mann, *Teachers' Manual*, p. 12. [119] Smith, *Clean*, p. 305.
[120] Wohl, *Endangered Lives*, pp. 65–6, 70. [121] R. Roberts, *Classic Slum*, p. 79.
[122] Shaw, *When I Was a Child*, p. 7. [123] BAWCA, 1:141, Alice Maud Chase, p. 30.
[124] Hudson, *Munby*, pp. 198–200. The following year, the 1865 Prisons Act stipulated that the hair of female prisoners was not to be cut except when necessitated by dirt, vermin or health. Male prisoners' hair was to be cut no 'closer than may be necessary for purposes of health and cleanliness'. Shorn prisoners were supposed to be allowed to grow their hair for several weeks before the end of their sentence to save them

Flesh and blood

The numerous descriptions of women, in particular, strip-washing behind curtains and locked doors in temporarily empty homes emphasises their desire for privacy and the challenge of its achievement. Michael Mason and Anna Davin both discuss the arrangements put in place by the poor to 'protect modesty', such as the erection of curtains to separate areas, or one sex leaving the premises while the other dressed.[125] But overcrowding must sometimes have meant a certain amount of discretion – turning a blind eye – was necessary to permit the processes of everyday life to continue. And as Davin also notes, the lack of privacy for undress does not appear to have been a universal concern.[126] In 1841 a Newcastle rector complained that it was impossible for a clergyman in his mining district to take his wife out visiting with him on account of 'the men washing half-naked in the presence of the women'. Likewise, a Barnsley solicitor claimed to have seen pit-girls 'washing themselves naked much below the waist as I passed their doors... and men young and old would be washing in the same place, at the same time'. He noted that the men and women were 'talking and chatting' to each other while they washed 'with the utmost unconcern', and concluded that 'the moral effect... must be exceedingly bad'.[127] Yet his description of their naked unselfconsciousness in a commonplace situation suggests quite the reverse.

Peter Jones found that the claim of nakedness was commonly invoked in pauper letters requesting parish relief. It denoted not literal nakedness, but a state of 'absolute need' and was calculated to elicit a favourable response by operating on the relieving officers' assumed belief in 'the absolute indecency of being forced out into the world without adequate covering for one's body'.[128] For middle-class observers like the Newcastle rector and Barnsley solicitor, and for evangelicals in particular, naked flesh was sinful, unclean, a temptation, and they were horrified to

---

'from observation and annoyance when released', but an 1889 Inquiry heard that 'the application of the rule as to hair-clipping is sometimes arbitrary and unequal'. *Prison Rules Inquiry. Report of the Committee of Inquiry as to the Rules Concerning the Wearing of Prison Dress, &c., Together with Minutes of Evidence and Appendices.* Parliamentary Papers 1889 LXI, pp. viii–ix.

[125] Michael Mason, *The Making of Victorian Sexuality* (Oxford University Press, 1994), pp. 141–3; Davin, *Growing Up Poor*, pp. 51–2.
[126] Davin, *Growing Up Poor*, p. 51.
[127] *Children's Employment Commission. Appendix... Mines. Part I.* Parliamentary Papers 1842 XVI, pp. 250, 676.
[128] P. D. Jones, 'I cannot keep my place', pp. 34–5. Jonathan Andrews makes a similar point. Jonathan Andrews, 'The (un)dress of the mad poor in England, c.1650–1850. Part 2', *History of Psychiatry*, 18:2 (2007), 131–56; 135.

discover that in some workplaces it was commonplace for employees to remove their clothing. In hot mills, for example, women often stripped down to their shifts and, like the miners, washed with men at communal facilities.[129] To Parliamentary Commissioners immorality seemed guaranteed since, as Mason emphasises, the 'strongly environmentalist bias' of middle-class opinion encouraged the belief that individuals who carried out intimate functions in close proximity were also likely to be engaging in sexual activity.[130] Karen Sayer points out that by masking the body clothing constructed 'the flesh as polluting' so that the exposed body 'came to be automatically treated as fluid, sexualised, dangerously unconfined'.[131]

Jennie Kitteringham highlighted a parallel reaction to the clothing of rural work girls. Coarse, tough, practical work garments were considered 'unwomanly', but less substantial clothing which revealed the contours of the body was seen as 'an invitation to promiscuity in the summer harvest fields'.[132] But it was in the mines that the situation was deemed most alarming. Here the Commissioners were confronted with an alien world characterised by physical strength, dirt and odour. When Sub-Commissioner Samuel Scriven descended a Staffordshire mineshaft, in 1841, he descended into hell. The scene he found in the cramped, dimly lit, workplace had, he said, 'something truly hideous and Satanic about it', arising from the heat, the contorted postures of the miners and the 'offensive odour from their excessive perspiration'. Still more shocking was the fact that the men were all 'naked or nearly so', and females worked in the same pits.[133] Sub-Commissioner Symons, finding in one Barnsley pit a group of men, boys and pubescent girls gathered around a fire, all 'stark naked down to the waist', declared it 'flagrantly disgraceful to a Christian as well as to a civilised country'.[134]

Symons's assertion echoed the imperial ideology which, in the name of civilisation, justified the imposition of dominant European morals and manners on subject groups. In Australia, says Margaret Maynard:

---

[129] *Factories Inquiries Commission. First Report... Employment of Children in Factories... D.1. Lancashire District.* Parliamentary Papers 1833 XX, pp. 42–4.
[130] Mason, *Making of Victorian Sexuality*, pp. 139–40.
[131] Karen Sayer, '"A sufficiency of clothing": dress and domesticity in Victorian Britain', *Textile History*, 33:1 (2002), 112–22; 118.
[132] Jennie Kitteringham, 'Country work girls in nineteenth-century England', in Raphael Samuel (ed.), *Village Life and Labour* (London: Routledge & Kegan Paul, 1975), pp. 73–138; p. 129.
[133] *Children's Employment Commission. Appendix... Mines. Part II.* Parliamentary Papers 1842 XVII, p. 127.
[134] *Children's Employment Commission. Appendix... Mines. Part I.* Parliamentary Papers 1842 XVI, p. 196.

146 'The struggle for respectability'

'Lack of clothing was seen as morally incompatible with the "superior" European way of life' and 'nudity became the site of a major cultural struggle to bring Aborigines within the sphere of Christian influence.' But still more troubling were white male convicts who sometimes worked naked in the fields and so became 'unacceptably close to the local male Aboriginal population in appearance, doubly transgressing accepted lines of racial and sexual order'.[135] Likewise Emma Tarlo argues that in colonial India: 'The "disgraceful" sight of the loinclothed boatmen' confirmed to Europeans 'the evolutionary inferiority of the Indian race – of its backwardness and barbarism'. It also 'revealed the blackness of the skin which was in itself regarded as a biological sign of racial inferiority'.[136]

In mines and factories, the workers' seeming indifference to nakedness similarly appeared to confirm their animalism, evolutionary retardation and need of salvation. This was compounded in the mines where the sooty blackness of the workers' skin could, for observers, seemingly create confusion about their racial identity.[137] Barry Reay draws attention to Munby's verbal and pictorial descriptions of pitwoman Eliza Hayes who, even as a surface worker, was 'about the very blackest pitwench' he ever saw. Reay quotes Anne McClintock who explains that Munby's sketch of Hayes depicts her not only as black from coal dust, but racially black, presenting:

a grotesque caricature of the stigmata of racial degeneration: her forehead is flattened and foreshortened; the whites of her eyes start grotesquely from her black face; her lips are artificially full and pale.

Munby gives no indication that he is consciously ascribing these stereotypical racial attributes to a white Lancashire woman, and unlike Symons he saw beauty beneath the blackness. But there is a parallel in his description of Hayes's 'Satanic blackness'.[138]

While Sub-Commissioner Symons worried about the pit girls' exposed breasts, when the girls gave evidence they seemed mostly unconcerned about the absence of a shift. Some, though, insisted that they always wore trousers. Seventeen-year-old Elizabeth Day, for example, said she was usually naked to the waist, and had been wearing a shift when

[135] Maynard, *Fashioned From Penury*, pp. 59, 62–3.
[136] Emma Tarlo, *Clothing Matters: Dress and Identity in India* (London: Hurst & Company, 1996), p. 34.
[137] Clare Rose similarly notes that: 'The terminology used for discussing working-class childhood was further clouded by contemporary definitions of "race" that elided class status and ethnicity.' C. Rose, *Making, Wearing and Selling*, p. 4.
[138] Barry Reay, *Watching Hannah: Sexuality, Horror and Bodily De-formation in Victorian England* (London: Reaktion, 2002), pp. 111–12.

Symons saw her only because she 'had had to wait, and was cold', but, she said: 'We always hurry in trousers.' It is difficult to ascertain whether this insistence on trousers indicates the witnesses' own priorities because the report documents only their answers, not the Commissioners' questions. The fact that females wore trousers did not necessarily mean their genitals remained covered and the responses of subsequent witnesses suggest that Symons then turned his attention to the question of whether the condition of the trousers permitted any bodily exposure. While fourteen-year-old Mary Holmes insisted her trousers did not get torn 'at all' (improbable given the working conditions, but perhaps she meant they did not get torn at the crotch), Rachel Tinker, aged thirteen, said 'they get torn between the legs'. The girls worked as hurriers, pulling the trucks of mined material to the shaft, and they did so with the aid of a chain which fastened to a belt around their waists, passed between their legs and attached to the truck. Ann Winchcliffe, aged ten, said of her trousers that 'the chain often tears them, and makes great holes in them between my legs'.[139] However, this still may not have meant that her genitals were visible, since the trousers were loose-fitting, the passageways along which the trucks were pulled were dimly lit, if at all, and a rear view of the hurriers as they worked would have been obstructed by the trucks they were pulling. It may therefore be that the trousers were worn for reasons of propriety – consciously exposed breasts being acceptable, but not female genitals – since Winchcliffe's evidence suggests they offered little protection from the chafing of the chain.

Practice varied. Symons identified the girls' gold ear-rings, at a nearby pit, as the chief means of determining their sex even though, when working underground, in addition to trousers and skull-cap they wore the female bedgown.[140] Similarly, it seems that women's attitudes to men working naked were mixed. Mary Barrett who, at fourteen, had spent five years as a Halifax hurrier, said she had 'got well used' to the men working naked, 'and don't care now much about it', but had been 'afraid at first, and did not like it'. In Lancashire, a thirty-eight-year-old female pit worker remembered, 'seeing a man who worked stark naked, and we would not go near him: we used to throw coals at him'.[141] There,

---

[139] *Children's Employment Commission. Appendix... Mines. Part I.* Parliamentary Papers 1842 XVI, pp. 244, 295–6.
[140] *Ibid.*, p. 194. In the photographs collected by Munby, virtually all the Wigan pit-brow girls are wearing gold hoop earrings. But he made no mention of them, despite his comment that the rolled-up aprons were 'perfectly useless – only retained as a symbol of sex'. TCLC, MUNB, 6, 29 September 1860; 3, 19 August 1859.
[141] *Children's Employment Commission. Appendix... Mines. Part II.* Parliamentary Papers 1842 XVII, pp. 122, 214.

clearly, the practice was unusual and in fact it seems that only a minority of adult men in certain areas worked completely naked. Elsewhere, and among younger males, one or two garments were retained. Hurrier Samuel Day and his colleagues worked in 'a shirt and nothing else on', but 'never naked'. Thirteen-year-old Charles Bayley, also a Yorkshire hurrier, testified that he and his workmates laboured 'with our trowsers on, and naked to the waist', or 'sometimes we take our trowsers off, and hurry in our shirts'.[142] The point, in either case, was that they always wore something that covered their genitals since, like the women's shifts, nineteenth-century men's shirts were long, reaching at least to the thighs and often further (although, clearly, they could ride up). All in all, the witnesses' responses suggest that the Sub-Commissioners' reports, designed to highlight the workers' lack of moral rectitude, served rather to advertise their own assumptions, anxieties and perhaps, as Frank Mort suggests, sexual proclivities.[143]

The Commissioners were convinced that scantily clad males and females working in close proximity must result in sexual improprieties, and some of the witnesses said they had either seen or been victims of libidinous behaviour. Patience Kershaw, the only female among some fifteen naked men and twenty boys at her Halifax pit said the latter 'take liberties with me sometimes, they pull me about', while Mary Glover, in Lancashire, claimed to have often seen 'men take liberties with the women'.[144] But many other women said they were never 'insulted' by men in the pit, and it seems unlikely they were doing so simply to safeguard their jobs since they were outspoken about other disliked aspects of their work. Furthermore, Jan Lambertz has highlighted the importance of friends and family in protecting female cotton-industry workers from abuse, or seeking redress when an abuse occurred, and the close-knit nature of many communities and workplaces may have acted as a break on sexual assault.[145]

In Halifax, for example, twelve-year-old hurrier Selina Ambler told Sub-Commissioner Scriven: 'The boys never dare *touch* us, if they did

---

[142] *Children's Employment Commission. Appendix... Mines. Part I.* Parliamentary Papers 1842 XVI, pp. 245, 276.
[143] Mason, *Making of Victorian Sexuality*, pp. 139–40; Frank Mort, *Dangerous Sexualities: Medico-moral Politics in England Since 1830* (London: Routledge, 2000), p. 38. We should not, however, forget the erotic potential of glimpsed flesh. See Richmond 'Stitching the self', p. 51.
[144] *Children's Employment Commission. Appendix... Mines. Part II.* Parliamentary Papers 1842 XVII, pp. 107–8, 214.
[145] Jan Lambertz, 'Sexual harassment in the nineteenth century English cotton industry', *History Workshop Journal*, 19 (1985), 29–61; 46–8.

Flesh and blood 149

my brother would "plump" [beat] them.'[146] A decade earlier, Sub-Commissioner Symons had pressed John Redman – for twenty-eight years a cotton-factory operative but at the time of inquiry a Manchester overseer of the poor and Sunday-school superintendent – on the moral effects of textile-factory work. Redman said that the average temperature in a cotton mill was 80°F, as a consequence of which the men 'generally work with their coats and waistcoats off... and without stockings, and the girls will take off their clothes, as far as decency will allow'. For Redman, the perils of this practice lay in the fact that the child workers, when allowed out of the factory, rushed away into the cold air without properly dressing which damaged their health. For Symons the danger lay in the potential for 'gross indecencies'. But according to Redman, 'moral evils' were kept in check by the spinners who were mainly married men, generally employed their own children or relatives as piecers, and even when they did not had 'a common interest as fathers in discountenancing indecencies of conduct and language', and set the tone for the unmarried spinners whose piecers were often their siblings.[147] This is not to dismiss or deny that, as Lambertz has shown, women and children were often placed in positions which left them vulnerable to sexual harassment and assault, but so they were in fully clothed workplaces.[148]

There was, then, no overarching working-class attitude toward nakedness and at certain times and in certain places, full, or more commonly partial, nudity was a practical response to difficult working conditions and largely unremarkable. As Jane A. B., a twenty-six-year-old cotton-factory worker, explained to Sub-Commissioner Symons when asked whether she had heard boy piecers making 'pert observations' about the girls when they undressed to start work: 'No, sir, it seemed to be quite an accustomed thing among them; they thought nothing about it.'[149] Furthermore, as Redman indicated with his qualification that factory girls removed their clothing *only to the limits of decency*, it is clear that the working classes did have sartorial moral codes, but the Commissioners neither recognised nor understood them. And more than one observer commented on the seemingly acceptable extent to which, in the name of fashion, wealthy women exposed their breasts. Munby, visiting the steamy boiling sheds of a Northwich saltworks, found the men naked to

---

[146] *Children's Employment Commission. Appendix... Mines. Part II.* Parliamentary Papers 1842 XVII, p. 124.
[147] *Factories Inquiries Commission. First Report... Employment of Children in Factories... D.1. Lancashire District.* Parliamentary Papers 1833 XX, pp. 41–5.
[148] Lambertz, 'Sexual harassment'.
[149] *Factories Inquiries Commission. First Report... Employment of Children in Factories... D.1. Lancashire District.* Parliamentary Papers 1833 XX, p. 38.

the waist, the women wearing 'thin shifts up to the breasts... their arms shoulders and bosoms being exposed on account of the heat – but not more than those of a lady at a ball'.[150]

Another largely impenetrable subject, as the Showalters discovered, is the management of menstruation, which also had implications for cleanliness and women's dress.[151] What little information there is suggests that, again, attitudes and practices varied, although the reasons are unclear. Alia Al-Khalidi, investigating nineteenth-century technologies for absorbing the menstrual flow, documented a new device which claimed to prevent 'the breakings out or inflamed chaps occasioned by the pellets of linen rag hitherto used', the 'pellets' suggesting a vaginal plug.[152] The Showalters, however, drawing a parallel with American practice, favour the idea of the 'menstrual napkin'.[153] A proposed trousseau for the wife of a working man, in 1888, tucks '24 towels' into the list of underclothing, rather than the household linen, indicating that they are sanitary towels.[154] Less clear, however, is whether this is what the readers would have been using, or whether this is what the middle-class author was encouraging the readers to use. But in her fictionalised autobiography, Margaret Penn, raised in a Lancashire agricultural community, explained that in the 1890s her grandmother knew her daughter was pregnant because she no longer needed 'those thick squares of Turkish towelling'.[155] Similarly, Elizabeth Roberts' oral history of north Lancashire between 1890 and 1940 found respondents relying on home-made sanitary towels formed from reusable pieces of old sheeting or towel, though with no explanation of how they were kept in place.[156]

Julie Marie-Strange identifies the cultivation of 'a new menstrual experience' in the nineteenth-century which was 'clean, odour free'.[157] But this was clearly a challenge for poor women. Elizabeth Roberts, noting that baths and hair-washing were prohibited for menstruating women

---

[150] TCLC, MUNB, 7, 4 October 1860. For a further example see Dorothy Wise (ed.), *Diary of William Tayler, Footman. 1837* (London: The St Marylebone Society, 1987), p. 36.
[151] Elaine and English Showalter, 'Victorian women and menstruation', *Victorian Studies*, 14:1 (1970), 83–9; 83.
[152] Al-Khalidi, 'Emergent technologies', 265.
[153] E. and E. Showalter, 'Victorian women', p. 86.
[154] TWL 5GFS/10/012, *Friendly Leaves*, February 1888.
[155] Margaret Penn, *Manchester Fourteen Miles* (London: Futura, 1982 [1947]), p. 40.
[156] Elizabeth Roberts, *A Woman's Place: An Oral History of Working-Class Women 1890–1940* (Oxford: Basil Blackwell, 1985), p. 18.
[157] Julie-Marie Strange, '"I believe it to be a case depending on menstruation": madness and menstrual taboo in British medical practice, c.1840–1930', in Andrew Shail and Gillian Howie (eds), *Menstruation: A Cultural History* (Basingstoke: Palgrave Macmillan, 2005), pp. 102–16, p. 112.

(and the striking contrast between this 'lack of hygiene' and the emphasis on cleanliness of the visible parts of the body), concludes that we 'can only speculate about the... discomfort, chafing and smell experienced by menstruating women', the damage to their self-esteem, and their fear of being detected.[158] But Roberts also found that other women simply allowed the blood to be absorbed by layers of underclothing and Patricia Crawford asserted that some nineteenth-century women 'did not use any pessaries or pads, for they feared that any cloth might prevent the menses from flowing'.[159] She gives no source for the information, but it fits with the idea of menstruation as a necessary and healthy purging which Sally Shuttleworth identifies and which Sharra L Vostral, writing about America, sees replaced in the later 1800s with a pathological concept of menstruation.[160] Also close to this idea, and in contrast with Roberts's concerns about smell and fear of detection, and Carol Dyhouse's emphasis on the shame and embarrassment women felt about menstruation, is the experience of mill-worker Selina Cooper.[161] Cooper claimed that in her Lancashire mill community, in the 1890s, menstrual blood was considered 'an attraction' and women used no sanitary protection so that 'all their petticoats would be covered in blood every month'. According to her daughter, Cooper made some towels for one girl whose incensed mother demanded, 'how was her daughter ever going to get off,' that is, married, if the men 'didn't know about this smell?' The girls wore open drawers and so the blood 'went straight down on to the floor, or on to the petticoats'.[162]

---

[158] E. Roberts, *A Woman's Place*, p. 18. Standish Meacham similarly noted that after childbirth women were restricted to having their hands, face and neck washed, while Mrs Layton, born in 1855, recorded that sometimes even this was prohibited. Meacham, *A Life Apart*, p. 70. Pember Reeves, *Life as We Have Known It*, p. 31.

[159] Patricia Crawford, 'Attitudes to menstruation in seventeenth-century England', *Past and Present*, 91:1 (1981), 47–73; 55 n. 41.

[160] Sally Shuttleworth, 'Female circulation: medical discourse and popular advertising in the mid-Victorian era', in Mary Jacobus, Evelyn Fox Keller and Sally Shuttleworth (eds), *Body/Politics: Women and the Discourses of Science* (New York and London: Routledge, 1990), pp. 47–68; Sharra L. Vostral, *Under Wraps: A History of Menstrual Hygiene Technology* (Plymouth: Lexington Books, 2008), p. 21.

[161] Dyhouse, *Girls Growing Up*, pp. 20–1.

[162] Liddington, *Life and Times*, p. 52. Similarly Jennifer Worth, a midwife working from an East London convent in the 1950s, was told by a nun about a 'dirty old man' who used to stand outside the nearby shirt-making factory and throw coins onto an adjoining grass bank which the low-paid female workers would scramble to get. '"It's degrading them," she said. "Those girls wear no knickers, you know. How can they afford such a luxury? That's what he's after, the debauched old satyr. And when they are menstruating they have no protection. The blood just runs down their legs. The smell is supposed to be enticing."' It is unclear when, precisely, this occurred, but Worth implies it was early in the twentieth century, before the First World War. Worth, *Shadows of the Workhouse* (London: Phoenix, 2009), pp. 156–7.

Cooper was a suffragette, and Strange identifies new narratives of menstruation at the turn of the twentieth century which, although connected with demands for women's rights and intended to liberate, potentially helped to cement 'conceptions of menstruation as problematic and taboo'.[163] This appears to be what is occurring in the Cooper narrative; she clearly saw the menstrual flow as a problem to be dealt with and hidden in a way that the girl's mother – and presumably the girl, and others at the mill – did not. But even when women did use sanitary towels or pessaries, many must have found it difficult to prevent outer clothes becoming stained with blood, especially when poverty meant they possessed only a very limited amount of underclothing.

Laundry

In the late-eighteenth and early-nineteenth centuries, the inculcation of 'a set of increasingly hegemonic ideas about the demonstration of decency and cleanliness', say Barbara Burman and Jonathan White, was facilitated by the easy availability of cheap, washable, cotton goods.[164] Daniel Roche detects, at the same time, a quest both for whiter linen, and 'a purified linen available to all'.[165] The inevitable result of this emphasis on sartorial cleanliness combined with the new ubiquity of washable cotton was an increase in laundry. But the inadequate water supplies and the cost of soap and fuel to heat water, which made bodily cleanliness a challenge for the poor, applied also – indeed more so – to laundry. And nineteenth-century England was a dirty place. Soot and smuts belched from chimneys and clung to clothing which trailed in refuse, mud, industrial waste, animal excreta and the overflow from cesspools, sewers and abattoirs.[166] Slum visitor Alice Lucy Hodson found the dirt 'so trying... nothing is ever really clean, for dust, fog, and smuts are continually depositing themselves'.[167] She was thinking of her own person, but she inadvertently highlighted the challenge for urban housewives, and late-nineteenth-century laundry manuals recommended

---

[163] Strange, 'I believe it to be a case', p. 114.
[164] Barbara Burman and Jonathan White, 'Fanny's pockets: cotton, consumption and domestic economy, 1780–1850', in Jennie Batchelor and Cora Kaplan (eds), *Women and Material Culture, 1660–1830* (Basingstoke: Palgrave Macmillan, 2007), pp. 31–51, p. 40.
[165] Roche, *Culture of Clothing*, p. 389.
[166] Wohl, *Endangered Lives*, pp. 81, 208–10. Wilson, *Sphinx in the City*, p. 29.
[167] Koven, *Slumming*, p. 192. See also, Peter Thorsheim, *Inventing Pollution: Coal, Smoke, and Culture in Britain Since 1800* (Athens, OH: Ohio University Press, 2006), pp. 63–4.

doing the laundry early in the day as there was then 'less smoke and dust'.[168]

Dirt and stains are most easily removed immediately, but for the poor with few changes of clothing this would often not have been possible. And some deposits would have been irremovable even with the swiftest action. So even though in the case of fabrics like cotton and linen 'clean' meant washed, it surely could not have meant stain-free. Non-washable fabrics posed a still greater challenge.[169] Even in the early twentieth century, men's outerwear, said Robert Roberts, 'was brushed but never really cleaned', or 'dabbed... with pungent patent liquids bought in twopenny bottles from the corner shop'.[170]

Laundry, like needlework and budgeting, was women's work. While young girls on their first venture into domestic service might soon find themselves up to their elbows in the wash tub, Edwin Grey recounted how, in the 1860s and 1870s, young men hired as live-in farm hands sent their washing home and had a clean shirt sent to them each week.[171] Others would have paid a laundress to wash their shirts, and although I am here concerned with domestic rather than professional laundering, they can, as Patricia Malcolmson shows, be difficult to separate, since in times of hardship many women took in, or went out to do washing.[172] 'There was plenty of people', Arthur Harding recalled, 'who would do a bit of washing 'cos even sixpence was a valuable bit of money.'[173]

Robert Roberts claimed that Salford men, sometimes encouraged by their wives, 'displayed virility by never performing any task in or about the home which was considered by tradition to be women's work'.[174] Similarly, Caroline Davidson says that in the nineteenth century working-class men who participated in domestic chores 'were considered either effeminate or eccentric', and therefore avoided it or did so only behind locked doors.[175] But Joanna Bourke argues that this is too simplistic. It was not the case that men did no housework, but the sexes typically performed different domestic chores. Shoe-mending, for example, was usually done by men and William Elliot, born in 1893, remembered that

---

[168] Calder and Mann, *Teachers' Manual*, p. 86. See also Florence B. Jack, *The Art of Laundry Work Practically Demonstrated for Use in Homes and Schools* (Edinburgh: T. C. and E. C. Jack and London: Whittaker & Co., 1898), p. 1.
[169] For the lengthy processes of satisfactorily cleaning and reviving woollen clothing, see Lemire, *Fashion's Favourite*, p. 93 n. 48.
[170] R. Roberts, *Classic Slum*, p. 38.   [171] Grey, *Cottage Life*, p. 58.
[172] Patricia Malcolmson, *English Laundresses: A Social History 1850–1930* (Urana and Chicago: University of Illinois Press, 1986), pp. xiii, 12–15.
[173] Samuel, *East End Underworld*, p. 42.   [174] R. Roberts, *Classic Slum*, pp. 53–4.
[175] Caroline Davidson, *A Woman's Work is Never Done: A History of Housework in the British Isles 1650–1950* (London: Chatto & Windus, 1986), pp. 187–8.

his father, whose income was a small weekly pension of seven shillings, 'seemed to be always mending our boots'.[176] However, Ellen Ross says that the rigid sexual division of household chores was often illusory, and in Martha Loane's experience as a district nurse, some husbands did 'the roughest part of the washing to spare their wives'.[177] But this was by no means a universal practice, and was performed as assistance to their wives whose responsibility it remained.

Laundry, as part of domestic economy, became a compulsory subject for girls in elementary schools in 1878, and from 1890 attracted a grant, but Carol Dyhouse suggests women resented the compulsion to send daughters to school to learn skills which, although many educationists thought otherwise, they could teach them at home.[178] And as Anna Davin shows, the necessity of a daughter's assistance on washdays, either to care for younger siblings or to help with the laundry itself, interrupted the schooling of many girls.[179] Their memories of childhood washdays are often pleasant. Londoner Mrs Layton, for example, looking back to summer washdays in the 1860s, remembered them as days of 'real sport' when she and her friends took younger brothers and sisters to the park.[180]

But, at least by the turn of the twentieth century, according to Martha Loane, the actual washing was adult work. Only 'a low type of mother' would solicit help from a daughter under fifteen, the accusation by neighbours that '[s]he lets her children stand at the wash-tub', being a severe disgrace.[181] This may have been associated with the clearer separation between child- and adulthood encouraged by compulsory education and the fact that washing was so physically demanding – to the extent that in some prisons laundry work was reserved for women sentenced to hard labour.[182] Before the spread of public washhouses, sufficient water for washing and rinsing had to be brought from the point of supply to the washplace, and disposed of afterwards. Large quantities of wet clothing and bed linen had to be hauled in and out of the tub, scrubbed, wrung and, where a machine was available, mangled, then hung out to dry. So 'unfeminine' was the work that Munby was incredulous when an

---

[176] Bourke, *Working-Class Cultures*, pp. 81–4, 89–94; BAWCA, 1:228, William Elliott, 'An octogenarian's personal life story', pp. 1, 5.
[177] Ross, *Love and Toil*, p. 69; Loane, *From Their Point of View*, p. 168.
[178] Dyhouse, *Girls Growing Up*, pp. 89, 91.
[179] Davin, *Growing Up Poor*, pp. 89, 102, 172, 178. See also, Turnbull, 'Learning her womanly work', p. 84.
[180] Llewelyn Davies, *Life as We Have Known It*, pp. 4–5.
[181] Loane, *From Their Point of View*, p. 168.
[182] P. Malcolmson, *English Laundresses*, pp. 30–2; Mayhew and Binny, *Criminal Prisons*, p. 194.

elegant young milliner claimed to sometimes take a day off work to go out washing. She eventually convinced him by removing a glove to reveal her 'small thin hand . . . sodden, as if from the washtub'.[183]

In contrast with her happy memories of childhood washdays, after years of laundering for her own family Mrs Layton declared washday to be 'an abomination in every house'.[184] Even with the benefit of a public washhouse, laundry remained a laborious task. In her fictionalised autobiography, Kathleen Woodward described her mother, in the early twentieth century, emerging 'pinkish purple, sweating':

'Wash, wash, wash; it's like washing your guts away. Stand, stand, stand; I want six pairs of feet; and then I'd have to stand on my head to give them a rest'.[185]

Successful laundry also required skill, knowledge and equipment. Different types of fabric – and different stains – required different treatment and water temperatures to ensure they came out as clean as possible, but did not shrink or felt. Coloured items had to be kept separate to prevent the transfer of dye. Starch had to be mixed to the right consistency and in the correct amount. Ironing in particular demanded expertise, to select the right sort of iron, to judge the correct temperature so that it would smooth effectively and not scorch. In poor homes a lack of equipment could also be a problem.[186] 'None but a complete slattern would use her red cloak as an ironing blanket', claimed *Cottage Comforts* in the early part of the century, suggesting that is precisely what some women did. It doubtless proved a good substitute in the absence of a dedicated cloth, and is a useful reminder of the varied functions of working-class clothing.[187]

Washday disrupted home life for all occupants.[188] On hot days Christopher Holdenby found the 'combined heat of the stove and steam of the copper' unbearable in the badly ventilated room where also meals were eaten.[189] In wet weather laundry had to be dried indoors, further reducing the space in already crowded homes. But warm weather was not necessarily more beneficial to the laundress. According to Lady Bell in Middlesbrough, if washing hung across the street blocked the carters' path, they would hook it off the line and throw it into the street so that it had to be washed again.[190] And Robert Roberts pointed out that

---

[183] TCLC, MUNB, 4, 3 February 1860.
[184] Llewelyn Davies, *Life as We Have Known It*, pp. 54–5.
[185] Kathleen Woodward, *Jipping Street* (London: Virago, 1983 [1928]), pp. 11–12.
[186] P. Malcolmson, *English Laundresses*, pp. 28–34.
[187] Copley, *Cottage Comforts*, p. 87. [188] P. Malcolmson, *English Laundresses*, pp. 22–3.
[189] Holdenby, *Folk of the Furrow*, p. 40. [190] Bell, *At the Works*, p. 231.

washing on the line could also be a site of anxiety since 'a poverty-stricken display could do one much social damage'.[191] Elizabeth Roberts says women soaked menstrual rags 'in buckets of cold water well away from the enquiring eyes of men or young children (some achievement in cramped houses)'.[192] But it would have been impossible to remove all the stains from either the rags or their petticoats and drawers, and these must also have been hung out to dry somewhere.[193] Doing this away from 'enquiring eyes' must have presented an even greater challenge than the soaking, but how it was achieved is a mystery.

Clothes storage

He took two waistcoats, and a pair of nankeen trowsers off the line in the room; there were two shirts and a pair of cotton stockings, wrapped up in an old table cloth at the end of the table... [He] took down my clock, after that he took down my husband's leather breeches from a nail.[194]

When Ann Codgell described to the Old Bailey the various items she said Richard Bowerman had stolen from her home in 1810, she also delineated a number of ways in which her husband's clothes were stored when they were not being worn. The nankeen trousers were on a line – perhaps originally hung up to dry, but left there to keep them out of the way – other items were wrapped in an old cloth, though we cannot be sure why, and his leather breeches were hung on a nail. In fact clothing was mostly folded rather than hung and given the increased use of cotton, which creases more easily than most woollen (though not linen) fabrics we must assume that, except when worn immediately after ironing, the clothes of the poor often had rather a creased appearance.

Hester C. Dibbits's analysis of probate inventories and wills in the Dutch Republic, notes the appearance of two new items of furniture in the second half of the eighteenth century: the wardrobe and the chest of drawers, both of which became 'typical bedroom furniture' in the 1800s. However, wardrobes were common only in the inventories of the wealthy and Dibbits notes that a wardrobe was a cupboard in which clothes

---

[191] R. Roberts, *Classic Slum*, p. 32. [192] E. Roberts, *A Woman's Place*, p. 18.
[193] Cold water only goes so far in removing blood stains. Curiously, the two laundry manuals cited in note 168 above, both contain instructions on removal of a variety of stains including mildew, wine, fruit, ink, paint, grease and tea, but neither mentions blood.
[194] Sarah Lloyd, 'Joys of the cottage: labourers' houses, hovels and huts in Britain and the British colonies, 1770–1830', in Joanne McEwan and Pamela Sharpe (eds), *Accommodating Poverty: The Housing and Living Arrangements of the English Poor, c.1600–1850* (Basingstoke: Palgrave Macmillan, 2011), pp. 102–21; p. 114.

could be either laid or hung. Although she assumes it became customary to hang clothes in the late eighteenth century she says nothing about the manner in which they were hung and, according to Judith Flanders, hangers did not come into use in Britain, even among the middle and upper classes, until the 1900s.[195] Still, in 1910–11, the middle-class *Every Woman's Encyclopædia* was complaining that the modern wardrobe was 'built on the lines of a linen-chest... with a few shelves, a few drawers', and just 'a corner where we are expected to hang out frocks'.[196] But however inadequate, the wardrobe was still an alien object to most of the poor. 'Wardrobes', said Arthur Harding, born in 1886, 'were practically unknown when I was a child. You put the same things on the next day. It was a question of sticking them on the chair when you went to bed of a night. If you had any best clothes, you kept them in the pawnshop.'[197] Ann Codgell might have done better to place her husband's clothes in the pawnshop since, as Madeleine Ginsburg notes, pawning Sunday clothes during the week not only provided ready cash for other purposes but provided safe storage – no insignificant matter given the prominence of clothing theft.[198]

Among the poor in the early part of the century, the main receptacles for storing clothes were boxes and baskets. Amanda Vickery stresses the importance of a personal locking storage box to Georgian servants who rarely enjoyed private living space and required a portable receptacle to move their possessions when they changed jobs.[199] She also notes employers' recognition that 'withholding a servant's belongings could be a useful tactic in delaying their departure'.[200] Still in the 1880s Hannah Mitchell, correctly guessing that her mistress would try to retain her clothes to prevent her leaving the situation without serving a month's notice, packed up her 'wardrobe, which was all contained in a small tin trunk' and put it outside for a friend to collect before announcing her imminent departure.[201]

---

[195] Hester C. Dibbits, 'Between society and family values: the linen cupboard in early-modern households', in Anton Schuurman and Pieter Spierenburg (eds), *Private Domain, Public Inquiry: Families and Life-Styles in the Netherlands and Europe, 1550 to the Present* (Hilversum: Verloren Publishers, 1996), pp. 125–45; pp. 139–40; Judith Flanders, *The Victorian House: Domestic Life from Childbirth to Deathbed* (London: Harper Perennial, 2004), p. 5.
[196] Anon., *Every Woman's Encyclopædia*, p. 700.
[197] Samuel, *East End Underworld*, p. 99.   [198] Ginsburg, 'Rags to riches', 126.
[199] Amanda Vickery, *Behind Closed Doors: At Home in Georgian England* (New Haven and London: Yale University Press, 2009), pp. 39–40.
[200] Amanda Vickery, *The Gentleman's Daughter: Women's Lives in Georgian England* (New Haven and London: Yale University Press, 1998), p. 184.
[201] Mitchell (ed.), *Hard Way Up*, pp. 68–9.

In his analysis of rural pauper inventories, Peter King presents transcripts of two: one compiled in 1810 and the other in 1812. The latter, he says, gives an insight into the 'relative richness of the material world' that some labouring families enjoyed, but the only dedicated clothes' storage in each list is one or more 'Clothes' or 'Close' baskets.[202] This, nevertheless, was superior to the storage facilities in Harding's deeply impoverished East London home at the close of the century, which comprised 'an old chest of drawers made out of tobacco barrels' and some orange boxes which 'were in great demand then. Cost nothing.'[203] Similarly, in early-twentieth-century Salford, Robert Roberts noted that the 'homes of the poor contained little or no bought furniture. They made do with boxes and slept in their clothes.'[204]

The lack of storage facilities reflected the small quantities of clothing the poor possessed, even at the end of the period. And this paucity of clothing, together with the lack of money and space to buy and house furniture meant that not only was the available storage limited, but it also had to accommodate a variety of items, including foodstuffs, with implications for both the appearance and the smell of the clothing kept in it. In Lambeth houses, for example, just before the First World War, Maud Pember Reeves found the only clothes storage to be 'the hook behind the door, and possibly a chest of drawers, which may partly act as a larder, and has... been used as a place in which to put a dead child'.[205] Christopher Holdenby described an agricultural labourer's cottage in which he lodged at the same period. The cottage was occupied by a husband, wife and their several children and was 'above average', yet the storage comprised only a 'tiny larder', one cupboard, which held 'the family nightgowns by day and day clothes by night', as well as food, cooking utensils and sewing equipment, and one chest of drawers: 'we all share it, and for the rest, use nails on the bare damp walls'.[206] We can imagine the clammy coldness on the skin of the clothes when taken from the nails.

Both Harding and Roberts remembered the introduction of furniture deals in the 1900s, offering 'a five-pound home for a shilling a week' or 'the "basic" "House of Furniture" complete, designed to fill the "one up and one down" home', at a cost of twelve guineas. Except for a dressing table, which may or may not have had drawers, neither contained any

---

[202] Peter King, 'Pauper inventories and the material lives of the poor in the eighteenth and early nineteenth centuries', in Tim Hitchcock, Peter King and Pamela Sharpe (eds), *Chronicling Poverty: The Voices and Strategies of the English Poor, 1640–1840* (Basingstoke: Macmillan, 1997), pp. 155–91; pp. 184–5.
[203] Samuel, *East End Underworld*, p. 22.   [204] R. Roberts, *Classic Slum*, p. 75.
[205] Pember Reeves, *Round About a Pound*, p. 52.
[206] Holdenby, *Folk of the Furrow*, pp. 40–2, 47.

dedicated clothes' storage and only after a couple of years, when much of the original debt had been paid off could the purchasers think about adding to their stock of furniture. Then, the 'first thing for a couple who could afford it', Harding said, 'was a wardrobe'. By the time he married in 1924, the 'bedroom suite' of sideboard, wardrobe and dressing table had appeared and was the first furniture Harding bought, 'to keep the clothes clean of bugs'.[207]

Working-class clothing in the nineteenth century would surely have presented a more crumpled appearance than is commonplace today. Not only has modern technology produced so many crease-resistant fabrics and laundry materials which reduce the need for ironing, but we own greater quantities of clothing which obviate the need for such repeated wear of the same garments, and we have far more dedicated storage space, especially to hang clothes when they are not in use. These factors, together with the customary weekly wash, mean that it is not, I think, unreasonable to suggest that nineteenth-century England as a whole looked rather less creased on Tuesday or Wednesday mornings than on Friday evenings.

* * *

Clothing and appearance were central elements of nineteenth-century working-class respectability. The observation of sartorial conventions, such as the display of appropriate dress on ritual occasions was not only understood but requisite, and a disproportionate expenditure on clothing – condemned by wealthier observers as a want of thrift – was condoned. Cleanliness was also important, although it is hard to gauge what constituted 'clean' when inadequate water supplies limited the washing of clothes and bodies. And here again, the improvements which gradually brought piped water to the homes of the wealthy, and public baths and washhouses to the more affluent working classes, served to further distance the poor who lacked even the few pence required to use them. Their bodies and homes appeared ever darker and dirtier in contrast with the increasing cleanliness of wealthier contemporaries, some of whom also coupled inner and outer purity so that the dirty and/or exposed body might be read as a sign of savagery and moral depravity. It is, though, impossible to generalise about working-class attitudes to morality in respect of bodily exposure and functions, since these appear to have varied greatly and with no evidence that the differences were geographically or temporally specific.

Although a collective endeavour in the family context, women, as with budgeting, bore a greater share of the responsibility for respectability. Of

[207] Samuel, *East End Underworld*, pp. 98–9; Roberts, *Classic Slum*, p. 35.

course, the two were closely connected, with a woman's skill in managing the available money and resources being central to the ability to present a respectable appearance. But the burden also fell on women because it was their job to do the laundry, to keep the children clean and, once again, to prioritise others' needs and desires above their own. And while an acceptable appearance, personal and familial, could be the occasion of great pride, equally its absence could generate immense shame and was a cause of self-inflicted as well as externally imposed social exclusion. Considering the relationship between age, employment and boys' clothes, Clare Rose concludes that 'even the poorest families were aware of the meanings of clothing... as nuanced markers of the familial and social position of the wearer'.[208] I would suggest that it was not '*even* the poorest families', but *especially* since they had the most at stake.

[208] C. Rose, *Making, Wearing and Selling*, p. 180.

6 The sense of self

> Clothing plays a considerable and active part in constituting the particular experience of the self, in determining what the self is.[1]

> Material artefacts... not only shape bodies and perceptions, but allow their possessors to establish their place in society.[2]

The role of clothing in self-determination can be positive and negative, creating feelings of both self-worth and worthlessness, belonging and exclusion. The small clothing stocks of the poor and their limited capacity to make clothing choices limited also the extent to which they could use dress to fashion and express identity. But this did not mean that they were entirely without agency and the very absence of clothing enhanced the significance of the garments they did possess. This chapter explores the relationship between poverty, appearance and self-determination. It begins with innovative readings of two autobiographies, the first written by Joseph Terry, born in Yorkshire in 1816, and the second by Louise Jermy, born in Hampshire in 1877.[3] Terry's, written in 1865 and part of the Burnett Archive of Working Class Autobiographies at Brunel University, extends to some 63,000 words and is unpublished, save for an extract in Burnett's edited collection, *Destiny Obscure*.[4] Jermy's autobiography, of nearly two hundred pages was published in 1934 and has been the subject of limited scholarly attention, but there appear to be few extant copies.

Michael Roper says that: 'Too often what goes missing from linguistic analyses is an adequate sense of the material.'[5] But fresh analysis of these two autobiographies, paying close attention to their frequent and

---

[1] D. Miller, *Stuff*, p. 40.
[2] Jennie Batchelor and Cora Kaplan, 'Introduction', in Jennie Batchelor and Cora Kaplan (eds), *Women and Material Culture, 1660–1830* (Basingstoke: Palgrave Macmillan, 2007), pp. 1–8; p. 1.
[3] BAWCA, 1:693, Joseph Terry. Jermy, *Memories*.   [4] Burnett, *Destiny Obscure*, pp. 52–8.
[5] Michael Roper, 'Slipping out of view: subjectivity and emotion in gender history', *History Workshop Journal*, 59 (2005), 57–72; 62.

often detailed references to dress, not only emphasises the material, but demonstrates how deeply and distinctively clothing, and its absence during the authors' formative years, shaped their individual and collective identities and mediated their relations with others.

Having considered the use of clothing for the creation of identity and self-presentation, the second part of this chapter explores how people assessed their own appearance – how they knew what they looked like. Taking Isobel Armstrong's idea of a 'scopic culture' I suggest that developments in the manufacture and processing of glass, which produced the cheval mirror, the plate-glass window and the camera lens, offered new modes of visual awareness and sartorial self-perception, and new ways of creating and disseminating normative ideals of personal appearance, which largely impacted negatively on the poor.

Joseph Terry: making the 'complete sailor'

As far as he could ascertain, Joseph Terry was born in Mirfield, Yorkshire, on Boxing Day, 1816. His father was a waterman with his own boat in which he transported coal and limestone around industrial Yorkshire.[6] Joseph also began working life as a waterman, later becoming head clerk for a miller and maltster before buying his own mill and then working in several cooperative ventures.[7] By the end of his autobiography, which seems unfinished, Joseph had just terminated his employment with the Huddersfield District Clothing and Provision Company and begun trading on his own account. On the way, he had been a Chartist, a Methodist and then a Unitarian, as well as an active supporter of the Co-operative movement. He had also married his 'beloved little' Sarah Daley, and though not wealthy Joseph was proud to have been able to provide for Sarah and their children – who numbered at least seven – as well as his niece who lived with them as nursemaid.[8]

As David Vincent says: 'The treatment of any aspect of an autobiographer's life is dependent upon the significance he attaches to it, and the connection he wishes to make between that aspect and the overall development of his personality.'[9] It is clear from Joseph's focus on his early identity as a waterman that it remained crucially important to him,

---

[6] BAWCA, 1:693, Joseph Terry, pp. 1–2.
[7] In this chapter I generally refer to Joseph Terry and Louise Jermy as Joseph and Louise, not to suggest a fallacious familiarity, but for clarity when other members of their families are introduced.
[8] BAWCA, 1:693, Joseph Terry, pp. 73, 78.
[9] David Vincent, *Bread, Knowledge and Freedom: A Study of Nineteenth-Century Working Class Autobiography* (London: Europa, 1981), p. 43.

despite his later occupational, political and spiritual achievements and interests. And it is equally clear that this identity was, to a great extent, created and expressed through clothing.

The autobiography opens with a utopian description of Mirfield at the time of Joseph's childhood, and his first experience of life 'on board' at the age of three or four. He wrote of his 'wonder and delight' at everything in the boat, the dangerous places they passed through, and his 'wild romantic' Uncle Ben. But, he said, 'the thing which is *of all others* impressed deeply on my mind at this age is the joy I felt when brother Jim & myself had our first new suit of what was considered a sailor[']s dress'.[10] 'Even before they were fully part of the working world', writes Clare Rose, 'poorer children's clothes reflected their parents' callings.'[11] The brothers' outfits were not the standard boys' sailor suits fashionable in the closing decades of the century, but miniatures of the adult waterman's costume 'of white woollen trousers and blue short check smock with woollen knitted cap, made to slip on the head, of a kind that would not blow off when on board in strong winds'. They were bought, Joseph said, 'at Ripon & father & mother went to buy them in the town'.[12]

How much of this Joseph actually remembered and how much he later gleaned from conversations with his parents we cannot know, but what matters is his insistence on the detail – the styles, colours, fabrics and place of purchase, which made them authentic watermen's outfits and the boys, therefore, authentic nascent watermen. He emphasises still further the inherent connection between the waterman's profession, identity and clothing in his description of Thomas Muffit who:

> was called the Waterman's Tailor, making a kind of suit which when put on showed the waterman at once, and it used to be said that six months' experience and one of his suits made a 'complete sailor'.[13]

Joseph was born at the tail end of the canal boom when construction had mostly ceased, but the waterways were still a vital and vibrant part of the industrial transport system. But he reached adulthood in the railway age which signalled the canals' decline. Canal historian Avril Lansdell explains that when poverty forced watermen out of their cottages and into permanent residence on their boats, they made distinct efforts to visually differentiate themselves from those who lived on land.[14] Joseph's determined identification with the watermen can therefore be read, in

---

[10] BAWCA, 1:693, Joseph Terry, pp. 1–4 (my emphasis).
[11] C. Rose, *Children's Clothes*, p. 101.   [12] BAWCA, 1:693, Joseph Terry, p. 4.
[13] *Ibid.*, p. 38.   [14] Lansdell, *Clothes of the Cut*, p. 13.

part, as a desire to proudly associate himself with a previously thriving, but subsequently beleaguered, community.

Pride, according to Joseph, was also a driving force behind the purchase of children's sailor clothes. 'Of course', he wrote:

> we were very young to assume such a dress, but the parents of children who were accustomed to be nearly always on board had pride over their offspring like other parents, & the Tailors who were accustomed to make sailors' clothing helped to foster their pride by making small dresses after the fashion of the larger ones.[15]

As Joseph's history unfolds, his idyllic childhood is shattered by a series of catastrophic events which destroy his mother's mental health and take his father away for extended periods. In these distressing circumstances the expression of parental pride and love materialised in the miniature sailor dress became a precious memory.

A year or two after the purchase of the outfits, the Terrys' boat was damaged and their horse and small savings lost in a storm. With difficulty, his father managed to resume business, 'until another accident befell us by which the vessel was entirely lost, & every vestige of property & means of living vanished'. His mother, who had become depressed after the first accident, suffered further mental deterioration and was admitted to the poorhouse. His father had to take wage labour at 'ten shillings a week & rations', and the boys went to stay with their paternal grandparents. When, after a couple of years his mother's health improved, his father placed her and Joseph in a cottage in Mirfield, brother Jim remaining with his grandparents. Their father, now working as a 'journeyman', was often away for weeks and Joseph and his mother had to manage on five shillings a week. Furthermore, her mental instability meant his mother was unable to properly lay out the money to best advantage and Joseph suffered 'much privation'. It was, he emphasised,

> utterly impossible for me were I ever so wishful to do so, to describe what I suffered for want of proper nourishment & clothing for a period of some two or three years, of from about my fifth to my seventh year. I had no shoes or stockings, & but very scanty clothing.[16]

Peter Jones has demonstrated how, in the late-eighteenth and early-nineteenth centuries, bare feet, especially children's, came to represent an extreme state of wretchedness.[17] It is on this aspect of his suffering that Joseph dwelt:

---

[15] BAWCA, 1:693, Joseph Terry, p. 4.   [16] *Ibid.*, pp. 5–9.
[17] P. D. Jones, 'I cannot keep my place', pp. 36–7.

> In the winter season my feet, & especially my heels & toes were much frostbitten, swollen & sore – so much so that after we were in better circumstance, & my parents could afford to clothe me better, it took years of care, scrubbing & washing to bring my feet into a proper and natural state.[18]

For Joseph, as for many of his contemporaries, the quantity and quality of his clothing became the measure of his material circumstances and a key factor in his physical well-being, the lack of clothing as detrimental to his health as lack of food.

Although his parents' circumstances gradually improved, they never regained the former level of comfort and security Joseph remembered, but he remained fiercely proud of them both and sought ways to identify with them. His brother Jim, he said, 'being older, stronger, and much stouter' was their grandparents' favourite, 'being called a "Terry", while I was more like mother and her family'. He writes always in the most loving terms of his 'poor dear mother', who possessed 'one of the tenderest hearts that ever beat in a human breast', but who never fully recovered her mental health. In contrast was his father, whose ancestors he knew to be:

> a fine hardy race, well built, very strong and muscular, good looking and of a peculiar cast of mind much inkeeping [sic] with their appearance. They were capable of high attainments in all they undertook, very few of them ever to my knowledge being common working men, but mostly Masters of some kinds of business, such as Farmers, Cattle Jobbers, Maltsters, Boat Owners, Captains of boats &c.[19]

His boat-owning father had followed this pattern of independence – as, subsequently, did Joseph when he became a mill-owner. And his father's actions during the storm which wrecked the family's fortunes showed that he also possessed the physical prowess of his forebears which Joseph so clearly admired. The storm occurred during the night, and fearing trouble his parents did not go to bed. His father smoked and dozed in a chair while his mother, the model of femininity, sat 'sewing, and keeping watch'. When the boat began to sink his mother noticed first and alerted his father. He rushed on deck and instructed his wife to hand up the two sleeping children. She managed to pass Joseph over without difficulty, but in her panic could not immediately find Jim. Her husband said she must either leave him or die herself:

> But what Mother could leave her child to perish? Not mine . . . [W]hile the boiling flood was gathering around her, and the hoarse voice of the storm mixed with the urgent entreaties of my father, she made a last effort to find the lost one,

[18] BAWCA, 1:693, Joseph Terry, p. 9.   [19] *Ibid.*, pp. 3, 6, 9, 13.

and this last effort was crowned with success. But my brother Jim, being a big, fat, heavy boy, it was with the greatest difficulty that she, now all but engulfed in the water, could hand him up to the ready and strong arms fully outstretched to receive him. But the task was by frantic and convulsive efforts accomplished, and the same strong arm with irresistible power seized her just in time to prevent her going down with the wreck.[20]

Joseph's (melo)dramatic account of the events was a combination of his own and his mother's memories, and he acknowledges her courage as well as his father's. But ultimately it was the 'irresistible power' of his father's 'strong arm' that ensured the family all survived.

Joseph subscribed to contemporary notions of gender roles. Fathers were strong and heroic, women tender and nurturing. And his mother's bravery nothwithstanding, in contrast with her 'iron-nerved' husband 'that moment of severe and untold anguish' she suffered when unable to find her son, resulted in 'a nervous shock which went with her to her grave, and entailed on our family in after days much painful affliction and sorrow'. She was not to blame; in Terry's eyes this was, for a woman, an understandable consequence of such an experience. But it robbed him of the capable model mother he remembered who had, 'watched over [him] with the greatest tenderness' when he was ill, baked bread, acted as the family 'cashier' and sat sewing while waiting for the storm to break.[21] He loved her dearly, but was effectively motherless and it was that remembered mother he longed for.

It was also such a mother he desired for his own children when he came to select a wife. He remembered looking, when 'a rough uncultivated little boy', through an open window on a visit to his grandmother and seeing:

a group of little girls . . . all very clean, and neatly dressed. The room was in perfect keeping with its inmates, and Mrs. Darley the mother who kept a respectable female school, their mother, seemed to my young vision like a guardian angel presiding over so many young inhabitants of a higher sphere. The impressions [sic] made on my young susceptible heart was a most powerful one. I felt that if ever I lived to be a man and could be so far improved and elevated as to be any thing like the approach of worthiness nothing would give my soul such delight as to call one of them my wife, and claim that sweet benign looking woman as my mother.[22]

At the age of twenty, and by then a waterman himself, Joseph rediscovered these girls and resolved to make nineteen-year-old Sarah Ann his wife. She eventually agreed to accept him as her suitor subject to their better acquaintance and her parents' approval. If Joseph were to win such a woman for his wife (and her mother as his own), he would

---

[20] *Ibid.*, pp. 5–6. [21] *Ibid.*, pp. 2, 3, 5, 6. [22] *Ibid.*, p. 39.

have to be such a man as his father. His work was about to take him away for several weeks and he paid a last visit to Sarah before departure. Determined to leave her with the best possible impression of himself, he dressed:

> in my sailor's dress, a kind of holiday uniform which consisted of cloth trousers, blue jacket and vest, black silk handkerchief tied loosely round the neck, check shirt, glazed oilcase hat, and light sailor's pumps or shoes fastened with buckles which were then much worn amongst us.

Again his detailed description of the colours, the fabrics and the accessories establish this as a very particular dress. 'It was', he said, 'a fine summers eve, all things were still and serene, as if nature content to be decked out in its most gorgeous habiliments stood still in its majesty to be admired.'[23] He could equally have been describing himself. We must assume Sarah Ann was impressed as she did, in time, become his wife and, from Joseph's account, they enjoyed a happy marriage.

As Joseph's lyrical prose demonstrates, he saw no incompatibility between muscular masculinity and a deep romanticism. For Joseph, the miniature sailor dresses worn by himself and his brother, were material proof of his parents' love before the family's disastrous change of fortune, the evidence, still, over forty years later, that it was circumstance, not parental rejection or deliberate neglect, that had left him shoeless, hungry and effectively orphaned. For Graham Dawson: 'Masculinities are lived out in the flesh, but fashioned in the imagination.'[24] When Joseph looked for a model of masculinity worthy of emulation, he found it in his memory of those early years when his father's waterman's outfit was the symbol of prosperous, independent manhood and identified him as a member of a proud and distinctive community. When, therefore, Joseph wanted to present himself as a promising prospective husband, he dressed in his waterman's clothes. And when he wrote the story of his life, even though he had ceased to be a waterman more than two decades earlier, it was the waterman's clothes he remembered and so fondly described. Although less than half-way through his autobiography Joseph said very little more about his clothing. This is explicable partly because his subsequent occupations did not have similarly distinctive costumes, but also because it was as a waterman that he had won a wife, created his own family and, therefore, established his masculinity.

---

[23] *Ibid.*, pp. 41–2.
[24] Graham Dawson, *Soldier Heroes: British Adventure, Empire and the Imagining of Masculinities* (London: Routledge, 1994), p. 1.

Louise Jermy: 'Not like other girls'

The Memories of a Working Woman, published in 1934, is the autobiography of Louise Jermy. She was born in 1877, the daughter of St John Withers, a labourer on the Broadlands estate in Hampshire, and his wife Selina, née Medley. Selina died in 1878 leaving her twenty-two-year-old husband with two young daughters, Louise, aged eighteen months, and Amy, aged three years. Like the Terry brothers, the sisters were sent to live with their grandparents until, at an unspecified point in their childhood, their father remarried and took his daughters to live with himself and his new wife in London.[25] Regenia Gagnier says that in her autobiography Louise related a life of 'perverted familial relations... aborted romance, and pronounced isolation'.[26] But she also revealed how, through clothing, she forged and asserted her own identity.

To the extent that Louise's autobiography is known at all, it is as 'the first written by a Women's Institute member' – which constitutes the opening sentence of the book's foreword, written by novelist, poet and Norfolk local historian, Ralph Hale Mottram.[27] Louise apparently wrote and published her *Memories* at the request of a Women's Institute member, but she said nothing about the Institute anywhere in her autobiography. For Mottram, it seems, the identities Louise gave herself – seamstress, domestic servant, daughter/wife/mother – were insufficient. He needed to give her a public status even though she does not appear to have required this herself – or rather, Louise created her public identity through writing and publication of her autobiography, not through association with others. After all, as I argue, the point of her book was to emphasise her difference, not her belonging.

Louise's title, *Memories of a Working Woman*, suggests she considered her various employments to be the outstanding features of her life and, together with the common life-cycle events they do, indeed, provide the chronological framework for her narrative. They are also the focus of the only dedicated scholarly study of Louise.[28] But Louise in fact said very little about the actual work she did, her real focus being relationships: with employers, with workmates, with her Sunday school teacher, with prospective husbands, but above all the complex and challenging

---

[25] Jane McDermid, 'Jermy, Louise Jane (1877–1952)', *Oxford Dictionary of National Biography*, Oxford University Press, 2004 www.oxforddnb.com; Jermy, *Memories*, Chapters 1 and 2.
[26] Regenia Gagnier, *Subjectivities: A History of Self-Representation in Britain, 1832–1920* (Oxford University Press, 1991), p. 49.
[27] Jermy, *Memories*, Foreword.
[28] Jane McDermid, 'The making of a "domestic" life: memories of a working woman', *Labour History Review*, 73:3 (2008), 253–68.

relationship with her parents. Dress was a crucial medium through which Louise's affective relationships were mediated, and she used it carefully and deliberately to align herself with her adored, idealised, birth mother, separate herself from her stepmother and enlist the support of her father, as his daughter, against her stepmother, as his wife.

Louise seems to have found all relationships difficult, and her feeling of alienation is manifested through repetitions that she was 'not like other girls'. The *Memories* open with her wondering whether the person who suggested she wrote them 'has said to herself, like many others have done, "She... is not like other people."' She immediately reinforced the point by presenting three names – three alternative identities – she had been given, which emphasised her difference. She had, she said, been called 'a Witch' because she was believed to 'possess the gift of second sight', also 'The Lady Louisa' because of the 'supreme scorn and disdain' with which she had once dismissed a particular incident, and '"Dynamite," owing to the startling manner in which [she] flew whenever... teased' by her workmates.[29] All this, which is in her opening paragraph, seems self-deprecating, but the autobiography reveals that Louise had a highly developed sense of self and self-worth, forged by her ability to survive extreme abuse and to earn her own living. She was at pains to explain that, if she was different, it was because of the things others had done to her, and clothes were the pivotal means by which she embraced her perceived oddity, expressed her sense of self-worth and created a distinct identity. She habitually wore black, for example, at a time when other young women wore it only for mourning or at an employer's insistence.

Having explained her different names, Louise launched into a story she heard from her father about her parents moving house soon after her birth. As Selina walked by the cart containing their possessions, Lady Mount Temple, the wife of her husband's employer, passed by and remarked that she was looking unwell. When Selina admitted she was cold, Lady Mount Temple removed her own coat and gave it to Selina to keep. It was, said Louise, a 'beautiful coat and cloak all in one of white wool and threaded with blue silk, the hood being lined with blue silk'. When Louise was fifteen, she inherited the cloak. It:

had been dyed and it was certainly out of date... but... as long as I possibly could, I wore it... I took it everywhere – it was scarcely ever out of my sight, and when I put it round me I often rubbed my face on the shabby old thing with loving remembrance of the act of kindness of a sweet and gracious lady. I believe I still have some fragments of the dear old thing even now.[30]

---

[29] Jermy, *Memories*, p. 1.   [30] *Ibid.*, pp. 2–3.

There is a strong fairy-tale atmosphere to Louise's account of how her mother came to possess the garment, the reason for which becomes apparent when Louise relates her early history. After her mother's death Louise went to live with her maternal grandmother. Her paternal grandmother 'was laundress to the great house' (Broadlands), and Louise remembered going with her cousin to fetch laundry from her, always using 'just the same paths as my mother had gone so many years before when my Lady gave her the cloak'. Calling in on this grandmother on her way home from school one day, Louise found her father there with a new wife, Mary, who was wearing 'a white hat with a large ostrich feather curling all round it. My father, she said, had paid thirty shillings for it for a wedding present to her, so that it was a very nice one.' Thirty shillings was, indeed, a very great deal of money for a labouring man to spend on a hat for his wife, even as a wedding present. Louise, swinging on the door, knocked the hat into a pail of water, but when punishment was threatened her stepmother intervened. She also forged a relationship with the sisters by giving each a necklace and sending them stockings which she had knitted herself, and Louise remembered that at this stage they got on very well.[31]

Soon, however, the girls moved to London to live with their father and stepmother, saying, 'goodbye to all [they] had ever known', by which, it rapidly becomes clear, Louise meant not only people, places and routines, but also care, affection and emotional security. Their father tried various employments with only moderate success, and the previously benevolent Mary, according to Louise's account, turned into the archetypal evil stepmother. Academically the sisters did well at their rather superior school, but Louise misbehaved and suspected this was because:

we were dressed so different to the rest. They had smart frocks and hair in curls or waves... but we had our hair cropped like boys, and... our dresses were very plain and we were made to wear plain linen pinafores.[32]

When Mary announced her intention to go out to work her husband, who had lost their savings in a failed business venture, objected and bought her a mangle so she could work from home. Eleven-year-old Louise was taken out of school to turn the mangle, collect and deliver the laundry. In contrast with her grandmother's laundry work, when Louise delightedly trod her mother's path and sometimes rode home in the wheelbarrow, now 'there was hardly time to get our food... my arms felt as if they would break, and my back ached so I could not sleep at night'. Additionally:

[31] *Ibid.*, pp. 11, 13–15.   [32] *Ibid.*, pp. 15, 20.

so irritable was mother with the everlasting work, that is was a word and a blow, and the blow often came first. I've been beaten with stair-rod, poker, broom-handle, knocked down and kicked up again.

Louise contracted tubercular hip disease, which she attributed to her maltreatment (although she had complained of leg pains before the abuse began), and at thirteen was 'partially crippled, in fact, for life'.[33]

At fourteen Louise was apprenticed to a dressmaker, against her stepmother's wishes because a fee was required and Louise earned no money – and, perhaps, because Louise was to go out and learn a skill while she had been restricted to home laundry work. Louise made good progress, but again felt alienated by her appearance:

Of course, I was different to all the other workers, their parents treated them like reasonable creatures, they were nicely dressed, while for the most part I was very shabby, being dressed always in something that somebody had left off.[34]

Then, during a particularly violent argument, her stepmother repeatedly struck Louise's head against an iron cistern which left her with recurrent fainting, headaches and confusion.

In contrast with her violent stepmother, the cloak Louise inherited at fifteen was a direct link with an imagined, idealised, birth mother. While her other second-hand clothes were symbols of poverty and degradation, the cloak was an heirloom, and when she rubbed her face on it, she invoked the tender caress of a loving mother in place of Mary's blows. Anthropologist Amiria Henare made a study of Maori cloaks, valued as ancestral treasures and the making, wearing and other ritual employment of which form 'tangible and substantive links between ancestors... and their living descendants'. While, for the Maori, generational transmission of the cloaks' construction techniques is as important as passing on the finished garments, Louise's mother neither made the cloak nor passed on to her daughter the techniques to make one of her own (although, of course, Louise's skills as a needlewoman were part of a wider and enduring female heritage). But also, for the Maori, both cloaks and techniques, 'allow for ancestral presence... they bear the *mana* (personal standing) and *wairua* (spirit) of people who died many years before' and become, as Miller notes, 'an abiding presence of that ancestor', and the 'exchange of cloth... an exchange of aspects of persons'.[35]

---

[33] *Ibid.*, pp. 28–9.   [34] *Ibid.*, p. 43.
[35] Amiria Henare, 'Nga aho tipuna Maori: cloaks from New Zealand', in Susanne Küchler and Daniel Miller (eds), *Clothing as Material Culture* (Oxford: Berg, 2006), pp. 121–38; pp. 122, 125, 134; Daniel Miller, 'Introduction', in Susanne Küchler and Daniel Miller (eds), *Clothing as Material Culture* (Oxford: Berg, 2006), pp. 1–19; p. 12.

Selina's cloak operated in a very similar way. It brought Louise's dead mother to her and literally enveloped her in Selina's imagined loving embrace.[36] And the act of kindness in giving the coat to Selina proved not only that Lady Mount Temple was 'a truly noble lady', but also suggested that Selina, by being deserving of such an act, had also possessed exceptional qualities. And so, even though the cloak was dated and shabby, Louise 'treasured it as if it had been gold' and claimed never to mind 'the smiles or the jeering remarks' it attracted, since it aligned her with the faultless imagined birth mother and distanced her from her despised stepmother.[37] For the Maori, the ritual use of cloaks at childbirth and baptism ceremonies also 'smoothed [the child's] passage ... from one phase of life into the next' and it is surely significant that Louise became so attached to the cloak as an adolescent, the point at which she was making the transition from child to adult and seeking a model for womanhood.[38]

Louise portrays her father as a weak man who turned a blind eye to the treatment she suffered at the hands of her stepmother who he allowed to rule the home and his children. 'If my father had any love for me he certainly didn't show it', she remarked. She determined to force it out of him by requesting a shilling a week for clothing which, she knew, would also force him to put her wishes above those of her stepmother, creating a division between husband and wife. He refused and so:

turning myself round I asked him if he would like to introduce me to any of the gentlemen of the firm as his daughter, seeing that he was one of the first foremen and in a good position . . . ? I think he saw all at once that I was no longer a child, and saw, too, how shabby I was, and told me to ask mother for a new dress. I said I would not, I was tired of wearing other people's cast-off clothes, which was all [I] ever got, and they were mostly quite unsuitable, that I had asked him, and should not ask anyone again, if my rags dropped off me.[39]

Louise was now sixteen and a competent seamstress, and a few days later her stepmother offered her 'a very pretty dress length', but Louise refused it. 'I wanted a black dress', she wrote, citing her 'awkwardness in getting up from the table' resulting from her hip disease, which meant previous clothes had been spoiled, whereas this would not be such a problem with a black dress.[40] But there was more to it. Her stepmother, she said, 'never really did like' her paternal grandmother, the laundress,

[36] According to Diane Atkinson, Hannah Cullwick also wore her deceased mother's clothes 'for years, not caring how old-fashioned they looked, enjoying feeling close to her mother'. Diane Atkinson, *Love and Dirt: The Marriage of Arthur Munby and Hannah Cullwick* (London: Macmillan, 2003), p. 19.
[37] Jermy, *Memories*, pp. 2–3.   [38] Henare, 'Nga aho tipuna Maori', p. 120.
[39] Jermy, *Memories*, pp. 28–9, 49–50.   [40] *Ibid.*, p. 50.

who Louise described as 'a very stately old lady', who always wore 'black silk... She would have a new black silk every five years, which was kept for state occasions, the oldest black being worn on washing days, the next on ironing days' and so forth. Louise also explained the old lady's love of fine linen before pulling herself up, stating: 'But this is not my life, only perhaps it explains itself as I am supposed to be like the two grandmothers more than anyone else.'[41]

Initially her father supported his wife in the dispute over Louise's desire for black fabric, arguing that most 'people had quite enough of black when they were obliged to wear it', that is, for mourning. Arguably Louise was in mourning, for her mother and the different life she would have led had she lived – she had put black ribbons on the cloak. Louise's response, however, was that she 'was *not like other girls*, at least I had been told so so often that I had come to believe it'. Her stepmother dismissed the matter, saying that Louise's sister would doubtless buy the dress length and her comment that 'it would not be spoilt in the making up, as Amy went to a good dressmaker', was an implicit slight on Louise's capability as a seamstress. At this, Louise's father:

suddenly turned to me and asked, supposing he let me have my money, could I make up decently enough to wear? I quickly said, yes, so that settled it. Mother was told to go with me to let me have just what I wanted and see what came of it. We went to the shop; I wanted a serge, she said I shouldn't have it, it was too old, and I really don't know how it would have ended, as I was determined to fight for that dress with a dogged persistence worthy of a better cause, when the shop man produced a piece of dress material which he assured me would suit me far better, and as he held it up and called my attention to the lovely gloss on it, I liked it at once, and although it cost a shilling more a yard than serge, she preferred to pay sooner than let me have the serge... I also chose buttons, linings, braid, etc., everything I should need.

This was an outright victory for Louise and the fact that her father had taken her part against his wife generated a camaraderie between them, even before the dress was made:

when father got the bill and received his change, he said, 'Come you know how to spend money, it's to be hoped you'll look a very fine bird when you get it all on,' and laughed at me, and I laughed back.[42]

Louise enlisted the help of the forewoman at work to provide a bodice pattern and when she had finished putting the dress together asked her stepmother for some black lace and orange ribbon to trim an old black hat. Again her stepmother objected to the colour, but again her father

---

[41] *Ibid.*, pp. 11–12, 15. [42] *Ibid.*, pp. 50–1.

intervened, and Louise used the ribbon to also trim the collar of a black silk vest to be worn under the bodice, and to make a 'puff' for the collar'. When she put the outfit on her father was:

amazed at the difference in my appearance... but agreed that at least I knew what suited me, declared that everything was suitable and pretty and the dress a perfect fit and success.[43]

Louise wore black all her life, which Gagnier attributes to a negative self-image centred on a 'conviction of her awkwardness and unattractiveness', and her work as a domestic servant: 'she wears black – the "decent black" of domestic servants, as Mayhew put it, "no ringlets, followers or scandals" – on and off the job'.[44] But Louise made the dress when she was sixteen, while still an apprentice dressmaker and with no plans for domestic service, which she did not begin until she was eighteen. And this was not sombre, anonymous black, but black with 'a lovely gloss on it', black enlivened by 'bright orange' trimmings. Louise did not wear black so that she could fade unnoticed into the crowd, but so that she would be distinctive. 'I was', she wrote, 'so thin that the waist measurement of the bodice was nineteen inches... I stood five feet nine and a half in my stockings... and save for a little colour in my lips I was very white.'[45] Tall, thin, the black and orange creating a striking contrast with her pallid complexion, habituated to being 'different', Louise had no intention of sinking into the background, but instead embraced and cultivated that difference to express her individuality and create a unique identity.

This was clearly a central episode in Louise's life – her account of it spreads across six consecutive pages in her autobiography – and in her recollection her relationship with her father changed after this. She believed 'he found his daughter more amusing and better company than he ever dreamt of', and began taking her to concerts, in contrast with the variety theatre which his wife preferred. When a neighbour suggested she had 'a young man' she 'didn't let it worry me for I was much too happy to know my father after all thought well of his daughter to want any young man's company or old man's either'.[46] Later she concedes that there always remained a rift between her father and herself, his intervention had come too late, but his willingness, through provision of the dress, to support her case against her stepmother, reduced the gap.

In *Jipping Street*, Kathleen Woodward wrote that she was, 'held fast', to her mother, 'by strong ties which existed without love or affection;

---

[43] *Ibid.*, pp. 51, 53.   [44] Gagnier, *Subjectivities*, p. 49.
[45] Jermy, *Memories*, pp. 53–4.   [46] *Ibid.*, pp. 54–5.

indissolubly I was bound'.[47] Louise and her stepmother were locked in mutual dislike and jealousy, but nevertheless maintained a similarly ambivalent mutual dependence. However poorly Louise thought Mary performed the role of mother she was the only one she had. And Mary, with small children of her own to look after, needed Louise's help, Amy having left home at the first opportunity. Temporary reconciliations were effected: Louise had cut out her black dress on the day of George V's marriage and Mary had gone to see what she could of the royal wedding. Returning home after an enjoyable day out, she was 'in an unusually good temper'. She told her husband to take Louise to see the illuminations and lent her various things to wear 'to make me look smarter', including a pair of unworn boots. Having experienced a brief release from drudgery she could afford to be generous, and the loan of clothing echoed her original efforts to befriend the sisters (and please her husband) through gifts of beads and stockings. But the amicability was only superficial. Mary persuaded Louise to give up dressmaking because it didn't pay well enough, and Louise, against her father's wishes, took up domestic service to get away from home because she was afraid of what she might do to Mary if she stayed.[48]

When Louise was in her early thirties, she suffered a period of severe depression and returned home. Her stepmother, fearing she was suicidal, watched over her and would sometimes talk about her own life. 'I saw', wrote Louise:

how in many ways, life had been a disappointment. It was at this time she told me, that for all she had worked to help father buy the house property, that never at any time had he given her more than enough to keep house on.

When Louise left home his father had blamed his wife, and from that time:

she had always to ask him for money for boots and dress, she never had any of her own, and also she said, 'If your father had listened to me, he would have gone to live up west, and taken up the cab business, but he would have his own way, and he lost nearly nine hundred pounds over it, so all my years of labour were wasted, and I've got nothing in the end. He says I can have what I want if I ask for it, but why should I always have to ask?'[49]

While, as Mary said, the family were not poor in absolute terms, her husband maintained a degree of authority over these strong-minded, strong-willed, adversarial women by denying them financial independence and forcing them to ask for the things they needed or wanted.

---

[47] Woodward, *Jipping Street*, p. 18.   [48] Jermy, *Memories*, pp. 52, 69, 71–4.
[49] *Ibid.*, p. 132.

David Vincent reminds us that many of the deepest emotional experiences are not verbal, and perhaps Mary should not have been surprised that, in the household of a man who expressed affection with a thirty-shilling hat, clothing became the vehicle through which relationships were forged, tested, broken and tentatively rebuilt.[50]

Glass and sartorial perception

Through mirrors and lenses glass makes us feel differently about ourselves.[51]

For Joseph Terry and Louise Jermy, clothes were both a means of self-validation and the chief medium through which – to borrow from Goffman – they created their 'front stage' personae, the versions of themselves they presented to the outside world. But the impression an individual believed he or she was making was not necessarily received in the same way. While this could happen to anyone, no matter what their class, status or income, the risk was greater among those with least resources to fashion a desired appearance, as William Tayler discovered:

The first time I went into the country, I was soposed to be a land surveyor; the last time I was there, at one place, they took me to be a school master or a bum bailey. At another place, they soposed me to be a beggar and was going to give me a half a pint of small beer; at another place they took me to be a thief or a insendrey and went for the Constable. Since then, I was soposed to be a tailor, once a grocer, two or three times a swindler and the other day, by a gentleman, if I was not a captain in the army! The last sertainly is the most respectable therefore I hope I am improveing in my apearance.[52]

Tayler, actually a footman, was in stable employment and so could afford to be amused by the misinterpretations of his identity, but such sartorial confusion was potentially disastrous. For observers, mistaking a 'thief', 'insendrey' or 'swindler' for a 'grocer' or 'gentleman', posed a threat to their personal safety and material security. For the wearer it might mean the difference between acceptance, good-will, respect and employment in a new community, or ridicule, violence, forcible detention or expulsion. But, for an individual like Tayler, knowing what he looked like posed something of a challenge.

In *Adam Bede*, set in the late 1790s, dairymaid Hetty Sorrel attempted to admire herself in her bedroom looking glass perched atop a chest of drawers. But she was frustrated by its:

---

[50] Vincent, *Bread, Knowledge and Freedom*, p. 41.
[51] Alan Macfarlane and Gerry Martin, *Glass: A World History* (University of Chicago, 2002), p. 3.
[52] Wise, *Diary of William Tayler*, p. 60.

numerous dim blotches ... which no rubbing would remove, and because, instead of swinging backwards and forwards, it was fixed in an upright position, so that she could only get one good view of her head and neck, and that was to be had only by sitting down on a low chair ... and she couldn't get near the glass at all comfortably.

We can imagine Hetty dipping and bobbing as she tries to position herself between the blemishes on this unaccommodating mirror. But even if it had not been marked and static, its diminutive size would still only have reflected a part of her body, not the whole – likewise the 'small redframed shilling looking-glass' to which she next turned, and the 'small hanging glass' she later borrowed from an adjoining room.[53]

Glass mirrors have been used in the West since at least the Roman period, and Alan Macfarlane and Gerry Martin highlight the scholarly association of mirrors with a heightened sense of individualism during the Renaissance.[54] But in the nineteenth century, says Isobel Armstrong, the 'full-length image of the body in a mirror was a new experience, often remarked'. It was part of a nineteenth-century fascination with glass and its reflective qualities, exemplified in the mid-century Crystal Palace, which gave birth to a 'scopic culture developed from the possibilities of just three vitreous elements ... the glass panel, the mirror, and the lens'.[55] I suggest that in sartorial terms the glass panel translates into the plate-glass shop window, and the lens into the camera – or rather, its product, the photograph – which together with greater ownership of mirrors increased visual self-awareness and new forms of selfperception.

Fontaine and Spufford both list looking glasses – common courtship gifts – among the goods carried by early-modern pedlars.[56] In his examination of Norfolk pauper inventories, Adrian Green identifies tea kettles and looking glasses as the two items which 'indicate change in the domestic experience of the eighteenth-century labouring poor', the looking glasses confirming, he says, that personal appearance was important for dignity. Yet only 16 per cent of the inventories referred to a looking glass, 'small – sometimes broken – pieces of mirror which the poor used to check their appearance before leaving the house'.[57] The

---

[53] George Eliot, *Adam Bede* (Ware: Wordsworth Editions, 1997 [1859]), pp. 124–5, 210.
[54] Macfarlane and Martin, *Glass*, pp. 16, 70–3.
[55] Armstrong, *Victorian Glassworlds*, pp. 1–3, 96.
[56] Fontaine, *History of Pedlars*, p. 185; Spufford, *Great Reclothing*, pp. 57, 89, 92. Margaret Spufford, *Small Books and Pleasant Histories: Popular Fiction and its Readership in Seventeenth-Century England* (Athens, GA: University of Georgia Press, 1981), pp. 116, 122, 168–9.
[57] Adrian Green, 'Heartless and unhomely? Dwellings of the poor in East Anglia and northeast England', in Joanne McEwan and Pamela Sharpe (eds), *Accommodating Poverty: The*

1810 and 1812 pauper inventories Peter King transcribed list, respectively, one and two looking glasses, but these two homes appear to have been particularly well-endowed, since only 19 per cent of his whole sample possessed one.[58] Alice Foley, born in 1891, could remember the 'cracked mirror hung on the small windowframe', nearby which 'dangled the family comb' in their 'dull and bleak back kitchen', indicating a very limited opportunity for sartorial self-appraisal even at the end of the century.[59] Nevertheless, by the early 1900s the emphasis on cleanliness combined with the growing focus on the home and changing furniture fashions, was increasing mirror ownership. Wash-hand stands, said Arthur Harding, who was working in the cabinet-making trade:

> became more ornate; they had a mirror fixed in the middle and side wings and they developed into the three-piece furniture: the sideboard and the wardrobe and the dressing table. In the end you had the dressing table with a lovely mirror in the middle.[60]

Such a dressing table, together with a tiled washstand, featured in the 12-guinea 'House of Furniture' described by Robert Roberts, but the mirror was still static, and still only returned a partial reflection of the body.[61]

Harding additionally recalled that around 1898 his father, also a cabinet-maker, began making overmantels, decorative plaster or carved-wood structures fixed to the wall above the mantelpiece and usually including a mirror. 'Everybody bought overmantles [sic]', said Harding:

> It was a new fashion about 1900. The poor always wanted an overmantle. Couldn't have a house without an overmantle... The bigger the better. Lovely glass in the middle and two side glasses... The cheapest ones were ten bob new in a shop.[62]

According to Robert Roberts, there existed 'a marked division between those houses which had an overmantel and those possessing no more than a plain shelf above the fireplace'.[63] Pember Reeves described the one-room Lambeth home of a family with four children. The furniture comprised a cot, bed, table, three chairs and a chest of drawers, but above the fireplace was 'an overmantel with brackets and a cracked

---

Housing and Living Arrangements of the English Poor, c.1600–1850 (Basingstoke: Palgrave Macmillan, 2011), pp. 69–101; p. 86.
[58] P. King, 'Pauper inventories', p. 162. [59] Burnett, *Destiny Obscure*, p. 94.
[60] Samuel, *East End Underworld*, p. 99. [61] R. Roberts, *Classic Slum*, p. 35.
[62] Samuel, *East End Underworld*, pp. 93, 97–8. The *Oxford English Dictionary* gives the first usage of 'overmantel' as 1882 in the upmarket *Harper's Magazine*.
[63] R. Roberts, *Classic Slum*, pp. 33–4.

looking-glass... The overmantel was saved for penny by penny before marriage, and is much valued.'[64]

However, the overmantel was prized as a status symbol and its mirror, as Hollander says, was 'not for looking in, but for looking at'.[65] Although it could be used to check personal appearance this was not its purpose, and like the wash-hand stand mirror it still permitted only a partial view of the body. The full-length mirror image, says Armstrong, was made possible by the nineteenth-century democratisation of the cheval glass – a framed, swing-mirror, large enough to reflect the whole body – and the introduction of the mirror wardrobe.[66] But this was a very limited democratisation, extending no lower than the middle classes, and for several mid- to late-nineteenth-century authors the novelty of the mirror for the working classes provided a key literary device.

In *The Water Babies* by the Christian Socialist and Darwinian evolutionist, Revd Charles Kingsley, the mirror's external revelation is the means of inner moral transformation for child chimney sweep Tom. Written in the 1860s, it is set in a northern town around 1820, before the use of climbing boys ceased, in law if not in practice. Tom 'never washed himself, for there was no water up the court where he lived', and '[h]e never had heard of God', except blasphemously. After getting lost while sweeping the chimneys of a large country house he emerged in a bedroom, 'the like of which he had never seen before'. It was 'all dressed in white; white window curtains, white bed curtains, white furniture, and white walls', on one of which was a picture 'of a man nailed to a cross, which surprised Tom much'. He was also puzzled by the presence of 'a washing-stand, with ewers and basins, and soap and brushes, and towels; and a large bath, full of clean water', assuming that anyone who needed such 'a heap of things all for washing' must be extremely dirty – yet there was no dirt in the room. Next he was astonished to see, on the bed, a 'snow-white coverlet' and a 'snow-white pillow' upon which lay a 'beautiful little girl' whose 'cheeks were almost as white as the pillow', and who, he thought, 'never could have been dirty'. And then he wondered:

'are all people like that when they are washed?' And he looked at his own wrist, and tried to rub the soot off, and wondered whether it ever would come off...
And looking round, he suddenly saw, standing close to him, a little ugly, black, ragged figure, with bleared eyes and grinning white teeth. He turned on it angrily. What did such a little black ape want in that sweet young lady's room? And behold,

---

[64] Pember Reeves, *Round About a Pound*, pp. 52–3.
[65] Anne Hollander, *Seeing Through Clothes* (Berkeley, LA and London: University of California Press, 1993 [1978]), p. 404.
[66] Armstrong, *Victorian Glassworlds*, p. 96.

it was himself, reflected in a great mirror, the like of which Tom had never seen before.

And Tom, for the first time in his life, found out that he was dirty; and burst into tears with shame and anger; and turned to sneak up the chimney again and hide.

The themes explored in Chapter 5 – the poor's difficulty in obtaining water, the ingrained occupational dirt, the contrast between that dirt and the cleanliness of the wealthy, the working-classes' perceived animalism, evolutionary retardation and need of salvation, the elision of class and race and the learned shame of dirtiness – coalesce in this scene in which the unfamiliar mirror becomes the instrument of almost biblical revelatory self-consciousness. It is also the humiliating prompt for Tom's reform, leading him to take flight, running, 'like a small black gorilla', through woods and across moors until he falls into a fever repeating the mantra, 'I must be clean, I must be clean.' He imagines he hears the white little girl saying to him, 'Oh, you're so dirty; go and be washed', and the bells ringing to call him to church. In a metaphorical act of immersive baptism, the 'heathen' Tom tumbles into a stream and is reborn as a water-baby and here, also, is the elision of physical and moral cleanliness. For when searchers 'found a black thing in the water, and said it was Tom's body, and that he had been drowned', they were wrong, because Tom had been washed 'so thoroughly, that not only his dirt, but his whole husk and shell had been washed quite off him, and the pretty little real Tom was washed out of the inside of it', and he begins a series of trials and adventures which lead to his salvation.[67]

For the Christian Socialist Kingsley, then, the mirror was an instrument of redemption and reform. But for Alice Fleming influenced, perhaps, by a childhood spent in what her brother, Rudyard Kipling, described as an 'establishment run with the full vigour of the Evangelical as revealed to the Woman' – the home of their foster mother – the mirror was an agent of vanity and destruction.[68] In Fleming's 1892 cautionary tale, 'Weekly payments: a humble tragedy', an 'oval looking-glass, on a varnished rosewood frame', tempts the young wife of plumber's assistant, Joe, to buy on credit with such disastrous consequences that she eventually commits suicide. The mirror has, she notes, 'a swing glass – Joe read to me about 'em, p'raps it's a cheval glass, too'. In Fleming's perception the fashionable cheval glass had replaced clothes as *the* consumer object

---

[67] Charles Kingsley, *The Water-Babies: A Fairy Tale for a Land-Baby* (London and Cambridge: Macmillan, 1863), pp. 3–4, 25–8, 32, 41, 53–7, 80.
[68] Rudyard Kipling, *Something of Myself for my Friends Known and Unknown* (London: Macmillan, 1937), p. 6.

of desire – even though the young woman is not sure what a cheval glass is. At 14s. 6d., though very shoddily made, it is way beyond her means and delivers her, fatally, into the hands of the tallyman.[69]

Our expectations mean that what we see in the mirror is different from what others see when looking at us, but a full-length reflection nevertheless equips the viewer with a much better impression of his or her overall appearance than is possible with a small mirror. It is, opined the middle-class *Every Woman's Encyclopaedia*, in 1910:

a great mistake to have a small glass and peep at yourself in sections... You go abroad then with a totally wrong impression of yourself, and have only to consult the eyes of the first man you meet to be speedily disabused of your pretensions.[70]

William Tayler would have known just what she meant. Inability to check overall appearance signals a way of conceptualising one's own visual impact that relies on the imagination, or on the reactions and observations of others. And even when wardrobes began appearing in working-class homes in the early twentieth century there is nothing to suggest they incorporated a mirror.

Rublack, noting the proliferation of visual media, especially portraits, in Renaissance Europe argues that: 'Growing attention to people's appearances must have had an impact on the very process of what people noticed when they looked at each other as well as on the sensation of being looked at.'[71] I would suggest that the ability to see, in one image, how this bodice relates to that skirt, or this jacket relates to those trousers, how the proportions of one part of the body relate to those of another, establishes in the viewer's mind an expectation that the body be considered as a cohesive whole and dressed accordingly. This has implications for what constitutes an orderly appearance, which work to the disadvantage of those who can only obtain a fragmented view. In the same way that the increasing brightness and airiness of elite spaces made the homes of the poor seem ever dirtier and danker, so, as the wealthy became more accustomed to a coordinated self-image, the poor were likely to seem even less tidily dressed. When the new mode of self-perception was formed unconsciously, and when judgements about the poor were made in ignorance of, or with disregard for, the material realities of poverty – the absence of the same opportunities for sartorial self-assessment – an untidy appearance might appear as wanton neglect. Breward notes that by the late-nineteenth century, 'dirt and

---

[69] Alice Fleming, 'Weekly payments: a humble tragedy', *Albemarle*, 1:2 (1892), 66–70.
[70] Anon., *Every Woman's Encyclopaedia*, p. 700.   [71] Rublack, *Dressing Up*, p. 24.

dishevelment' were equated with 'immorality and a perceived lack of respect for a basic sanitary code'.[72] Rather than being seen as the unavoidable consequence of inadequate water supplies, washing facilities, clothing stocks and visual aids, a disordered appearance could be interpreted as a wilful disregard for social convention.

Armstrong also identifies the nineteenth century as the 'era of public glass', facilitated by the abolition, in 1845, of excise tax on glass and an 85 per cent reduction in price by 1865. 'Plate glass,' she says, 'mirrors, and chandeliers, gave a sheen to urban experience.' Shops multiplied so that in London a 'continuous glazed thoroughfare ran from East to West, from Whitechapel... to Oxford Street and down to the western end of Piccadilly'.[73] This new reflective urban world, gas-lit by night, provided passers-by with continual reminders of their corporeal existence, heightening awareness of appearance, drawing attention to the fact that people moved through the world in *clothed* bodies, allowing – forcing – comparison with others. Breward notes that the abundance of mirrors in gin palaces and music halls increased 'the sense of palatial grandeur', but 'also intensified an atmosphere of critical surveillance, both of others and of the self'.[74] If some of the poor took the opportunity of public glass to obtain a full-length image of themselves and improve it, doubtless, for others, multiple reflections served to highlight sartorial inadequacy, about which they could do very little.

But a third element of the scopic culture, the photograph, introduced simultaneously with the spread of the cheval mirror and public glass, did offer an increasingly affordable, if less immediate, means of visual self-appraisal. Perceived as the 'Art of Truth', presenting 'a perfect and faithful record', it became, says Hollander, 'the defining representational medium of its age' and came to govern 'the perception of human looks'.[75] Peter Hamilton, John Tagg and Jennifer Green-Lewis align this medium, also, with the middle classes and officialdom, stressing its use for social classification by anthropologists, criminologists, physicians, social investigators and philanthropists, and reminding us that its inherent reproducibility allowed users 'to disseminate images of the normal and the abnormal'.[76] This again tended to discriminate against the poor whose

---

[72] Breward, *Hidden Consumer*, p. 90.
[73] Armstrong, *Victorian Glassworlds*, pp. 1, 43, 134.
[74] Breward, *Hidden Consumer*, p. 222.
[75] John Tagg, *The Burden of Representation: Essays on Photographies and Histories* (Basingstoke: Macmillan, 1988), p. 78; Hollander, *Seeing Through Clothes*, pp. 452–3; Peter Hamilton and Roger Hargreaves, *The Beautiful and the Damned: The Creation of Identity in Nineteenth Century Photography* (Aldershot: Lund Humphries, 2001), p. 109.
[76] Hamilton and Hargreaves, *The Beautiful and the Damned*, p. 60; Tagg, *Burden of Representation*, Chapter 3; Jennifer Green-Lewis, *Framing the Victorians: Photography and the*

images were frequently taken or commissioned by people with money and status, often for their curiosity, propaganda or sociological value (and not always with the subject's knowledge), who determined how they would be portrayed.

But for those who could afford it, says Tagg, 'to have one's portrait done' was an assertion of rising social status.[77] And the decreasing cost and easy availability of photography allowed some of the poor, if not the very poorest, to occasionally commission their own photographs. The Gernsheims note that photography as a profession is absent from the 1841 census, but twenty years later 2,879 photographers were recorded. During the same period the number of portrait studios in London rose from three to over two hundred, and: 'Every town of note, and even some villages, boasted one or more photographers, and travelling photographic vans made the round of outlying country districts.' Street photographers appeared in London in 1857 and photography became a sideline for traders such as ice-cream sellers and tobacconists who would provide a 'likeness' for 6d., or possibly less, and as the technology improved and the popularity of photography rose, the price dropped.[78]

Photography, says Tagg, allowed 'the extension of a "procedure of objectification and subjection", the transmission of power in the synaptic space of the camera's examination'. For Tagg this is largely negative, but he also acknowledges that any power relation 'can be modified or deflected'. He sees this in terms of 'resistance', but I would also suggest appropriation, evidenced by Hannah Mitchell who discovered that a photograph could be a potent instrument of self-affirmation.[79] Born in Derbyshire, in 1871, Mitchell grew up with a poor self-image which she attributed to her mother's favouritism of her sisters whom she perceived to be more attractive. At sixteen, Mitchell was working as a dressmaker's assistant under the supervision of 'Miss T.', a 'refined, well-educated young woman', who 'urged attention to personal appearance and correct speech'. This was a temporary job, and as a souvenir of their time together, Mitchell and her co-workers had their photograph taken:

Miss T. in the centre in a fawn dress trimmed with brown ribbon, Miss N. sharp-featured but smart in a dark red frock which suited her admirably. Miss K., tall and very handsome, always wore black. Mona with her bright eyes and dark curly

---

Culture of Realism (Ithaca, NY and London: Cornell University Press, 1996), Chapters 5 and 6.

[77] Tagg, *Burden of Representation*, p. 37.

[78] Helmut Gernsheim and Alison Gernsheim, *The History of Photography: From the Camera Obscura to the Beginning of the Modern Era* (London: Thames & Hudson, 1969), pp. 234, 241.

[79] Tagg, *Burden of Representation*, pp. 92–3.

hair wearing a dark frock with some bright coloured trimming, myself in a black velvet frock with a slim waist, closely buttoned down the front with pearl buttons; my hair, now light brown and abundant, piled high in the prevailing fashion.

This photograph, still one of Mitchell's 'most treasured possessions' half a century later, marked:

a sort of milestone in my life; showing me to myself, for the first time, as an attractive girl, with the kindly and genuine appreciation of my fellow workers, it did much to lessen the inferiority complex from which I suffered badly at that time.[80]

Hamilton says photography 'offered ways of visualising things which had not been "seen" hitherto', and Green-Lewis identifies the camera as 'an instrument of revelation'.[81] Looking at her own image Mitchell saw herself anew, almost as though she was looking at another person. She was not the 'miserable, puling creature' her mother had declared her, but a respected member of a group of well-dressed, attractive young women.[82] By showing her what she wore the photograph also showed Mitchell who she was – or had become. Green-Lewis, examining the use of photography in the treatment of the insane, notes physician Benjamin Rush's early-nineteenth-century (pre-photographic) idea to create visual records of patients and display them in a gallery. His idea, she says, was 'to bind groups of persons who had been previously separated', in this case doctors and patients, the well and the sick.[83] Similarly, for Mitchell, the photograph bound her to a group of young women of a type from which she had previously felt separated. While photographic images were achieved neither as easily nor as swiftly as a glance in the mirror, they were less ephemeral, and Hannah Mitchell faced the world with a greater knowledge of her visual image than William Tayler, who was so dependent on other people's reactions to gauge his sartorial impact.

* * *

Clothing was integral to people's sense of self, self-confidence, self-worth and identity. For Joseph Terry and Louise Jermy it was a vital tool in the negotiation of relationships and the transition from boy/girl to man/woman. But where the dispossessed Terry used his sailor's dress to embrace a collective identity which linked him to a proud and distinctive lineage, the alienated Jermy used her clothing to celebrate and assert her perceived difference. Living, mainly, on a boat, in the 1820s and 1830s, the young Joseph Terry's concept of his own visual impact

[80] Mitchell (ed.), *Hard Way Up*, pp. 54, 58, 71–2.
[81] Hamilton and Hargreaves, *The Beautiful and the Damned*, p. 114; Green-Lewis, *Framing the Victorians*, p. 3.
[82] Mitchell (ed.), *Hard Way Up*, pp. 72, 54.
[83] Green-Lewis, *Framing the Victorians*, p. 149.

would probably have been greatly reliant on his observations of others similarly dressed and on people's reactions to him. Jermy, working as an apprentice dressmaker at the close of the century, was much more likely to have had access to a large mirror and the opportunity, therefore, to observe and assess her overall appearance.

Jermy, who lived until 1952, may also have had many photographs taken of her and she may have come to own a sizeable mirror. In the late-nineteenth and early-twentieth centuries, however, both were largely beyond the reach of the poor. Among the wealthy a superabundance of reflected images that familiarised them with the visual impact of their own, full-length, frequently-washed, clothed bodies, created a normative sartorial aesthetic dependent on cleanliness and an awareness of one's own appearance as seen by others. The spread of photography allowed an increasing proportion of the working classes also to exploit the positive potential of this new visual self-awareness. But all of this worked to the disadvantage of the poor who, in their dark and ill-equipped homes could, like Hetty Sorrel, still only see themselves, if at all, a bit at a time and wash themselves infrequently. Certainly, shop windows and mirrors, pubs, theatres and gin palaces offered the possibility of full-length surveillance, but by then the viewer was already outside, presenting him- or herself to the world. For those with negligible financial resources the reflections could as easily have presented further reminders of inadequacy and an added source of shame and embarrassment as an opportunity for sartorial adjustment and self-improvement.

7 'The bowels of compassion': clothing and the Poor Law

> The object of this Club is to promote good Conduct, to check wastefulness and vice, and to encourage the Poor in the habit of small savings, that they may be thereby enabled to supply themselves with Clothing, with the aid of the subscriptions of other wealthier neighbours.[1]
> (Rules of the Kettleburgh Penny Clothing Club, 1837)

Dress was such a powerful means of self-expression for Joseph Terry and Louise Jermy because they were able – albeit sometimes with difficulty – to exercise considerable choice over their style of clothing. But for many of the poor even second-hand clothes and the fabrics for home manufacture were beyond their means, forcing them to seek assistance from the parish or charity, which compromised their sartorial self-determination and self-expression.

The 1601 Poor Law Act, which remained virtually unchanged for over two hundred years, made each parish responsible for the support of its poor who were unable to maintain themselves, financed through the levy of local poor rates. Some assistance, known as indoor relief, was provided in residential workhouses, but most aid came as outdoor relief – cash or goods, including clothing, distributed to the poor living in their own homes. According to Steven King, a considerable portion of parish resources under the Poor Law was devoted to clothing both the indoor and outdoor poor, and he says that parishes clothed their poor well as a matter of civic pride. The mounting cost of outdoor relief led to cutbacks and demands for reform, resulting in the 1834 Poor Law Amendment Act. This aimed to abolish outdoor relief for the able-bodied, making the abhorrent workhouse the only assistance available to them, but King

---

[1] *Kettleburgh Penny Clothing Club* [Rules] (Framlingham, 1837). An earlier version of this chapter appeared in *Textile History*. Vivienne Richmond, '"Indiscriminate liberality subverts the morals and depraves the habits of the poor": a contribution to the debate on the Poor Law, parish clothing relief and clothing societies in early nineteenth-century England', *Textile History*, 40:1 (2009), 51–69, www.maneypublishing.com/journals/tex and www.ingentaconnect.com/content/maney/tex.

argues that outdoor clothing relief continued throughout the opening decades of the nineteenth century and under the new Poor Law.[2]

Peter Jones subsequently set out to test King's thesis with a study of Hampshire and St Martin-in-the-Fields, Westminster, concluding that in these places clothing provision remained an important parish function up to 1834. In the first part of this chapter, I too test the argument. Drawing on Poor Law records from Sussex and Kent I argue that here, and therefore potentially elsewhere, parish clothing relief virtually ceased in the 1820s as a result of the debate about Poor Law reform which intensified from the late eighteenth century, and that abolition of outdoor clothing provision was a specific goal of the new Poor Law Commissioners. The second part of the chapter examines the proliferation of penny clothing societies, a form of self-help charity. Jones argues that these were a supplement to parish provision, but my findings demonstrate that clothing societies were intended as a replacement for, not an addition to, parish provision.[3]

The decline of outdoor clothing relief

In 1783–85 annual poor relief expenditure in England and Wales averaged £2 million. By 1829–33 it had risen to an average £6,700,000 per annum via an 1818 peak of over £7,800,000.[4] Poor rates soared particularly in the over-populated wheat-producing agricultural areas that Mark Blaug termed 'Speenhamland counties', where parish doles, based on family size and the price of bread, supplemented low wages. The period from 1813 to the end of the 1830s was especially bleak for English agriculture and in Speenhamland counties poor relief per head was generally higher than elsewhere. In 1802 it averaged 12s. in the former compared with 8s. in non-Speenhamland counties, rising to 13s. 8d. and 8s. 7d. respectively by 1831, with Sussex the highest-spending county throughout.[5]

The combination of inflated prices and static or depressed wages at the end of the Napoleonic Wars in 1815 put new clothing still further beyond the reach of many. Its increased cost is illustrated by the contracts

---

[2] S. King, *Poverty and Welfare*, pp. 157–8; S. King, 'Reclothing the English poor, 38.
[3] P. Jones, 'Clothing the poor'. Jones actually refers to clothing clubs rather than societies, and the terms 'clothing society' and 'clothing club' were used interchangeably. For continuity, and to distinguish them from commercial clothing clubs, I have used 'society' throughout except where a particular organisation styled itself 'Club'.
[4] Eric J. Evans, *The Forging of the Modern State: Early Industrial Britain 1783–1870* (Harlow: Longman, 1983), p. 402.
[5] Blaug, 'The myth of the old Poor Law', p. 164.

to supply drapery to the workhouse at St Paul's, Deptford. For example, between 1809 and 1813 men's blue kersey cloth coats were supplied for 7s. or 7s. 6d. each, but by early 1816 the price had doubled to 14s. 6d., while men's drab breeches rose from 5s. in 1813 to 7s. 4d. during 1815–16, and Peter Jones identifies this as a period of '"crisis" in clothing the poor', apparent in the 'upsurge of... charitable bequests of clothes'.[6] Poor relief records in Rotherfield, Sussex, and Deptford, Kent, show that parish clothing provision in both also responded to the rising distress. In Rotherfield, with a population of just over two thousand, the overseers in February 1811 considered a typical 27 requests for clothing and granted two-thirds.[7] By January 1813 requests had increased to 51 and again two-thirds were granted. The clothing given was robust working dress, including shoes, breeches, gowns, stockings, petticoats, shirts, waistcoats, round frocks (smocks), greatcoats and bedgowns.[8]

This rise in parish clothing provision was mirrored in Deptford, on the London border of north-west Kent. A semi-urban district with a population of 12–13,000, Deptford was quite different from rural Rotherfield. As home to the Royal Dockyard and the Navy victualling depot, the French wars brought some employment to Deptford, but also rising prices and a steep rise in poor rates.[9] In the parish of St Paul's, during the first quarter of 1810, the Overseers' Minutes show 35 items of clothing – shoes, shifts, petticoats and shirts – granted in outdoor relief. During the same quarter in 1817, outdoor clothing relief in St Paul's reached a peak with 211 items being granted.[10]

This would seem to agree with King's and Jones's suggestion of responsive parish clothing provision. However, King also negates claims that 'buying second-hand or poor-quality cloth and clothing was the [parish] norm', and goes so far as to suggest that some overseers were supplying paupers with 'fashionable clothing'.[11] Styles strongly contests this, arguing that parish clothing was 'consistently cheap, coarse and undecorated. Paupers received the minimum of sartorial sufficiency, barely matching, let alone surpassing, non-pauper adults at the lowest point

---

[6] LLHAC, SPD/4/3, Churchwardens and Overseers Committee (COC) Minutes 1809–13; LLHAC, SPD/4/4, COC Minutes 1813–17. Clothing supplied for women followed a similar pattern. P. D. Jones, 'I cannot keep my place', p. 36.
[7] Population figures given at 'Rotherfield', *The Weald of Kent, Surrey and Sussex*, www.thesussexweald.org.
[8] ESRO, PAR 465/7/1, Rotherfield Request Book [RRB] 1810–11; ESRO, PAR 465/7/2, RRB 1812–13.
[9] Jess Steele, *Turning the Tide: The History of Everyday Deptford* (London: Deptford Forum, 1993), pp. 49, 60, 93.
[10] LLHAC, SPD/4/3, COC Minutes 1809–13; LLHAC, SPD/4/4 COC Minutes 1813–17.
[11] S. King, *Poverty and Welfare*, p. 158.

of the family poverty cycle.'[12] At St Paul's, Deptford, the records show regular quarterly payments to contractors for new drapery and shoes for the workhouse, which appear to have also formed the stock from which outdoor paupers were supplied.

Although it is difficult to assess the quality of the goods in the absence of samples, the low prices – 3s. for a pair of men's breeches and 7½d. per yard for camblett for women's gowns in 1823, for example – suggest the quality was far from superior. Furthermore, the fact that still in 1825 as in 1786 the contractors were quoting, for example, for blue kersey cloth coats and waistcoats and 'Breeches of strong brown Russia Drab' for men, and blue serge for women's gowns, certainly militates against any suggestion of fashionable dress.[13] The consistent purchase of blue cloth and clothing also suggests a uniform appearance, a policy Styles associates with the abolition of badging which, from 1697 had compelled parish paupers to wear 'upon the shoulder of the right sleeve of the uppermost garment... a large Roman P together with the first letter of the name of the parish or place whereof such poor Person is an inhabitant'.[14] The badging law was repealed in 1810, but Deptford was dressing its paupers uniformly before this and either ignored, or was ignorant of, the badging repeal. In 1817 it ordered that workhouse paupers attending church were to be provided with coats 'marked according to Act of Parliament', and from that year the contracts to supply the workhouse show 'coats of blue kersey cloth with Badge'.[15] There is, then, little in Deptford to suggest that the overseers provided anything except essential clothing for its paupers, or that the supply was an advertisement of civic pride.

Parliamentary Reports on the Poor Laws in 1817 and 1818 demanded a reduction in poor relief expenditure as it rose to nearly £8 million a year.[16] In both Rotherfield and St Paul's, parish clothing provision was one area where savings were made. At Rotherfield, in January 1823, only three requests for clothing were granted, compared with over thirty in the same month a decade earlier.[17] Local opposition to clothing relief was evidenced by landowner Lord Sheffield who around 1815 wrote to the parish officers in Fletching, eleven miles from Rotherfield, insisting

---

[12] Styles, *Dress of the People*, p. 275.
[13] LLHAC, SPD/4/7, COC Minutes 1822–25; LLHAC, SPD/4/2, COC Minutes 1785–93.
[14] Styles, *Dress of the People*, p. 274; *A Bill To Amend so much of an Act, passed in the 8th & 9th year of King William the Third, as requires poor Persons receiving Alms to wear Badges.* Parliamentary Papers 1810 I, p. 1. (Intituled an Act 7 June 1810.)
[15] LLHAC, SPD/4/5, COC Minutes 1817–1820.
[16] Mark Blaug, 'The Poor Law report reexamined', *The Journal of Economic History*, 24 (1964), 229–45; 231; Evans, *Forging of the Modern State*, p. 402.
[17] ESRO, PAR 465/7/5, RRB 1820–24.

they had no power to relieve the poor out of the workhouse with any kind of clothing. Assistance, he said, should come from charitable sources and be directed towards the 'industrious and well-disposed poor'.[18] By 1832 virtually the only clothing given by the Rotherfield overseers as outdoor relief was for boys and girls starting out in service, partly as a bargain made with prospective employers to relieve the parish of other maintenance costs. The Rotherfield Request Book records, for example, that in January 1823, Mrs Ovenden of Salters Green agreed to 'keep Lois Frost till Ladytide if the Parish will allow her Clothes as others. Granted.'[19]

At St Paul's in the first quarter of 1825, 65 items of clothing were granted, a significant reduction from the 211 of 1817. And during the fourteen months between December 1825 and January 1827 a total of just 11 items were distributed as outdoor clothing relief.[20] Furthermore, the St Paul's workhouse supply contracts indicate that these reductions cannot simply be explained by a corresponding fall in prices. Certainly, the cost of some garments did drop, the breeches, for example, falling to a stable 4s. to 4s. 6d. during 1823–7 – a little less than the 1813 price. But other garments remained expensive. By 1822 the cost of men's coats had decreased only to a steady 13s. to 13s. 6d., still nearly twice their price a decade earlier.[21] The extreme reductions in clothing provision suggest a determined effort to reduce outdoor relief.

The abolition of outdoor clothing relief was warmly embraced by the Poor Law Commissioners who, by 1839, were claiming that across the country the 'practice of allowing clothing to adult paupers out of the workhouse appears to be so rare, as not to call for any remarks' on their part.[22] They were exaggerating; implementation of the reforms was uneven and the main target of the 1834 Amendment Act was the rural

---

[18] ESRO, SPK P.6, Private correspondence of Lord Sheffield, 1811–19. Undated letter from Lord Sheffield to the parish officers of Fletching.
[19] ESRO, PAR 465/7/5, RRB 1820–24; ESRO, PAR 465/7/6, RRB 1828–30; ESRO, PAR 465/7/7, RRB 1830–31; ESRO, PAR 465/7/9, RRB 1832–33. Peter Jones highlights the prevalence of this practice in his analysis of poor relief in Ringwood, Hampshire, in the 1810s and 1820s. P. D. Jones, 'I cannot keep my place', 41–3.
[20] LLHAC, SPD/4/15, COC Order Book 1819–25; LLHAC, SPD/4/7, COC Minutes 1822–25; LLHAC, SPD/4/8, COC Minutes 1825–29.
[21] LLHAC, SPD/4/3, COC Minutes 1809–13; LLHAC, SPD/4/4, COC Minutes 1813–17; LLHAC, SPD/4/7, COC Minutes 1822–25; LLHAC, SPD/4/8, COC Minutes 1825–29. Clothing supplied for women followed a similar pattern.
[22] *Copies of correspondence between the Poor Law Commissioners and the Boards of Guardians of the Ledbury and Cricklade Unions, relative to supplying clothes for new-born infants on their quitting the workhouse; – also, of applications to the commissioners on providing clothes for infants born in the workhouse.* Parliamentary Papers 1846 XXXVI, p. 16.

south.²³ But there is no doubting the Commissioners' intentions. By 1846 they were condemning even the provision of outdoor relief clothing to boys and girls entering service, believing the 'practice of making allowances of clothing to the children of able-bodied labourers going into service [which] appears to prevail in many Unions' tantamount to granting 'premiums upon pauper apprenticeships'.²⁴

But nothing demonstrates so forcefully the Commissioners' determination to implement the reduction of clothing relief, and the ambivalence of those charged with its execution, as the 1839 Minute outlawing the issue of clothing to short-term inmates leaving workhouses, based on the belief that many clad themselves in rags before admission in the knowledge that they would be reclothed on discharge. Each workhouse was managed by a Board of Guardians which reported to the Poor Law Commissioners, but the day-to-day running of the workhouse was in the hands of a master and matron appointed by the Guardians. Inmates could quit the house after giving three hours' notice, but any request for parish clothing to take with them had to be considered by the workhouse Guardians at their weekly meetings. In December 1845 the Ledbury Guardians granted the master and matron discretionary permission to clothe children born in the workhouse when they left. The Commissioners' Secretary, Edwin Chadwick, reminded the Ledbury Guardians they had no authority to delegate such powers prompting local JP, the Revd Edward Higgins, to write to the Commissioners, confident that they were not possessed of the full facts. 'On Saturday... last', he wrote, 'it being quite dark, and raining in torrents, a naked infant, and cold as ice... was brought to my door by a labourer and his wife.' The child belonged to a local woman who had left the Ledbury workhouse earlier that day, 'very thinly clad' and seventeen days after giving birth. She had insisted on her right to leave the workhouse, at which point:

the baby clothes were taken from the baby, and the baby was handed over to the mother, naked, whereupon she took off her own flannel petticoat, and a threadbare shawl, and with the infant so covered, she started for her mother's... and on her way exposed the infant.

The workhouse, Higgins pointed out, was 'a test of destitution' and inmates were 'therefore, to enter it destitute. The infant is born in the house, and of course brings no clothes with it; is it to be sent out

---

²³ Alun Howkins, *Reshaping Rural England, A Social History 1850–1925* (London: HarperCollins, 1991), p. 74.
²⁴ *Copies of correspondence...* Parliamentary Papers 1846 XXXVI, pp. 16–17.

naked in all seasons and weather?' Exasperated, he argued that the clothing for an infant cost only 2s. 6d., a 'paltry sum' unlikely to 'tempt a woman to immure herself in a workhouse for three weeks and upwards'. The Commissioners were not persuaded; 'the words "any child born in the workhouse"', they said, 'might... be taken to extend to a child of ten years old, and such child might be leaving the workhouse without any parents'. They consented 'to the Guardians authorizing the master to give clothing to infants leaving the workhouse with their mothers, and having been born therein, the mother having no clothes for the child', but cautioned against any liberality that might encourage pregnant women to enter the workhouse to obtain clothes for the expected child.[25]

The Ledbury case prompted revelations of similar incidents and Guardians elsewhere sought guidance and clarification from the Commissioners. Even as correspondence continued between Higgins and Chadwick, early in January 1846, news reached the Commissioners of Elizabeth Butcher who, the previous month, had given birth in a Wiltshire workhouse and left it with her baby who had been 'stripped of the union clothes'. The child was later found drowned. The Commissioners cannot have been pleased when the Coroner reported that, after returning a verdict of wilful murder against Elizabeth Butcher, the jury expressed:

their surprise, that the deceased infant should have been stripped of her clothing, and suffered to leave the workhouse in a state of nakedness, with its mother utterly destitute and unable to shelter it from the inclemency of the weather. They are also grieved to add, that they find other cases of the same character have been similarly treated before quitting the workhouse, by order of the Board.

One witness stated that although Butcher had not applied to the Guardians 'for additional clothing it was admitted by the master that it was generally understood amongst the female paupers, that any such application would have been refused'.

Another inmate testified that four years earlier she had given birth in the workhouse and left without clothes for the child having been refused them by the Board.[26] Two weeks after the Butcher drowning *The Times* brought the Ledbury case to national attention by reproducing an article from the *Worcestershire Chronicle*. A note by the *Chronicle*'s editor stated that if the Ledbury Guardians had 'turned the child out of the [workhouse] without a shred of clothes to its back, they would really

---

[25] *Ibid.*, pp. 3–5, 17.   [26] *Ibid.*, pp. 6, 8, 11, 14.

deserve to be indicted as accessories before the fact'. The new Poor Law, he thought, had 'the property of Medusa's head and turns the hearts of those who assist to put it into operation into stone'.[27] The implication was that the refusal of baby clothes, the most basic provision for a new child, stripped vulnerable post-partum mothers of all hope for their offspring and made death a seemingly better future for them than a life of poverty.

The spread of clothing societies

The cutbacks in parish relief left the poor dependent on other strategies, in particular charitable assistance. While Utilitarianism informed the New Poor Law of 1834, from the late eighteenth century the nature of philanthropy was largely determined by what Boyd Hilton terms moderate Anglican evangelicalism. While only a minority of the population, he says, would have identified themselves as Evangelicals, its social influence was much more pervasive and in terms of philanthropy, the key term for moderate evangelicals was self-help.[28] Evangelicals deemed social stratification providential and so aimed to relieve rather than eradicate poverty. As a Sussex curate explained in 1828:

> It is not in the power of any of us to relieve all who suffer, nor, even were our means of doing good as ample as the kindest heart could wish, would it be proper that we should interfere in every case to avert the penalty intended to discourage extravagance and vice in this present world.[29]

Evangelicals believed eternal salvation was available to all, but had to be earned through the constant avoidance of sin. For the poor this meant proving again and again that they were deserving of assistance, by being grateful and deferential, adhering to good moral conduct and, especially, by demonstrating their willingness to help themselves. For the rich, salvation required them to assist those less fortunate than themselves, but caution was required since, as the Revd Becher in Southwell explained in 1828, 'indiscriminate liberality subverts the Morals and depraves the habits of the Poor'.[30] It encouraged idleness and improvidence, thereby

---

[27] 'Child Murder', *The Times*, 24 January 1846, p. 6.
[28] Boyd Hilton, *The Age of Atonement: The Influence of Evangelicalism on Social and Economic Thought, 1795–1865* (Oxford: Clarendon, 1988), pp. 16, 26, 91.
[29] John Barlow, *The Probable Effects of Clothing Societies in Improving the Habits and Principles of the Poor* (London: C. J. G. and F. Rivington, 1828), p. 19.
[30] John Thomas Becher, *The Anti-pauper System; Exemplifying the Positive and Practical Good, Realized by the Relievers and the Relieved, Under the Frugal, Beneficial, and Lawful, Administration of the Poor Laws, Prevailing at Southwell, and in the Neighbouring District* (London: W. Simpkin and R. Marshall, 1828), p. 30.

sinfully assisting the recipient on the path to hell and so threatening the salvation of the giver. A particular evangelical target was cash doles since, as the Revd Close of Cheltenham explained, without constant vigilance 'MONEY, or even anything that can be SOLD ... will soon be turned into the means of intoxication'.[31] There was no perfect solution, but a partial remedy lay in helping the poor themselves acquire what they needed, rather than simply handing it over. The 1789 *Instructions for Cutting Out Apparel for the Poor*, for example, advocated selling boys' breeches, waistcoats and coats separately, rather than as a complete suit, to make purchase more affordable, the author explaining that 'donations of money or clothing ... have been found too often to defeat the salutary purpose for which they were intended'.[32]

Chief among the new self-help schemes was the clothing society. Parish-based, established and managed principally by Anglican clergy, clothing societies supplemented the weekly deposits of the poor – usually between 1*d*. and 6*d*. – with premiums subscribed by wealthier neighbours. These varied, but never exceeded the depositor's savings and were commonly 4 shillings and 4 pence – or 52 pence, the equivalent of a depositor saving a penny a week for a year. At the end of the year the total sum was laid out on clothing and sometimes bedding. Clothing societies therefore satisfied the twin demands of self-help and assistance in kind. They fostered self-respect and a degree of self-reliance, encouraged the responsible management of household income and provided a channel for contact between the classes, since membership by the poor often depended on nomination by a wealthy subscriber – and where it did not the manager retained the right of veto.[33] The societies also aimed to reduce the poor rates, a fact made most evident by the stated exclusion from many of 'any able-bodied labourer [who] shall consent to receive parochial relief'.[34]

The earliest society I have traced was established in Painswick, Gloucestershire, in 1796, recommended in an 1802 report of the Society for Bettering the Condition of the Poor.[35] Although the report mentions two further clothing societies, near Birmingham, few seem to have been

---

[31] General Society for Promoting District Visiting, *The District Visitor's Manual. A Compendium of Practical Information and Facts, for the use of District Visitors* (London: J. W. Parker, 1840), p. 123.

[32] Anon., *Instructions for Cutting Out*, pp. iii, 54–5.

[33] For typical clothing society rules see *Kettleburgh Penny Clothing Club*.

[34] F. Litchfield, *Three Years Results of the Farthinghoe Clothing Society With a Few Remarks on the Policy of Encouraging Provident Habits Among the Working Classes* (Northampton, 1832), p. 5.

[35] Society for Bettering the Condition and Increasing the Comforts of the Poor, *Reports* (1802), vol. III, p. 332.

founded before the 1810s. But from then on, as the debate about Poor Law reform reached a climax, clothing clubs proliferated. By the end of the 1830s societies had been established in many counties in the southern half of the country, including Buckinghamshire, Devon, Essex, Norfolk, Northamptonshire, Somerset, Suffolk, Sussex, Warwickshire and Wiltshire.[36] Except Somerset, all were among Mark Blaug's 'Speenhamland counties', the rural districts where Poor Law officers 'had come to heed the alarm at the rising burden on the rates' and were looking for ways to check expenditure on outdoor relief.[37]

Jones asks why the poor would spend their own money on clothes 'that may well have been available from the parish'. He concludes that the clothing societies' attraction was the greater opportunity for independent provision, citing the Revd Williams of Shalbourne, who stated that the clubs in his parish were 'of little benefit to [the poor], *because what they derive from the Club now they derived from the parish before the club*; and it is no sort of benefit to the poor man any more than it contributes to the support of his independence'.[38] But the clothes were simply not available from the parish. Jones was assessing two Wiltshire societies in 1831 and 1834, respectively, before and in the same year as the new Poor Law was introduced. Williams was giving evidence in 1838 to a Parliamentary Select Committee on the Operation of the new Poor Law – after the attempt to outlaw outdoor relief. Earlier in his evidence Williams had been at pains to emphasise that since the introduction of the 1834 Act the local Poor Law Guardians had consistently refused applications for outdoor relief. The Clothing Club, he said, had been established within the past three years and he cited the restriction on outdoor relief as 'One

---

[36] D. Capper, *Practical Results of the Workhouse System, as Adopted in the Parish of Great Missenden, Bucks*, 2nd edn (London: Hatchard and Son, 1834), p. 63; 'Almshouses' [Exeter], *GENUKI*, genuki.cs.ncl.ac.uk/DEV/Exeter/ExeterHist1850/; 'Upminster: Introduction and manors', *A History of the County of Essex: Volume 7* (1978), pp. 143–153, www.british-history.ac.uk; George Cotterill, *A Pastoral Address to the Members of Clothing Clubs*, 3rd edn (London: Longman, Brown, Green and Co. and Norwich: J. Tippell, 1846); William White, *History, Gazetteer, and Directory, of Norfolk, and the City and County of the City of Norwich* (Sheffield, 1836), p. 474; Litchfield, *Three Years Results*; SHL, B.834, *Hinton Clothing Club* [rules]; *Kettleburgh Penny Clothing Club*; *Rules for the Clothing Club at Stutton* (1833); *Rules of the Ubbeston Provident Clothing Society* (Halesworth, 1833); *Rules of the Ufford Penny Clothing Club* (Woodbridge, 1834); Barlow, *Probable Effects*, 'Introductory Statement'; Sylvia Margaret Pinches, 'Charities in Warwickshire in the eighteenth and nineteenth centuries', PhD, University of Leicester (2001), pp. 170–2; P. Jones, 'Clothing the poor', 29–30.
[37] Blaug, 'The myth of the old Poor Law', 158, 167, 178. Kent, where the Deptford clothing society was well established by 1858 (year of inauguration unknown), had the highest poor relief expenditure of non-Speenhamland counties between 1802 and 1831. *Ibid.*, 178–9.
[38] P. Jones, 'Clothing the poor', 31 (Jones's emphasis).

Cause of it'. Significantly, Williams points out that parishioners gained from 'the Club' what they had obtained from the parish *'before the club'*, the implication being that 'the Club' had *replaced* parish provision.[39] Jones is correct that the Clothing Club offered the opportunity to obtain the same items previously supplied by the parish in a more independent fashion, but the poor joined it partly because they had little option.

By 1833 the Revd Capper in Buckinghamshire, recommending a system of self-help pauper management, thought it necessary to give only a minimal description of a clothing society, 'since this kind of club is so general throughout the country', and other casual references testify to the societies' proliferation.[40] In 1849 Charlotte Brontë's eponymous heroine, Shirley, bent on being 'saved by works', apprenticed herself to the philanthropic Miss Ainley in view of her own 'ignorance about clothing societies, and such things', while ten years later Harriet Martineau approved of English women's agricultural work, the earnings from which 'improves the family diet, and subscribes to the clothing club'.[41] Michael Rose claims that from the 1870s private charity, under the auspices of the Charity Organisation Society was 'to be re-organised... and worked in closer co-operation with the poor law system', but the close relationship between cutbacks in outdoor relief and the establishment

---

[39] *Report from the Select Committee of the House of Lords appointed to examine into the several Cases alluded to in certain Papers respecting the Operation of the Poor Law Amendment Act; and to report thereon... Part I*. Parliamentary Papers 1837–38, XIX, p. 102. There is a further point: when Williams refers to 'the Club' it is not at all certain that he is referring to the Clothing Club. The statement Jones quotes comes in the middle of a discussion of Friendly Societies, also known as Benefit Clubs. The beginning of the statement reads, 'The Benefit Clubs are of little Benefit to them.' Williams has previously explained that parishioners pay 4*d*. per month into the Clothing Club and the discussion later continues as follows:

In this Clothing Club do you limit them to a Penny a Week?
Yes, we do...
[W]hat is the Deduction per week from their Means of maintaining their Family for the sake of those Clubs?
The Club is 1*s*. 3*d*. a Month, and the other is 4*d*. a Month; that would be 1*s*. 7*d*. a Month...
Do they get any thing in the Club towards the Funeral, in the Case of the Death of the Subscriber?

There is a clear distinction between 'the Club', which the references to funeral expenses identify as the Friendly Society, and the 'Clothing Club' which is elsewhere distinguished as the 'Penny Club'. *Report... respecting the Operation of the Poor Law Amendment Act... Part I*. Parliamentary Papers 1837–38, XIX, pp. 102–3.

[40] Capper, *Practical Results*, p. 81.

[41] Charlotte Brontë, *Shirley* (London: Penguin, 1985 [1849]), pp. 262, 266; Anon. [Harriet Martineau], 'Female Industry', *The Edinburgh Review*, 222 (1859), 293–336; 299.

of clothing societies suggests this was occurring much earlier in the century.[42]

Often where a clothing society was established, so were similar clubs for coal and footwear. They developed at the same time as other self-help institutions, such as friendly societies, which spread most rapidly in industrial areas. In the southern counties where clothing societies proliferated, agricultural labourers showed little inclination to establish friendly societies. Here, as poor rates peaked and clothing societies were introduced, the gentry and clergy took it upon themselves to establish friendly societies for the labourers, run on a similar basis to clothing societies, to encourage them to look to their own resources in times of need.[43] Lemire identifies initiatives like clothing societies as part of a normalised, pervasive and inclusive savings culture, arising from the increasingly cash-based nineteenth-century economy. This was manifested in organisations such as the Trustee and Post Office savings banks which, although aimed at the modest saver, remained inaccessible to many. But clothing and boot societies formed part of a range of measures, including penny, school and co-operative banks, which made saving accessible to all but the very poorest. They also promoted what Lemire terms 'provident consumerism': saving for the purpose of responsible consumption and the (appropriately modest) material rewards of thrift.[44] Clothing societies were also often attached to schools, where they could inculcate the principles of self-help in the young.[45]

In rural areas, in the opening decades of the nineteenth century, Anglican clergy were accused of pluralism, absenteeism and pastoral neglect.[46]

---

[42] Michael E. Rose, 'The disappearing pauper: Victorian attitudes to the relief of the poor', in Eric M. Sigsworth (ed.), *In Search of Victorian Values: Aspects of Nineteenth-century Thought and Society* (Manchester University Press, 1988), pp. 56–72; p. 62.

[43] P. H. J. H. Gosden, *The Friendly Societies in England 1815–75* (Manchester University Press, 1961), pp. 23–4, 41, 52–3, 60; Martin Gorsky, 'The growth and distribution of English friendly societies in the early nineteenth century', *The Economic History Review*, 51 (1998), 489–511; 493–7; Simon Cordery, *British Friendly Societies, 1750–1914* (Basingstoke: Palgrave Macmillan, 2003), pp. 49–51; Nicola Sian Reader, 'Female friendly societies in industrialising England, 1780–1850', unpublished PhD thesis, University of Leeds (2005), pp. 63, 89, 223.

[44] Lemire, *Business of Everyday Life*, pp. 141, 157, 159, 163–5, 166–7.

[45] *School Savings Banks. Nominal Return of Schools in Receipt of Annual Grants which have Savings Banks attached to them for the use of the Children, stating whether they are Penny Banks, or whether they are in connection with the Post Office Savings Bank, and showing, in each Case, the Sums Deposited and Withdrawn, and the Number of Depositors, for the Year ending on the 31st day of August 1877.* Parliamentary Papers 1877 LXVII.

[46] James Obelkevich, 'Religion', in F. M. L. Thompson, *The Cambridge Social History of Britain 1750–1950*, 3 vols (Cambridge, 1993), vol. III, pp. 311–56; pp. 314, 319; Howkins, *Reshaping Rural England*, p. 66.

The Church responded by increasing resident, active clergy, and Howkins cites the establishment and management of clothing societies as one of the ways this new activity was expressed.[47] The young Revd Ellman, who in 1838 assumed the curacy of the Sussex parish of Berwick, exemplified the new model clergy. The Rector, he explained, 'took no interest in the parish, he never drove over the eight miles from Lewes even once during the six and a half years I remained here as Curate'. But Ellman 'visited the people constantly' and, in addition to a Dame School, started 'Clothing and Coal Clubs'.[48]

But a second wave of clothing society creation occurred in the third quarter of the century as anxiety about the derogatory effects of urban and industrial life increasingly centred on the metropolis.[49] This was followed by renewed concern about outdoor relief and misdirected philanthropy resulting in a 'Crusade' against outdoor relief.[50] In 1869 George J. Goschen, President of the Poor Law Board, 'warned metropolitan guardians about the "alarm which might arise on the part of the public" if double distribution persisted involving both statutory relief and charity'. For Goschen 'relief rationalization' could best be organised by a voluntary agency and he looked to the newly formed Charity Organisation Society (COS) to do it.[51] The COS was never particularly effective, but its formation was a manifestation of an anxious climate convinced of the need once more to curtail indiscriminate philanthropy and encourage the principle of self-help which had gained increased emphasis with the publication of Samuel Smiles's phenomenally successful book on the theme a decade earlier.[52] It was during this period that London clothing societies appear to have multiplied most rapidly, and in urban areas the clergy viewed them as a favourable alternative to 'Satan's favourite haunt' – the pawnshop.[53] The clergy were aided by troops of district visitors whose 'fiscal evangelism' urged upon those they visited the expediency of joining the clothing society, while the society itself provided a

---

[47] Howkins, *Reshaping Rural England*, pp. 68–70.   [48] Ellman, *Recollections*, pp. 138–9.
[49] Stedman Jones, *Outcast London*, p. 12; See also M. Rose, 'The disappearing pauper', p. 60.
[50] Anne Summers, 'A home from home – women's philanthropic work in the nineteenth century', in Sandra Burman (ed.), *Fit Work for Women* (London: Croom Helm, 1979), pp. 33–63; p. 51; Mary MacKinnon, 'English Poor Law policy and the crusade against outrelief', *The Journal of Economic History*, 47 (1987), 603–25; 612.
[51] Robert Humphreys, *Sin, Organized Charity and the Poor Law in Victorian England* (Basingstoke: Macmillan, 1995), p. 5.
[52] Samuel Smiles, *Self-Help, With Illustrations of Character and Conduct* (London: John Murray, 1860).
[53] Tebbutt, *Making Ends Meet*, p. 113.

good premise for what were often unwelcome visits, since visitors could collect the pennies in the course of their rounds.[54]

Clothing society regulations

Jones questions why clothing society depositors 'opted for precisely the same kinds of practical, hard-wearing textiles' available from the parish or other charitable sources. He concludes that it was due to the poor's moral rejection of opulence in favour of utilitarian clothing which signified 'simplicity, honesty and hard work... fairness, "natural justice" and social responsibility'.[55] But apart from the fact that this necessary everyday clothing was no longer available from the parish, Jones underplays the restrictions clothing societies placed on the goods they supplied. The societies existed not only to assist with clothing provision, but also to regulate depositors' moral behaviour. The Kettleburgh Penny Clothing Club was typical in its ambition to 'promote good Conduct, to check wastefulness and vice', at the same time that it encouraged 'small savings' to help the poor 'supply themselves with Clothing'. Societies excluded members if they, or their dependants, were 'guilty of a felony' or 'habitual drunkenness, of tippling in Alehouses... neglect of the Sabbath, thieving, or any gross act of immorality', which might include 'becoming pregnant while unmarried' or a baby arriving too soon after marriage. Regularity was encouraged through the levy of halfpenny fines for non-payment of a weekly instalment, and expulsion, with the forfeit of all monies paid, if the omission continued.[56]

But moral regulation was also attempted through the clothes themselves by stipulating that only 'useful and necessary clothing' could be obtained. The purchase of 'any smart articles of dress, or finery of any kind' was prohibited in the belief that among the poor they bespoke depravity, inappropriate aspiration and a want of thrift. The Stutton Clothing Club in Suffolk was typical, permitting only the purchase of 'Calico, Flannel, Stuffs, Checks, Handkerchiefs, Shawls, Cloaks, Fustian... Waistcoats and Stockings'.[57] Clad in their practical garments,

---

[54] Edward L. Cutts, *Address to District Visitors* (London: Society for Promoting Christian Knowledge, 1873), pp. 16–17; Lemire, *Business of Everyday Life*, p. 163.
[55] P. Jones, 'Clothing the poor', 32.
[56] *Kettleburgh Penny Clothing Club; Rules of the Haveningham Provident Clothing Society* (Halesworth: 1833); Litchfield, *Three Years Results*, pp. 4–5; ESRO, PAR 496/9/3/1, Rules of the Uckfield Clothing Society.
[57] *Kettleburgh Penny Clothing Club; Rules for the Clothing Club at Stutton.*

clothing society members were to be emblems of thrift, piety and industry, whose reward of better clothing for their exemplary conduct was to be an incentive to emulation among their peers. The success of this attempted social control is, however, doubtful. Since membership often required subscriber nomination, those who joined clothing societies were likely to be the 'respectable' poor who were already thrifty and industrious. But respectability did not, as Jones implies, inevitably lead to a rejection of 'finery' in favour of 'honest' textiles. Rather, these were all that could be obtained from the clothing societies and items for Sunday and holiday wear had to come from other sources, such as the clothes sent home by daughters in service.

It is also rather doubtful how much 'finery' could have been obtained with clothing society money even if the depositors had been given free reign. The society in Ripe, Sussex, for example, paid a flat 4s. 4d. premium. Of the forty depositors in 1855, four saved 1d. weekly, ten 2d., seventeen 3d., six 4d. and three 6d. At the end of the year (assuming no missed payments and therefore no fines), the seventeen depositors saving threepence a week would each have received 17s. 4d. (3 × 52d. + 4s. 4d.). While this was a useful sum, Ripe appears to have permitted only a husband or wife to join the society (although children could join the Sunday School clothing society), and it would probably have been necessary therefore to share the 17s. 4d. between the needs of several people. Furthermore, clothing society money was often used to buy sheets and blankets, leaving less to spend on clothing. The Ripe accounts show that depositors bought drapery, shoes and ready-made clothes, but drapery predominated. Of the total £39 9s. 2d. laid out in 1855, comprising the premiums, adults' and schoolchildren's deposits, £33 3s. 2d. was spent on drapery £1 2s. 6d. on shoes and £5 3s. 6d. on ready-made clothing.[58] Given the challenges of cutting out, discussed in Chapter 4, it is also possible that some societies provided cut-out garments, ready for making up, rather than a length of cloth. If so, this may have reduced the depositors' control over the style of garments available.

Although clothing society membership was predicated on respectability, the spectre of pauper fecklessness haunted the managers. Fearful that the money might be diverted from its intended purpose, deposits were rarely returned in cash. Instead, many societies issued depositors with a ticket to exchange for goods at a specified local retailer. Edwin Grey, who grew up in a Hertfordshire village during the 1860s and 1870s where, as 'with most other villages there was a . . . clothing club',

---

[58] ESRO, PAR 462/26/1, Account Book of Ripe Parish Clothing Club 1854–69; ESRO, PAR 462/25/5/1, Records of the Ripe Sunday School.

explained that even then the packages of goods could not be taken home immediately, since they had first to be 'looked over by the Rector's daughters and other local ladies to ensure that all the contents were good, warm, useful articles, and no so-called finery'.[59] Some societies feared that even the tickets might be used to clear 'old debts, &c.', and arranged for tradesmen to bring their goods to the village meeting room where, under supervision, depositors made their choice.[60] In the most cautious societies depositors stated what articles they required and the committee bought and distributed them. Lemire points out that although a feature of the nineteenth-century culture of savings was that it offered an alternative to the accumulation of surpluses as material goods for subsequent liquidation as necessary, it did not altogether replace it, and when pressed for money the poor were liable to turn anything they could into cash.[61] As a final safeguard, therefore, some clothing society managers reserved indefinitely the right to see, on demand, the goods purchased to ensure they had not been sold or pawned.[62]

Clothing societies and class relations

While the rules and regulations appear repressive and authoritarian, clothing societies did offer the poor a greater degree of independence than parish provision. As the Revd Williams explained to his parishioners: 'If you subscribe to this Society you claim this as a Right, whereas in the other Case you throw yourself upon the Parish.'[63] But somewhat paradoxically, the clothing society ideology of what might be termed supervised self-reliance sought to reinforce paternalistic class relations at the same time as it encouraged independence.

In the early decades of the nineteenth century yearly hiring and living-in of agricultural labourers declined, particularly in the southeast, increasingly replaced by hiring for the week, day or hour. Under the old system, payment of a guaranteed wage had been made in lump sums once or twice a year, enabling the immediate purchase of necessary items. Under the new system there was no guaranteed annual income and labourers received smaller sums more frequently, which demanded different management. Furthermore, as Keith Snell has shown, in most of southern England real wages fell from the early 1800s, while lack of continuity of employment and increasing sexual division of labour, which

---

[59] Grey, *Cottage Life*, pp. 38–9.   [60] Capper, *Practical Results*, p. 81.
[61] Lemire, *Business of Everyday Life*, p. 147.   [62] Litchfield, *Three Years Results*, p. 5.
[63] *Report... respecting the Operation of the Poor Law Amendment Act... Part I*. Parliamentary Papers 1837–38, XIX, pp. 102–3.

reduced female employment opportunities in many agricultural areas, led to a further decline in household income.[64]

The change in hiring arrangements together with enclosure and the aspiring gentility of the farmer employers led to physical and social separation between labourer and farmer. The Swing riots of 1830–31 further widened the gap and were, to wealthier neighbours, evidence of the moral degradation and lawlessness of the agricultural labouring poor.[65] Howkins claims that '[t]he rural poor seemed to many to be completely alienated from their "betters", a separate, secret people, impervious to change and influence'. But as farmers came to recognise the reciprocity between themselves and their labourers, the one unable to work the land without assistance, the other unable to maintain his family without employment, they sought reparation of the rift. The result, says Howkins, was a renewed paternalism, expressed in the selection of key rituals, 'especially those around the gift to revive carefully controlled idyllicist notions of rural social life and order'.[66] By subscribing to clothing societies, farmers and gentry apparently affirmed community hierarchy while assisting the poor and engendering in them contentment, gratitude and deference. For the Revd Barlow in Sussex, clothing societies were the means by which to best 'make the poor feel the value of their own exertions', while simultaneously inspiring in them a sense of 'grateful attachment' towards their superiors.[67]

The connection between employer as donor and employee as recipient in clothing societies, and the extent to which the societies pervaded and impacted on rural domestic economics, is clarified by an analysis of the depositors and subscribers in the Ripe Parish Clothing Club. Ripe is a Sussex agricultural village adjoining Berwick where the Revd Ellman established a clothing society in the 1830s. In 1851 Ripe had a population of 382 of whom 260 were aged eleven and over.[68] The Clothing Club was opened in 1854 and attracted forty-two depositors, all adults.[69] Thirty-four of these can be identified in census material, thirty-two of whom were agricultural labourers or their wives or widows

---

[64] Blaug, 'The myth of the old Poor Law', p. 171; Barry Reay, *Rural Englands: Labouring Lives in the Nineteenth Century* (Basingstoke: Palgrave Macmillan, 2004), pp. 34–5; Snell, *Annals of the Labouring Poor*, pp. 29–34, 45, 51–60.
[65] E. J. Hobsbawm and George Rudé, *Captain Swing* (London: Pimlico, 1993).
[66] Howkins, *Reshaping Rural England*, pp. 65, 75. [67] Barlow, *Probable Effects*, p. 22.
[68] *Census Returns of England and Wales, 1851* (Kew: The National Archives of the UK: Public Record Office, 1851), HO 107 1643 [Ripe]; C. J. Barnes, *Sussex (East) Census – 1851 Index* (Hastings: C. J. Barnes, 1994).
[69] ESRO, PAR 462/26/1, Account Book. 'Adults' refers to persons aged eleven and over, the age at which males here entered full-time agricultural labour.

and only one of whom had potentially never been married.[70] According to the 1851 census, there were fifty family units in Ripe where the head was either an agricultural labourer or his widow and, allowing for the uncertainties caused by members who shared the same name, the thirty-two agricultural-labouring Clothing Club depositors represented a minimum of twenty-seven and a maximum of thirty-two families. So of the total fifty family units, at least 54 per cent, and possibly 64 per cent, had a depositor in the Clothing Club. Of these, only a small, mostly elderly, minority had no dependent children, the remainder each having between one and eight.[71] The majority of Clothing Club depositors were, then, from households where the head was an agricultural labourer or his widow, and where there were dependent children, and over half of the total agricultural-labouring households in Ripe had a Clothing Club depositor.

Ten of the fourteen subscribers to the Ripe society between 1854 and 1869 can be identified. Of these, six were farmers employing, apart from domestic servants, between one and twenty-six persons. The remaining four were an innkeeper, the rector, the previous incumbent's wife and a landed proprietor. In the case of two subscribers whose identity is uncertain, but for whom in each case there are two possibilities, one alternative in each instance is that they were farmers.[72] In Ripe, then, the majority of non-clerical subscribers were farmer-employers and the majority of depositors were agricultural labourers. The probability that the farmers were supporting their own employees is increased by a 1902 appeal for subscribers. 'In former years', it said, 'many of the Employers subscribed to the Club, in order that their own work-people might partake of its benefits.'[73] Anne Digby found that in Norfolk farmers preferred to give perquisites such as 'subscriptions for a clothing club rather than rises in money wages which were difficult to alter later'.[74]

In terms of the connection between clothing societies and the reduction of parish relief, it is surely significant that half of the fourteen Ripe Clothing Club subscribers served as Overseers or Guardians of the Poor between 1856 and 1865.[75] The only depositor to receive outdoor relief

---

[70] *Census Returns... 1851*, HO 107 1643 [Ripe]; Barnes, *Sussex; Census Returns of England and Wales, 1861* (Kew: The National Archives of the UK: Public Record Office, 1861), RG 9 588 [Ripe].
[71] *Census Returns... 1851*, HO 107 1643 [Ripe]; Barnes, *Sussex*.
[72] ESRO, PAR 462/26/1, Account Book; *Census Returns... 1851*, HO 107 1643; *Census Returns... 1861*, RG 9 588 [Ripe]; Barnes, *Sussex*; Ellman, *Recollections*, pp. 16, 275.
[73] ESRO, PAR 462 7/30/1, *Ripe Magazine*, December 1902.
[74] Anne Digby, *Pauper Palaces* (London: Routledge & Kegan Paul, 1978), p. 22.
[75] ESRO, PAR 462/12/3, Vestry Book of the Parish of Rype in the County of Sussex, 1855–1874.

during this period was Joseph Townsend who obtained a pair of half boots in 1862 'because he is an imbecile and earns 7/- a week'. Outdoor relief to other parishioners was restricted to funeral expenses and the infirm, the unemployed able-bodied being sent to the workhouse.[76] King notes an increasing tendency to blame the failings of the poor themselves for their poverty, and clothing societies can be seen as shifting responsibility from the parish to the poor.[77] Ratepayers were still providing aid through clothing society subscriptions, albeit on a voluntary rather than a compulsory basis, and so could argue that if the poor were not adequately clothed it was not for want of assistance, but because of their own improvidence.

The same agricultural labourer-depositor/farmer-subscriber pattern prevailed in Rotherfield, fifteen miles from Ripe, which in 1861 had a population of 3,413 and where approximately 36 per cent of all heads of households were clothing society depositors. The figure is lower than in Ripe, but Rotherfield, being a larger community, had a larger mix of classes and occupations.[78] While some societies, such as Ripe, allowed both men and women to become depositors in the adults' society, others, such as Rotherfield, permitted only the head of the household to join. As such, the only female members were widows, and the vast majority of depositors were able-bodied men, which is significant for two reasons. First, although historians have subsequently shown them to be mistaken, it was the perception of the architects of the 1834 Act that able-bodied men were the main recipients of outdoor relief – and therefore the main targets of the cutbacks – which ties the clothing society still more firmly to the 1834 amendments.[79] Second, Lemire links the self-discipline required for saving with the self-control required for sexual continence and identifies both as facets of respectable masculinity.[80] But requiring men to be the depositors in clothing and boot societies was a deviation from, and possibly a challenge to, women's responsibility for both domestic financial management and clothing provision.

While the employer-subscriber/employee-depositor model of clothing societies appears to support ideas of the gift as a means of instilling deference and gratitude, the societies may in fact have inspired a lesser

---

[76] ESRO, G12/20/2, General Ledger of West Firle Union; ESRO, G12/1a/1, West Firle Union Minute Book.
[77] S. King, *Poverty and Welfare*, p. 105.
[78] *Census Returns... 1861*, RG 9 574 [Rotherfield]; ESRO, PAR 465/17/1, Rotherfield Clothing Club Book; ESRO, AMS 1189, Rotherfield Clothing Club Report 1867.
[79] Blaug, 'The myth of the old Poor Law', 177; M. Rose, 'The disappearing pauper', p. 64.
[80] Lemire, *Business of Everyday Life*, p. 161.

degree of 'grateful attachment' than earlier charitable initiatives which required no financial input from the recipient. Marcel Mauss suggested that an unreciprocated gift makes the recipient inferior, because it places them in the donor's debt.[81] Alan Kidd argues that the nineteenth-century requirement that the recipient be 'deserving' was an attempt to alter the one-way character of the charity relationship by making the condition of being deserving 'a mediated "return" for the charitable gift'. Kidd limits the nature of being 'deserving' to a display of gratitude and deference, long an assumed part of the charitable relationship, unvalued except where it was lacking, but in the nineteenth century re-valued as reciprocity.[82] By requiring the recipient to contribute at least as much as, and usually more than, the value of the gift they received, clothing societies provided a greater degree of reciprocity in the gift relationship and so diminished the deference due. King argues that in the early decades of the century the most ragged poor were not the recipients of parish clothing relief, but those who disdained such assistance and in their struggle for independence were forced to tolerate a very low standard of clothing.[83] Such individuals may have found the self-help nature of clothing societies more acceptable than the old clothing doles which had to be personally solicited and justified.

The scarcity of northern clothing societies

Clothing societies provided a reliable and semi-independent source of new, serviceable clothing which labourers needed for everyday wear. Admittedly, a Wokingham schoolmaster who had fallen 'into evil ways' absconded with the clothing club money, but generally the weekly pence, once deposited, were safely away from temptation and theft.[84] Also, in contrast with the pawnshop and the tallyman, the societies offered a premium rather than charging interest and the goods were generally obtained at a discount. Assistant Commissioner Austin, reporting his findings on the agricultural areas of Wiltshire, Dorset, Devon and Somerset in 1842, considered that:

---

[81] Marcel Mauss, *The Gift: The Form and Reason for Exchange in Archaic Societies*, trans. W. D. Halls (London: Routledge, 1990 [1923–4]), p. 65; See also Stedman Jones, *Outcast London*, pp. 251–2.
[82] Alan Kidd, 'Philanthropy and the "social history paradigm"', *Social History*, 21:2 (1996), 180–92; 186–7.
[83] S. King, 'Reclothing the English poor', 47.
[84] Lisa Spurrier, 'Absconding with the clothing club money', *The Berkshire Echo: The Newsletter of Berkshire Record Office*, No. 22 (January 2003), p. 2.

a great change has been effected for the benefit of the labouring classes within these few years by the clothing clubs... The effect of these clubs has been very great in increasing the linen and clothes of the labourers' families since their establishment.

Austin had examined the society at Blandford, Dorset, and he detailed some of the benefits to both depositors and tradesmen. At Christmas the former were:

entitled to purchase of the tradesman appointed to supply the club, to the amount of their respective shares of the funds, any plain articles of dress or of household linen. The tradesman of the club, in consideration of the large sum of money thus laid out, and promptly paid at his shop... supplies the best articles of the description wanted at a price rather lower than he could afford to sell them to the labourer dealing with him in the ordinary way.[85]

But while clothing societies proliferated in southern agricultural districts and the capital, they were much rarer in northern industrial and mining areas.[86] Even in northern agricultural areas they appear less common than in their southern counterparts. Witnesses to the Parliamentary Commission investigating the employment of women and children in agriculture in 1842–3 constantly testified to the presence and usefulness of clothing societies in the southern counties, but in Yorkshire and Northumberland they were far fewer and often in decline. The Clerk of the Beverley Union, for example, thought benefit clubs were on the increase, but 'Clothing Clubs very rare'.[87] Occasional examples occur in some northern industrial towns such as Leeds and Manchester, but only one individual who gave evidence to the 1833 Factories Inquiry Commission mentioned a clothing club, and this at precisely the time when their establishment in the southern agricultural districts was reaching its first peak.[88]

There are several possible reasons for this relative absence. Clothing societies' close connection with Poor Law reform and the latter's focus on rural areas probably inhibited their spread in northern industrial areas since even a decade after the Amendment Act the 1844 Outdoor Relief Prohibitory Order was issued to rural, not urban unions. It took another eight years for an urban equivalent and then, as Robert Humphreys says, the Order 'lacked even the surface stringency of its rural predecessor'.[89]

---

[85] *Reports... Women and Children in Agriculture*. Parliamentary Papers 1843 XII, pp. 22–3.
[86] The Society in Iford, Sussex, for example, continued until 1931. ESRO, PAR 403/26/1, Iford Clothing Club Accounts 1890–1931.
[87] *Reports... Women and Children in Agriculture*. Parliamentary Papers 1843 XII, p. 312.
[88] *Factories Inquiries Commission. First Report... Employment of Children in Factories... C.2. North-eastern District*. Parliamentary Papers 1833 XX, p. 14.
[89] Humphreys, *Sin, Organized Charity*, p. 17.

Not until 1875, and in the wake of the textile industry crises of the 1860s, did the Manchester Board of Guardians take decisive action to limit outdoor relief.[90]

Clothing societies' minimal presence in northern mining and factory areas may also have been due to higher incomes among workers in those industries, compared with southern agricultural labourers, which more easily facilitated the outright purchase of clothing. And, as discussed in Chapter 3, industrial areas tended to have more varied opportunities for independent clothing acquisition than their southern rural counterparts. Worker-led friendly societies and, later, trades unions were established earlier in industrial areas than in agricultural districts, suggesting a preference for independent self-help rather than paternalistic schemes.[91] Additionally, in industrial towns, high infant mortality rates and – where there was an anatomy school nearby – the 1832 Anatomy Act permitting the release for dissection of the unclaimed bodies of paupers dying in workhouses, meant that spare pennies were more likely to be devoted to the burial society. The Anatomy Act, says Ruth Richardson, 'appears to have been an important stimulus to the very rapid growth of friendly and burial societies'.[92]

In mining areas the population 'was notoriously restless and unsettled' and so lacked the stability that the extended deposit period of the clothing society required.[93] Contemporary sources also cited the lack of paternalism. Parliamentary Sub-Commissioner Lichfield claimed in 1842 that in the northernmost counties '[t]he arrival of the pitmen is the signal for the departure of the gentry', with the result: 'that active benevolence of the higher ranks which induces them to visit the habitations of the working classes; to counsel, guide, and instruct them ... are here wholly deficient'.[94] The influence the 'higher ranks' might have exercised, had they stayed, is debatable and probably more significant, given the prevailing Anglicanism of clothing societies, was the predominance of

---

[90] Kidd and Roberts, *City, Class and Culture*, p. 55.
[91] E. H. Hunt, 'Industrialization and regional inequality: wages in Britain, 1760–1914', *Journal of Economic History*, 46:4 (1986), 935–66. For trades unions see also Henry Pelling, *A History of British Trade Unionism* (Middlesex: Penguin, 1963), Chapter 3. For friendly societies see footnote 43 above. John Styles also noted regional variations in clothing provision in eighteenth-century England, although different from those in the nineteenth. Styles, 'Clothing the north', p. 160.
[92] Evans, *Forging of the Modern State*, p. 154; Richardson, *Death, Dissection*, pp. 83, 203–7, 275.
[93] Raphael Samuel, 'Mineral workers', in Raphael Samuel (ed.), *Miners, Quarrymen and Saltworkers* (London: Routledge & Kegan Paul, 1977), pp. 1–97; p. 67.
[94] *Children's Employment Commission. Appendix... Mines. Part I.* Parliamentary Papers 1842 XVI, p. 533.

non-conformity in many industrial and mining areas.[95] Lichfield noted that the Methodists had 'chiefly, and in several districts exclusively, undertaken the charge of providing religious instruction in the collieries' simply because colliery villages were generally established after the parish church had been built and their situation was determined by proximity to the pit, which was often some miles from the church. Methodist chapels, on the other hand, tended to be erected after the villages were established and, therefore, in the villages themselves, making them more accessible.[96]

Witnesses to an 1842–3 Parliamentary inquiry claimed that a dislike of charity was characteristic of northern labourers, but northern independence could only be achieved with money.[97] The northern poor needed help as much as the southern agricultural labourers, but few would obtain it from clothing societies although definitive reasons for this have yet to be uncovered.

Clothing societies at the close of the century

Clothing societies were in the ascendancy as rural peddling was in decline and by channelling money into clothing societies, which bought only from specified local tradesmen, they may have contributed to the rural pedlar's demise. But if clothing societies posed a threat to this traditional mode of retailing, they also provided custom for new trade initiatives. In 1889 the Bon Marché department store in Brixton, south London, boasted 'a vast and varied collection of Novelties for the Spring Season... equal in assortment to those in the West End' alongside a promise of 'Special Terms given to Clothing Clubs, Dorcas Societies, Charitable Institutions &c'.[98] It should not, though, be imagined from this that local clothing societies were supplying depositors with these 'novelties'.

According to shop owner L. E. Neal, clothing societies also inspired new trade practices. Enterprising retailers, he said:

organised schemes of a similar kind in connection with their own shops. They extended the scope by throwing it open to the public generally, and added various attractions, such as permission to purchase against the deposits before the club book had been made up.[99]

---

[95] There were Non-conformist clothing societies – Charles Booth, for example, mentioned some run by Wesleyan missions in 1902 – but they do not appear to have been common. Booth, *Life and Labour... Third Series: Religious Influences*, vol. VII, p. 204.
[96] *Children's Employment Commission. Appendix... Mines. Part I.* Parliamentary Papers 1842 XVI, p. 533.
[97] *Reports... Women and Children in Agriculture.* Parliamentary Papers 1843 XII, pp. 335, 337–9. See Chapter 2 for northern poverty.
[98] LMA, P95/ALL2/29, *All Saints, Clapham Park, Church Magazine*, April 1889.
[99] Lawrence E. Neal, *Retailing and the Public* (London: Allen & Unwin, 1932), p. 59.

Furthermore, Coopey et al. cite the 'small weekly payments' of clothing societies as one of the 'pre-existing patterns of saving and spending' on which both shop credit rotation clubs and the new mail-order traders modelled their credit facilities. And just like clothing societies, the watch clubs out of which mail-order trading developed fined participants for late payment of instalments.[100]

New trade and established charity coexisted and many clothing societies continued until the early 1930s, closing their books only when the Poor Law was gradually dismantled after 1929, indicating that not only their origin but also their termination was connected with the Poor Law. Although depositor numbers in some societies were declining by the close of the 1800s, others were flourishing. In Abbey Dore, Herefordshire, the thirty-two members of 1869 were, by 1909 down to just four, but in Eardisley, only twelve miles south, the 1868 membership of eighty-six was virtually unchanged in 1884, at eighty-nine.[101]

Societies often survived longer in the urban areas, since in many rural communities membership numbers dwindled as rural populations shrank, and more specifically the socio-economic group from which depositors had chiefly been drawn – agricultural labourers with young families – declined. The persistent efforts of the District Visitors helped the continuation of urban societies, but so too did their popularity among the depositors. As late as 1885 a new society was formed at Lancaster Gate, London, when the wives of the navvies constructing Westbourne Park Station requested the organisers of their mothers' meeting to establish a Savings' Bank and Clothing Club.[102] Often subscriber rather than depositor numbers declined despite the repeated exhortations of managers to their wealthier parishioners. In Windsor, annual support of £100 from Queen Victoria notwithstanding, the parish magazine in 1894 felt it 'only right to inform intending depositors . . . that some alteration will probably have to be made in the rules, as the Annual Subscriptions do not now cover the amount of the Gratuity that for several years past has been added to each card'.[103]

* * *

My findings from Sussex and Kent disagree with King's and Jones's claims that up to and beyond the 1834 Poor Law Amendment Act,

---

[100] Coopey et al., pp. 79, 81, 85.
[101] HRO, AC 16/64, Abbey Dore Clothing Club Accounts 1869–1909; HRO, AN 91/122, *Eardisley Parish Magazine*, December 1868, March 1885.
[102] LMA, P87/CTC/47, *Christ Church, Lancaster Gate, Parish Magazine*, June 1885.
[103] See *Oxford English Dictionary* definition of club: '1890 *Times* (Weekly ed.) 3 Jan. 15/3 Her Majesty contributes £100 annually to the funds of the Royal Clothing Club at Windsor'; *Old Windsor Banner*, March 1894.

parishes were concerned to provide paupers with generous quantities of good-quality, even fashionable, clothing. Although there was a rise in provision in the first two decades of the 1800s, the clothing supplied was of inferior quality, possibly stigmatic, and followed by a steep decline, even before the 1834 Act. Initially a response to calls for a reduction in poor relief spending, the decline subsequently reflected the Poor Law Commissioners' resolve to abolish outdoor clothing relief. In its stead arose clothing societies which, in line with the new focus on accounting discussed in Chapter 2, sought to impose habits of responsible financial management on the poor and, under the evangelical ethos of self-help, required recipients to demonstrate their worth, by making a monetary contribution to their own support and adhering to a set of moral precepts. Following the pattern of official concern about poor-relief spending, the societies spread rapidly in the rural south and later in London, but remained less widespread in the north.

Cut-backs in out-relief and the implementation of the new Poor Law met with fierce opposition, including rioting, but I have found no evidence of resistance to clothing societies. Historians have argued that opposition to change in the Poor Law was based on the poor's assumption of right to relief. Acceptance of self-help schemes does not challenge this argument, but does suggest the poor were flexible about the form relief might take. Many, as beneficiaries of Speenhamland-type systems, were long accustomed to relief being a supplement to, not a replacement for, wages, and were thus equally accustomed to a combined programme of personal contribution and external assistance. Self-help schemes simply put such arrangements on a more formal and reliable footing. Whereas each request for parish clothing relief had to be justified and risked rejection, once accepted into the clothing society the petitioner became a depositor with a guaranteed, if variable, annual return.

Clothing societies helped with the provision of a basic, utilitarian wardrobe. Depositors with surplus resources might be able to supplement this with other, perhaps more decorative, items from different sources. Edwin Grey claimed that in his Hertfordshire village during the 1860s and 1870s two travelling shopkeepers, a draper and a boot-seller, from nearby St Alban's supplied goods to the cottagers which they paid for in weekly instalments. Grey had 'no doubt that a good bit of the so-called finery so carefully debarred and tabooed from the clothing clubs was bought by the young women from these sources'.[104] It is, though, doubtful how many clothing society depositors would have been able to afford this, and the regular deposit of even just a few pence was beyond the means of some, which excluded the very poorest and most in need.

---

[104] Grey, *Cottage Life*, p. 39.

Lynn Hollen Lees argues that the amended Poor Law 'worked effectively to enforce social distance between paupers and the rest of Victorian society', and the clothing societies, so intimately entwined with the Poor Law, were no exception.[105] They created a division even between those able and unable to commit to a weekly penny, the 'deserving' status conferred by membership meaning that those too poor to join were not only denied the opportunity of better clothing, but their morality was also potentially called into question.

[105] Lynn Hollen Lees, *The Solidarities of Strangers: The English Poor Laws and the People, 1700–1948* (Cambridge University Press, 1998), p. 151.

8   'An urgent desire to clothe them': ladies' clothing charities

> I think it is scarcely possible for any lady to go among a set of ragged children without feeling an urgent desire to clothe them better.[1]
>
> (Sarah Trimmer, 1787)

A minority of clothing societies were established and managed by women, but the executive positions were usually held by Anglican clergy and churchwardens, who were necessarily male, with women serving on the Committees that chose and inspected the clothing. But as Dickens scoffed in 1839, a proliferation of other charities was established, managed and run by women. There was:

> the ladies' soup distribution society, the ladies' coal distribution society, and the ladies' blanket distribution society... the ladies' dispensary, and the ladies' sick visitation committee... the ladies' child's examination society, the ladies' bible and prayer-book circulation society, and the ladies' childbed-linen monthly loan society.[2]

Dickens was derisory, but his list indicates the wide range of philanthropic work in which middle- and upper-class women were engaged at a time of limited state welfare provision. And while he also sneered at the 'enviable amount of bustling patronage' with which the maternity society endowed the 'ladies', charity work provided occupation and purpose for many women who had no need, or opportunity, of paid employment, as well as material aid to the poor.[3]

It is curious that, excepting the 'childbed-linen monthly loan society', Dickens includes no clothing charities since, as Frank Prochaska says, needlework, being at 'the heart of female culture in the nineteenth century... was crucial to women's philanthropy'.[4] And both where clothing

---

[1] Sarah Trimmer, *The Oeconomy of Charity* (London, 1787), p. 47.
[2] Dickens, *Sketches by Boz*, p. 52. For women's philanthropic work see F. K. Prochaska, *Women and Philanthropy in Nineteenth-Century England* (Oxford, Clarendon Press, 1980).
[3] Dickens, *Sketches by Boz*, p. 55.
[4] F. Prochaska, 'A mother's country: mothers' meetings and family welfare in Britain, 1850–1950', *History*, 74:242 (1989), 379–99; 390.

societies did and did not exist, a plethora of alternative initiatives were established, and these are examined in the first part of this chapter.[5] Some existed for the sole purpose of providing clothing, whereas others provided clothes as one of a range of services, but all testified to the scale of deprivation and the ingenuity of the philanthropic impulse. Some, like Dorcas societies and maternity boxes, were well-established schemes, others, like mothers' meetings, were new ventures, but they all fell into two main types: those in which the actual manufacture of clothing was done by 'ladies', their children, or their servants, and those in which the sewing was done by the beneficiaries with ladies acting as facilitators or employers. Almost all, however, moved to a system of self-help, requiring financial input from the recipients, even if they had originally simply given away clothing free of charge. And while most supplied the poor with new, rather than second-hand garments, as in the clothing societies, they were invariably utilitarian.

Just as it became more difficult for clothing societies to attract subscribers, so women's widening horizons, new leisure activities and changing religious practices made it harder for charities to recruit sufficient volunteers. This coincided with the growing realisation that poverty was the result of environmental rather than divine causes, which prompted new ideas about how, and by whom, it should be relieved. The result was the development, in the 1880s, of more efficient charitable schemes, such as the Needlework Guilds, which operated on a regional rather than parochial scale, offered female organisers greater participation in public life and made links between private charity and civic responsibility. Another was the jumble sale, an efficient, self-help initiative, largely free from the utilitarian constraints and moral regulation of most other clothing charity, and an instant success among both organisers and the poor.

Local clothing charities

Clothing for childbirth presented particular challenges for the poor, especially as families grew and resources shrank. It is a messy business even when there are no complications, but even more so when poor health and multiple pregnancies frequently led to miscarriages and haemorrhages, soiling both the mother's clothes and the bed linen. Standish Meacham reports that at the turn of the nineteenth and twentieth centuries brown paper was used to protect the bed, which a later

---

[5] As the established church, and the denomination with the largest number of professed adherents throughout the century, the focus in this chapter is charity provided by, or connected with, the Anglican church. However, other denominations also provided a great deal of charitable assistance along the same lines, examples of which are included.

midwife says was 'entirely effective', but it is unclear when it was introduced and how widely it was used.[6] Furthermore, according to one mother, even in the late nineteenth century, only her face, neck and hands were washed after the delivery, 'and it was thought certain death to change the underclothes under a week. For a whole week we were obliged to lie on clothes stiff and stained.'[7] And, if the child itself was to be kept in any semblance of cleanliness, several changes of clothing were required, especially if laundry had to wait until the mother could resume her place at the washtub.

Assistance came in the form of the maternity box – Dickens's 'childbedlinen monthly loan society' – a box, bag or basket of clothing and bedding for a newborn child and the expectant mother, lent to poor women at the time of their confinement. Even in 1789, *Instructions for Cutting Out Apparel for the Poor* noted that the maternity box had 'a claim to notice from long experience of its utility'.[8] Two subsequent needlework manuals, the 1808 *Lady's Economical Assistant* and the 1838 *Workwoman's Guide*, also gave instructions for stocking a maternity box (Table 8.1, Columns A, B and C), the half century between the *Instructions* and the *Workwoman's Guide* serving to slightly increase the garments for the mother, but greatly reducing those for the baby.[9] Whereas the 1789 baby

---

[6] Meacham, *A Life Apart*, 70; Jennifer Worth, *Call the Midwife: A True Story of the East End in the 1950s* (London: Phoenix, 2012), p. 12.
[7] Margaret Llewelyn Davies (ed.), *Maternity: Letters from Working Women* (London: Virago, 1984 [1915]), p. 32. The woman appears to be referring to bed sheets, rather than her own clothes, although it is not clear – and even so, lying on filthy sheets for a week would obviously have soiled her own clothes.
[8] Anon., *Instructions for Cutting Out*, p. vii.
[9] In a posthumously published essay, Janet Arnold revealed that the author of *The Lady's Economical Assistant* was Anne Streatfield of 'The Rocks', Uckfield, Sussex. A family tree compiled, and kindly supplied to me, by the late local historian Simon Wright shows that the surname is actually spelled 'Streatfeild', and that the Streatfeilds were an established Sussex family which Anne joined when she married Richard Thomas Streatfeild (the Mr R. T. Streatfeild Arnold was unable to identify) in 1801. Arnold also mentions *Instructions for Cutting Out Apparel for the Poor* as a forerunner of *The Lady's Economical Assistant*. The copy of *Instructions* in the British Library bears the name of its owner, in manuscript, on the title page: Anne Shuttleworth, which, as Wright's family tree also shows, was Anne Streatfeild's maiden name. Since she therefore owned a copy of the *Instructions* at least seven years before publishing *The Lady's Economical Assistant*, it is reasonable to assume that it was both a model for her own book and one she thought would bear improvement. (The possibility that Anne Shuttleworth also wrote the *Instructions* is precluded by the fact that she was only nine years old when it was published.) The later Streatfeilds continued the philanthropic work, Anne's grandson Richard, a churchwarden, being listed as one of the managers of the Uckfield Clothing Society in 1894. Janet Arnold, '*The Lady's Economical Assistant* of 1808', in Burman (ed.), *The Culture of Sewing*, pp. 223–33; ESRO PAR 496/9/3/1, Rules of the Uckfield Clothing Society. For a history of the Streatfeild family see Simon Wright, 'The Streatfeild family and The Rocks estate', *Hindsight*, 6 (2000), 46–61.

Table 8.1. Items for maternity boxes and ladies' infants as stipulated in *Instructions for Cutting Out Apparel for the Poor* (1789), *The Lady's Economical Assistant* (1808) and *The Workwoman's Guide (1838)*

A	B	C	D
Instructions for Cutting Out Apparel for the Poor (1789) MATERNITY BOX	*The Lady's Economical Assistant* (1808) MATERNITY BOX	*The Workwoman's Guide* (1838) MATERNITY BOX	*The Workwoman's Guide* (1838) LADIES' INFANTS
FOR THE BABY:	FOR THE BABY:	FOR THE BABY:	12–18 SHIRTS
6 SHIRTS	4 SHIRTS	3 SHIRTS	2–4 FLANNEL BANDS
6 CAPS	4 CAPS	3 CAPS	2–3 FLANNEL CAPS
6 UNDER CAPS	2 BEDGOWNS	1 FLANNEL CAP	6–12 NIGHT CAPS
2 BEDGOWNS	2 FROCKS	3 NIGHT-GOWNS	3–6 DAY CAPS
2 FROCKS	24 NAPKINS	2 FLANNEL GOWNS	4–6 NAPKINS (DOZENS OF)
24 SQUARES OF DOUBLE DIAPER	2 FLANNEL BLANKETS	12 NAPKINS	4–6 PILCHERS
1¾ YARDS OF WHITE BAIZE FLANNEL	2 ROLLERS	1 FLANNEL BAND	6–12 PINAFORES
	2 PAIR OF STAYS AND FLANNEL COATS	2 SOFT TOWELS	4–6 BEDGOWNS
FOR THE WOMAN:	2 UPPER PETTICOATS	FOR THE WOMAN:	3–4 FIRST DAY-GOWNS
2 SHIFTS		2 SHIFTS	3–4 NIGHT-FLANNELS
2 SKIRTS	FOR THE WOMAN:	2 NIGHT JACKETS	3–4 DAY FLANNELS
1 PAIR OF SHEETS	1 LARGE BEDGOWN	2 CAPS	
2 PILLOW-CASES	2 CALICO NIGHT GOWNS	1 FLANNEL PETTICOAT	1–2 FLANNEL CLOAKS
	2 SKIRTS	1 FLANNEL GOWN (OR SHAWL)	2–3 FLANNEL SHAWLS
	1 PAIR OF SHEETS	1 PAIR OF SHEETS	4–6 ROBES
		1 ROLL OF FLANNEL, 4 BREADTHS LONG, AND ½ YARD DEEP	4–6 PETTICOATS
			4–8 SOCKS
			1 HOOD
			1 CLOAK OR PELISSE

required six shirts, six caps and twenty-four napkins, the 1838 infant apparently needed only half that number.

The Workwoman's Guide also included a list of the garments deemed necessary for ladies' infants (Table 8.1, Column D), recommending a much greater quantity of each item than for the children of the poor – twelve to eighteen shirts rather than three, for example, and four to six dozen napkins instead of twelve. This is partly explained by the fact that laundry was commonly performed only every four or six weeks in wealthy households and so more clothes were needed to ensure a fresh supply between washes. But there is also a whole range of clothing which the child of wealthy parents apparently required, but its poor counterpart did not: separate night and day caps, pilchers (flannel wrappers worn over the napkins), pinafores, a variety of gowns and flannels, cloaks, shawls, robes, petticoats, socks, a hood and a cloak.

Even where the same garments were stipulated, 'the quality of the materials, of course, must differ'. Hence, babies' nappies were to 'be made of soft diaper, or, if for the poor, old sheeting, table-linen, or strong fine linen answers well' – rich babies were to have 'soft' cloth against their tender skin, the poor only 'strong' and possibly recycled. The style of garments also differed for rich and poor, the former to have longer skirts, for example, since those of the 'latter would soon be tumbled and dirty'.[10]

The boxes were to be promptly returned after one month, the contents complete and washed and so ready for the next recipient, but this again raises the question of what constituted 'clean'. One of the great benefits of boxes which contained clothes and bedding for the mother must have been that that they prevented the woman's own clothes and sheets becoming soiled so that they were fit for use after her confinement. The loan items on the other hand, even with careful washing, must have become increasingly stained.

Like the maternity box, the Dorcas society was a long-standing initiative which extended either side of the nineteenth century.[11] 'The Dorcas', and its variations such as the ladies' working party, solicited subscriptions to buy materials to make into clothes for distribution among the poor and was named after a New Testament figure who made clothes for the widows of Joppa. Most societies had honorary members, who provided the money to cover expenses, and working members who undertook to make the garments. The latter met regularly to carry out the work, providing a social opportunity for the 'ladies' as well as clothing for the poor. Many continued year after year, the workers agreeing to produce a minimum quantity of clothing, often one garment a month. Others were temporary institutions established for specified periods. Sydenham, for example, organised working parties which met on each of the five Tuesdays in Lent, producing 166 garments in 1888 for donation to the nearby Bell Green Mission.[12]

[10] A Lady, *The Workwoman's Guide*, pp. 16, 29, 25.
[11] There are still Dorcas societies attached to churches and chapels, especially in America, carrying out a range of charitable work including clothing provision.
[12] LLHAC, A89/98/23, *Sydenham Churches of S. Bartholomew and S. Matthew, Parish Magazine*, April 1888.

While refuges and missions, particularly those in urban areas, solicited old clothing for the poor – St Bartholomew and St Matthew at Sydenham, for example, ran a Depôt for Left Off Clothes – most ladies' clothing charities supplied new garments and mainly of the same serviceable kind issued by the clothing societies.[13] Indeed, there is a remarkable consistency in the garments these organisations supplied to the poor. In 1814 The Ladies' Benevolent Society, Liverpool, purchased calico for shifts, coloured and white flannel, linsey and grogram for petticoats, striped linen and cotton for bedgowns, ginghams for babies' bedgowns, check, diaper and cambric muslin for caps.[14] Nearly eighty years later the organisers of the St Jude's, South Kensington, Dorcas Society were still soliciting contributions of 'flannel, calico, and warm material for frocks and petticoats'.[15]

Women in more affluent areas were encouraged to sew for the poor elsewhere and Gareth Stedman Jones says that from the 1860s onwards, East London 'was a by-word for chronic and hopeless poverty', attracting particular attention.[16] In Shropshire, for instance, the ladies of Whittington formed an East London Working Party.[17] But East London's impoverished pre-eminence provoked rivalry closer to home. At St Mildred's in Lee, Lewisham, for example, collectors of old clothing for the Southwark poor insisted that, 'South London has stronger claims upon us by far than the East End, and it is not known by everybody that in some parts of it the poverty is quite as heartrending.'[18] Junior organisations nurtured juvenile philanthropy, inculcating the duty of care in the next generation of charity workers. Christ Church, Lancaster Gate, was one of many parishes which established a Ministering Children's League to encourage middle-class children to help their poorer neighbours. By the end of its first year, 1885, it had 101 members who had made 'over 400 articles of clothing and amusements' for distribution to 'poor children in various poor parishes of London'.[19]

The evangelical emphasis on self-help is evident in the move made by many ladies' charities from the free distribution of clothing to the

---

[13] *Ibid.*, February 1888.
[14] *The Fifth Annual Report of the Ladies' Benevolent Society, Liverpool* (Liverpool, 1815), p. 9.
[15] *St. Jude's, S. Kensington* [parish magazine], January 1894.
[16] Stedman Jones, *Outcast London*, p. 99.
[17] *The Parish Magazine for Oswestry, Whittington, Moreton, Welsh Frankton, The Lodge, Trefonen and Other Neighbouring Parishes*, March 1885, November 1885, December 1889.
[18] LLHAC, A83/21/91/2, *St. Mildred's, Lee, Parish Magazine and Parochial Record*, December 1890.
[19] LMA, P87/CTC/47, *Christ Church, Lancaster Gate, Parish Magazine*, January 1885, March 1885, June 1885, December 1885; LMA, P87/CTC/60, *Christ Church, Lancaster Gate, Parochial Report*, 1900.

requirement of some financial input, or demonstration of deserving status, on the part of the poor. The maternity box frequently evolved into the Maternity Society which, like clothing societies, required regular contributions from the expectant mother. At Camden Church, Camberwell, for example, mothers in the 1890s were asked to 'lodge weekly sums for their benefit, and when "The Loan Bag" is needed, each depositor receives the total amount she has been able to enter, with a bonus'.[20] Dorcas societies and working parties began to sell the clothing they produced at or around cost price, as opposed to simply giving it away, and purchasers often had to obtain an entrance ticket to the sales from a subscriber or District Visitor. So, in 1899, the District Visitors at St Margaret's, Lee, distributed 805 tickets to the poor to enable them to buy 'at cost price' the produce of the Needlework Society.[21] Several schemes served a dual function by employing the poor to make clothes and then selling them to others at reduced cost. The work was funded by subscribers who could nominate poor women who wished to work.[22]

Unsold clothing was sometimes donated to the sale in a nearby district rather than simply given to the needy. In 1889, for example, the St Augustine's Dorcas Society in Lewisham raised £2 17s. at its Annual Sale, and the unsold work, 'value 13s. 1d., was sent as last year as a donation to the Society at St. Mildred's, and disposed of at their Sale'.[23] By the close of the century even the Ministering Children's League at Christ Church had established a Penny Branch for working-class children, its 206 members meeting fortnightly to 'do various kinds of work for their Stall at the Annual Sale'.[24]

Mothers' meetings

Mothers' meetings were established around mid century and supplied poor women with serviceable materials at a reduced price, which they made up into clothing for their families under the supervision of the lady organisers. Some meetings ran their own clothing society while others accepted payment by instalment for the materials. Camden Church, Camberwell, was typical with members making 'weekly payments for

---

[20] LMA, P73/CAM/105, *Camden Parish Magazine*, July 1891.
[21] LLHAC, A58/18/F2/1, St. Margaret's Lee, District Visiting Society Minute Book, November 1899–December 1933.
[22] See, for example, LMA, P89/ALS/149, *All Souls, Langham Place, Parish Magazine*, December 1892, December 1893; LLHAC, A64/12/290, *St. Philip's, Sydenham* [parish magazine], January 1891, March 1891.
[23] A83/21/91/2, *St. Mildred's, Lee, Parish Magazine*, February 1890.
[24] LMA, P87/CTC/60, *Christ Church, Lancaster Gate, Parochial Report*, 1900.

materials, which are purchased at the Mission Hall, and made up during the meetings or may be taken home when fully paid for'.[25] While the women sewed, one of the ladies read aloud some edifying literature.

The meetings enabled women to do in company necessary work that they might otherwise have had to do in isolation, thereby legitimising social intercourse which in other circumstances might have been regarded as idleness. According to Flora Thompson, the meetings 'were clearing-houses for gossip, but that did not make them less enjoyable'.[26] But Mrs Layton, a member of the Women's Co-operative Guild, where meetings were managed by working women themselves, presents a different viewpoint:

I had attended Mother's Meetings, where ladies came and lectured on the domestic affairs in the workers' homes that it was impossible for them to understand. I have boiled over many times at some of the things I have been obliged to listen to, without the chance of asking a question. In the Guild we always had the chance of discussing a subject.

Angered by the supervisors' patronising attitude, Mrs Layton abandoned the mothers' meetings as did another Guildswoman who did not 'have patience to listen to the simple childish tales that were read... and did not like to feel we had no voice in its control'. Above all she objected to the inability of the 'ladies' to really understand the women's problems, and

the feeling in speaking to the ladies that after consulting this one, that one and somebody else, a little charity might be given – the tradesman perhaps who has always had your custom in better circumstances, he knows all about your business when you present your charity ticket. This sort of thing to honest working people hurts their feelings of independence.[27]

The implication is that the mothers required no moral spur to independence, merely the financial means to achieve it. Nevertheless, there were up to a million regular attendees at mothers' meetings where cheap materials and the opportunity to exchange skills and knowledge boosted family clothing stocks.[28]

Mothers' meetings offered other benefits, such as a Christmas sale of clothes, a provident fund, or an annual treat at which 'valuable parcels

---

[25] LMA, P73/CAM/105, *Camden Parish Magazine*, October 1891.
[26] F. Thompson, *Lark Rise*, p. 433.
[27] Llewelyn Davies, *Life as We Have Known It*, p. 40.
[28] Prochaska, 'A mother's country', 379.

of clothing, household linen & c.', were distributed.[29] The contents of these parcels were donated by well-wishers who may have bought them at the sales of work organised by the ladies' working parties. A sale of work at St Mildred's, Lee, for example, was open not only to the poor themselves, but also to ladies seeking 'suitable and useful... gifts for the poor', especially at Christmas.[30] And those who wished to support their local sale of work, but were unable to produce something themselves, were encouraged to purchase items from clothing stalls at bazaars or other sales of work and donate them to the local sale. So, in 1890, members of the Lancaster Gate Women's Home Mission Association were invited to purchase from the University College Hospital Bazaar items for the Mission's own sale in December.[31]

The parochial clothing charities were, then, not isolated institutions but a network of interrelated and interdependent organisations, and the variety of clothing-related charity that might be found in a single area is demonstrated by the list of 'Classes and Parish Work' in the January 1895 edition of the St Margaret's, Lee, parish magazine. On Monday mornings deposits for the Clothing and Boot Clubs were received at the Parish Room where, in the afternoon, one of two mothers' meetings was held. On Tuesdays 'the Ladies of the Committee of the Needlework Society', which employed poor women to make charity clothing, met to 'superintend the cutting out of the materials, to issue tickets, and to receive back the work'. On Fridays, the Ladies Working Party gathered to make 'useful articles of clothing in aid of Home and Foreign Missions'. St Margaret's also ran a branch of the Girls' Friendly Society which would almost certainly have taught needlework, and finally it lent out maternity bags and welcomed donations of 'cast-off clothing and old linen... as applications are continually being made for each and all of them'.[32]

Although my emphasis has been on Anglican charities, other denominations, including those ministering to immigrant communities, offered similar help with clothing. During the second half of the century the Ladies Clothing Society attached to the Manchester Jews' School provided pupils with clothing twice a year, the gift dependent on the good behaviour of both the pupils and their parents.[33] In East London,

---

[29] LMA, P93/ALL1/15/1, *All Saints, Mile End New Town, Parish Magazine*, December 1886; LLHAC, A83/21/91/2, *St. Mildred's, Lee, Parish Magazine*, January 1881; LMA, P73/CAM/105, *Camden Parish Magazine*, October 1891, February 1892.
[30] LMA, P94/ALL/10, *All Saints, Aden Grove, Green Lanes, Stoke Newington, Parish Magazine*, December 1903.
[31] LMA, P87/CTC/47, *Christ Church, Lancaster Gate, Parish Magazine*, May 1890.
[32] LLHAC, A78/18/J/1, *St. Margaret's, Lee, Parish Magazine*, January 1895.
[33] GMCRO, M 346, Jews' School Ladies' Clothing Society Minute Book 1885–1937.

The Ladies' Society of St George's German Lutheran Church made a winter distribution of clothing to the children of poor families in the 'Little Germany' area of Whitechapel.[34] The Mothers' Meeting at nearby Bethnal Green Road Congregational Church devoted time each week to 'receiving pence on account of material required, and supplying goods for making up' and occasionally held a 'Sale of Garments at low prices'.[35] And the London Wesleyan Mission, Shadwell, distributed old and new clothing, ran sewing classes and employed local poor women to produce clothing as a form of 'Help-myself-Society'.[36] In south London, Madame Cecilia, Religious of St Andrew's Convent, Streatham, extolled the virtues of Roman Catholic mothers' meetings where lectures were given on topics including cutting out and needlework, and which often had 'some provision for selling garments, boots, or materials at reduced prices and by instalments', as well as maternity boxes for loan.[37] Some organisations helped any who came to their door, others only members of their own faith or congregation. A woman who in 1881 made an application for clothing to the District Visitors at the Anglican Emmanuel Church, Maida Hill, for example, was told that being a Roman Catholic, the Roman Catholic Communion should provide for her.[38]

Much charity work was motivated by compassion and a genuine sense of duty or responsibility. It also gave purpose and meaning to the circumscribed lives of many middle- and upper-class women and the transposition of their domestic skills to the wider community offered them participation and influence in the public sphere. But it could also be abused. Joseph Arch, for example, recalled that in his childhood village in the 1830s there was 'a most despotic parson's wife, a kind of would-be lady pope', who 'could be uncommonly nasty when she chose', and who required the poor women of the village to curtsey to her in church before taking their seats. 'You may be pretty certain', said Arch, 'that many of these women did not relish the curtsey-scraping and other humiliations they had to put up with', but a great deal of charity was dispensed from the parsonage and so with 'families to think of, children to feed and clothe somehow; and when so many could not earn a living wage', the

---

[34] THLHLA, TH8662/82, Protocol Book, Society of Ladies for Clothing the Children of Poor German Families, 1868–1883.
[35] THLHLA, W/BGU/8/1/15, 'Mothers' meeting', *The Annual Record for 1890*, p. 20.
[36] Anon. [Peter Thompson], *London Wesleyan Mission, East. Record of Work For 1892–3, With Facts and Incidents* (London: J. & B. Dodsworth, 1893), pp. 33–5, 75–6, inside back cover.
[37] Madame Cecilia, Religious of St. Andrew's Convent, Streatham, *Girls Clubs and Mothers' Meetings* (London: Burns & Oates, 1911), pp. 114–21.
[38] LMA, P89/EMM/7, Emmanuel Church, Northwick Terrace, Maida Hill, District Visitors' Record of Relief Granted 1881–1892.

women curtsied. Arch's mother, however, would not. When the parson's wife demanded that the girls at the village school 'were to have their hair cut round like a basin, more like prison girls than anything else', Mrs Arch refused to have her daughters' hair cut. As a result the family 'never received a farthing's-worth of charity' which was 'given regularly, and as a matter of course, from the rectory to nearly every poor person in the village'.

Arch attributes his mother's defiance to her 'shrewd, strong-willed, and self-reliant' character, which doubtless played a part. But also, Arch's father was in the highly unusual position for a shepherd of owning the house in which the family lived, having inherited it from his coach-builder father. And so while his wages were small and the family suffered periods of privation, ameliorated by his wife taking in laundry, Mrs Arch did not have to accommodate the major expense of rent in her domestic budgeting. Other mothers simply could not afford to offend the parson's wife.

Arch proudly identified with his bold, self-assured mother and was similarly resistant when, as a father himself, he too was faced with a despotic vicar's wife. Around 1860 he took one of his daughters, aged nine, to Warwick market and bought her a beaded hairnet which caught her fancy. She wore it to school, but when the parson's wife visited:

Up she marched to the child and said, 'I shall not allow you to come to school with a hair-net on – we don't allow *poor people's* children to wear hair-nets with beads, and if you dare to come to school this afternoon with that trumpery on, I shall take it off and teach you a lesson.'

She dropped the matter when Arch threatened to summons her.

The parson's wife clearly included Arch among the poor. But as with his mother, Arch's confident defiance rested on his financial position as much as his legal rights, and few agricultural labourers could have afforded the ninepence he had paid for a child's hairnet.[39] Arch may not have been wealthy, but he was an expert hedger and ditcher, a carpenter and roofer in his spare time, and the possessor of a freehold cottage, all of which combined, says Alun Howkins, to give him 'real independence of master and squire'.[40] Thus the family's experiences demonstrate not only the potential for tyrannous self-aggrandisement that charity work offered, and the desire to outlaw the poor's use of 'finery', but also the difficulty of

---

[39] Arch, *From Ploughtail to Parliament*, pp. 7–8, 17–18, 51–2.
[40] Alun Howkins, 'Arch, Joseph (1826–1919)', *Oxford Dictionary of National Biography*, Oxford University Press, 2004, www.oxforddnb.com.

delineating 'the poor', and the intimate relationship between economic independence and personal – sartorial – liberty.

The 1880s: women, charity and civic cooperation

The 1880s were a period of 'social crisis', characterised by economic depression and unemployment, riots and strikes.[41] There was, says Jose Harris, a 'collapse of archaic rural communities, an explosion of migration to great cities, a rapid rise in living standards for those in secure employment', and an extension of the franchise, but also 'increased insecurity and unemployment for a large minority'.[42] Writing in 1945, Helen Lynd described the 1880s as the decade when 'an ideology half a century old yielded to a new phrasing of social problems and an effort to find new paths to their solution'.[43] Charles Booth conducted his mammoth survey of London as public attention was drawn to the extent and perceived dangers of urban poverty by publications like Andrew Mearns' *The Bitter Cry of Outcast London* (1883) and William Booth's *In Darkest England and the Way Out* (1890). Poverty began to be seen not 'as the normal condition of the working population but as a "problem" that was concentrated upon specific social groups and social misfortunes', but with potentially dangerous consequences for 'the wider body politic'.[44]

The result was an impulse 'to improve, reform, rationalize, and revolutionize social institutions and to bring them into harmony with the perceived requirements of the modern world', and charity work was no exception.[45] Janice Helland, for example, has documented the revival in the 1880s of British and Irish home industries in which elite women, rather than making charity goods themselves, trained the poor in craftwork and secured elite commercial markets for their produce so they could earn their own livings.[46] The 1880s also saw the appearance of Needlework Guilds and jumbles sales, both of which aimed to clothe the poor more efficiently than the labour-intensive mothers' meetings, maternity and Dorcas societies, but have been largely ignored by historians.[47]

[41] J. Steele (ed.), *Streets of London*, p. 6.
[42] Harris, *Private Lives, Public Spirit*, pp. 5, 239.
[43] E. P. Hennock, 'Poverty and social theory in England: the experience of the eighteen-eighties', *Social History* 1:1 (1976), 67–91; 68–9.
[44] Harris, *Private Lives, Public Spirit*, p. 239.   [45] *Ibid.*, p. 36.
[46] Helland, *British and Irish Home Arts*, pp. 13–14; Janice Helland, 'Working bodies, Celtic textiles, and the Donegal Industrial Fund 1883–1890', *Textile*, 2:2 (2004), 134–55; 137–8.
[47] Madeleine Ginsburg is the exception. Ginsburg, 'Rags to riches'.

Needlework Guilds continued the practice of making new clothing for the poor, but were organised on a much larger scale than previous clothing charities and separated the work of production and ultimate distribution. And although the aims and operation of Needlework Guilds and the home industries' revival differed, in other respects, as I demonstrate below, they had much in common. Jumble sales remained local, but dealt in used clothing thereby removing the time-consuming work of garment production, and they offered a less paternalistic approach to clothing charity.

Efficiency was necessary because new forms of social and philanthropic work, career opportunities, leisure activities and changing patterns of religious observance were making it increasingly difficult to recruit women to do the more traditional – and, to many, mundane – aspects of charity work such as sewing for the poor. Church attendance fell between the late 1880s and 1914, particularly among middle- and upper-class Anglicans, who had been the key providers of much parish welfare. The reasons for this decline are contested, but Jose Harris believes religion was quickly becoming a more private issue, and Hugh McLeod says that by the early twentieth century many churches were finding it difficult to maintain a wide programme of charitable activities because of a shortage of voluntary workers.[48]

The Church was also facing serious financial challenges. Between the 1830s and 1890s, building construction, maintenance and repair costs, as well as clergy salaries, rose as the number of church buildings increased by over 40 per cent, and the number of beneficed clergymen almost doubled. At the same time, regular guaranteed income was reduced with the abolition of compulsory church rates in 1868 and the removal of pew rents in some churches.[49] Building and maintenance of schools were also expensive priorities, especially when the expansion of non-denominational schools after the 1870 Education Act challenged the Church's educational supremacy. These various economic problems left congregations deep in debt, yet there was no reduction in the lists of parochial charities which, in the face of persistent need, they felt duty-bound to support.[50] It is no surprise that in 1903 Charles Booth noted the frequent references in Church of England reports 'to the

---

[48] Hugh McLeod, *Secularisation in Western Europe, 1848–1914* (Basingstoke: Macmillan, 2000), pp. 199–202; Harris, *Private Lives, Public Spirit*, p. 176.

[49] R. Currie, A. Gilbert and L. Horsley, *Churches and Churchgoers: Patterns of Church Growth in the British Isles Since 1700* (Oxford University Press, 1977), pp. 60, 111, 196–7, 213; Stephen Yeo, *Religion and Voluntary Organisations in Crisis* (London: Croom Helm, 1976), p. 79.

[50] Yeo, *Religion*, pp. 79, 157.

absorption of time in raising funds', which were often required as much for the maintenance of church fabric as for the support of impoverished parishioners.[51]

McLeod cites increased leisure time and activities as a contributory factor to declining middle-class Church attendance. 'Between about 1875 and 1885', he says, 'dinner parties, trips into the country, boating, cycling, golf... began to take up the Sundays of the urban middle class', so that by the 1900s Sunday in England was 'no longer a day dominated by religion'.[52] Women also had many other calls on their time. They were being admitted to higher education, the professions and other employments including clerical work, nursing and teaching. They were serving on School Boards, parish and district councils, as Poor Law Guardians, district and workhouse visitors and rescue workers. Judith Walkowitz identifies 'an army' of middle- and upper-class women 'who went "slumming"', citing Louisa Hubbard's estimate of 20,000 paid, and 500,000 voluntary social workers by the close of the century. Female urban charity workers, says Walkowitz, went 'in search of adventure, self-discovery, and meaningful work'. She describes their experiences in terms of 'interest', 'change', 'excitement', 'power' and 'prestige', while, in contrast, traditional charity workers 'became the object of ridicule and derision as "old maids"'.[53] When, for example, G. K. Chesterton needed a foolproof disguise for a gang of criminals in his 1905 story *The Club of Queer Trades*, he made them members of a Dorcas society: stereotypical black-clad spinsters who looked what 'men of the world would call dowdy', and whose conversation consisted of 'strong and advanced' 'views on the subject of pinafores'.[54]

Needlework Guilds

Needlework Guilds were begun in Dorset in 1882 by 'Giana', Lady Georgiana Wolverton who, being requested to supply clothing for an orphanage, decided to ask her friends to contribute two garments each and to create a supply of clothing 'for free distribution among the hospitals, homes, and poor parishes of the county'. Ginsburg identifies Needlework

---

[51] Booth, *Life and Labour... Third Series: Religious Influences*, vol. VII, p. 82.
[52] Hugh McLeod, *Religion and the People of Western Europe 1789–1989* (Oxford University Press, 1997), p. 115. Jose Harris believes the 'threat to organized religion from the new recreational culture' has been exaggerated, but also notes the 'muted' religious character of Edwardian Sundays. Harris, *Private Lives, Public Spirit*, p. 178.
[53] Walkowitz, *City of Dreadful Delight*, pp. 53–4, 57, 58, 63–8. See also Ross, *Love and Toil*, pp. 15–17.
[54] Denis J. Conlon (ed.), *The Collected Works of G. K. Chesterton VI* (San Francisco: Ignatius Press, 1991), p. 112.

Guilds as the 'most systematic attempt to distribute clothing to the poor', and they were established in Britain, North America and parts of Europe.[55] The Guilds supplied the utilitarian garments characteristic of Victorian charity clothing, the Middlesex Guild, for example, reminding members that underclothing for women and girls was to be 'neat and plain, and without lace trimmings'.[56] But the Guilds differed from the existing local clothing charities, which they aimed to supplement, not supplant, in several respects. First, rather than supplying the poor directly, their chief object was to provide clothing 'to ministers of denominations, town missionaries, the managers of hospitals, orphanages, and nursing societies' – in effect, welfare professionals, who would then distribute the clothing to individual recipients.[57] Second, they were established on a county or borough basis, rather than the parochial focus of most clothing charities. Third, donors could make the clothing at home when it suited them (and possibly with the aid of a sewing machine), or buy it, rather than attending a regular working party. Fourth, the Guilds were (ostensibly) non-denominational and, finally, they required members to supply just two garments, and no subscriptions, each year, despite which they operated on a vast scale.[58] The Middlesex Needlework Guild, for example, collected 20,115 garments in 1897, which it distributed in just over 100 grants to parishes, missions, hospitals, orphanages, almshouses and other homes, rescue and maternity societies, across London and Surrey.[59]

Although, therefore, the Needlework Guilds continued the tradition of elite women supply clothing for the poor, they did so much more efficiently than most previous schemes and were, to a great extent, a reaction against probably the best-known of nineteenth-century female charity events: the bazaar. Organised by middle- and upper-class women, who also made the majority of the trinkets and novelties on sale, bazaars became a popular fund-raiser from the 1820s.[60] Although they continued

---

[55] Ginsburg, 'Rags to riches', 129; Burke MacArthur, *United Littles: The Story of the Needlework Guild of America* (New York: Coward-McCann, 1955), pp. 21–7.
[56] LMA, P83/MRK/109/43, Middlesex Needlework Guild. Rules. (1897) p. 5.
[57] 'Birmingham and District Needlework Guild', *Birmingham Daily Post*, 17 October 1885, p. 7. Branch secretaries did sometimes distribute clothing to poor individuals in their locality, but this was not the Guilds' purpose.
[58] Lady Wolverton in fact originally asked members to provide between two and six garments a year, but two soon became standard. According to Burke MacArthur, the rationale for this was that recipients would have 'one to wear and one to wash'. *The Standard*, 16 October 1882, p. 3; MacArthur, *United Littles*, p. 28.
[59] LMA, P83/MRK/109/42, Middlesex Needlework Guild. Report for 1897 (1897), pp. 10–14.
[60] Whitlock, *Crime, Gender*, p. 61.

throughout the century, Prochaska notes that '*The Times*, the best guide to the most fashionable fancy fairs in London', advertised twenty-one bazaars in 1875, but only sixteen in 1895. He attributes the reduction to increased advertising in local newspapers at the expense of *The Times*, but even taking into account those advertised in the local press he discusses very few after 1875.[61] Bazaars, says Tammy Whitlock, were 'expected to have a certain scale of grandeur and spectacle'.[62] This emphasis on materialism and display attracted criticism, and as Alice Taylor's examination of the Boston Antislavery Bazaar reveals, although it was an annual event the range of activities required for its successful execution stretched across the entire year, and could be time-consuming and exhausting.[63] It was, an inaugural newspaper announcement explained, with the intention 'to wean women from the habit of doing useless fancy work, and to direct their industry into a better channel' and tap into 'a rich mine of mis-applied energy', that Lady Wolverton devised the Dorset Needlework Guild:

The knitting of a pair of stockings for a deserving old man will not occupy half the time required to crochet an elaborate antimacassar, and will be considerably more useful; a warm petticoat, capable of imparting almost endless comfort to an aged sister, will be a far less tedious task than the 'stitch, stitch, stitch' of a couple of yards of embroidery.[64]

But if bazaars wasted women's time in the production of unnecessary fancy goods, they also provided them with the experience in business, organisation and management necessary to run an enterprise on the scale of the Needlework Guilds.[65]

The Birmingham and District Needlework Guild will serve to illustrate in a little more detail the scope and nature of the operations and ambitions of the Guilds and their managers. It was established in 1883 and 'increased very rapidly'. Donors sent their garments to local branch collectors who forwarded them to regional centres which, in turn, forwarded them to the central Guild. By 1891 the Birmingham Guild had

---

[61] Prochaska, *Women and Philanthropy*, pp. 49, 50–2.
[62] Whitlock, *Crime, Gender*, p. 56.
[63] *Ibid.*, p. 61; Julie Roy Jeffrey, '"Stranger, buy... lest our mission fail:" the complex culture of women's abolitionist fairs', *American Nineteenth Century History*, 4:1 (2003), 1–24; 11–15; Alice Taylor, '"Fashion has extended her influence to the cause of humanity": the transatlantic female economy of the Boston Antislavery Bazaar', in Beverly Lemire (ed.), *The Force of Fashion in Politics and Society: Global Perspectives from Early Modern to Contemporary Times* (Farnham: Ashgate, 2010), pp. 115–42; pp. 119–20, 125.
[64] *Sheffield and Rotherham Independent*, 21 October 1882, p. 12.
[65] A. Taylor, 'Fashion has extended', p. 136.

nine centres which that year collected 34,261 garments and during its first eleven years it collected and distributed nearly a quarter of a million garments.[66]

The 'giant proportions' of the Birmingham Guild's work were something of which its Council was proud and jealous. Noting in 1886 that the London Guild had grown bigger than Birmingham, which had been the largest, the latter stated its intention of regaining and ever retaining the lead. The Honorary Secretary considered that the Guild, 'ought never to be contented until every woman and girl in Birmingham who could sew had promised to make two garments each year'.[67] When Lady Newport, the President, received a letter from Lady Wolverton proposing to start a Warwickshire Guild, the response was that 'a rival guild so very near to their own would be a very great mistake' and that the Birmingham Guild was in any case planning to extend its own reach to incorporate 'the three surrounding counties', which it soon did.[68]

Needlework Guilds wished their clothing to go to the 'deserving', but their role as intermediary bodies meant they had only limited powers to ensure this. Lady Newport, for example, 'expressed a hope that the clergy and the authorities of the institutions who received grants would make the best use of the garments', intimating that, in her opinion, they had not always done so. Similarly, she urged branch secretaries who gave clothing to individuals, 'not to give away their things in a hurry, but to keep them until they were quite sure of having discovered recipients who needed and would appreciate them'. Hearing that Guild clothing had been pawned, Birmingham also marked all its clothing with a Guild stamp and enlisted the help of the Chief Constable to encourage pawnbrokers to refuse pledges of stamped clothing.[69]

Ginsburg claims that the Guilds were '[n]on-sectarian and classless', but they had a Christian – and sometimes Anglican – bias.[70] Lady Newport, for example, told the members that an organisation like the Guild would be needed 'so long as this world lasted' because: 'Was it not said nearly two thousand years ago by their Blessed Lord, "The poor ye have always with you"?' And while the Mayor of Birmingham, in 1891, insisted that '[r]eligious and political differences were unknown'

---

[66] *Birmingham Daily Post*, 17 October 1885, p. 7; 18 October 1886, p. 5; 2 November 1891, p. 4; 30 October 1893, p. 3.
[67] *Birmingham Daily Post*, 18 October 1886, p. 5.
[68] *Birmingham Daily Post*, 17 October 1887, p. 7; *Birmingham Daily Post*, 15 October 1889, p. 7.
[69] *Birmingham Daily Post*, 14 October 1890, p. 7; *Birmingham Daily Post*, 30 October 1893, p. 3.
[70] Ginsburg, 'Rags to riches', 129.

in the Guild, his claim was somewhat undermined by a statement that 'the Nonconformist branch at Dudley had withdrawn from the guild'.[71] The formation, in 1886, of a national Catholic Needlework Guild, also indicates denominational divisions.[72] And while the Birmingham Guild 'implored each secretary... never to feel satisfied until every woman of every class in her district belongs to it', members were expected to provide the materials for the garments they made which excluded poorer women from membership.[73] Similarly exclusive was the suggestion that the money for materials be raised by members keeping a money-box, 'into which each of their gentlemen friends should be asked to put a shilling or more'.[74]

The success of Needlework Guilds was largely reliant on the involvement of aristocratic women. In the 1887 Birmingham Needlework Guild report, for example, a resolution proposed by Lady Newport was seconded by Lady Dudley, and a vote of thanks to the four general secretaries, who included the Hon. Mrs Henley Eden, was proposed by Lady Peel and seconded by the Hon. Mrs Calthorpe.[75] Aristocratic patronage was also a key characteristic of the home industries revival and Helland points out that although the hands-on organisation of the 1886 Highland Home Industries and Arts exhibition in Golspie was mostly done by local middle-class women, it was the name of Anne, Duchess of Sutherland, who opened the exhibition, that 'provided the exhibition's cachet and attracted wealthy aristocratic patrons'.[76] Similarly, the Birmingham Needlework Guild was founded by Mrs Henry Edmunds, who became its Secretary, and the vast majority of its members were middle class.[77] But it is Lady Newport, as President, whose name recurs throughout newspaper reports of the Guild's activities, who opened the annual meetings, who read messages from the Mayor, who announced the numbers of garments received and branches formed, and who urged the members to greater achievements.

The role of philanthropy in providing women with a political voice and political influence has long been established. Clare Midgley, for example, has demonstrated how, from the late eighteenth century, as

---

[71] *Birmingham Daily Post*, 2 November 1891, p. 4; *Birmingham Daily Post*, 30 October 1893, p. 3.
[72] Catholic Needlework Guild, *Twenty-Second Annual Report of the Portsmouth Diocesan Division* (Portsmouth, 1908).
[73] *Birmingham Daily Post*, 18 October 1886, p. 5.
[74] *Birmingham Daily Post*, 30 October 1893, p. 3.
[75] *Birmingham Daily Post*, 17 October 1887, p. 7.
[76] Janice Helland, 'Rural women and urban extravagance in late nineteenth-century Britain', *Rural History*, 13:2 (2002), 179–97; 188.
[77] *Birmingham Daily Post*, 17 October 1885, p. 7.

part of the domestication and feminisation of the anti-slavery campaign, women harnessed female control of the domestic budget to boycott the purchase of slave-produced sugar.[78] In the 1880s new philanthropic initiatives continued to provide elite women with a presence in the political sphere at both national and local levels. Helland shows, for example, how Lady Aberdeen used costumes purchased from Celtic Revival industries to demonstrate her support for Irish Home Rule.[79] In Birmingham, Lady Newport forged an increasingly intimate relationship between the Needlework Guild and the civic authorities to become closely, and publicly, aligned with local politics. In 1885 the Mayor permitted the Guild to hold its annual meetings at the town Council House and to use two rooms as a sorting and distribution depot. By 1889 the Mayor was actually attending the annual meeting, together with the chairman of the Health Committee (the borough hospital having been a beneficiary of the Guild's clothing grants) and the Town Clerk, and the Mayor's attendance (or apologies) became customary thereafter. But a major coup occurred in 1891 when the annual meeting, previously held in the drawing room of the Council House, moved to the Council Chamber and after the Mayor had opened the proceedings 'Viscountess NEWPORT then took the mayoral chair, which was vacated by his Worship'. Thus, in a series of steps, reported in the main Birmingham newspaper 'renowned for its large readership, liberal values and its role in fostering civic pride', the separation between civic duty and private charity dissolved, propelling Lady Newport into the very seat of local government.[80]

Jumble sales[81]

Ginsburg argues that the rise of self-help led to the appearance of jumble sales and the demise of Needlework Guilds.[81] But in fact Needlework

---

[78] Clare Midgley, 'Slave sugar boycotts, female activism and the domestic base of British anti-slavery culture' *Slavery and Abolition*, 17:3 (1996), 137–62; 143. See also, Whitlock, *Crime, Gender*, p. 67; Jeffrey, 'Stranger, buy...', 2–3; A. Taylor, 'Fashion has extended', pp. 121, 123.

[79] Janice Helland, 'Embroidered spectacle: Celtic Revival as aristocratic display', in Betsey Taylor FitzSimon and James H. Marphy (eds), *The Irish Revival Reappraised* (Dublin: Four Courts Press, 2004), pp. 94–105. For female philanthropy in the craft revival movement as a means of political participation, see also A. Anderson, 'Victorian high society', p. 316.

[80] *Birmingham Daily Post*, 17 October 1885, p. 7; *Birmingham Daily Post*, 15 October 1889, p. 7; *Birmingham Daily Post*, 2 November 1891, p. 4; 'Birmingham Daily Post', *19th Century British Library Newspapers*, 0-find.galegroup.com.catalogue.ulrls.lon.ac.uk/.

[81] Earlier extended versions of this discussion on jumble sales appear in Vivienne Richmond, 'Rubbish or riches? Church jumble sale purchases in late-Victorian England', *Journal of Historical Research in Marketing* 2:3 (2010), 327–41; Vivienne Richmond, 'The English Church jumble sale: parochial charity in the modern age', in Ilja Van Damme and Jon Stobart (eds), *Modernity and the Second-Hand Trade: European Consumption*

The 1880s: women, charity and civic cooperation   231

Guilds and jumble sales flourished simultaneously and the ideology of self-help long predated both. Ginsburg also cites the *Oxford English Dictionary* which gives 1898 as the first use of the term 'jumble sale'.[82] But the earliest sale I have traced was a decade earlier, in 1888, in the south London parish of St Mary Newington and the reader familiarity assumed in the report of the sale suggests it was not St Mary's first.[83] In 1891, the editor of an Essex magazine, fearing that 'readers may not know what a Jumble sale is', felt it necessary to 'just mention' that it was 'a sale of disused articles of clothing, &c., which the working classes are glad to purchase'.[84] But the following year, although an illustration in the *Graphic* (Fig. 8.1) described jumbles sales as 'A new way of raising money for charitable purposes', the accompanying article said they had already:

come to be a recognised institution in parish work, and in many instances to be as highly appreciated an adjunct to Church work as the mother's meeting or the boot and blanket club itself.[85]

By the mid 1890s, from Sussex to Lancashire via Essex, Middlesex, Berkshire, Warwickshire, the West Midlands, Worcestershire, Shropshire and Staffordshire, people were collecting, sorting and ticketing for the annual jumble sale.[86] And while Ginsburg is right to state that the jumble sale was 'quick to develop once its advantages were recognized', she thought it had been initially 'slow to catch on' in the country, whereas my research, based primarily on Anglican parish magazines, found jumble sales were equally popular, almost from the outset, in both urban and rural areas.[87]

Most jumble sales offered a range of household goods as well as clothing, but invariably clothes and footwear formed the bulk of the items on

Cultures and Practices 1700–1900 (Basingstoke: Palgrave Macmillan, 2010), pp. 242–58, reproduced with permission of Palgrave Macmillan.

[82] Ginsburg, 'Rags to riches', 130.
[83] *St. Mary Newington Parish Magazine*, October 1888.
[84] *Loughton Parish Magazine*, December 1891.
[85] 'At a jumble sale', *Graphic*, 19 November 1892, p. 616.
[86] ESRO, PAR 342/7/1/5, *Forest Row Parish Magazine*, December 1894; MALS, L108/1/23, *Emmanuel Parish Magazine*, January 1897; *Loughton Parish Magazine*, December 1891; *Pinner Parish Magazine*, April 1895; *Old Windsor Banner*, December 1895; *The Alscot Magazine*, July 1896; *St. Paul's, Balsall Heath, Parish Magazine*, January 1894; *Evesham Parish Magazine*, June 1896; *The Parish Magazine for Oswestry*, February 1895; *Kinver Parish Magazine*, January 1896. Other London sales can be found, for example, in, LMA, P89/ALS/149, *All Souls, Langham Place, Parish Magazine*, May 1892; *St. Luke's, Camberwell Parish Magazine*, July 1894; LMA, P95/ALL2/29, *All Saints, Clapham Park, Church Magazine*, February 1894; *S. Jude's Whitechapel* [parish magazine], October 1892; *St. Jude's, S. Kensington*, [parish magazine], April 1894; *S. James'* [Euston] *Parish Magazine*, August 1896.
[87] Ginsburg, 'Rags to riches', 130–31.

Fig. 8.1. E. F. Brewtnall, 'A Jumble Sale: A New Way of Raising Money for Charitable Purposes', *Graphic* 1892.

sale and were first on the list of requested donations. Camden Church was sure that:

> Friends returning from their holidays will doubtless find many ARTICLES OF WEARING APPAREL which though useless now to them may be just the thing a poorer neighbour needs and will gladly pay a trifle for.
>
> BOOTS, 'however old are better than none,' and these are therefore useful for our purpose...
>
> BOYS' AND MENS CLOTHING are a great boon to our poor, so are also pieces of OLD CARPET and OIL CLOTH.[88]

Jumble sales, in selling goods to the poor rather than simply giving them free of charge, were self-help initiatives. One vicar spoke for many when he claimed that the articles by 'the mere fact of being *bought* were probably valued more than they would be if *given*', articulating the belief that the moral and material elevation of the poor was to be achieved through their own financial investment.[89] But according to the report in a Clapham parish magazine, a jumble sale benefited not only the poor, but everyone involved in its production and beyond:

> It is not often that anything gives such general gratification as this Sale has done; the donors of the various articles are glad, for they have freed their houses from things which they did not want; the purchasers are pleased, for they got at a low price things which are useful to them, and the School Managers are grateful, for £33 is a most acceptable addition to our School Funds.[90]

Donors, buyers, the local school would all gain from the simple process of gathering and selling second-hand items.

Jumbles sales were, as one report noted, 'a really "economic" method of helping the poor'.[91] Unlike bazaars, maternity and Dorcas societies, there were no goods to be produced and therefore no capital was required to purchase items or materials as doles or for resale. They were also efficient. Donations could be solicited by a simple appeal in the parish magazine, perhaps followed up with a distribution of handbills, and most organisers asked donors to bring contributions to a central collection point, often the sale venue. All that remained was the sorting, pricing and actual sale of the goods.[92] The profits from jumble sales were applied to a variety of causes including mission-room and parish-nurse funds. But the church itself was also a major beneficiary as at Whitchurch, Warwickshire,

[88] LMA, P73/CAM/105, *Camden Parish Magazine*, August 1893.
[89] LLHAC, A83/21/91/2, *St. Mildred's, Lee, Parish Magazine*, December 1890.
[90] LMA, P95/PAU 1/25, *St Paul, Clapham* [parish magazine], May 1892.
[91] LMA, P79/MTW/43, *St. Matthew's, Upper Clapton, Service Paper*, April 1892.
[92] LMA, P92/TRI/75, *Holy Trinity, Southwark, Parish Magazine*, April 1896.

where the proceeds were shared between 'The East Window, the Clock, [and] the Parish Library'.[93] And so instead of being a drain on parochial finances, jumble sales actually made money for the Church. This was a significant factor, given the financial challenges it was facing, although it seems to have placed the Church in competition with its impoverished parishioners. Indeed, one Dorset appeal for donations for a jumble sale, the proceeds of which were to be devoted to repair of the church's 'Tower Pinnacles', went so far as to cast the churchwardens – charged with raising the necessary funds – as the 'deserving poor'. Although the tone was tongue in cheek, and relied on readers' existing knowledge that jumble sales provided material aid to the needy, the parish poor received no mention in the appeal at all.[94]

Prochaska dismisses jumble sales as 'inferior bazaars'. Certainly, the two were very different. Bazaars focused on new goods, sold to the middle and upper classes, and usually offered an array of refreshment stalls and side shows to induce customers to linger.[95] Jumble sales sold secondhand items to the poor, only occasionally offered refreshments or other attractions and numerous reports of the stalls being 'cleared in about half-an-hour' noted the swiftness of the proceedings.[96] However, jumble sales and local bazaars made comparable profits but with the former requiring considerably less effort. The average takings at fifty-six jumble sales held between 1889 and 1901, reported in the parish magazines I examined, were around £21.[97] In comparison, Prochaska found that a provincial bazaar might expect to make about £27, with some raising less than £2.[98]

Jumble sales, like bazaars, were organised predominantly by women – the 'energetic Committee of twelve ladies' who 'arranged and conducted' a Staffordshire sale was typical – and, as with the Needlework Guilds, the experience of organising a bazaar equipped many women to organise a jumble sale.[99] Alice Taylor described the cooperation between British and American women which resulted in shiploads of donated goods for the

---

[93] *Aldenham Parish Magazine*, March 1898–December 1907. *The Alscot Magazine*, September 1897.
[94] DHC, PE/SH/CW/4/4/20, 'Notice for a rummage sale to pay for the repair of the tower pinnacles', Sherborne Parish, 1889.
[95] Prochaska, *Women and Philanthropy*, pp. 47, 59–61.
[96] LMA, P95/ALL2/29, *All Saints, Clapham Park, Church Magazine*, July 1898.
[97] It is not always clear whether the sums declared are takings or profits. Where both are stated, net profits have been used for the calculation.
[98] Prochaska, *Women and Philanthropy*, pp. 50–1, 53. The figure of £27 is calculated by dividing £28,817 by 1,083, the latter being the number of fancy sales at which the former was raised.
[99] *Kinver Parish Magazine*, January 1896.

Boston anti-slavery bazaars leaving British ports in the 1840s and 1850s, and transatlantic exchange is also evident in the early jumble sales which were often called by other names including rummage sale, American Fair and Grand American Rummage Sale.[100] Indeed, bazaars and jumble sales were sufficiently connected to sometimes be held in conjunction. All Saints', South Acton, advertised 'The Afternoon and Jumble Sale', with the former, held at the time when middle-class women paid social calls, designed to dispose of a number of items left over from a recent bazaar. The Jumble Sale, in contrast, opened at 7.30 p.m. – the close of the working day – and was 'a splendid and advantageous... opportunity for getting rid of old clothes of all descriptions and much that is ordinarily termed rubbish'.[101]

One of the chief leisure activities that drew women away from traditional charity work was shopping. Brian Nelson even goes so far as to claim that shopping functioned 'in the same way that the Church had previously done, by providing women with a haven outside the home, in which to sit, think, and find solace'.[102] But Judith Walkowitz aligns London shopping with philanthropic 'slumming' rather than meditative escapism. Access to both the West End shops and East End poor 'depended on new public services and transportation that facilitated the movement of respectable women across urban spaces', and Walkowitz says that some middle-class women viewed charity work and shopping as appropriate and 'roughly equivalent recreational activities'.[103] The jumble sale may also have been associated with the rise of shopping as a leisure activity, and in particular department stores, which multiplied from the 1870s.[104] With their focus on fashion and novelty, department stores encouraged a culture of consumption and, therefore, attracted criticism from moralists.[105] But if buying a new item released its predecessor

---

[100] A. Taylor, 'Fashion has extended', p. 133; *The Parish Magazine for Oswestry*, December 1892; LMA, P73/CAM/105, *Camden Parish Magazine*, January 1893, May 1893, January 1894, April 1894. Jumble sales are still known as rummage sales in America.
[101] LMA, DRO/056/028, *All Saints, South Acton, Church Monthly*, March 1898.
[102] Rachel Bowlby, *Just Looking: Consumer Culture in Dreiser, Gissing and Zola* (London: Methuen, 1985), pp. 4, 19. Brian Nelson, 'Introduction', in Émile Zola, *The Ladies' Paradise* (Oxford University Press, 1998), p. xvii; Also, for the department store as a social space for women see Wilson, *Adorned in Dreams*, p. 150.
[103] Walkowitz, *City of Dreadful Delight*, pp. 46, 47, 49, 53.
[104] There is disagreement about what constitutes a department store and consequently the precise date of its first appearance. P. Horn, *Behind the Counter: Shop Lives from Market Stall to Supermarket* (Stroud: Sutton Publishing Ltd, 2006), pp. 101–2; Erika Diane Rappaport, *Shopping for Pleasure: Women in the Making of London's West End* (Princeton, NJ and Woodstock, UK: Princeton University Press, 2000), p. 29.
[105] Nelson, 'Introduction', p. xi; Bowlby, *Just Looking*, p. 3. For a full discussion of women and shopping, see Rappaport, *Shopping for Pleasure*.

to the jumble sale there was justification for a purchase. This kind of philosophy even permeated jumble sale appeals. The parish magazine for Alderminster, Warwickshire, in 1897 urged readers to 'give the tradesman a chance, and your poorer neighbours an opportunity', by parting with an unused item rather than keeping it in case of future need.[106]

The expansion of women's activities, whether for work or pleasure, also risked exposing them to the accusation that they were neglecting their domestic duties. The Anglican Church, says Brian Heeney, repeatedly cited the home as 'woman's appointed sphere', particularly during the last quarter of the century and beyond when female emancipation appeared to threaten family life.[107] Jumble sales were an opportunity to show that the threat was unfounded. By the simple act of clearing out and donating unwanted articles – which might include taking them to the collection point and being seen to do so, or discussing with others what had been found and disposed of – women could publicly demonstrate that they were still attending to their housekeeping.

Jumble sales, then, offered several potential benefits to organisers, but what of the poor? The illustration of a Halifax sale in the *Graphic* article shows a busy, crowded event with an array of articles on offer, the 'lady' assistants in their bonnets and bustles clearly distinguishable from the female customers in their northern shawls (Fig. 8.1).[108] A Camberwell parish magazine was far from atypical when it reported 'the avidity with which men, women, and children contended for possession of the goods and chattels which covered the tables' and the 'crowds flocking in' to its 1893 jumble sale.[109] Only occasionally is such anecdotal hyperbole supplemented by more statistical accounts, but where these exist they tend to support the claims. *The Alscot Magazine*, for instance, which covered five rural Warwickshire parishes across a four-mile swathe, reported that 'at least 260 persons passed [through] the gates' of the July 1896 Whitchurch Rummage Sale.[110] The Census shows that in 1891 Whitchurch had a population of 194, which by 1901 had shrunk to 175, so the sale must have attracted customers from neighbouring villages.[111] Furthermore, one of those villages held its own sale just two months after the Whitchurch event and in most cases, as in

---

[106] *Alscot Magazine*, August 1897.
[107] Brian Heeney, *The Women's Movement in the Church of England 1850–1930* (Oxford University Press, 1988), pp. 9–10, 15–16.
[108] Note also the clogs of the man on the right trying on the coat which is much too large for him.
[109] LMA, P73/CAM/105, *Camden Parish Magazine*, May 1893.
[110] *Alscot Magazine*, July 1896.
[111] *Census of England and Wales, 1891, Area Houses and Population, Vol. I, Administrative and Ancient Counties* (London: HMSO, 1893), p. 367; *Index to the Population Tables for*

the Alscot parishes, the sale was repeated at least annually.[112] The fact that customers were willing to pay an entrance fee – usually 1d. – further testifies to the sales' appeal and utility. However, while this modest fee helped to maximise profits, it would have been sufficient to exclude the very poorest who were perhaps those most in need of the goods on offer.

Presumably the style, quality, condition and price of the clothes were attractions, although reliable evidence of these is scarce. But in contrast with so many other clothing charities, there appears to have been no attempt to prohibit 'finery', and while the sorting and pricing process might have provided an opportunity to remove 'unsuitable' items, there is nothing to indicate that this occurred. A minority of sales restricted admission to local residents who were probably known to the organisers, distributed entrance tickets to specific individuals, such as members of Mothers' Meetings, or reserved 'the right of refusing to anyone, (1) admission, and (2) sales, without assigning any reason'.[113] The stated purpose of these restrictions was to prevent entrance by second-hand dealers, although clearly they could have been used to bar anyone the organisers deemed undesirable. But there is no evidence of parallels with the clothing societies' overt attempts to regulate moral behaviour through the exclusion of drinkers or unmarried mothers.

The evangelical ideology which accepted the social hierarchy and deemed different types of possessions appropriate for the different classes, was declining at the end of the century, replaced by 'religious liberalism'.[114] The Christian Socialist revival argued that poverty was a social problem, not the result of personal sin. Its practitioners were relatively few and generally with '"advanced" socialist or left-wing liberal views', but they included many senior clerics and were influential. The result, says Gerald Parsons, was that by 1900 the Church was much less concerned about social control.[115] As Charles Booth put it: 'The Evangelical body within the Church of England has fallen on difficult times... The general movement of taste and habit in religion, as well as in life generally, has been in the direction of greater brightness.'[116] David Garland highlights the 'practicable socialism' of the university settlement

---

England and Wales in the County Volumes of the Census Report, 1901 (London: HMSO, 1903), p. 271.

[112] *Alscot Magazine*, November 1896, June 1897, August 1897.

[113] *Aldenham Parish Magazine*, July 1899; *Pinner Parish Magazine*, April 1895, December 1897; LMA, P95/ALL2/29, *All Saints, Clapham Park, Church Magazine*, May 1898.

[114] McLeod, *Religion*, pp. 113, 115.

[115] Gerald Parsons (ed.), *Religion in Victorian Britain*, vol. II (Manchester University Press, 1988), pp. 51–2, 55, 60.

[116] Booth, *Life and Labour... Third Series: Religious Influences*, vol. VII, p. 53.

movement, which also began in the 1880s and aimed to 'bind classes by friendship'.[117] 'Like male socialists and New Liberals', says Walkowitz, some female philanthropists 'came to reject a view of poverty as moral failure in favor of a more structural explanation, focused on unemployment, underemployment, and insufficient wages'.[118] They also looked increasingly to the state to take action, with philanthropy, says Brian Harrison, 'losing its plausibility as an over-all national solution to social problems'.[119]

This is not to claim that paternalism and deference had vanished, swept aside by an all-consuming spirit of egalitarianism; the very fact that jumble sales were organised by the wealthy for the poor indicates the continuance of 'them and us' in the social order. And in contrast to the self-congratulatory reports in the parish magazines, Robert Tressell's account of the jumble sale – portrayed through fiction but reflecting the author's very real anger at the social divide – presented it as one of 'the farcical, imbecile measures' by which

well-to-do inhabitants and the local authorities attempted – or rather, pretended – to grapple with the poverty 'problem'... On the day of the sale the parish room was... filled with all manner of rubbish, with the parson and the visiting ladies grinning in the midst.[120]

Perhaps, then, the poor quality of much jumble-sale merchandise obviated the need for censorship. While St Paul's Balsall Heath noted that 'kind friends sent us much good clothing', many appeals for donations emphasised quantity rather than quality.[121] Camberwell was far from unique when it claimed that 'anything and everything, broken or bent, worn or torn, old or new, will sell'.[122] Organisers determined the utility of second-hand items in clear class terms. In Loughton, for example, the parish magazine delineated the benefits to be gained from a forthcoming sale: '*first*, it will enable many of our parishioners to clear out of their houses a good deal of old rubbish; *secondly*, it will be a great benefit to our poorer brethren in giving them an opportunity of purchasing at a very small cost many useful things'.[123] There appears to have been some form of alchemy in process transforming, in the space of two phrases, 'rubbish' into 'useful things'.

---

[117] David Garland, *Punishment and Welfare: A History of Penal Strategies* (Aldershot: Gower, 1985), p. 121.
[118] Walkowitz, *City of Dreadful Delight*, p. 55.   [119] Harrison, *Peaceable Kingdom*, p. 256.
[120] Robert Tressell, *The Ragged Trousered Philanthropists* (Oxford University Press, 2005 [1914]), p. 345.
[121] *St. Paul's Balsall Heath Parish Magazine*, January 1894.
[122] *St. Luke's Camberwell, Parish Magazine*, July 1894.
[123] *Loughton Parish Magazine*, December 1891.

Also, despite the 'thirst for fashion' and novelty encouraged by department stores, less affluent middle-class women extended their budgets by buying and selling used clothes, rather than simply giving them away, and renovating garments to lengthen their use.[124] The condition of garments by the time they reached the jumble sale may, therefore, have left much to be desired. The thirteen budgets for the 'minimum necessary annual cost of clothing' for a working-class woman collected by Rowntree, and discussed in Chapter 2, each allowed for only one dress and in four instances this was bought at a jumble sale.[125] These dresses were for everyday wear which, as Maud Pember Reeves discovered, claimed very low priority in the household budget and could be extremely shabby.

Six of the remaining nine dresses in Rowntree's budgets were described as 'second-hand', which may simply indicate the different terminology the contributors used, or may denote their differentiation between jumble sale goods and those obtained from other second-hand outlets. If the latter, it is difficult to determine the basis of the differentiation, but price does not appear to be a key factor. The four jumble sale dresses each cost between 4s. 6d. and 7s. 6d., compared with between 4s. 6d. and 8s. 6d. for the other second-hand ones. A more noticeable contrast is between all the second-hand dresses and the remaining three, each of which were new and cost 10s. 0d.[126]

In fourteen of Rowntree's fifteen budgets for men's everyday clothing, the coats, vests and some trousers are 'second-hand'.[127] There is no mention of jumble sales, although many of the sales' requests for donations specifically included men's clothing. Perhaps no jumble sales were held when these men required clothing, or the second-hand clothes included jumble-sale purchases, because according to Arthur Harding, whose mother used to steal clothing from church jumble sales to sell to second-hand dealers, men's clothing was 'very saleable', and the fact that organisers tried to exclude second-hand dealers also testifies to the clothing's resale value. However, while Harding said that 'good children's clothes', like men's garments, 'were worth money', his mother 'didn't trouble about women's clothes at all'.[128] It is not clear whether this was because of their poor quality, or because the low priority of women's clothing meant there was little market for it.

---

[124] Joanne Entwistle, *The Fashioned Body: Fashion, Dress and Modern Social Theory* (Cambridge: Polity Press, 2000), pp. 131–2, 232–4; Barbara Burman, 'Made at home by clever fingers: home dressmaking in Edwardian England', in Burman (ed.), *The Culture of Sewing*, pp. 33–53; pp. 40–1.
[125] Rowntree, *Poverty*, pp. 395–6.   [126] *Ibid.*, pp. 55, 395–6.   [127] *Ibid.*, pp. 393–4.
[128] Samuel, *East End Underworld*, p. 25.

Rowntree's budgets aside, there is little specific information on the price of jumble sale goods. Most reports comment only on the 'merely nominal' or 'very low prices', which are reflected in the sales' modest profits.[129] Oral evidence gathered by Ginsburg, who points out the comparatively high cost of women's second-hand clothing in Rowntree's budgets, revealed jumble sales to be 'a staple of parish life' at the turn of the century and 'the prices in pence rather than shillings'.[130] It is also not clear how, and by whom, prices were set. Although advance pricing by the organisers seems to have been common there was also the possibility of on-the-spot negotiation.

While jumble sales appear to have been eagerly attended, there is no evidence that the poor preferred them to other second-hand outlets. Jumble sales may simply have extended the range of used-good markets, rather than offering better quality, variety or prices which probably varied between and within jumble sales. And even if jumble sales were preferred, the ability to buy clothes from them probably often rested largely on one occurring at the same time as the need for a particular garment. Tight budgets left even the most prudent housewives little opportunity for speculative purchases against future need and when a garment wore out it required replacement as soon as possible and could not wait for the next jumble sale. On the other hand, we know that the poor strove to acquire elements of 'Sunday best' and the fact that Rowntree's York women bought their day-to-day dresses at jumble sales does not mean they did not sometimes buy items of holiday clothing there too. Hodson suggests that the northern market hall, offering a full range of products at low prices under one roof, operated as a version of the department store for the more affluent working classes.[131] Perhaps the jumble sale served a similar function for the poor, with its promise of a bargain, opportunity to socialise with friends and neighbours, and a 'large and strange collection of articles for sale' – which might include 'silk hats and old fenders, a patent fire-escape and paper fans, bonnets and books, coats and crockery'.[132] Certainly this is how a *Daily Express* journalist viewed a 1913 Islington sale, organised to raise money for the paper's fund to assist impoverished women: '8 p.m. – Doors opened, and an eager multitude, bent on bargains like any woman at Whiteley's or Selfridge's almost run in.'[133]

* * *

[129] LMA, P79/MTW/42, *St. Matthew's Upper Clapton, Service Paper*, May 1889; LMA, P95/ALL2/29, *All Saints, Clapham Park, Church Magazine*, May 1898.
[130] Ginsburg, 'Rags to riches', 130–1.
[131] Hodson, 'The municipal store', p. 103.
[132] LMA, P95/PAU 1/25, *St Paul, Clapham* [parish magazine], April 1892.
[133] *Daily Express*, 30 January 1913, p. 7.

Literary references to female philanthropy indicate how culturally embedded women's charity work had become, and given the relationship between needlework and femininity, discussed in Chapter 4, it is unsurprising that a very great deal of that work was directed toward providing the poor with clothing. But the scale and range of their work also testifies to the enduring struggle of the poor to clothe themselves and their families. For much of the century most clothing charities echoed the clothing societies, providing new but strictly utilitarian clothing, being religiously affiliated and motivated, and operating increasingly on a self-help basis which required a monetary contribution from the recipients and therefore excluded the most needy. Also like the clothing societies, many organisers deemed the poor in need of moral improvement and saw clothing charity as an opportunity to effect it.

Toward the end of the century social unrest and instability, expanding horizons for women, new leisure activities, the influence of liberalism diluting that of evangelicalism, and the understanding that poverty was a human rather than divine creation, produced a changed philanthropic environment. The result was the introduction of more efficient, modern forms of clothing charity, which operated on a larger scale than the traditional local initiatives, but in tandem with them, were less concerned to restrict the style of clothing and were not necessarily denominational. The jumble sale proved to be the most enduring and among the most popular with both organisers and buyers. Yet even this humble institution, by charging an entrance fee and selling, rather than giving away the goods, still remained beyond the reach of the very poorest.

9 'We have nothing but our clothes': charity schools and servants

The final two chapters are concerned with uniforms, which proliferated in the nineteenth century and allowed their wearers even less control over their clothing than those dependent on charity or parish aid. Uniforms helped to impose a visual order on the increasingly anonymous and crowded cities, to signal who did what, who to ask for assistance – on the railway, in the restaurant, or when in difficulty. A smart corporate uniform could be worn with pride, a symbol of authority, knowledge and responsibility. But uniforms subdue individuality and are, says Jennifer Craik, 'all about control not only of the social self but also of the inner self and its formation'.[1] Increasingly, in the nineteenth century, uniforms were used to mould and reform characters, to discipline, and it is these functions with which I am concerned.

I begin with charity school pupils, particularly girls, and the role of uniform in preparing them for their expected careers as domestic servants, whose numbers rose rapidly in the nineteenth century with the growth in number and changing role of middle-class women. Mistresses' desire to mark a greater separation between themselves and their staff led to the imposition of uniforms on female domestic servants, intensifying clothing as a key site of tension between mistress and servant. This was further exacerbated when employers tried also to regulate servants' off-duty dress, the invasion of personal liberty denying them freedom of expression and reflecting a belief that servants were the property, rather than the employees, of their mistresses.

Charity school uniforms

Missing or unreliable records make it impossible to calculate the number of children attending English charity schools at the beginning of the nineteenth century. For example, Mary Gladwys Jones, historian

---

[1] Jennifer Craik, *Uniforms Exposed: From Conformity to Transgression* (Oxford: Berg, 2005), p. 4.

of the charity school movement, points out that although 'thousands' of schools for educating the poor were established in the eighteenth century, returns made by the Society for the Promotion of Christian Knowledge (SPCK) give the identical figures of 1,329 schools and 23,421 scholars in both 1723 and 1799.[2] Nevertheless, it is certain that the schools were attended only by a minority of children, but a significant minority which numbered thousands rather than hundreds. And while Craik says that 'charity schools were essentially workhouses for children and ... financed by levies on parish members', they were founded and funded by a variety of organisations and individuals, mostly from religious motivations.[3]

Most charity schools clothed their pupils, evidenced in the numerous Bluecoat schools which derived their name from the uniform, and school trustees and masters giving evidence to the 1816 Select Committee on the education of the 'lower orders' in London cited the provision of clothing as a chief reason why parents sought a charity school place for their children.[4] However, most schools kept the uniform of the period in which they were established, usually between the sixteenth and eighteenth centuries. Boys at Bluecoat schools, for example, wore a form of Tudor dress consisting of a long blue coat, white neckbands, yellow stockings, Holbein cap and buckled shoes. Also some uniforms were derived from clerical dress and retained elements of this. By the nineteenth century, therefore, these uniforms were decidedly antiquated. In the 1840s, for example, Stephen Forsdick, the son of a gamekeeper, attended The Free School in Watford, Hertfordshire, where the boys wore the uniform of its foundation in 1704:

suits ... of a dark frieze cloth, with knee breeches and cutaway coats ... black shoes and white stockings. The caps were flat with red tassel on top and red band around the crown. We also wore a white Bib, like those worn by the clergy of the Church of England.[5]

Benefactors and other wealthy observers romanticised these picturesque costumes.[6] From the early 1700s, 'Londoners flocked in their

---

[2] Mary Gwladys Jones, *The Charity School Movement: A Study of Eighteenth-Century Puritanism in Action* (Cambridge University Press, 1938), pp. 19, 24.
[3] Craik, *Uniforms Exposed*, p. 58.
[4] *First Report. Minutes of Evidence... Education of the Lower Orders of the Metropolis.* 1816, Parliamentary Papers 1816 IV, p. 80.
[5] BAWCA, 1:242 Stephen Forsdick, 'Untitled', pp. 2–3; The school is now Watford Grammar School and its website gives 1704 as the foundation date, whereas Forsdick gives the date as 1656. 'History of the School', *Watford Grammar School for Boys*, www.watfordboys .org.
[6] Phillis Cunnington and Catherine Lucas, *Charity Costumes of Children, Scholars, Almsfolk, Pensioners* (London: A. and C. Black, 1978), p. 63. See also Elizabeth Ewing, *Women in Uniform Through the Centuries* (London: Batsford, 1975), pp. 22–5.

244   'We have nothing but our clothes': charity schools and servants

thousands' to see the combined pupils of the London and Westminster charity schools take part in an annual street procession and church service held, from 1782, at St Paul's Cathedral, and attended by the clergy, civic officials and royalty.[7] The children received a new outfit once a year – often, in the case of the girls, made by themselves – and wore it for the first time on these occasions. By the mid nineteenth century the congregation numbered 13,000 persons of which approximately 5,000 were the school pupils. Writing in 1851, the Revd T. B. Murray, Prebendary of St Paul's and Secretary of the SPCK, noted that: 'The costume of the boys and girls, which is provided new for this day, is what some may style quaint and old fashioned.' This was because it reflected the fashions of the Queen Anne period, 1702–14, during which most of the schools had been founded.[8] According to the *Graphic*'s report of the 1870 Anniversary celebration: 'A prettier or more touching spectacle can hardly be imagined.' The 'effect of the differently-coloured costumes' was 'most striking and picturesque'. The children were displayed on benches 'erected in the form of a Roman amphitheatre', emphasising the children's role as performers in a drama staged for the entertainment of the monied.[9]

In 1865 Arthur Munby visited the Bluecoat School on the Isle of Wight, where the girls were aged between eleven and fourteen. Typically, Munby was enchanted by their uniform which comprised:

close white cap no border, short frock of blue serge, sleeves end above elbow & bare arms, tippet and apron of bluecheck (sometimes white), red waistbelt with date 1761 in front, and most picturesque straw hat with narrow red ribbon: broad brim drawn down at sides like Hogarth's milkmaids, original of bonnet in fact.[10] (Fig. 9.1)

Not only did the girls have to wear a uniform one hundred years out of date, they also had to proclaim it on their belts.

Much of Munby's enchantment with the girls stemmed from the fact that his secret fiancée, and later wife, maid-of-all-work Hannah Cullwick, had attended the Shifnal Bluecoat School, in the 1830s, where she wore a uniform very similar to that of the Isle of Wight pupils. Seeing the girls from the Parish School of St Andrew's Holborn playing together, 'all drest alike, in short frocks of blue serge & capes to match' and 'close white

[7] M. G. Jones, *Charity School Movement*, p. 60.
[8] T. B. Murray, *The Children in St. Paul's. An Account of the Anniversary of the Assembled Charity Schools of London and Westminster, in the Cathedral Church of St. Paul* (London: SPCK, 1851), pp. 5, 6, 9, 10, 20.
[9] 'Anniversary Festival of Charity Children in St. Paul's', *Graphic*, 11 June 1870, p. 660.
[10] TCLC, MUNB, 33, 25 May 1865.

 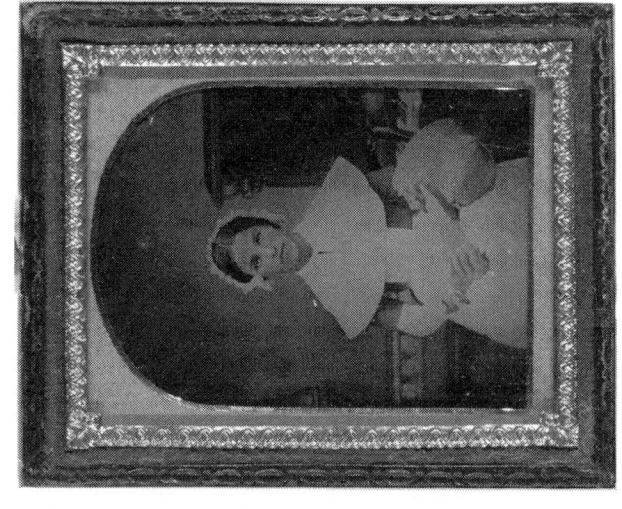

Fig. 9.1. Left: Girls from Bluecoat School, Isle of Wight, 1865. Right: Uniform of the Blue School, Shifnal, the school Hannah Cullwick attended.

caps of old world shape', prompted Munby to rhapsodise: 'So Hannah played with her fellows, in *her* charity-dress.' A month later, travelling to Crystal Palace to hear the singing of the 'girls of the Blue School at Tottenham, 1736', during what seems to have been something of a tour of charity schools, he again romanticised 'their charming antique dress – which she once wore' (see Fig. 9.1).[11]

There is little evidence of how the pupils viewed their education or their clothes. As places were limited and admission often dependent on benefactor nomination, being a charity school pupil was an indication of favour. Also, for the vast majority of the pupils, the clothing was of greater quantity and better quality than they would otherwise have possessed. Doubtless some took pride in their charity-school uniforms, but its antiquated style and the fact that it advertised the children's poverty could make them the targets of ridicule or contempt.[12] This may have increased during the century with the growth of state-funded education, where uniforms were not worn and which meant school attendance was no longer the privilege of a favoured minority.

Cullwick's own account of her charity uniform makes a striking contrast with Munby's sentimental musings, and is a moving and powerful testimony to the stigma and humiliation it engendered. Cullwick was admitted to the Bluecoat school through the patronage of her mother's former employer and left at the age of eight, the anguish caused by the uniform indelibly impressed on her mind though a pupil for no more than three years.[13] Over three decades later, when distressed by her sister's affected superiority, she wrote in her diary that:

she *must* remember how I loved [her] & did all I could, dressing her up as smart as possible & playing with her, & tho' I wore the charity dress myself I didn't want *her* to wear it. If I put anything else on myself the lads used to call me 'proud *Nance*'.

Still more potently, she recalled her feelings when, aged fourteen, she heard that her mother had died, which appears to have been the most devastating experience of her life. 'I'd quite lost my love for living', she wrote, 'as I had when I wore the charity dress.'[14]

Craik says blue was commonly chosen as the colour of charity-school uniforms because it was the cheapest dye, but according to Jonathan Andrews, blue, associated with the Virgin Mary, was the colour of

---

[11] TCLC, MUNB, 33, 9 May 1865; 33, 16 June 1865.
[12] P. Cunnington and Lucas, *Charity Costumes*, pp. 55–6.
[13] Atkinson, *Love and Dirt*, p. 10.
[14] L. Stanley (ed.), *Diaries of Hannah Cullwick*, pp. 37, 260, 298.

Christian charity.[15] In either case, the clothing reminded the children they were recipients of charity, and according to Lees they 'heard multiple sermons on the need to abjure nasty habits and remain clean and tidy, while their teachers took every opportunity to remind them of their inferior heritage and negligible prospects'.[16] The education they received was designed to fit them for manual work, and when Munby visited the Isle of Wight Bluecoat school, the mistress told him, in front of the girls: 'We give them plain [education] suited to station in life: they become under-servants, "some are little scrubs", some do needlework'. She then invited Munby, a total stranger with no official connection to the school, to manually inspect a girl's clothing, to which she unresistingly submitted: '"Williams, come forward,"... mistress bids me feel her frock, her apron, she standing meekly.'[17]

'The need to shape minds and bodies finds in uniform a valuable aid', says Daniel Roche, and Craik, echoing Foucault, contends that the role of school uniforms is to shape 'the self to create conditions for the habitus of the docile body', docility meaning 'teachable, submissive, tractable and easily managed – not just passive but primed (ready and alert) for instruction'.[18] These were among the most desirable qualities in the domestic servant.[19]

Female servants' dress

Domestic service was the largest single female occupation in nineteenth-century England, and remained so until at least the 1930s, its numbers rising from just over three-quarters of a million in 1851 to nearly 1,400,000 million in 1891.[20] Many girls entered the occupation at the age of twelve or thirteen, some younger – Hannah Cullwick was just eight when she took up her first position in 1841.[21] Most remained in service until marriage or throughout their working lives if they remained single. In 1880 42 per cent of female domestic servants were under the age of twenty.[22] In a large household the female servants ranged, in descending order, from the housekeeper to cook and ladies' maids, parlour-, house

---

[15] Craik, *Uniforms Exposed*, p. 59; Andrews 'The (un)dress of the mad poor...Part 2', 137.
[16] Lees, *Solidarities of Strangers*, p. 54.   [17] TCLC, MUNB, 33, 25 May 1865.
[18] Roche, *Culture of Clothing*, p. 228; Craik, *Uniforms Exposed*, pp. 52, 231 n. 2. Foucault, *Discipline and Punish*, Part III, Chapter 1.
[19] Leonore Davidoff, *Worlds Between: Historical Perspectives on Gender and Class* (Cambridge: Polity, 1995), p. 27.
[20] *Ibid.*, p. 22; Burnett, *Useful Toil*, p. 130. Combined figures for England and Wales.
[21] L. Stanley (ed.), *Diaries of Hannah Cullwick*, p. 35.
[22] Davidoff, *Worlds Between*, p. 22.

and nurse-maids down to the scullion at the bottom. But as Edward Higgs and Theresa McBride have shown, most servants worked in more modest homes, with just one or two other servants, or often alone as a maid-of-all work.[23] Domestic service was a low-status, residential occupation with no legal regulation. For lone maids especially, hours were long, the working and living conditions often poor, the labour arduous and the isolation intense, all of which made effective workers' associations virtually impossible.[24]

Servants enjoyed little personal autonomy and according to Leonore Davidoff, as alternative employment opportunities multiplied, offering greater freedom, servants remained in 'pre-industrial, almost biblical, subordination' to their employers.[25] Subsequent studies offer a more nuanced picture of the employer–servant relationship, showing that servants had long challenged employers' authority through either open or covert acts of rebellion, and their unwillingness to tolerate unreasonable employer demands increased during the late nineteenth and twentieth centuries.[26] And Davidoff questioned whether 'servants internalized a belief in their own unworthiness'. Hannah Cullwick's testimony suggests they were themselves unsure.[27] 'At the charity school', she wrote:

I was taught to curtsy to the ladies & gentlemen & it seem'd to come natural to me to think them *entirely* over the lower class & as if it was our place to bow & be at their bidding, & I've never got out o' that feeling somehow.

This, written in 1873, over thirty years after she left the school, chimes with Munby's Bluecoat account and suggests that Cullwick had thoroughly absorbed her education in deference in which the uniform played such a vital role. She also recorded her 'fear' of being thought 'set up or

---

[23] Edward Higgs, 'Domestic service and household production', in Angela V. John (ed.), *Unequal Opportunities: Women's Employment in England 1800–1918* (Oxford: Basil Blackwell, 1986), pp. 125–50; p. 136; McBride, *Domestic Revolution*, p. 20.

[24] Burnett, *Useful Toil*, pp. 164–5.   [25] Davidoff, *Worlds Between*, p. 18.

[26] Vickery, *Gentleman's Daughter*, p. 184; Steedman, *Labours Lost*, pp. 184–96; Reay, *Microhistories*, p. 148; Selina Todd, *Young Women, Work, and Family in England 1918–1950* (Oxford University Press, 2005), pp. 148–50; Delap, *Knowing Their Place*, pp. 26–8, 49–50, 70; Laura Schwartz, *A Serious Endeavour: Gender, Education and Community at St Hugh's, 1886–2011* (London: Profile Books, 2011), pp. 113, 122; Alison Light, *Mrs Woolf and the Servants* (London: Penguin Fig Tree, 2007), Chapter 3 especially. See also Carolyn Steedman, *Master and Servant: Love and Labour in the English Industrial Age* (Cambridge University Press, 2007), pp. 137–45, which considers cordial as well as confrontational relationships between employers and servants in the late eighteenth and early nineteenth centuries.

[27] Davidoff, *Worlds Between*, pp. 27–8.

proud'. She was, she said '*born* to *serve*, & *not* to order', and hoped to 'always keep the same humble spirit'.

But as Cullwick approached her thirtieth birthday she realised she 'must be quite a woman now, though I don't feel any different than I ever did except in feeling lower in heart I think, for I've bin a servant now 20 years or more'. Acceptance of her servility is here tempered with the suggestion of dissatisfaction at her status, and her recognition that twenty years of domestic service has left her in a state of arrested development. And in contrast with her claim that service was her birthright, she continues by saying that it was Munby who had taught her 'the beauty in being nothing but a common drudge', and that it had 'been difficult to learn thoroughly'. On the one hand, therefore, she attempts to act out the humility she has learned, but there is a part of her that resists. And while she was undoubtedly a hard and loyal worker, she did not hesitate to defend herself against injustice from either employers or Munby. As Liz Stanley notes, Cullwick was no puppet, but a woman 'of much power and pride... strong-willed and stubborn'.[28]

Female domestic service changed in the nineteenth century. Previously, it had commonly been connected with the productive capacities of the employer's home, with the maid working under the command of, but alongside, the mistress in the dairy or textile production, as well as participating in household work. 'Servants', says Weatherill, 'were a necessity in maintaining the household of middle rank without excessive toil. They were not a luxury or a form of conspicuous consumption; they were a fundamental part of domestic life.'[29] In the relative absence of domestic appliances in the nineteenth century, servants were still necessary for the smooth running of middle- and upper-class homes. But with the expansion of the middle classes, the withdrawal of the women from manual labour and the separation of work and home, the dominant concern, says Leonore Davidoff, became 'social placement and social closure', established through conspicuous consumption and the possession of 'deference givers' – servants.[30] But this often meant embedding total strangers in the family home. Servants, says Kate Summerscale, were 'often feared as outsiders who might be spies or seducers, even aggressors... the serpent in the house'.[31] Employers' manuals dispensed advice on how to spot an unreliable servant, *Trusler's Domestic*

---

[28] L. Stanley (ed.), *Diaries of Hannah Cullwick*, pp. 9, 85, 125, 282.
[29] Weatherill, *Consumer Behaviour*, p. 139.   [30] Davidoff, *Worlds Between*, p. 23.
[31] Kate Summerscale, *The Suspicions of Mr Whicher: or The Murder at Road Hill House* (London: Bloomsbury, 2008), pp. 145–6.

Management in 1819, for example, warning that 'Dressy servants' were 'women of suspicious character'.[32]

Complaints about working-class women's attempts to dress above their station and their love of 'finery' were rife and formed 'part of the long-standing misogynous discourses that stretched back into early Christianity and beyond'.[33] All women were ostensibly open to accusation, but some were particular targets. Munby found it 'refreshing' to see, one Sunday in Scholes in 1860, the majority of young women wearing 'local dress' of 'short striped kirtle ' and 'clean cotton jacket, pink or cream colour... and strong shoes (not clogs on Sunday)'. But he was alarmed at two others among them, 'in bloated muslin dresses, trinkets, bandeaued hair, & all other the (*sic*) borrowed fripperies of a higher class' who, in a different setting, he would have assumed were prostitutes. He discovered, however, 'that they were <u>dressmakers</u>' and: 'Their degradation therefore was natural.'[34] Milliners and factory workers also attracted criticism for their sartorial display, but none more so than female domestic servants whose persistent self-adornment was a recurrent trope in nineteenth-century publications.[35]

Lemire notes that in the late eighteenth century domestic servants 'maintained the most fashionable appearance of all wage-earners'.[36] This was in great part due to their proximity to the fashions of the middle and upper classes, but also the expanding choice of cheap cotton fabrics increased the ability of working-class women to own more, and more colourful, clothes. The result was a perceived blurring of social boundaries, and the impossibility of telling mistress from maid became a frequent complaint. When, in Mrs Trimmer's cautionary tale, *The Servant's Friend*, first published in 1787, the mistress tells her new cook, Susan, that she dresses inappropriately for her situation, Susan responds: 'So I am too fine for madam! is she afraid I shall be taken for the mistress?'[37] When defining the superior status of their employers became

---

[32] John Trusler, *Trusler's Domestic Management, or the Art of Conducting a Family, with Economy, Frugality & Method* (Bath, 1819), p. 56.
[33] A. Hunt, *Governance of the Consuming Passions*, p. 218.
[34] TCLC, MUNB, 6, 30 September 1860 (Munby's emphasis).
[35] Munby claimed it was 'well known that the factory girls of Manchester earning 18/ a week or more, drink gin so besottedly that they have often nothing left to wear but their working suit'. TCLC, MUNB, 6, 29 September 1860. Styles also stresses the perceived 'sartorial extravagance' of domestic servants in the eighteenth century. Styles, *Dress of the People*, p. 277.
[36] Lemire, *Fashion's Favourite*, p. 96.
[37] Sarah Trimmer, *The Servant's Friend; an Exemplary Tale Designed to Enforce the Religious Instructions Given at Sunday and Other Charity Schools: by Pointing Out the Practical Application of Them in a State of Service*, 7th edn (London, 1808 [1787]), p. 54.

a significant aspect of the servant's role, it was essential to maintain separation between them. Dress restrictions increasingly became the means by which this was attempted.

A flood of literature exhorted servants to dress modestly, often contrasting the exemplary neat dress and meek disposition of one servant with the sartorial and personal boldness of her wilful colleague. In *The Servant's Friend*, housemaid Kitty is a former charity-school girl whose uniform appears to have achieved its self-abnegatory purpose. She dresses in a serviceable 'camlet gown... black quilted petticoat, worsted stockings, and leather shoes', and is shocked when the new cook, Susan, appears in her Sunday dress of 'silk gown, curls at her ears, her hair half way down her back, a fine gauze cap, with lappets and streamers, a flounced petticoat, and long train to her gown'. Susan is also bad tempered, deceitful, prefers ballads, romances and fortune-telling books to the Bible, visits friends instead of going to church, plays cards, drinks and gets up late, brings in a poor woman to do her work, paying her in food and drink stolen from her mistress, and is eventually dismissed without a reference and 'reduced to down-right beggary'![38] Her dress, then, is not only problematic in itself, but emblematic of a range of transgressive behaviours which will inevitably lead to her downfall.

The Servant's Friend was one of numerous tracts written for pupils at charity and Sunday schools, not least those founded by its author, Mrs Trimmer, an evangelical Anglican whose *Oeconomy of Charity* (1787) was 'one of the most influential works on how and why Sunday and charity schools should be established'.[39] Sunday schools were attended by three-quarters of English working-class children in the mid nineteenth century and a still greater number thereafter.[40] There would have been few children, therefore, who were not exposed to the literature, which aimed to foster the habits of modesty and obedience requisite for a life of compliant servitude. Frequently, it invoked biblical authority to support the demand for modest dress. An SPCK publication, for example, rather dubiously interpreted Peter's command to wives to reject 'outward adorning... of wearing of gold, or of putting on of apparel' in favour of 'the ornament of a meek and quiet spirit', as a directive to servants to '[d]ress neatly and simply'.[41]

---

[38] Trimmer, *The Servant's Friend*, pp. 53, 55, 62.
[39] Barbara Brandon Schnorrenberg, 'Trimmer, Sarah (1741–1810)', *Oxford Dictionary of National Biography*, Oxford University Press, 2004, www.oxforddnb.com.
[40] K. D. M. Snell, 'The Sunday school movement in England and Wales: child labour, denominational control and working-class culture', *Past & Present*, 164 (1999), 122–68; 126.
[41] A. C. W., *Rules for Young Women* (London and Oxford: SPCK, c.1873), p. 10.

Manuals such as *Trusler's Domestic Management* aimed to instruct inexperienced young wives how to manage their servants. And while *Trusler's* told employers to look to a servant's dress for clues to her character, it also placed responsibility on the mistress to avoid exposing the servant to temptation, since this might have potentially dire consequences:

> a drawer, a closet, &c. left open by accident... may tempt her to make free with a bit of ribband or tape, or a skein of silk or thread, which may lead afterwards to a freedom that may endanger her liberty or her life.[42]

The crime will be the servant's and it is her life or liberty that will be forfeited, but the irresponsible employer will be an accessory before the fact. And the perceived need for constant vigilance, the assumption that the maid is always a potential thief reveals the perceived inherent unease in the employer–servant relationship.

Servants were commonly given cast-off clothes by their employers, either for their own use or to send home to relatives.[43] For ladies' maids, cast-off clothes were an expected perquisite, and, according to one manual, the quantity and style of clothing likely to be acquired was a key factor in their choice of position.[44] But Harriet Martineau advised that a responsible mistress would give her maid 'such only of her dresses as can be made up again with neatness and propriety'.[45] In 1849 the corrupting effects of giving ladies' maids unsuitable garments seemed proven when, throughout her trial for murder, former lady's maid Maria Manning wore a 'rich black satin dress', a cast-off from her aristocratic mistress.[46] Manning had bludgeoned a man to death to obtain his money, and the black dress became a key focus of the contemporary commentary on the celebrated case, the implication being that it had cultivated in her an irresistible desire for luxury. Rumours and myths about the dress abounded; Edmund Gosse, for example, remembered learning 'that Mrs Manning was hanged in black satin, which thereupon went wholly out of fashion'.[47] Her biographer dubbed Manning *The Woman Who Murdered Black Satin*, but while she was, indeed, hanged in the dress, her association with the fabric had no derogatory effect on sales.[48] Indeed,

---

[42] Trusler, *Trusler's Domestic Management*, p. 41.
[43] As Margot Finn says, this is a point that Flora Thompson repeats throughout *Lark Rise*. Finn, *Character of Credit*, pp. 83–4.
[44] Anon., *The Management of Servants. A Practical Guide to the Routine of Domestic Service* (London: Warne and Co., 1880), p. 172.
[45] Anon. [Harriet Martineau], *The Guide to Service; The Lady's Maid* (London, 1838), p. 40.
[46] Dorothy Margaret Stuart, *The English Abigail* (London: Macmillan, 1946), p. 209.
[47] Edmund Gosse, *Father and Son: A Study of Two Temperaments* (London: Penguin, 1989 [1907]), p. 108.
[48] Albert Borowitz, *The Woman Who Murdered Black Satin: The Bermondsey Horror* (Columbus, OH: Ohio State University Press, 1981), pp. 291–6.

according to one contemporary report, the female jail staff envied no one more 'than Calcraft, the hangman... when he carried away the rich dress of the defunct female convict', doubtless to sell.[49]

As well as receiving their mistresses' old clothes, ladies' maids received higher wages than the majority of female servants. The 1869 edition of Beeton's *Household Management*, for example, gave the upper limit of a lady's-maid's wages as £25 compared with £16 for a maid-of-all-work.[50] Additionally, in order to groom and dress her mistress, and maintain her wardrobe, a lady's-maid was 'thoroughly to understand the business of dressmaking... hair-dressing and getting up of fine linen', which she might equally apply to herself.[51] The lady's maid was, therefore, the most likely to be mistaken for a mistress. But probably not her own; while presenting an appearance that did credit to her mistress's status she was not to rival her, and while she was to maintain an interest in dress and fashion it was to remain, to some extent, vicarious. And even the mistress's cast-off clothes would have been of limited use to the servant trying to emulate her, since the fact that the mistress had discarded them would suggest either that they were showing signs of wear, or that the fashion had been superseded.

Even if a lady's maid could sometimes be mistaken for a member of the middle classes, there were various ways in which the monied could make sartorial distinctions between themselves and the majority of their social inferiors.[52] As cotton gained increasing ascendancy over linen and wool in the clothing of the poor, the wealthy used it less. The Cunningtons list: 'Muslins, cambric, bombazine, jaconet, sarcenet, lutestring, poplin, satin, printed cottons, crape' as the materials used for fashionable ladies' day dresses between 1800 and 1810. By the 1840s the list comprises: 'Cloth, merino, alpaca... Striped silks... levantine, foulard, chiné silk, Grenadine, taffeta plaided and broché, barege, organdy, tarlatan, gingham'.[53] The cotton muslins, jaconet and prints have gone and although cotton fabrics are still represented in the organdy, tarlatan and gingham they are greatly outnumbered by fabrics made of silk, wool or a mixture of the two. Hannah Cullwick, arriving at a new post late one afternoon in 1867, noticed that her mistress 'was dress'd only in a plain cotton dress'. Although 'it wasn't a *lilac* print', these having become the

---

[49] Anon., *An Account of the Last Days, Confessions, and Executions of the Mannings, for the Murder of Patrick O'Connor, at Bermondsey* (Leith: C. Drummond, 1849), p. 10.
[50] Isabella Beeton, *The Book of Household Management* (London: Ward, Lock and Tyler, 1869 [1859–61]), p. 10.
[51] Anon., *The Management of Servants*, p. 173.
[52] John Styles makes a similar point about the late eighteenth century. John Styles, 'Involuntary consumers? Servants and their clothes in eighteenth-century England', *Textile History*, 33:1 (2002), 9–21; 18.
[53] C. W. and P. Cunnington, *Handbook of English Costume*, pp. 358, 428.

habitual morning wear of domestic servants, 'but a red and white plaid', she was clearly surprised that her employer was wearing a cotton dress at all.[54]

Ladies' maids formed a minority of servants, and the small wages of the vast majority of servants were sufficient in themselves to ensure that mistresses need have no fear of sartorial competition. Hannah Cullwick earned £8 per annum in her positions as nursemaid, under-housemaid and scullion between 1849 and 1851. As a maid-of-all-work and then a general servant, between 1856 and 1868, her wages rose from £16 to £21 per annum, but by the time she was earning the higher rate she was thirty-five years old and had been in service for twenty-seven years.[55] Furthermore, the dirt and physical labour of their daily work ensured that few servants would be mistaken for anything other than what they were. Cullwick recorded that her hands were '*grener'd* as we say in Shropshire. That is, the cracks in our hands ingrain'd with black lead and that, so that even scrubbing will not fetch it out'.[56] Although it must be acknowledged that Cullwick had a singular fascination with dirt, the existence of a colloquial term for the condition indicates that it was not peculiar to her. Munby was able to identify 'numbers of maidservants' among the crowd attending a 'Grand Review' of troops at Windsor Palace because '[u]nless she be a lady's maid . . . Her hands show work; and if gloved, you still see they are larger than a lady's'.[57]

While, again, large, work-roughened, female hands were, as Barry Reay says, 'one of Munby's special fetishes', and he was more alert to them than most, body language also played a part.[58] The maidservant, Munby said 'has not the selfconscious selfrestraining (*sic*) dignity of a lady, nor the sprightly vanity of a milliner, nor the rude simplicity of a country girl living at home'.[59] More simply, there was a distinctive difference in gait and grace between those who passed their time at dancing classes and those who spent their days bending and kneeling to clean steps or work in the field.

Nevertheless, the desire of employers to assert status and authority, to make clear distinctions between themselves and their staff, to impose order on their homes, and to make servants as unobtrusive as possible, meant that by the 1860s the vast majority of domestic servants were uniformed. Where an 1824 manual instructed servants simply to dress plainly in 'a stuff gown, or a dark-coloured cotton one, and a stuff

---

[54] L. Stanley (ed.), *Diaries of Hannah Cullwick*, p. 59.
[55] Atkinson, *Love and Dirt*, pp. 20, 21, 25, 46, 47, 135, 152, 166, 171–2. In 1868 she also worked very briefly as a cook for £22 a year. *Ibid.*, p. 168.
[56] L. Stanley (ed.), *Diaries of Hannah Cullwick*, p. 61.   [57] Hudson, *Munby*, p. 272.
[58] Reay, *Watching Hannah*, p. 127.   [59] Hudson, *Munby*, p. 272.

Female servants' dress 255

Fig. 9.2. A general servant in Marylebone, 1872.

petticoat', by 1880 *The Management of Servants* was demanding that 'at breakfast and during the day... the parlour maid wears a print dress, white apron, and white cap', while at afternoon tea women servants were to 'wear dresses of dark materials, white aprons, and white caps' and special shops opened selling servants' uniforms and allied requisites.[60] Looking out of his London window one morning in 1868 Munby could see the maidservants at work in six houses: 'Fourteen young women; all drest alike, in pale lilac frock, white cap, white apron, bare arms' (Fig. 9.2).[61]

According to Flora Thompson, when young girls entered service employers provided their caps, aprons and print dresses. In fact servants were more usually expected to provide their own uniforms and two pages later Thompson described accompanying her friend Martha to her

---

[60] Anon., *The New Female Instructor. Or, Young Woman's Guide to Domestic Happiness; Being an Epitome of all the Acquirements Necessary to Form the Female Character, in Every Class of Life: With Examples of Illustrious Women, etc.* (London, 1824), p. 373; Anon., *Management of Servants*, p. 79; Adburgham, *Shops and Shopping*, p. 195.

[61] Hudson, *Munby*, p. 251.

first job interview where the prospective employer instructed Martha to: 'Tell your mother I shall expect her to fit you out well. You will want caps and aprons. I like my maids to look neat. And tell her to let you bring plenty of changes, for we only wash once in six weeks.' Furthermore, Martha's mother had anticipated this, telling her to request an advance of wages from the employer to purchase the necessary articles, the expense frequently posing a challenge, sometimes prohibitive, to those entering service.[62] In 1904 thirteen-year-old Kate Taylor began work as a farmhouse general servant on a wage of 15d. per week. Unable to buy 'the necessary print for dresses and hessian for aprons', her employer advanced the money and stopped it from her wages. 'I worked', wrote Taylor, 'without wages for six months, and each evening, Sundays included, I sat behind her chair and sewed.'[63] The 1910 *Every Woman's Encyclopaedia* directed that: 'Print dresses, with neat white aprons and caps, should be worn for mornings . . . A black dress, pretty muslin apron and cap, should be worn in the afternoon', and that in the case of low wages 'the mistress will often give the maid material for one black dress, or provide her caps, aprons, cuffs, etc.; but this is a voluntary matter'.[64]

The afternoon uniform of female domestic servants was extended to women performing similar work in public settings, such as chambermaids and waitresses. In 1872 Munby visited the Queen's Theatre, Long Acre, where he was:

shown to the boxes by a girl drest as a sort of parlourmaid; with a saucy little white cap on the top of her head, and a dainty white apron and bib over her black frock . . . we saw her five fellows, all in the same neat livery.[65]

Twelve years later, in the Health Exhibition dining room, he found '40 young women waitresses, each in livery of black frock, large white apron and bib, large white cap, corkscrew hung from the waist'.[66] As ever, Munby found the costume picturesque, but for many domestic servants the uniform, and particularly the outdated cap, became the 'outward and visible sign of servility' and a site for employer–servant conflict.[67]

House steward William Lanceley cautioned against too rigid an attitude on the part of employers recalling a mistress who:

was dead against dress . . . and although it was a most comfortable place, two years was about the longest servants stayed in it. They left for no other reason than the restriction in dress.[68]

---

[62] F. Thompson, *Lark Rise*, pp. 157, 159–60.   [63] Burnett, *Destiny Obscure*, p. 308.
[64] Anon., *Every Woman's Encyclopaedia*, p. 14.
[65] TCLC, MUNB, 40, 25 January 1872.   [66] TCLC, MUNB, 52, 6 August 1884.
[67] Burnett, *Useful Toil*, p. 167.
[68] William Lanceley, *From Hall-Boy to House Steward* (London: E. Arnold, 1925), p. 152.

The uniforms were not necessarily intrinsically unattractive. Minnie Frisby, working as a servant in the early 1890s, had a mistress who was very particular about her own dress and liked her maid to also be well turned out. 'Mrs. Tapp always like (*sic*) me to be smart and dressed in my black by 12 o'clock', wrote Frisby.

I really never saw her cross but about once, and then it was because she had given me a lovely dress length (black of course) for a Xmas present, and my Mother had let someone make it old fashioned; Mrs. Tapp said they had spoilt it. I also remember her making me a lovely afternoon apron; she worked hours at it in the drawing room, scalloped all the edges; yes, she liked me to be smart.[69]

McBride suggests employers' concern with their servants' dress was linked to their role as indicators of the employers' social position. Frisby's duties included answering the door to visitors and her mistress's insistence on a 'smart' dress ensured her maid conveyed a good impression of the household. Even so she supplied it only as a Christmas gift, and no matter how attractive, the dress and apron were still a uniform.

Many employers also tried to restrict servants' off-duty dress. In 1855 the *Family Economist* opined that a mistress was entitled to require her servants to spend some of their wages on 'neat and creditable clothing', but '[b]eyond this she may have no right to interfere'. But this was disingenuous since it continued with the recommendation that 'by a judicious use of her influence she may restrain them from running into extravagance and inconsistency of dress', including the tendency to 'a more showy style of dress'. It united a '*love of finery*' with 'untidiness and uncleanliness' as well as '*slovenliness*' and highlighted, as especially inappropriate for domestic servants, 'silk gowns and silk stockings, blonde, lace, feathers and artificial flowers, bracelets, necklaces, rings and earrings', as well as decrying the use of curl papers in the hair, not only because of the resultant 'long pendant ringlets', but because the time spent applying the papers could be more usefully spent mending their clothes.[70] '[A]s to our dressing in style, surely when our money is well earned we can dress as we like, so long as we are neat and clean in their houses', wrote 'Three Domestics' to the *Daily News*.[71] And Lanceley recalled that the directive to servants to dress in 'simple attire' in a house where he worked 'did not prevent them from buying smart clothes', but led them to deceive. As the clothes could not be worn in sight of the mistress, when a servant wished to go out in her finery, 'some of the other servants would help her to slip out and would let her in on her return'.[72] While many employers

---

[69] BAWCA, 1:250, Minnie Frisby, p. 18.
[70] 'The dress of female servants', *The Family Economist*, 4 (1855), pp. 21–2.
[71] *Daily News*, 9 September 1897, p. 6.

would doubtless have considered this conclusive proof of the connection between showy dress and dishonesty, the deceit, far from being inherent, was provoked by their own unreasonableness.

Mayhew claimed that female servants' efforts to dress well were doomed attempts to make them 'attractive to men of a higher class'.[73] But this ignores the personal pleasure of self-adornment, and when Lanceley cautioned employers not to be over-restrictive about dress it was because, he said: 'Most servants have sisters and brothers in business houses, especially those whose homes are in London, and they like to meet their own kin on something like the same footing.'[74] This, then, had nothing to do with emulation of social superiors, but a desire for the dignity of peer equality.

As new employment opportunities for working-class women multiplied, employers found it increasingly difficult to attract and retain staff, giving rise to the Servant Question which, in the 1870s, became a topic of lively debate in newspapers across the country. In 1872 the *Leeds Mercury* claimed it had become 'the most interesting of all topics to the vast majority of the English middle classes'. The *Mercury* complained of both the number and quality of servants. Noting a Scottish attempt to form a servants' union it called also for an organisation to benefit employers by acting as a source of trained servants, the present supply being 'far more independent than their predecessors... fonder of dress, and less ready and able to work'.[75] A response from 'A Father of Servant Girls' did not dispute the 'flimsiness of wearing apparel' among domestic servants, but said mistresses were to blame since 'girls always were girls in this respect, and as the ladies lead in extravagance and gaudiness in dress, so will the girls follow as far as they can'.[76] This was a view shared by Eliza Lynn Linton. A staunch opponent of female emancipation, Lynn Linton identified the management of servants as women's 'own special work', and a field in which they should lead by example:

The extravagance of living, of dress, of appointments, which is one part of the servant disorder – because maids, being women, will trick themselves out in finery to attract as much admiration as their mistresses... whence do these come save from women[?][77]

In his 1876 manifesto, *The Scarcity of Domestic Servants*, London footman Herbert Miller recorded that he had asked 'milliners, dressmakers, factory girls and others likely to make good servants', why they chose

---

[72] Lanceley, *From Hall-Boy*, p. 190.   [73] Mayhew, *London Labour*, vol. IV, p. 258.
[74] Lanceley, *From Hall-Boy*, pp. 151–2.   [75] *Leeds Mercury*, 22 April 1872, p. 2.
[76] *Leeds Mercury*, 7 May 1872, p. 6.
[77] *Hampshire Advertiser*, 13 May 1876, p. 7. Lynn Linton's article appeared first in the *Belgravia* magazine and was reproduced in several provincial newspapers.

their particular trades in preference to domestic service even if it meant they earned less. Domestic service, they replied, involved, 'an almost total loss of personal liberty' and was 'regarded as low and degrading'. A factory girl, earning 10*d*. a day, claimed to be 'above that poor scum what mustn't wear a feather or a ribbon, or breathe the fresh air, without asking somebody's leave, and because I likes my liberty'.

Miller, like Lanceley, also recommended greater tolerance on the part of employers. He proposed the formation of an employer's association whose members agreed to four 'privileges and concessions' for their employees. Second on the list, after a change of name from servant to 'Domestic Attendant', and before regulation of free time and a guaranteed reference on leaving employment, was: 'That no restrictions shall be placed on dress when off duty; and when on duty, only that which may be necessary to insure respectability.' Nothing, he said had 'done so much to make servitude unpopular amongst women as the restrictions placed upon the dress of servants'. Miller took the essentialist view that for women of all classes, 'it is as much a part of their nature to decorate their persons to the best advantage as it is for them to breathe', but when outlining the consequences of denying servants this freedom he returned to the issue of peer respect. Was it, he asked:

> fair or politic to expect servants to dress in such a fashion that when they appear in public their calling is patent to everybody, and are thus rendered a mark for the insults of omnibus conductors, butchers' boys, porters, and others?[78]

The use of uniforms continued until the eventual demise of domestic service in the Second World War and Miller's suggested association came to nothing. But employers were sometimes forced to make concessions over dress and appearance if they wished to retain their servants. In 1872 a seventeen-year-old London servant reluctantly complied with her new employer's insistence that she cut the tail off her dress and wore aprons with bibs to them, but she absolutely refused to take the pads out of her hair, 'large chignons being then the fashion'.[79]

* * *

The uniforms of charity-school pupils and domestic servants demonstrate the gulf in understanding between the different classes. Where schoolchildren shrank from the stigma of charity dress, the wealthy enjoyed the spectacle of its picturesque display. Employers seeking to establish their authority and status, and fearing the dilution of visual

---

[78] Herbert P. Miller, *The Scarcity of Domestic Servants; The Cause and Remedy. With a Short Outline of the Law Relating to Master and Domestic Servant* (London, 1876), pp. 16–17, 52–3, 57–9.

[79] Llewelyn Davies, *Life as We Have Known It*, p. 28.

social distinctions, sought to couple demure dress with moral rectitude and finery with vice. Servants, desiring peer conformity and the pleasure of self-adornment were resentful of restrictions on their sartorial freedom. Uniforms sought to render their wearers pliant, obedient and subservient, but the human spirit is not so easily subdued, and while exhortations to servants to dress plainly and economically were articulated in a diversity of cultural productions throughout the period, the need to do so suggests that employers were losing the battle, or at least gaining no ground. For servants, living in someone else's home, often in a poorly furnished room, with little time or possessions of their own, dress offered one of the few opportunities to exercise some autonomy, creativity and personal expression. As one servant told her mistress, who had thought her dress 'rather extravagant':

'Well, ma'am, you see this is the way of it. You have your own house and many things to take pride in, and show what you are – but we have nothing but our clothes'.[80]

[80] *Daily News*, 11 September 1897, p. 6.

10 'The greatest stigma and disgrace': lunatic asylums, workhouses and prisons

Lunatic asylums, workhouses and prisons were transformed during the nineteenth century. Under the influence of both evangelicalism and Utilitarianism, these three major public institutions replaced simple confinement with a reforming or curative process which aimed to prepare inmates for their productive and participatory return to the wider community. Clothing, especially uniforms, played a vital part in these reforming programmes. In the late eighteenth century it was not unusual for some lunatic asylum patients to be entirely naked. Uniforms were introduced in the nineteenth century, but almost immediately began to be dispensed with in favour of varied dress on the grounds that they inhibited the restoration of mental health. Uniforms were used in some workhouses under the old Poor Law, but after the 1834 Amendment Act they became more widespread and their purpose more punitive. However, by the close of the century their appropriateness for elderly paupers was being questioned. In the asylums and workhouses, therefore, at least for some inmates, the use of uniforms diminished. But in prisons, as long-term incarceration replaced transportation, all convicted criminals became uniformed and the emphasis on uniform dress only increased as the century proceeded.

In the second half of the century the combined inmates of prisons, workhouses and asylums nearly doubled from 166,682 in 1851 to 316,616 in 1901. Although at both dates this represented approximately one per cent of the total population, the spread across the institutions altered. While the workhouse and prison populations each rose by just over 50 per cent, the compulsory construction of county lunatic asylums from 1845 saw the number of patients increase more than fivefold, from 16,426 to 90,767.[1] In 1851 the asylum and workhouse populations were fairly evenly divided between men and women. This was still the case for

---

[1] *Census of Great Britain, 1851. Population Tables. II. Ages, Civil Condition, Occupations, and Birth-Place of the People: with the Numbers and Ages of the Blind, the Deaf-and-Dumb, and the Inmates of Workhouses, Prisons, Lunatic Asylums, and Hospitals.* Parliamentary

asylums in 1901, although males accounted for three-fifths of workhouse inmates. But in prisons, male inmates greatly outnumbered female. On Census day in 1851, 22,451 of the 26,855 inmates of the various prisons of Great Britain were male. Similarly, in 1901, 14,636 of the 17,480 persons detained in the civil prisons of England and Wales were male.[2]

The workhouse inmate was by definition a pauper, and the poor formed the majority of both prison and asylum populations. The occupational tables of the 1851 census show that the largest occupational group for males in all three types of institution was 'Labourer (branch undefined)', followed by agricultural labourer. Among the females the largest single occupational group by a wide margin was domestic servant, followed by significant numbers of milliners, washerwomen, charwomen and seamstresses. 'Gentlemen' accounted for only 306 of the total inmates of all three institutions, and 'Gentlewomen' 312.[3]

The preponderance of labouring men and women in prisons reflected their disproportionate representation in the populace generally, and the very needs borne of poverty could lead to criminal activity. The new public lunatic asylums erected from 1845 were built specifically to house pauper 'lunatics', which David Wright says led to an 'exodus' of lunatics from workhouses and gaols, where they had previously been confined but often not recorded, into the new public asylums.[4] But, as Elaine Murphy shows, many designated lunatics remained in workhouses where, in some instances, special wards were expanded to accommodate more inmates.[5] According to Steven Cherry, by 1859 the nation's lunatic asylums housed 17,608 patients which, he says was twice the lunatic population then in workhouses, which still means that there were nearly 9,000 pauper lunatics in the latter.[6] The key, says Murphy, was 'treatability', so that the 'acutely mad were welcome in the asylum, idiots and old dements' were not.[7] By Census day 1901 there were 14,972 insane persons in the

---

Papers 1852–53 LXXXVIII (I), pp. cccxi–xx; *Census of England and Wales. 1901. General Report with Appendices*. Parliamentary Papers 1904 CVIII, pp. 157, 161, 163–4.

[2] *Census of Great Britain, 1851. Population Tables. II.* Parliamentary Papers 1852–53 LXXXVIII (I), p. cxvii; *Census of England and Wales. 1901.* Parliamentary Papers 1904 CVIII pp. 161–3.

[3] *Census of Great Britain, 1851. Population Tables. II.* Parliamentary Papers 1852–53 LXXXVIII (I), pp. cccxii, cccxv, cccxxiii, cccxxv, cccxxvi, cccxxxii, cccxxxiv.

[4] David Wright, 'Getting out of the asylum: understanding the confinement of the insane in the nineteenth century', *Social History of Medicine*, 10:1 (1997), 137–55; 155.

[5] Elaine Murphy, 'Workhouse care of the insane, 1845–90', in Pamela Dale and Joseph Melling (eds), *Mental Illness and Learning Disability Since 1850: Finding A Place for Mental Disorder in the United Kingdom* (London: Routledge, 2006), pp. 24–45; pp. 27, 32, 39.

[6] Steven Cherry, *Mental Health Care in Modern England: The Norfolk Lunatic Asylum/St Andrew's Hospital c.1810–1998* (Woodbridge: Boydell Press, 2003), p. 51.

[7] Murphy, 'Workhouse care of the insane', p. 32.

workhouses of England and Wales, and Murphy says some 16 per cent of pauper lunatics were living in workhouses, except in London where a 'financial inducement' to move pauper lunatics from workhouses to asylums had reduced the proportion to 2 per cent.[8]

Wright believes the admission of pauper lunatics to asylums was 'a pragmatic response of households to the stresses of industrialization'. He calls for a new approach to the study of the asylum which focuses less on the history of psychiatry and more on nineteenth-century changes in household structure and the role of the family in the processes of caring for those with mental health problems and admitting them to institutions.[9] Akihito Suzuki's analysis of interviews with the families of labouring men admitted to Hanwell Asylum supports such an approach and, perhaps, helps to explain the large number of pauper lunatics. Suzuki found that the major lay explanations for the causes of insanity were the inter-related issues of anxiety about, or the experience of, poverty and unemployment, and 'the psychological strains caused by stressful domestic situations'. Furthermore, while those in authority believed idleness to be detrimental to mental health, the patients' families stressed 'the endless struggle to earn enough' and 'the psychological risk of overwork and exhaustion'.[10]

Clearly, then, there was a close link between pauper lunatic asylums and workhouses. As Peter Bartlett says, the county lunatic asylum was 'an institution legally based in the Poor Law, with Justices of the Peace in charge, and reliant on Poor Law officials to control and process admissions'.[11] It was Poor Law medical officers who authorised the transfer of inmates from workhouses to asylums and, ironically, Suzuki found that the workhouse was among the most commonly cited 'symbols of anxiety and fear of economic ruin which led to the mental diseases of those sent to the Hanwell Asylum'.[12] Suzuki also draws parallels between the new regimes in prisons and asylums, both of which, he says, aimed at efficient operation along military lines which stemmed from the large number of military veterans who found work in the civil service after the Napoleonic Wars. He claims an abundance of interconnections between asylum and prison staff, pointing out, for example, that

---

[8] *Census of England and Wales. 1901.* Parliamentary Papers 1904 CVIII, p. 157; Murphy, 'Workhouse care of the insane', pp. 39, 40.
[9] Wright, 'Getting out of the asylum', 139, 149–55.
[10] Suzuki, 'Lunacy and labouring men', pp. 120–3.
[11] Peter Bartlett, 'The asylum and the Poor Law: the productive alliance', in Joseph Melling and Bill Forsythe (eds), *Insanity, Institutions and Society 1800–1914* (London and New York: Routledge, 1999), pp. 48–67; p. 51.
[12] *Ibid.*, p. 50; Suzuki, 'Lunacy and labouring men', p. 126.

John Godwin, who was briefly appointed Governor of Hanwell Asylum in 1844, was a retired army officer who had previously applied for a position as prison governor. Roche emphasises the disciplinary potential and purpose of uniforms and demonstrates that the style of uniforms eventually imposed upon English nineteenth-century prisoners derived directly from the *ancien régime* military.[13]

For Suzuki, the asylum policy of non-restraint was as much a bureaucratic as a medical and humanitarian strategy, aimed at the maintenance of perfect order.[14] Likewise Bartlett highlights the maintenance of order as a priority in the workhouse, and says the asylum was necessary to ensure this by providing a place of removal for disruptive lunatic workhouse inmates.[15] According to David Garland, late-Victorian penal institutions served to separate 'the lowest sections of the working classes – the poor, the lumpenproletariat, the "criminal classes"', from 'their more "respectable" peers', to create 'a definite social division' between them which was strengthened by the economic difference between unskilled and skilled workers.[16] Garland does not say how this differed from the situation earlier in the century, but it is true that the erection of separate workhouses, asylums and prisons accommodated the desire to classify individuals, as poor, mad or criminal (and often in the case of the criminal lunatic asylum, as poor, mad and criminal) and to isolate them from the wider community. All three institutions also operated systems of further internal classification. In the workhouses inmates were categorised by age, sex, health, ability to work, marital status and behaviour. Also, asylums with mixed private and public patients classified and housed them according to their economic standing.[17] Many asylums also practised 'treatment by classification' under which 'people identified in a particular way from diagnosis and behaviour were "treated" or rather managed, in broadly similar ways'.[18] Prisons classified by gender, age,

---

[13] Roche, *Culture of Clothing*, Chapter 9.
[14] Akihito Suzuki, 'The politics and ideology of non-restraint: the case of the Hanwell Asylum', *Medical History*, 39:1 (1995), 1–17; 11–13, 16. Similarly, Allan Beveridge employs military imagery to describe Thomas Clouston, the Physician-superintendent of the Royal Edinburgh Asylum from 1873, as 'the supreme commander of an army of Asylum staff'. Allan Beveridge, 'Life in the asylum: patients' letters from Morningside, 1873–1908', *History of Psychiatry*, 9:36 (1998), 431–69; 432.
[15] Bartlett, 'The asylum and the Poor Law', pp. 56–7.
[16] Garland, *Punishment and Welfare*, p. 38.
[17] Rebecca Wynter, 'Good in all respects': appearance and dress at Staffordshire County Lunatic Asylum, 1818–54', *History of Psychiatry*, 22:1 (2011), 40–57; 45.
[18] Frank Crompton, 'Needs and desires in the care of pauper lunatics: admissions to Worcester Asylum, 1852–72', in Pamela Dale and Joseph Melling (eds), *Mental Illness and Learning Disability Since 1850. Finding A Place for Mental Disorder in the United Kingdom* (London: Routledge, 2006), pp. 46–64; pp. 59–60; See also Leonard D. Smith,

crime, sentence, length of stay and behaviour. And in all three institutions, clothing aided classification.

Although dress, and uniform in particular, was integral to the reforming and classificatory programmes of asylums, prisons and workhouses, as well as their orderly functioning, it has only recently begun to attract discrete scholarly attention. For example, in *The Most Solitary of Afflictions*, the update of his seminal 1979 *Museums of Madness*, Andrew Scull notes the nakedness prevalent in many asylums in the early years of the century, but is silent about when, why and in what manner the inhabitants became clothed.[19] So familiar and politically sensitive are prison uniforms that it seems astonishing that Juliet Ash, in her 2010 analysis of prison clothing, *Dress Behind Bars*, was able to claim 'this is an uncharted area of study'.[20] Like Ash, most historians who have examined asylum, prison or workhouse dress, have focused on one type of institution. Beginning with a brief history of the introduction, or increasing use, of uniforms in all three institutions, this chapter emphasises the close links between them, in particular the military influence on their operation. However, it continues by showing that despite their shared reforming purpose, the institutions' different types of inmate and the different reasons for their incarceration led to divergent clothing policies – policies which, nevertheless, all explicitly recognised and sought to exploit, either positively or negatively, the self-affirmatory and transformatory power of dress.

'Cure, Comfort, and Safe Custody': Public Lunatic Asylums in Early Nineteenth Century England (London: Leicester University Press, 1999), p. 192.

[19] Andrew Scull, *The Most Solitary of Afflictions: Madness and Society in Britain 1700–1900* (New Haven: Yale University Press, 1993), p. 127; Andrew Scull, *Museums of Madness: The Social Organisation of Insanity in Nineteenth-Century England* (London: Allen Lane, 1979). Elaine Showalter pays some attention to asylum dress, mentioning both Conolly and Granville who are discussed below, but only in relation to women. Elaine Showalter, *The Female Malady: Women, Madness and English Culture, 1830–1980* (London: Virago, 1987), pp. 84–5. Prison uniforms became as much a part of the disciplinary procedure as the isolation and work that Michel Foucault highlights, yet he is silent on the subject. Foucault, *Discipline and Punish*, pp. 231–44. Seán McConville's monumental work on English local prisons, despite three chapters entitled 'Enforcing Uniformity' which deal with issues such as discipline, labour and diet, is almost equally silent. Seán McConville, *English Local Prisons 1860–1900: Next Only to Death* (London: Routledge, 1995). Michael Ignatieff mentions early intentions to impose a uniform in the new penitentiaries, but says nothing about its implementation or the clothing issued. Michael Ignatieff, *A Just Measure of Pain: The Penitentiary in the Industrial Revolution 1750–1850* (Harmondsworth: Penguin, 1989 [1978]), pp. 93–4, 96. Philip Priestley and Michelle Higgs give descriptions of Victorian prison dress but being brief are necessarily rather generalised. Philip Priestley, *Victorian Prison Lives: English Prison Biography, 1830–1814* (London: Pimlico, 1999), pp. 19–22; Michelle Higgs, *Prison Life in Victorian England* (Stroud: Tempus, 2007), pp. 23–5.

[20] Juliet Ash, *Dress Behind Bars: Prison Clothing as Criminality* (London and New York: I. B. Tauris, 2009), p. 2.

Lunatic asylums

it grovelled, seemingly on all fours; it snatched and growled like some strange wild animal: but it was covered with clothing.[21] (*Jane Eyre*, 1847)

For Jane Eyre, encountering for the first time Rochester's mad wife, clothing was the only thing that distinguished 'lunatic' from animal. In fact, in the early nineteenth century, some of those diagnosed as mad were not afforded even this dignity, and although Jonathan Andrews argues that the 'failure to clothe the insane was neither as extreme nor as constant as has been claimed', conditions varied between and within asylums.[22] Select Committee reports in 1814 and 1816 identified deficiencies in every aspect of the asylum experience including the patients' clothes. There were complaints about insufficient parish provision of clothing for pauper patients in private madhouses and the staff issue of parish clothing to private patients to maximise profits. Even at the close of the eighteenth century some medical practitioners still perceived the insane to be insensitive to, and unaffected by, extremes of cold and pain, as well as unable to dress themselves. And so while the owner of a Bath asylum, instead of dressing his patients during the winter, 'sowed (*sic*) them up in a blanket', witnesses reported seeing patients across the country 'perfectly naked upon straw'.[23] Incontinent patients were particularly likely to be left naked, and when clothing was provided it was often second-hand and of poor quality.[24]

For the first half of the century, most 'madhouses' were privately owned, there was little regulation, and few counties took advantage of 1808 legislation allowing them to levy a rate for asylum construction. Exceptions were Lancaster and Wakefield, opened in 1816 and 1818 respectively, and which in 1828 physician Sir Andrew Halliday cited among the 'best regulated public asylums in England'.[25] Both clothed and occupied their patients, instead of leaving them idle and improperly dressed. These were aspects of 'moral treatment', which came into use in the late eighteenth century and which, Anne Digby explains, 'meant a concentration on the rational and emotional rather than the organic

---

[21] Charlotte Brontë, *Jane Eyre* (London: Everyman/J. M. Dent, 1996 [1847]), p. 292.
[22] Andrews, 'The (un)dress of the mad poor... Part 2', 149.
[23] *Report from the Committee on Madhouses in England*. Parliamentary Papers 1814–15 IV, pp. 11, 17, 20–1; *First Report: Minutes of Evidence Taken Before the Select Committee Appointed to Consider of Provision Being Made for the Better Regulation of Madhouses, in England*. Parliamentary Papers 1816 IV, pp. 6–7.
[24] Jonathan Andrews, 'The (un)dress of the mad poor in England, c.1650–1850. Part 1', *History of Psychiatry*, 18:1 (2007), 5–24; 16–17. Andrews, 'The (un)dress of the mad poor... Part 2', 133, 143–4.
[25] Andrew Halliday, *A General View of the Present State of Lunatics, and Lunatic Asylums, in Great Britain and Ireland, and in Some Other Kingdoms* (London, 1828), p. 17.

causes of insanity', and encompassed a variable 'range of non-medical treatments designed to involve the patient actively in his recovery'.[26] In her study of the York Retreat, a Quaker asylum which opened in 1796 and practised moral treatment, Digby says that what made it so special was 'the unexpected *normality* of life there... patients were encouraged, as far as their illness allowed, to participate fully in a domestic pattern of life: to dress in ordinary clothes'.[27]

Moral therapy also included the abandonment of mechanical restraints such as leg irons, chains and straitjackets, which were often replaced with specially devised clothing. John Conolly, from 1839 physician at the Hanwell Asylum, was among the most prominent and enthusiastic advocates of this practice. Inspired by Robert Gardiner Hill, the medical officer at Lincoln asylum, Conolly issued 'strong dresses' – garments made from material which was difficult to tear – to patients who destroyed or removed their clothing. Leather binding around collars and cuffs thwarted those who tried to destroy them with their teeth, while 'warm boots, fastened round the ankles by a small lock' protected the feet of patients who would not lie down. The 'varied contrivances' had 'variable results', but within months of his appointment Conolly announced that the use of 'the strait-waistcoat, the muff, the restraint-chair, and of every kind of strap and chain designed to restrain muscular motion' had been discontinued.[28]

Conolly saw a role for clothing in the treatment of all patients, not only the refractory, believing '[s]loveliness of dress', was 'unfavourable to mental composure'.[29] The clothing was to be new, adjusted to the seasons, not irritating to the skin, kept in good order and tidily worn. Female patients were not to 'go about bareheaded', it being 'not natural to the woman to neglect the dress of her head'. And he expressed his 'extreme disapprobation' of the 'excesses of economy' which placed 'male pauper lunatics in... second-hand clothing which does not fit them, or in old leather breeches, and soldiers' jackets, dyed'.[30]

---

[26] Smith, '*Cure, Comfort and Safe Custody*', pp. 189–90; Anne Digby, 'Moral treatment at the Retreat, 1796–1846', in W. F. Bynum, Roy Porter and Michael Shepherd (eds), *The Anatomy of Madness: Essays in the History of Psychiatry*, 2 vols (London and New York: Tavistock Publications, 1985), vol. II, pp. 52–72; p. 53.

[27] Anne Digby, *Madness, Morality and Medicine: A Study of the York Retreat, 1796–1914* (Cambridge University Press, 1985), p. 51.

[28] John Conolly, *The Treatment of the Insane Without Mechanical Restraints* (London: Smith, Elder and Co., 1856), pp. 193–4, 199.

[29] John Conolly, *An Inquiry Concerning the Indications of Insanity, with Suggestions for the Better Protection and Care of the Insane* (London: John Taylor, 1830), p. 199.

[30] John Conolly, *The Construction and Government of Lunatic Asylums and Hospitals for the Insane* (London: John Churchill, 1847), pp. 60–3.

In 1845 the Lunatics Asylums and Pauper Lunatics Act compelled every county and borough in England and Wales to provide suitable facilities for their pauper lunatics and the accompanying Lunacy Act appointed six paid (and between two and five honorary) Lunacy Commissioners to monitor, regulate and annually inspect the asylums.[31] The Commissioners reserved most praise for those asylums operating along the lines advocated by Conolly whose refined and expanded theories were published in an 1856 treatise in which he argued that some habits generally considered deranged, such as 'hoarding up strange finery of beads and lace', were, in fact, evidence of a residual self-respect on which asylum staff should capitalise. He dismissed those who considered money spent on clothing to be wasted, assuring them that: 'The poor patients in the county asylums fully appreciate the comfort of a Sunday-dress; and the liberality which supplies a decent suit of clothes, or a neat gown and cap selected by the wearer, is by no means thrown away.'[32]

Initially, public asylums introduced uniforms for the patients and Rebecca Wynter found that even when a uniform was not intentional, bulk clothing purchase produced a uniform appearance among pauper patients.[33] At first, Conolly too favoured uniforms and at Hanwell the men wore grey broadcloth and the women gowns of grey linsey. But Conolly quite rapidly moved to variety of dress for female patients, claiming that it was impossible to soothe some unless they were allowed to wear their own clothes. In contrast, he believed uniforms for male pauper patients contributed 'greatly to their general good appearance, as a variety of male dress cannot be so neatly preserved as to avoid a miscellaneous shabbiness' as women's dress. However, style was important and at Hanwell he recommended the substitution of a short coat for the round jacket disliked by many of the men, and a little variety to be permitted by allowing the men to choose the colour and kind of their hats and neck-handkerchiefs.[34]

Opposition to asylum uniforms increased with the passage of time.[35] In 1876 J. Mortimer Granville, with the benefit of twenty years' study of lunacy, penned the *Lancet* Commission on Lunatic Asylums reports. According to Granville, insanity resulted from a lack of self-control and was 'an affair of three w's – worry, want, and wickedness'. Cure was 'a matter of three m's – method, meat and morality', and in Granville's method clothing was second in importance only to food. He was even

---

[31] Andrew Roberts, '5: The Lunacy Commission', *The Lunacy Commission, A Study of its Origin, Emergence and Character*, studymore.org.uk/5s.htm.
[32] Conolly, *Treatment of the Insane*, p. 89.   [33] Wynter, 'Good in all respects', 46.
[34] Conolly, *Construction and Government*, pp. 61–2.
[35] Smith, *'Cure, Comfort and Safe Custody'*, p. 276.

more strongly opposed to uniforms than Conolly, believing they encouraged institutionalisation. 'I cannot imagine', he wrote, 'a more depressing sensation than that produced by being put into an asylum uniform. It looks so like providing for a lengthened residence', which ran counter to the aim of fitting patients for return to the outside world. He attributed insistence on uniforms among asylum committees and medical attendants to 'an exaggerated notion of the value of... "discipline,"' and 'fear of the Commissioners, who are much too ready to set down any omission in the matter of dress to neglect or parsimony'.[36]

Like Conolly, Granville thought the effects of uniforms more pernicious among females, and that women's (innate) desire for attractive clothing could be used to manage them. 'Dress', he said, 'is woman's weakness, and in the treatment of lunacy it should be an instrument of control, and therefore of recovery.' At the West Riding Asylum he had been 'much struck with the ingenuity displayed' with regard to dress claiming that 'a little cheap trimming' had made the female patients' dresses 'so attractive that they come to be worn with pride'. But even among the men, Granville believed 'the avoidance of a dull uniformity, indicative of a permanent separation from society', to be essential. Granville also believed variety of clothing would even obviate the need for 'strong' dresses. Half the patients who tore their clothing did so, he claimed, because it irritated their skin, the other half because they 'do not like their costume'. While he thought it unwise 'to pander to the morbid whims of the insane', or to give in to violence, he believed 'some concession... to a strongly indicated wish for better clothing' would aid recovery. He also advocated allotting 'the best attire... to patients as the reward of especially good conduct and the most intelligent self-control'.[37] Dress, then, was to be both a means of recovery and a reward for its achievement.

Granville's reference to 'the best attire' indicates the varied quality or condition of clothing not only between but within asylums, which is corroborated by inspectors' reports. In 1870, for instance, at Cornwall County Asylum, while some private patients 'were but poorly dressed', the inspectors had 'the satisfaction of reporting favourably of the personal condition and clothing of the pauper patients'. But at Derby County Asylum, while '[t]he women especially were remarkably clean and well dressed', there were a larger number than usual of the men wearing strong

---

[36] J. Mortimer Granville, *The Care and Cure of the Insane. Being the Reports of The Lancet Commission on Lunatic Asylums 1875–6–7 For Middlesex, the City of London and Surrey*, 2 vols (London: Hardwicke & Bogue, 1877), vol. II, p. 173.
[37] Granville, *Care and Cure of the Insane*, vol. I, pp. 52–3.

dresses, and 'much less neatness in their clothing generally than in the female division'.[38] The Commissioners consistently praised variety of dress, especially among female patients, and condemned the continued use of 'strong dresses' for refractory patients. At Barming Heath, Kent, in 1880, for example, they found 'no special fault', but there was 'room for improvement'. For the women, they said, 'a little outlay in ribbon and other cheap material... would achieve a good deal, and patients then caring more for their dress would probably acquire better ways, and generally recover some selfrespect (sic)'.[39]

Ten years later they applauded the introduction of 'variety of colour and texture' in the women's dresses, but still wished to see many more 'with white collars, relieving the sombreness of their dress, and lending an appearance of contrast to their complexions and dark hues of their gowns'. At Chartham the material of the women's gowns was 'good enough, but the make... far too careless', and the 'buttonless or unbuttoned condition' of the men's clothes indicated neglect by the male attendants.[40] By the close of the century, the inspectors still found eighteen patients at Hanwell in strong dresses, though 'of an unobstrusive (sic) character', and hoped that the physician at the Claybury Asylum, London, would 'be able to devise some less repulsive form of strong dress for the women'. But, on the whole, phrases such as 'bright and varied', or 'satisfactory and creditable to those in charge' characterised their reports and at Stafford their major complaint was the danger posed by female patients being in possession of the long hat pins then in fashion.[41]

The inspectors' reports indicate a continuing and increasing concern with the style and quality of the patients' clothing, and a trajectory of continual improvement. Whether the patients' and their families agreed is rather more difficult to ascertain. To be branded a lunatic was stigmatic and patients' first-hand accounts of the asylum experience are rare.[42] But one example was published in 1867, its anonymous author subsequently

---

[38] *Lunacy. Copy of the Twenty-Fourth Report of the Commissioners in Lunacy to the Lord Chancellor.* Parliamentary Papers 1870 XXXIC, pp. 125, 130.
[39] *Lunacy. Copy of the Thirty-Fourth Report of the Commissioners in Lunacy to the Lord Chancellor.* Parliamentary Papers 1880 XXIX, pp. 230–1.
[40] *Lunacy. Copy of the Forty-Fourth Report of the Commissioners in Lunacy to the Lord Chancellor.* Parliamentary Papers 1890 XXXC, pp. 197, 199.
[41] *Lunacy. Copy of the Fifty-Fourth Report of the Commissioners in Lunacy to the Lord Chancellor.* Parliamentary Papers 1900 XXXVII, pp. 315, 316, 320, 348.
[42] In Porter's study of the autobiographies of 'mad people', the only two English nineteenth-century lunatic autobiographers on whom he focuses, John Clare and John Perceval, were incarcerated in private asylums. Roy Porter, *A Social History of Madness: Stories of the Insane* (London: Weidenfeld & Nicolson, 1987), pp. 76–81, 167–88.

identified as John Weston, a patient in the Bristol Borough Asylum, which opened in 1861.[43] On admission Weston was issued with precisely the kind of clothes Conolly had so deplored in 1847 – second-hand, ill-fitting, uncomfortable, and with no adaptation for the change of climate:

> an old check shirt, buttoning at the back, and so loose at the neck that it fell down low in front, and when the gingham necktie was on, left a space uncovered just at the wind-pipe... an old cloth jacket and waistcoat, all open at the chest, and the mouth of the sleeves so loose as to resemble a mandarin's oriental overall, and old washed white corduroys, without drawers... This proved to be the garb, winter and summer, with perhaps some dead man's old shoes, newly fortified with patches on the toes.

For Weston this shabby institutional dress was emasculating; when he changed it for his own clothes on release he felt himself to be 'putting off the pauper, and once more putting on the man'.[44]

In asylums which housed both pauper and private patients, better clothing, or permission to wear their own, was part of what the wealthy paid for.[45] In the day-room Weston had seen two other patients, 'dressed in their own clothes – gentlemen, I was told – private patients'. His own clothing improved only because the asylum garments were allocated to a specific ward and he happened to be moved to one which chanced to have better clothing. A patient from his previous ward seeing Weston in the exercise yard teased him saying: 'Oh, I suppose you won't speak to me now that you are promoted. You are so proud of your fine clothes.'[46]

As far as the inspectors were aware, separate Sunday clothing was becoming commonplace. At Lincolnshire Asylum in 1880 they were told that 'Sunday suits are given... to those of the men who can appreciate the luxury; the very dirty and demented being alone without such suits. The women have a Sunday change of dress, also.'[47] But the inspectors did not visit on Sundays and so were reliant on the word of the asylum officials. Weston found that there was, indeed, a different Sunday dress

---

[43] Jane Hamlett and Lesley Hoskins, 'Comfort in small things? Clothing, control and agency in county lunatic asylums in nineteenth- and early twentieth-century England', *Journal of Victorian Culture*, 18:1 (2013), 93–114; 99.

[44] Anon. [John Weston], *Life in a Lunatic Asylum: an Autobiographical Sketch* (London, 1867), pp. 13, 100.

[45] Leonard Smith, '"Your very thankful inmate": discovering the patients of an early county lunatic asylum', *Social History of Medicine*, 21:2 (2008), 237–252; 245; Wynter, 'Good in all respects', 45–6.

[46] Anon., *Life in a Lunatic Asylum*, pp. 13, 51. Allan Beveridge found similar discrepancies between pauper and private patients, as well as instances of the 'demoralizing and degrading' effects of asylum clothing, in this case uniforms, at the Royal Edinburgh Asylum. Beveridge, 'Life in the asylum', 433, 453.

[47] *Lunacy.... Thirty-Fourth Report*. Parliamentary Papers 1880 XXIX, p. 252.

at Bristol – but only for the select few who attended a nearby church and were therefore seen in public.[48] The issue of Sunday best to asylum inmates recognised its social and cultural significance, but its restricted distribution and identification as a 'luxury' suggest it had not become routine asylum practice as Conolly had recommended in 1856.

The history of asylum dress is not a simple unbroken narrative of improvement, and Diana Gittins notes that at Severalls Hospital in Essex, uniform clothing, albeit with variation of colours and patterns, was worn until 1960.[49] But the transition from leg iron to hat pin was profound, although according to Foucault, dressing asylum patients in ordinary clothes was part of an invidious transition from 'physical constraint' to 'self-restraint', the clothes imposing an artificial normality which only masked and silenced the madness.[50] And Akihito Suzuki, who thinks Conolly was a good administrator, but a poor psychiatrist, believes his insistence on good, comfortable, patient clothing was simply part of his endeavour to maintain order among the 'super-sensitive and hyper-irritable' patients.[51] But as Leonard Smith says, such interpretations ignore the genuinely humanitarian (if imperfectly realised) intentions that lay behind reform in the new institutions.[52]

Workhouses

The 1834 Poor Law Amendment Act not only restricted the issue of clothing as outdoor relief, but in its attempts to make the workhouse the only source of relief available to able-bodied paupers increased the numbers of those compelled to don the workhouse dress. But both before and after 1834, as with prisons and lunatic asylums, whether or not an indoor pauper was required to wear workhouse clothing, and whether that clothing constituted a uniform, depended on when and where he or she was incarcerated.[53] Under the Old Poor Law, some parishes appear to have supplied clothing only as needed by each individual, some issued a regulation and punitive uniform, while others stipulated that workhouse clothing be worn but it is by no means certain that it was intended as a disciplinary measure.

In 1797, for example, Eden found that inmates at a Shrewsbury workhouse were to be clothed only 'if thought necessary' to 'avoid infectious

---

[48] Anon., *Life in a Lunatic Asylum*, p. 39.   [49] Gittins, *Madness in its Place*, pp. 1, 134–5.
[50] Foucault, *Madness and Civilization*, pp. 236–7.
[51] Suzuki, 'The politics and ideology of non-restraint', 15.
[52] Smith, 'Cure, Comfort and Safe Custody', p. 276.
[53] See, for example, Norman Longmate, *The Workhouse: A Social History* (London: Pimlico, 2003), pp. 93, 138–9, 145, 178; Digby, *Pauper Palaces*, pp. 38, 45, 146, 155, 157, 165.

distempers'.[54] But at Laleham, Middlesex, in 1805, the rules for the new workhouse proposed that resident paupers were to 'wear the parish Uniform', and punishments for bad behaviour were to include 'Distinction of Dress'.[55] At Greenwich in 1828, inmates were also required to wear the house dress, but here the Contractor was to supply:

> good sufficient Shoes, Hats, Bonnets, Caps, and Wearing Apparel of all kinds, as well Linen as Woollen, two things of each sort for every poor person admitted into the Workhouse, suitable to their age and sex.

Furthermore, the linen, night caps and stockings were to be changed every Sunday morning and wigs were to be provided 'for such as wear them or require them, in the judgment of the Churchwardens, Overseers, and Governors and Directors'.[56] If the inmates were so liberally supplied in practice, the quantity of clothing, the specification of linen and wool, the stipulation that the clothing be 'good', the suitability for age and gender, and the provision of wigs, supports Steven King's claim of generous parish provision.[57]

But the implicit benevolence of the Greenwich overseers would have dismayed George Nicholls who, in a series of letters to the local newspaper, reproduced in an 1822 pamphlet, detailed the 'improvements' he had made in the management of the poor at Southwell, Nottinghamshire. Nicholls believed that if a poorhouse was necessary it should be only for the 'aged infirm and needy', and the rules

> should be so strict and repulsive, – the living, the clothing, and the comforts provided in it, should be of such a description, as not to excite a desire for partaking of them among others.

His desire was 'to see the *Poor House* looked to with dread by our labouring classes, and the reproach for being an inmate of it extend downwards from Father to Son'.[58]

The heavily annotated copy of Nicholls's Southwell pamphlet at the British Library was the property of Edwin Chadwick, architect of the 1834 Poor Law Amendment Act under which parishes were grouped into Unions and required to erect a workhouse. On admission, inmates were to surrender their own clothes and assume 'the workhouse dress', which 'shall, as far as may be practicable, be made by the paupers in

---

[54] Eden, *State of the Poor*, vol. II, p. 627.
[55] LMA, DRO 21/64, All Saints' Laleham Vestry Minute Book, 1803–1848.
[56] Joint Vestry, *Papers relating to the Parishes of St. Giles and St. George Bloomsbury. Abstract of the Contract for Maintaining the In-door Poor of the Parish of Greenwich* (London, 1826–51).
[57] See Chapter 7.
[58] An Overseer [Sir George Nicholls], *Eight Letters on the Management of Our Poor, and the General Administration of the Poor Laws* (Newark, 1822), pp. 18–19.

the workhouse'.⁵⁹ Although, as Longmate points out, the regulations did not require the clothing to be a uniform, as Wynter found in the lunatic asylums, economies of scale meant that in practice it always was.⁶⁰ Economy also meant clothing was issued from stock, so it was a matter of chance whether inmates were given garments that fitted them, and the same clothes were reissued to inmate after inmate.

Like prisons and asylums, workhouses aimed at moral reform of the inmates. When ten-year-old Charles Shaw entered the Chell workhouse in 1842 he was 'roughly disrobed, roughly and coldly washed, and roughly attired in rough clothes'.⁶¹ The clothing of Kent workhouse boys and their schoolmaster in a photograph taken around 1870 is in a shocking condition. While each boy appears to have a full suit of trousers, jacket or smock and neckerchief, they are badly torn, the trousers in particular, and stained.⁶² Such 'rough clothes' were part of the harsh conditions that aimed to instil a desire never to return. And even if paupers were sometimes better clad in the new workhouse than they had been prior to admission, the stigma of residence generally outweighed the material advantage.⁶³ 'I dread the workhouse', a blind tailor told Mayhew, 'for the workhouse coat is a slothful, degrading badge. After a man has had one on his back, he's never the same.'⁶⁴

Disregard of important social and sartorial customs could further compound the humiliation of wearing workhouse dress. Clare Rose notes that workhouse boys of all ages might be dressed in the same style, denying them the clothing changes that for other working-class boys marked the transitional stages from child- to adulthood.⁶⁵ The boys in the Kent photograph appear to be wearing wooden clogs, commonly issued because they were cheap, but virtually unknown in southern England outside the workhouse. When, as adults, John Castle and his brother entered the Witham workhouse in 1836 they were 'ordered to strip and put on the regimentals of the Union'. These consisted of 'a pair of thick leather breeches', at a time when breeches had generally been replaced by trousers, 'leather coat, low shoes, ribbed stockings and a hairy cap with peak'. When the brothers got leave to visit relatives one Sunday, there was no change of clothing and Castle was pleased to borrow a suit

---

⁵⁹ *Poor Law Amendment Act. Copies of Orders, &c. issued by the Poor Law Commissioners relating to the Poor Law Amendment Act; with an account of money expended for the relief and maintenance of the poor, &c. in England and Wales from 1834 to 1840 inclusive*. Parliamentary Papers 1841 XXI, p. 10.
⁶⁰ Longmate, *The Workhouse*, p. 93.   ⁶¹ Shaw, *When I Was a Child*, pp. 97–8.
⁶² J. Worth, *Shadows of the Workhouse*, photographs between pp. 166–7.
⁶³ Digby, *Pauper Palaces*, p. 146.   ⁶⁴ Mayhew, *London Labour*, vol. I, p. 344.
⁶⁵ C. Rose, *Making, Selling, and Wearing*, p. 36.

from a cousin to avoid paying calls in the Union 'regimentals'.[66] Some thirty-five years later Munby, coming across two young women from the Kensington workhouse, noted their old-fashioned dress. 'Many people', he said, 'turned round to look at these two lasses in their coarse and lowly dress, so different from the Sunday finery of the milliners, & even of the servants, around.'[67]

It was, says Steven King, 'above all old age that could generate chronic long-term need and marginality for those not anyway caught in the culture of endemic poverty', and as the report of the 1851 Census noted: 'In the workhouses are found some of the oldest people in the country.'[68] As able-bodied young men, the Castle brothers were the prime targets of the punitive new Poor Law but as the century progressed the workhouse population increasingly consisted of elderly paupers who, simply owing to 'the scanty earnings of their class', had been unable to provide for old age.[69] Of the 126,488 paupers resident in the workhouses of England and Wales in 1851, 18,489 were aged seventy or above, and the elderly were far more likely to be long-term residents than younger paupers.[70] While they sometimes received more sympathetic treatment than the able-bodied, the Act made no provision for this, and with the recognition that their poverty was no fault of their own, concern about their plight mounted. In 1892 the *Bristol Mercury*, for example, reported that the Islington Union had 'decided upon a distinctly revolutionary change' by providing 'ordinary clothes' instead of the 'hideous and degrading' workhouse uniform, for inmates aged over sixty to wear when out in public. The Clapham and Wandsworth Guardians were considering the same policy and the *Mercury* looked forward to the time when Bristol would follow suit, considering that both the elderly and children should be free from the 'stigma' of 'distinctive dress'.[71] While this was a step forward, the amendment was limited to the public display of the paupers' clothing, not the essential sense of shame it often instilled in the wearer, whether or not it was exposed to public view.

In 1893 the Royal Commission on the Aged Poor was established to inquire into poor relief provision for the elderly. W. E. Knollys, Chief General Inspector and Assistant Secretary to the Local Government

---

[66] Burnett, *Destiny Obscure*, pp. 275–6.
[67] TCLC, MUNB, 40, 28 January 1872. Needless to say, Munby thoroughly approved of them.
[68] S. King, *Poverty and Welfare*, p. 255; *Census of Great Britain, 1851. Population Tables. II.* Parliamentary Papers 1852–53 LXXXVIII (I), p. cxxvii.
[69] *Bristol Mercury and Daily Post*, 18 April 1892, p. 5.
[70] *Census of Great Britain, 1851. Population Tables. II.* Parliamentary Papers 1852–53 LXXXVIII (I), pp. cxvi, cxvii.
[71] *Bristol Mercury and Daily Post*, 18 April 1892, p. 5.

Board which, since 1871, had been responsible for Poor Law administration, gave evidence on workhouse clothing 'outside the metropolis', which he believed to be commensurate with the more enlightened London Unions, such as Islington. On admission, he said, men would be issued with:

> A cloth cap or felt hat, a working-day suit, coat, waistcoat, and trousers of moleskin or corduroy; and another suit, a Sunday or liberty suit, of gray or brown tweed, or blue pilot cloth, two shirts (cotton), two shirts (flannel), two pairs of drawers, two pairs of hose, one pair of boots, two neckties, and two pocket handkerchiefs.

The clothing for female inmates consisted of:

> Two gowns of serge or linsey, two upper petticoats, two flannel petticoats, two flannel chemises, two calico chemises, two pair of hose, a pair of stays, a pair of boots, two aprons, two nightgowns, one neck-shawl, woollen, for the winter, one neck-shawl, cotton, for the summer, two handkerchiefs, two caps, one woollen for winter wear, and the other muslin for summer wear, and a bonnet and shawl, such as would be worn by any other woman outside the house.

In practice, however, universal provision was neither so liberal nor so respectful of sartorial convention. When pressed, Knollys admitted that he had known workhouses where the inmates were not provided with Sunday clothing, which had prevented them attending church, and that the question of whether they should be provided with two suits was 'a matter for the discretion of the guardians'. And while he initially claimed that: 'Anything in the shape of uniform is now avoided as much as possible', he was subsequently able to say only that 'the effort is being made in an increasing number of instances to prevent anything like a uniform for inmates of workhouses'.[72]

The Commission resulted in an 1895 circular, recommending more 'comforts' to elderly workhouse inmates, including permission to wear their own clothes, but as Pat Thane says, this advice was 'followed slowly and unevenly'.[73] Photographs of the St Pancras and St Marylebone workhouses in London, published respectively in 1897 and between 1904 and 1906, show row upon row of elderly paupers in almost identical clothing (Fig. 10.1).[74] The text accompanying the St Pancras image conceded

---

[72] *Royal Commission on the Aged Poor. Minutes of Evidence Taken Before the Royal Commission on the Aged Poor. Days 1 to 26. Vol. II.* Parliamentary Papers 1895 XIV, p. 47.
[73] Pat Thane, *Old Age in English History: Past Experiences, Present Issues* (Oxford University Press, 2000), p. 192.
[74] See also the photographs of elderly female paupers at Poplar Workhouse, c.1905, and male paupers at St Pancras Workhouse, c.1906, in J. Worth, *Shadows of the Workhouse*, between pp. 166–7.

Fig. 10.1. Top: Dining Hall, St Pancras Workhouse, c.1897. Bottom: Dining Hall, St Marylebone Workhouse, c.1905.

that the refuge offered to the inmates 'as their only home for long years' was neither 'luxurious or attractive', while observers of the St Marylebone photograph were invited to first: 'Tarry awhile at the porter's lodge, and watch the incomers before they lose some of their individuality.'[75] The images are a powerful testament to the endurance and depersonalising effect of uniform dress and demonstrate one of the reasons why, according to Akihito Suzuki: 'Old age and the attendant reduction or loss of income loomed large in the mental landscape of working-class men.'[76]

Prisons

Quite suddenly there appeared a person dressed in the most extraordinary garb I had ever seen outside a pantomime. It was my first close view of a convict... The whole clothes were of a peculiar kind of brown (which I have never seen outside a prison), profusely embellished with broad arrows... A short jacket, ill-fitting knickerbockers, black stockings striped with red leather shoes. Whether he wore a shirt or not, I cannot say... It sounds more or less like a bicycle suit, but it is not. There is something about the whole cut of prison clothes which is seen nowhere else.[77]

In 1889, a Committee of Inquiry was established to investigate 'the Rules concerning the Wearing of Prison Dress'. Its final report contained an appendix, 'Prison dress historically considered', written by the Committee's Secretary, Major Arthur Griffiths, a prison inspector who had been deputy governor of three prisons.[78] According to Griffiths, when the prison reformer John Howard made his first inspection of English prisons, in 1777, he found clothing provided in just three, Warwick, Reading and Nottingham, where he believed its purpose was to reduce the spread of gaol fever, which posed as great a threat to judge and jury as it did to prisoners. Visiting the new gaol at Horsham, Sussex, two years later Howard noted with approval that the men wore a green striped uniform. The clothing was, he believed, better than that in which many were admitted, it prevented the surrender of prisoners' own clothes as bribes to warders, and aided detection of escapees. As Griffiths pointed out, the government signalled its approval of prison-issue clothing when

---

[75] Anon., *The Queen's Empire: A Pictorial and Descriptive Record* (London, Paris and Melbourne: Cassell and Company Ltd, 1897), p. 276; George R. Sims (ed.), *Living London*, 3 vols (London, Paris, New York and Melbourne: Cassell and Company Ltd, 1906), vol. II, p. 100.
[76] Suzuki, 'Lunacy and labouring men', p. 125.
[77] Jabez Spencer Balfour, *My Prison Life* (London: Chapman and Hall, 1907), pp. 36–7.
[78] Bill Forsythe, 'Griffiths, Arthur George Frederick (1838–1908)', *Oxford Dictionary of National Biography*, Oxford University Press, 2004, www.oxforddnb.com.

it passed legislation in 1794 authorising the erection of a penitentiary on Jeremy Bentham's plan, which stipulated that inmates were to be clad in a 'state of tightness and neatness superior to what is usual even in the improved prisons'.[79] However, that penitentiary never materialised and forty years later Joseph Gurney, visiting northern prisons with his sister, Elizabeth Fry, found them united only in their diversity of practice.[80] As Thomas Fowell Buxton put it: 'Some prisons provide a dress, others do not; some prisoners are comfortably clad, and some are almost naked.'[81]

The introduction of prison uniforms was gradual and uneven, reflecting the tension between the local authorities on the one hand and the ultimately triumphant government officials and penal reformers on the other. The former, often resistant to central interference, were under pressure from rate-payers, who financed the prisons, to house offenders as cheaply as possible. The latter, as transportation declined, sought an alternative in long-term imprisonment, centrally and consistently administered. But equally significant was the introduction, alongside the traditional goals of incarceration and punishment, of new notions of repentance and reform in which the uniforms played a key role.

The National Penitentiary at Millbank, opened in 1816, was the first prison built and directly managed by the government. As a reformed prison the inmates' own clothes were taken away, and a prison dress provided.[82] Seven years later, the Gaol Act of 1823 attempted to impose a degree of uniformity on the running of the nation's local prisons and stipulated that a prison uniform could be imposed if those in charge thought it 'expedient', although pre-trial prisoners were to be compelled to wear prison clothing only if their own was inadequate or needed to be confiscated 'for the purposes of justice'.[83]

By 1841 over £17,000 was spent annually on prison clothing in England and Wales, but its distribution was uneven.[84] Generally, town and borough gaols, like debtors' prisons, did not provide clothing except on

---

[79] *Prison Rules Inquiry*... Parliamentary Papers 1889 LXI, pp. 69, 89.
[80] Joseph John Gurney, *Notes on a Visit Made to Some of the Prisons in Scotland and the North of England, in Company with Elizabeth Fry. With Some General Observations on the Subject of Prison Discipline* (London, 1819), p. 114.
[81] Thomas Fowell Buxton, *An Inquiry Whether Crime and Misery are Produced or Prevented, by our Present System of Prison Discipline* (London: J. and A. Arch, 1818), p. 71.
[82] Buxton, *An Inquiry*, pp. 103–5.
[83] *A Bill for Consolidating and Amending the Laws Relating to the Building, Repairing, and Regulating of Certain Gaols, Bridewells, and Houses of Correction, in England and Wales*, Parliamentary Papers 1823 I, p. 9. (Intituled an Act 18 June 1823.)
[84] *Seventh Report of the Inspectors... Prisons... I. Home District.* Parliamentary Papers 1842 XX, p. 205.

Table 10.1. Examples of clothing issued to prisoners compiled from data in the prison inspectors' 1842 report

Garment	Millbank Penitentiary M	Millbank Penitentiary F	Bedford County House of Correction, Bedfordshire M	Bedford County House of Correction, Bedfordshire F	Colchester County House of Correction, Essex M	Colchester County House of Correction, Essex F	Coldbath Fields House of Correction, Middlesex M	Coldbath Fields House of Correction, Middlesex F
Stays, busk and lace		1						
Bonnet and shawl		1						
Night cap	1	2		1				
Day cap	1	2	1	1	1	1	1	1
Jacket	1		1		1		1	
Waistcoat	1		1		1		1	
Trowsers (pair)	1		1		1		1	
Shirt	3		1		1		1	
Stockings (pair)	3	3	1	1	1	1	1	1
Handkerchief	6	7	1	1			1	2
Shoes (pair)	2	2	1	1	1	1	1	1
Braces	1							
Gown		1		1		1		1
Petticoat		1		1		1		1
Linsey woolsey petticoat		1						
Flannel petticoat				1				1
Shift		3		1		1		1
Coloured apron		2						
White apron		1						
Wrapper								1

an individual basis when absolutely necessary, while county gaols and houses of correction did, although few were as liberal as Millbank (see Table 10.1). As the first prison inspectors were not introduced until 1835 – and then only five in number – the standard of dress a prisoner could expect depended largely on the extent to which justices and prison governors chose to comply with central instructions and recommendations. At St Alban's, for example, in 1842, the inspectors discovered pre-trial prisoners compelled to wear the prison dress in direct contravention of the Gaol Act, despite the Secretary of State having written to the visiting justices about it.[85]

Prison dress also varied according to the regime under which inmates were confined. In 1842 the opening of the 'model prison' at Pentonville and the introduction of the 'separate system' ensured offenders had ample time to ponder the enormity of their sins by prohibiting all communication between them. To this end, male inmates wore 'a peculiar brown cloth cap', the peak of which, said Mayhew, 'hangs so low down as to cover the face like a mask, the eyes alone of the individual appearing through the two holes cut in the front'. Females under the separate system wore 'small black alpaca veils'. The masks and veils were abolished when the prisons came under central government control as tending 'to depress the spirits' of the wearers.[86] One prisoner who spent three months under the separate system, during which he 'never even saw the face of the man next to me', declared he 'should ha' been dead long afore now' if it had continued.[87]

Inspectors generally favoured uniforms and by mid century their earlier complaints about incorrect imposition gave way to criticism of partial or total absence. They argued that a full suit of clothes would reduce recidivism and thus further cost,

> for if a man should wear out his own clothes... in prison, he will be unable to undertake a respectable employment on his discharge from prison, and will be thus exposed to an additional temptation to criminal courses.[88]

By 1865 all convicted criminals were required to wear a prison uniform and when the 1877 Prison Act brought all prisons under central government control, it made no further alterations to the 1865 dress regulations although abuses continued.[89] But from 1898 convicted offenders were to be placed in one of three divisions. Division I prisoners were allowed to wear their own clothes, while Division III prisoners, who were expected to form the majority, were to wear the standard prison uniform. Division II was a new category of privileged prisoners who were to be kept apart from those in Division III, to wear a different uniform and to receive

---

[85] *Ibid.*, p. 139.   [86] Mayhew and Binny, *Criminal Prisons*, pp. 141–2, 524.

[87] Anon., *Her Majesty's Prisons. Their Effects and Defects. By One Who Has Tried Them*, 2 vols (London: Sampson Low, Marston, Searle, and Rivington, 1881), vol. I, p. 202.

[88] *Fifteenth Report of the Inspectors Appointed, Under the Provisions of the Act 5 & 6 Will. IV. c.38, to Visit the Different Prisons of Great Britain*. Parliamentary Papers 1850 XXVIII, p. 33.

[89] Robert Wilkinson, *The Law of Prisons in England And Wales, Being the Prison Act, 1865 (28 & 29 Vict. C.126) and The Prison Act, 1877 (40 & 41 Vict. C.21), With an Analysis of Acts; Notes; A Selection of Other Acts, and Portions of Acts Still in Force Relating to Prisons; and a Full Index* (London: Knight & Co., 1878), p. 119.

more letters and visits. But the Act did not make clear who should be placed in which Division. Prisoner classification had previously been carried out by prison officers, who, for some years, had been able to place certain prisoners, such as those without previous convictions or whose crime was thought to be out of character, in a Star Class, so named because its members' uniforms bore a red star. The new Act aimed to transfer classification to the courts which might place in Division II prisoners who would previously have been placed in the Star Class.[90] But the imprecision of the legislation left the exasperated Governor of Durham Prison having to further sub-divide those in Division II

into star and ordinary, resulting in the anomalous appearance of prisoners in the already select costume of the 2nd division with the additional distinction of red stars, in order to avoid their mixing with notoriously habitual criminals in the same division.[91]

The blueprint for institutional uniforms was provided by the military where the struggle to accommodate both 'general uniformity and distinctive variety' was resolved by the use of varying 'facings, collars and linings'.[92] These were also used in the prisons and supplemented with the application of a series of badges, such as those worn by the Star Class. Badging the poor had a long history. The London charity-school children who processed through the street to St Paul's each wore a 'badge of their benefactors' bounty', and the badging of parish paupers is discussed in Chapter 7.[93] But prison badging assumed a bewildering complexity. At Millbank in the 1860s, for example, where marks were awarded for good behaviour, first-year prisoners wore

their registered number printed on a drab badge on the left arm, and no facings on the jacket; for the second year in the third class, when the badge and facings are black, with the number of the man printed in red on the badge... At the expiration of two years, if the prisoner has earned his full complement of marks... he is promoted to the second class, the badge and facings for which are yellow, the printing of the number being in black... After three years' servitude, and earning the requisite marks, the man is promoted into the highest, or first class, the badge and facings of which are blue, with the numbers printed in black.[94]

---

[90] *Prison Act, 1898. Copy of Circular, Dated 25th April, 1899, Addressed to the Chairman of Each Bench of Magistrates Calling Attention to the Prison Act, 1898, and the Rules Made Under It.* Parliamentary Papers 1899 LXXIX, pp. 3–4.
[91] *Report of the Commissioners of Prisons and the Directors of Convict Prisons, with Appendices.* Parliamentary Papers 1900 XLI, pp. 264–5.
[92] Roche, *Culture of Clothing*, pp. 243, 246.
[93] M. G. Jones, *Charity School Movement*, p. 75.
[94] Anon., *Five Years' Penal Servitude*, pp. 84–5.

Prison rules were mainly devised with men in mind since they formed the vast majority of the prison population, and the 1889 Prison Rules Inquiry concerned itself almost entirely with male prisoners. But female prisoners were also badged and colour-coded. At Woking in the 1880s there were four stages of confinement. In the first two the women wore brown, with green in the third and navy blue in the fourth stages, although no matter what the colour every article was 'stamped with a "broad arrow," the convict's crest'.[95] At Tothill Fields prison Munby noted that each prisoner had a badge on her sleeve to indicate her status:

> Those with a white vertical stripe were thieves: those with a red, savage assaulters: a red disc meant good conduct, and a red ring round the arm distinguished the convicts proper – women sentenced to penal servitude.[96]

There is, said Daniel Roche, 'nothing less uniform than the uniform which reflects both the desire for distinction and that for conformity'.[97] This was, perhaps nowhere better illustrated than in the late-Victorian prisons where the aim of suppressing individual identity as part of the reforming process had to be reconciled with the ability to identify individuals, and to indicate differences between them, both to punish the recalcitrant and encourage the penitent. The uniform aimed to present a *tabula rasa* on which the wearer's chronological and moral progress was charted. But just as each number was unique, the systems of badging and colour coding restored to the wearer an ever greater degree of individuality, compromising the uniform's homogenising intent.

Reactions

The Committee of the 1889 Prison Rules Inquiry concluded that, among prisoners, there were few objections and little resistance to wearing uniform. But this was based on the evidence of just twenty-three witnesses, all male and only five of whom were, or had been, prisoners, and the

---

[95] Florence Elizabeth Maybrick, *Mrs Maybrick's Own Story, My Fifteen Lost Years* (New York and London: Funk and Wagnalls Co., 1905), pp. 106–7. According to the former Prison Service Museum (now incorporated with the Galleries of Justice Museum, Nottingham) 'the original broad arrow mark was allegedly part of the heraldic symbol of Henry, Earl of Romney, Master General of the Ordnance 1693–1702, who was asked by the king to find some way of preventing crown property from being stolen, and used the device to mark everything'. Its first application to prison uniforms is uncertain but seems to be around 1850. (My thanks to Dot at the Prison Service Museum for this information, sent in an email, now deleted.) Margaret Maynard, however, notes that it was being used in the Australian penal colony, simply to identify government property, by at least 1827. Maynard, *Fashioned From Penury*, p. 21.
[96] TCLC, MUNB, 11, 30 November 1861.   [97] Roche, *Culture of Clothing*, p. 239.

Committee also recognised that 'an outward acquiescence' might often be 'accompanied by a repugnance to the dress as humiliating and degrading, and tending to confound those guilty of slight offences with habitual criminals'.[98] How the majority of inmates viewed their uniforms is hard to establish. It is clear from the quality of their writing that most of the small number of prisoners who left a personal record of their incarceration were, like Edward Callow and the anonymous 'One Who Has Tried Them', educated people. Their purpose was often to claim their innocence or to plead extenuating circumstances, and they comprised the smallest portion of the prison population.[99] It is possible that the privations of prison life seemed harder to them because they were accustomed to a higher standard of living – very few inmates would, like MP turned fraudster Jabez Balfour imprisoned at Wormwood Scrubs in 1895, have complained that what they 'really missed more than anything else in prison was the morning tub'.[100]

As with nineteenth-century autobiographies more generally, accounts of prison life written by men far outnumber those by women making it still harder to access a representative female perspective. Wealthy American poisoner Florence Maybrick, who complained that '[t]he law in prison is the same for the rich as the poor', clearly considered herself superior to the general run of prisoners.[101] Similarly, according to Jabez Balfour, Pentonville 'swarmed – literally swarmed – with vermin', but this was understandable given that most of the inmates were of the '"street arab" class' and 'as filthy in their personal habits as they are lawless and debauched in their lives'.[102] While it would be wrong to assume these prejudices were peculiar to the monied, it is true that the prison dress was for many inmates an improvement on their usual clothing. *Startling Disclosures!* which in 1878 gave an account of life in the City Prison, Holloway, noted that '[m]any prisoners, especially those from the agricultural districts, had never been so well off before for clothing, food, and shelter', and the same applied to many urban offenders.[103] Mayhew watching the boys exercising at Tothill Fields prison, claimed that he could tell 'by their shuffling noise and limping gait, how little used many of them had been to such a luxury as shoe leather', although ill-fitting prison-issue footwear should not be discounted as a possible reason for their impeded walking. However, a

---

[98] *Prison Rules Inquiry.* Parliamentary Papers 1889 LXI, p. vi.
[99] Anon. *Five Years' Penal Servitude*; Anon., *Her Majesty's Prisons.*
[100] Balfour, *My Prison Life*, p. 16.   [101] Maybrick, *Mrs Maybrick's Own Story*, p. 89.
[102] Balfour, *My Prison Life*, pp. 133–5.
[103] Anon., *Startling Disclosures! Six Months of Hard Labour in the City Prison, Holloway, by One Who Was There, and Remand to Newgate* (London: Curtice and Co., 1878), p. 35.

mud-lark told Mayhew that he liked prison because 'while he staid (*sic*) there he wore a coat and shoes and stockings', and planned to return the following winter as 'it would be so comfortable to have clothes and shoes and stockings then, and not be obliged to go into the cold wet mud of a morning'.[104] Perhaps for some, temporary loss of liberty was an acceptable price for respite from intolerable living conditions.

Others both resisted the prison clothing and used clothing as a form of resistance. Hats and caps were worn 'in a hundred different ways' to lend individuality to the uniform, skirts were made fuller with coals and hammock ropes, and wire from dinner cans used to stiffen stays.[105] Although women who so modified their clothing were disciplined, officials could interpret their concern with appearance as a natural, if undesirable, feminine trait. But protests involving violent or sexual behaviour disrupted prevailing notions of appropriate gendered behaviour. Mayhew observed with interest a twelve-year-old girl 'crouching in a corner' of a punishment cell 'with only one garment wrapt around her, and her blue prison clothes torn into a heap of rags by her side'. A day or so later he was pleased to see her back in her own cell where, 'clad in another prison dress' she was a model of feminine conformity, 'reading a book', and appearing 'quiet and subdued'.[106] Seth Koven suggests that workhouse inmates destroyed their clothing to claim an element of control over their lives, simultaneously venting outrage at their treatment and forcing the provision of new clothing.[107] Although the girl Mayhew saw appeared tamed, she too had made her protest and forced the authorities to reclothe her.

Margaret Maynard notes that convict women in the Australian penal colonies 'developed subtle strategies of resistance, including scandalising officials', and that their sexual conduct was the key gauge by which their behaviour was assessed.[108] In England, female prisoners exploited the potential of 'inappropriate' sexual behaviour to scandalise, and their strategies were decidedly unsubtle. Munby, in 1862, heard from a contact in the Government Prisons Office several accounts of the 'shamelessness' of female prisoners at Millbank where a 'favourite practice' was

to expose their persons to the grave official men who have to visit them: that to this end a woman will suddenly slip off all her clothes at once, in the presence

---

[104] Mayhew and Binny, *Criminal Prisons*, p. 402; Mayhew, *London Labour*, vol. II, p. 155.
[105] Helen Gordon, *The Prisoner. A Sketch* (Letchworth: Garden City Press, 1911), p. 2; Anon., *Five Years' Penal Servitude*, pp. 68–9; Mayhew and Binny, *Criminal Prisons*, p. 185. Anna Clark records similar modification of uniforms by women in Irish workhouses. Anna Clark, 'Wild workhouse girls and the Liberal imperial state in mid-nineteenth century Ireland', *Journal of Social History*, 39:2 (2005), 389–409; 392.
[106] Mayhew and Binny, *Criminal Prisons*, pp. 528, 530.   [107] Koven, *Slumming*, p. 69.
[108] Maynard, *Fashioned From Penury*, pp. 25, 56.

of these gentlemen; or be found by them in her cell, *standing on her head* on the bed, her clothes of course falling downwards from the waist.

Another woman,

> during a call from the chaplain, suddenly stripped and threw herself on the bed, calling to him to 'come on'... another escaped from the female warders, and ran naked about the prison green, pursued by the men, whom she eluded for some time by her nudity... a third climbed on to the roof of the building stark naked, and continued dancing there in sight of all the jailers, till the hose of the fire engine was set to play upon her![109]

In contrast, at Springfield prison in Essex, where male inmates had only one shirt each, leaving them shirtless during the laundry process, they protested not by stripping but by refusing to remove or wash their clothes.[110]

When clothing removal is reported by prison inspectors it is almost always carried out by women, and in lunatic asylums it was particularly associated with, and deemed especially depraved in, female patients.[111] Such overtly sexual behaviour, the polar opposite of quiet subjugation, ran counter to the ideal of feminine chastity, modesty and asexuality. Munby, though seemingly quite excited by the women's actions, was uncertain whether to attribute them to 'mere depravity' or 'a prurient nympholepsy'.[112] Also, while men were regularly required to enter female prisons – the prison inspectorate and clergy, for example, were exclusively male – women very rarely entered men's prisons. Bodily exposure by women therefore had much greater shock potential than when performed by men. Anna Clark describes how an Irish workhouse priest, witness to an assault by male officers on a female inmate in which her clothes were thrown 'completely over her head', found the 'scandalous, abominable and obscene' episode 'so horrifying it made him almost too faint to hold his pen'.[113]

Work was part of the reforming programme in asylums, workhouses and prisons, and a great deal of it was related to the production and maintenance of inmates' clothing. Prisoners also produced clothing for the prison staff, for other institutions and for slop manufacturers, often in

---

[109] TCLC, MUNB, 12, 1 February 1862.
[110] *Seventh Report... Prisons... I. Home District.* Parliamentary Papers 1842 XX, pp. 81, 83.
[111] See for example, *Ibid.*, p. 92; Andrews, 'The (un)dress of the mad poor... Part 1', 17; Crompton, 'Needs and desires', pp. 53–4. Crompton notes that masturbation was the corresponding concern about male lunatics.
[112] TCLC, MUNB, 12, 1 February 1862.
[113] Clark, 'Wild workhouse girls', 394. See also the discussion, in Chapter 5, of female bodily exposure.

vast quantities. In 1853 Pentonville's prisoner-tailors, for example, produced 'more than 5,000 jackets, 4,000 vests, and nearly 7,000 trousers, besides repairing 4,500 old ones'. Check-lining, twill for handkerchiefs, around 10,000 yards of shirting and 5,000 yards of sheeting and towelling, all for use by the convicts were also manufactured each year.[114] But the work provided further opportunities for resistance. At Millbank, in 1827, male prisoners sent their clothes to the laundry in small bundles inside which they concealed letters, written on leaves from a prayer book, requesting female correspondents. The female prisoners who staffed the laundry replied, making ink from the blue-stone used for washing and in one instance sending also 'a heart... worked with grey worsted on a flannel bandage'.[115]

Around the same time a group of female prisoners passed around a piece of yellow serge on which were embroidered plans for a conspiracy to murder the chaplain, the matron and a female officer: 'Watch yor time – stab am to the hart in chaple; get round them and they can't tell who we mean to stab.'[116] Decades later Suffragettes also communicated by stitching messages on pieces of waste material circulated inside cotton reels, and embroidered 'VOTES FOR WOMEN' on the tails of the men's shirts they were compelled to make, appropriating the most 'feminine' of skills to protest against sexual inequality and subvert the reforming intent.[117]

Dress as punishment

The purpose of prison uniforms was a central issue in the 1889 Prison Rules Inquiry. Arthur Balfour, who briefed the Committee on the Inquiry's parameters said it had, 'been pointed out that, as a matter of history, prison dress was originally intended as a benefit to the prisoner, not as a punishment'. Similarly, Sir Edmund du Cane, Chairman of the Commissioners of Prisons, stated his certainty that it had been introduced 'solely' in conformity with 'the modern idea that prisons should be administered in an orderly manner', since:

the idea of humiliating and degrading prisoners, and especially of making a spectacle of them... is quite opposed to modern principles and practice, and belongs rather to the period when stocks and pillory were in use.

---

[114] Mayhew and Binny, *Criminal Prisons*, pp. 155–6.
[115] Arthur Griffiths, *Memorials of Millbank and Chapters in Prison History* (London, 1875), pp. 147–9.
[116] *Ibid.*, pp. 159–60.
[117] Mary S. Allen, *Lady in Blue* (London: Stanley Paul and Co., 1936), p. 18.

288 'The greatest stigma and disgrace': lunatic asylums and prisons

But in his appendix to the Committee's report, 'Prison dress historically considered', Arthur Griffiths was adamant that when the first English penitentiary was established at Gloucester in 1785, along the lines recommended by Howard, the rules stated that a uniform was to be worn 'as well to humiliate the wearer as to facilitate discovery in case of escape'. Griffiths also maintained that 'the disciplinary aspect of dress was never lost sight of even by those whose motives were mainly philanthropic'. Reformers, he said,

> were strongly in favour of prison dress, because they had observed that it was the rule in the best managed gaols . . . the prisoners were under better control; they were more industrious, more submissive, more amenable to those reformatory influences which even a century back had been already accepted as a guiding principle of treatment.[118]

Whatever the original purpose, the use of different uniforms and the complex system of facings and badges to signify different types of prisoner and behaviours, militate against arguments that prison uniforms served no punitive purpose. The prison uniform was the site of a complex interweaving of administration, health, discipline and punishment, and while the report of the 1889 Prison Rules Inquiry shows that the Committee were convinced of the utility of prison uniform on sanitary, disciplinary and organisational grounds, they also recognised that prison dress was associated with 'all that is vile and shameful' and 'tending to confound those guilty of slight offences with habitual criminals'.[119] Furthermore, in both prisons and workhouses clothing was also employed more overtly as a form of punishment and humiliation.

Mayhew described the pauper street cleaners whose clothing was stamped with the parish to which they belonged and which, as he pointed out, was simply a different form of badging from that outlawed in 1810.[120] Even worse, the smocks issued to pauper labourers in one London parish had been 'marked, with sufficient prominence, "CLERKENWELL. STOP IT!"', intimating 'that the labourers were not only paupers, but regarded as thieves, and expected to purloin the parish dress they wore'. Following public criticism, the 'STOP IT!' was removed and the smocks '*merely* lettered "CLERKENWELL"'.[121] As his emphasis indicates, Mayhew was opposed to any form of pauper branding, but when the *Bristol Mercury* petitioned for leniency toward elderly paupers in 1892, it still maintained that it was appropriate for 'loafers' to 'bear some badge

---

[118] *Prison Rules Inquiry*. Parliamentary Papers 1889 LXI, pp. iii, 1, 44, 69, 70.
[119] *Ibid.*, p. vi.   [120] See Chapter 7.   [121] Mayhew, *London Labour*, vol. II, p. 244.

that they are maintained at the public expense'.[122] This attitude not only suggests that the Poor Law had been little affected by the new ideas about poverty as a man-made problem, which were informing more enlightened approaches to charitable clothing provision, but emphasises the punitive intent of the workhouse uniform for other classes of pauper. Still, in the early twentieth century 'able-bodied men from some Northern poorhouses', wrote Robert Roberts, 'worked in public with a large P stamped on the seat of their trousers'. Interestingly, while Roberts acknowledged the attendant humiliation he also thought the stamp prevented the pauper 'absconding to a street market where he could have exchanged his good pants for a cheap pair – with cash adjustment'. This suggests that in Salford, at least, the parish supplied trousers of reasonable quality and that the humiliation lay only in the stamped P, not in their style or fabric.[123]

But some workhouse paupers were also punished by being placed in dress which differed in colour or style from that of other inmates. Even after the practice was banned in 1839, many Poor Law Unions dressed unmarried mothers in yellow, it being, says Margaret Maynard, the traditional European colour of disgrace.[124] In 1841 it became lawful for Guardians to distinguish 'disorderly or refractory paupers' by placing them for forty-eight hours in 'a dress different from that of the other inmates'.[125] In prisons different colours and styles of clothing were used not only to classify, but also to punish prisoners. At Millbank Mayhew saw a female convict who had torn her prison dress wearing a canvas dress 'strapped over her claret-brown convict clothes...fastened by a belt and straps of the same stuff, and...held tight by means of a key acting on a screw attached to the back'.[126]

Early prison uniforms were often parti-coloured. Margaret Maynard says they were probably first used in the model Gloucester Reform Gaol, which opened in 1791, and in the New South Wales penal colony were introduced for prisoners doing hard labour 'to brand their ill conduct with a public mark of disgrace and to distinguish them from the better behaved'.[127] In England more sensitive governors dispensed with these

---

[122] *Commission on the Aged Poor.* Parliamentary Papers 1895 XIV, p. 47.
[123] R. Roberts, *Classic Slum*, p. 21.
[124] Longmate, *The Workhouse*, p. 157. Longmate cites the example of Andover where unmarried mothers were dressed 'in an ordinary frock, but with a broad yellow stripe down it'. See also, Digby, *Pauper Palaces*, p. 153; Maynard, *Fashioned from Penury*, p. 20.
[125] *Poor Law Amendment Act. Copies of Orders... 1834 to 1840 inclusive.* Parliamentary Papers 1841 XXI, p. 19.
[126] Mayhew and Binny, *Criminal Prisons*, p. 272.
[127] Maynard, *Fashioned From Penury*, pp. 18–19.

on the grounds that: 'The man seems to become an object to all observers, and to shrink from himself where there is that sort of dress.'[128] But as uniforms became more common, parti-coloured clothing was used more extensively to mark out disorderly prisoners, or those convicted of more serious crime. In the 1870s, 'One Who Has Tried Them' was intrigued by a fellow inmate who sported:

> a combination of dark chocolate and the brightest canary yellow, arranged in alternate patches, the front half of one trouser-leg yellow, the back half chocolate, and in the other leg the front half chocolate and the back half yellow, and a jacket and waistcoat to match.

This was the dress of felons while those convicted of lesser crimes wore brown uniforms.[129] There was also a yellow and drab parti-coloured uniform for those who attempted to escape, which at Pentonville was accompanied by 'low shoes' since the usual heavy boots 'would be formidable weapons to attack the officers with'.[130] And Edward Callow described the 'black dress man' in a neighbouring cell at Dartmoor who, as punishment for assaulting an officer was fettered and clad in a parti-coloured suit of black and drab, the breeches buttoned down the sides to allow them to be put on and off without removing the fetters.[131]

Not only fetters, but also straitjackets and other garments which restricted bodily movement remained in use for refractory prisoners. Mayhew was shown a canvas straitjacket 'with black leathern sleeves, like boots closed at the end, and with straps up the arm'.[132] Some had 'a large circular piece of heavy sole-leather sewed on the front, to make it still more stiff and unyielding'. The sleeves were supposed to be long enough to allow the arms to extend full length inside them, but according to one autobiographer many were not, so that the immobilised arms were 'forced to bend at the elbows and the doubled fists pressed with great force against the bottoms of the pockets'. This use of restrictive clothing was occurring at the same time as it was being dispensed with in lunatic asylums as injurious to mental health, and it is indicative of their damaging potential that prison straitjackets were so uncomfortable that at Woking doctors employed them to ascertain whether a prisoner was genuinely pleading mental illness or 'putting on the balmy'.[133]

---

[128] *Report from the Select Committee on the State of Gaols, & c.* Parliamentary Papers 1819 VII, p. 333.
[129] Anon., *Her Majesty's Prisons*, vol. I, pp. 195–7.
[130] W. B. N. [Lord William Beauchamp Nevill], *Penal Servitude* (London: Heinemann, 1903), pp. 135, 138.
[131] Anon., *Five Years' Penal Servitude*, p. 166.
[132] Mayhew and Binny, *Criminal Prisons*, p. 273.
[133] Bidwell, *Forging His Chains*, pp. 497–500.

Dress as punishment 291

Punishment could also be imposed by withholding certain types of clothing. Suffragette Hannah Mitchell, briefly imprisoned in Strangeways in the early twentieth century, complained that 'the absence of garters and knickers made one feel almost naked'.[134] Inspectors' reports suggest that, at least in the second half of the century, male prisoners were quite commonly issued with drawers or lined trousers, and that by the end of the century women were universally supplied with shifts. Stays were common though not universal, but women's drawers a rarity even though their use among working-class women was becoming more widespread. Mayhew and Binny had reported flannel drawers in the mid-century female clothing stores at Wandsworth, but these were issued only to the small minority who were wearing them on admission and who would undoubtedly have been among the more affluent inmates.[135]

Juliet Ash notes that the Millbank regulations stipulated that the clothing was to be 'made of cheap and coarse materials', and she argues that the requirement that the clothing be 'coarse and uncomfortable indicates how bodily punishment was to be maintained as part of the humiliation of prison life'.[136] Coarse, however, did not necessarily mean rough and irritating, but inferior quality, and the materials of ordinary working-class dress were commonly described by their owners as 'coarse', denoting their basic and functional nature. For poor inmates, the quantity of clothing supplied at Millbank would almost certainly have been greater than they possessed independently, and if the quality was not better, it was probably no worse. For Hannah Mitchell at Strangeways, bodily punishment and humiliation through clothing centred not on the use of uncomfortable materials, but the denial of intimate garments. Leigh Summers argues that the 'uncompromisingly ugly' appearance of workhouse and prison corsets may have acted as a psychological extension of the women's incarceration, reminding them 'of their reduced or expunged femininity'.[137] But the provision of even an inferior corset at least acknowledged their femininity.[138]

* * *

While economies of scale and a shared reforming intent meant that uniforms were initially introduced in the new lunatic asylums, workhouses and prisons of nineteenth-century England, their withdrawal or

---

[134] Mitchell (ed.), *Hard Way Up*, pp. 147–8.
[135] Mayhew and Binny, *Criminal Prisons*, p. 524.
[136] Ash, *Dress Behind Bars*, pp. 18–19.   [137] L. Summers, *Bound to Please*, p. 16.
[138] Gittins implies the same when she notes that in the 1950s bras and corsets were not issued to female patients at an Essex 'lunatic asylum'. Gittins, *Madness in its Place*, p. 135.

adaptation to take account of the different reasons for incarceration suggest that perhaps nowhere in nineteenth-century England was an understanding of the psychological power of clothing expressed more clearly than in its residential institutions. Its stigmatising potential was manifested in the official use of terms such as 'repulsive', 'humiliating' and 'degrading' to describe institutional clothing, in inmates' and patients' resistance to it, and in the issue of distinctive dress to the refractory. Its self-affirming effect was recognised in the use of clothing as a means of reward and in the modification, albeit imperfect, of the clothing issued to asylum patients and elderly paupers, who had committed no offence, to facilitate their social integration.

The use of clothing in pauper lunatic asylums also throws up a curious contrast. The aim of nineteenth-century asylums was to replicate, as far as possible, within the asylum the conditions of the patients' life outside to aid their recovery and discharge. But while working-class women outside the asylum were continually criticised for their love of 'finery', in the pauper lunatic asylums this was encouraged as a healthy sign of normality. Conolly deemed utilitarian clothes the 'outward signs of poverty', which women discarded 'as soon as they are raised above the lowest condition of pauperism'. There was, he said, no greater mistake 'than that of supposing that being dressed in unbecoming clothing, in stuff gowns and in mob-caps, is either a virtue in itself, or an incentive to virtue'. Where employers, moralists and philanthropists attempted to confine the poor to 'useful and necessary clothing', arguing that its value lay not only in its practicality but also in the moral influence it exerted, Conolly argued that:

Such sentiments form part of a gloomy and selfish system, including mortifications and degradations, especially unfavourable to goodness of any kind, and only gratifying to those who impose them.[139]

As Conolly realised, pride in dress and personal adornment was not an automatic sign of moral laxity or improvidence but an indication of self-respect.

[139] Conolly, *Construction and Government*, pp. 61–2.

Conclusion
No finery

> Edwardians were socially stratified into those who wore tailor-made clothes, those who wore new ready-mades, and those who wore only other people's cast-offs.[1]

Laurence Fontaine credits pedlars with increasing the comfort of English homes in the sixteenth and seventeenth centuries, concluding that 'it was the poorest who profited most', from the cotton and canvas fabrics they carried, using them to make 'shirts and spare sets of clothes and underclothes'.[2] Margaret Spufford discovered 'the surprising fact' that in the seventeenth century 'many of the children of inventoried people below the level of gentry were relatively well-clad; indeed, almost all of them had some new clothes'.[3] In the eighteenth century, says Beverly Lemire, 'standards of material sufficiency' rose 'ever higher'. The reduced price of cotton allowed the more affluent labourers 'the undreamt-of luxury of several changes of clothes, of a sort that could be restored to pristine perfection through judicious washing', and John Styles agrees that '[p]lebeian men and women could realistically expect to own duplicates of many items of clothing'.[4]

This relative abundance continued in the nineteenth century when urbanisation and the cheap, mass-produced, ready-made, cotton garments of industrialisation accelerated the erosion of the 'rustic' homemade – and sometimes home-spun – wool and linen clothing of the former predominantly rural economy, changing the style of working-class dress. With the simultaneous expansion of retailing methods, including more shops, new forms of credit and the introduction of mail order,

---

[1] Paul Thompson, *The Edwardians: The Remaking of British Society*, 2nd edn (London: Routledge, 1992), pp. 287–8.
[2] Fontaine, *History of Pedlars*, p. 188.
[3] Margaret Spufford, 'The cost of apparel in seventeenth-century England, and the accuracy of Gregory King', *The Economic History Review*, New Series, 53:4 (2000), 677–705; 704.
[4] Lemire, *Fashion's Favourite*, pp. 56, 60, 93; Styles, *Dress of the People*, p. 322.

greater use of advertising and a general rise in living standards as the century progressed, access to new clothing improved and the quantity of garments people could expect to own increased. But if this suggests a continuous trajectory of improvement, it is interrupted by the poor. In the eighteenth century, says Lemire, the poor 'were never provided with more than the perceived basics in clothing', but rising consumption elevated the standard of what constituted 'an acceptable minimum of clothing'.[5] However, in the nineteenth century, and into the twentieth, many working people, both in and out of employment, lacked even a basic full set of clothes let alone a change, and the improved wardrobes of those who prospered highlighted the deprivation of those who did not.

Steven King detects, 'an underclass of poor people emerging from the mid-eighteenth century onwards who would spend much of their lifetimes in poverty and who were likely to pass on that poverty to their own children and to share their poverty with brothers, sisters and friends'.[6] In the nineteenth century these people formed a *sartorial* underclass, visually distinct and socially marginalised – sometimes even as they participated. While Charles Shaw recalled the new clothes, bought on credit from tailors and dressmakers, worn by the children in his mid-nineteenth-century Charity Sunday procession, a Salford woman remembered a second-hand 'bit of a frock' bought for 'sixpence ha'penny' from the dingy Flat Iron Market for her Sunday school Whit Walk in the early 1910s. Her mother washed and ironed it, and 'put a bit of ribbon round', but it was still a second-hand dress. Furthermore, she said:

I used to walk in my bare feet, and they used to put me right at the front of the band when we were going up Regent Road. We had no money, y'see... the poorest children were sent straight to the front, and we all got clapped, people clapping it up.[7]

She seems to have enjoyed being the focus of attention, despite its cause, and there was evident sympathy for her plight expressed in the special treatment. But this was poverty singled out and paraded as difference. It is doubtful whether her mother viewed it so positively, and many of the watching parents would also have been conscious that only a twist of fortune, reversible at any moment, separated their children from the same fate. And while ritual occasions emphasised the lack of clothing, it was also apparent on a daily basis since working-class life continued to

---

[5] Lemire, *Fashion's Favourite*, p. 108.   [6] S. King, *Poverty and Welfare*, p. 254.
[7] Davies, *Leisure, Gender and Poverty*, pp. 125–6.

be lived largely on the streets, despite improvements in housing toward the end of the century.

With the growing realisation that poverty was a human rather than divine creation, the concept of 'the poor' as the generalised mass of the labouring people changed to a specific sub-group of the working classes. But for all the painstaking work of social investigators definitions of 'poverty' and 'the poor' remained elusive. Booth, at the end of the century, could draw a poverty line at an income of 18–21s. a week, but an array of factors – budgetary skills, family size and ages, location and occupation, personal needs and priorities – meant poverty could not be measured by income alone.

In any case, the vast majority of people did not identify poverty by enquiring about earnings, they simply looked. People therefore made strenuous efforts to avoid looking poor. Arthur Goffin recalled that among his work colleagues in the Beccles print trade at the close of the century there were those who spat and took snuff, using their aprons instead of handkerchiefs. But there were also:

many clean and well dressed men who abhorred such behaviour... These men took a pride in their appearance, always wearing collar, tie and hat. It has always astounded me when I think of how this appearance, indeed culture, was achieved in the environment in which so many of these men had to live.[8]

Being decently dressed, despite unfavourable circumstances, was a defining characteristic of 'respectability'. But for many of Goffin's workmates the ability to present a respectable appearance depended not only on their own efforts, but also on the labour and sacrifices of their wives. It was women who managed the budget and juggled resources, decided what to go without when clothing was needed, what to put in pawn and when to take it out, whether to clothe a child in flammable fabric or let it go cold(er). It was women also who bore the responsibility for making, mending, washing and ironing their families' clothing, ensuring that even if they were shabby they were not ragged. And it was women who put their own needs last. All this was necessary to establish their credentials as good housewives and hence good women, and largely determined their families' collective respectability. If few internalised this ideology as literally as Betsy B., a forty-five-year-old Birmingham housewife admitted to a lunatic asylum in 1858 convinced that her body contained mangles and sewing machines, they nevertheless felt the weight of the burden and suffered the distress of impotence when their resources were inadequate for their needs.[9] As a despairing widow told Rowntree and Kendall: 'When

---

[8] BAWCA, 1:271, Arthur Goffin.   [9] Crompton, 'Needs and desires', p. 55.

I've seen other children with warm clothing, and mine jealous... then I haven't known what to say.'[10]

The consequences of inadequate clothing were not simply physical discomfort and threats to health – frostbitten feet, chills and respiratory diseases. Insufficient or inappropriate clothing stymied personal creativity, denying the poor the escapism and pleasure of self-adornment and its potential for inner as well as external transformation. It also reduced life chances so that people born into poverty could find themselves caught in a vestimentary vicious circle, unable to obtain the work that would allow them to buy better clothing because they were inadequately dressed, but unable to buy the requisite clothing through lack of work. Bill Lancaster notes that assistants in the large department stores of the later nineteenth century came from 'diverse social backgrounds', and the position was regarded as 'a definite step up' for young working-class men and women. But, he says, few daughters of agricultural labourers would have been among them simply because of the prohibitive cost of the necessary clothing.[11] There appears to have been a broad consensus among nineteenth-century officials that agricultural labourers fared worse than urban and industrial workers, but poverty found a home everywhere, and some of the worst was in the urban slums. In London in the 1880s, says Walkowitz: 'Without respectable attire, workingmen ran the risk of arbitrary arrest and conviction for nuisance activities if they ventured out of their own locale.'[12] And so, for want of decent clothes, the poor might find themselves geographically confined to pauperised communities where ambition and aspiration could easily be stifled.

Wherever possible in this volume I have let the poor speak for themselves, to explain their own priorities – what was important to them and why – through their autobiographies and the testimony they supplied to parliamentary and social investigators. What emerges, clearly and forcefully, is that the social, emotional and psychological significance of clothing equalled and often surpassed its importance for bodily comfort. Clothes do indeed, as Daniel Miller argues, constitute who people are, and for both wearers and providers identity was forged, as well as expressed, through what they wore. When Joseph Terry donned his first miniature sailor suit he became a waterman, mentally as much as visually. And his parents, through being able to provide the clothes and thereby so explicitly and proudly enlist their son in the canal community,

---

[10] Rowntree and Kendall, *How the Labourer Lives*, p. 175.
[11] Bill Lancaster, *The Department Store: A Social History* (London: Leicester University Press, 1995), p. 141.
[12] Walkowitz, *City of Dreadful Delight*, p. 42.

became good parents just as surely as they did when they rescued their boys from the storm. And so those who were denied the opportunity to dress themselves or their dependants as they wished were also denied a part of themselves. When John Weston put on the asylum clothes he was no longer an independent, individual man but simply another indeterminate, impotent pauper. And the imposition of uniforms on charity-school children, servants, prisoners and workhouse inmates as part of a training in obedience which attempted to remove all freedom of expression can, taking Barthes theory of clothes as language and dress as speech, be interpreted as an attempt to use clothing to silence the poor.

Many witnesses testified to the shame and ostracism engendered by deficient clothing, the delayed breeching while the necessary money was saved, the Sabbath seclusion for want of Sunday best. But some also detailed how they used dress to enhance self-esteem and project a distinctive, positive self-image; and for both Joseph Terry and Louise Jermy it was the major conduit through which they negotiated significant relationships. But dress was also the means by which they both traversed the often difficult internal transition from adolescence to adulthood and their accounts illuminate our understanding of the way that the self was – and is – perceived, fashioned and embodied, and emphasise clothing's integral part in that process. Our understanding of self-perception is also extended through consideration of the emergent nineteenth-century scopic culture of mirrors, plate glass and photographs. The revelatory, luminous new world it created heightened people's consciousness of their visual impact, forming an expectation among the elite that the dressed body should present an ordered cohesive appearance. This largely worked to the disadvantage of the poor, since it emphasised their dark, squalid homes and sartorial shortcomings. Similarly, exploration of what cleanliness meant, not only for the poor but the working classes in general, questions the extent to which people outside the elite were able to achieve the changing standards of cleanliness identified by previous scholars, and suggests that this was yet another area in which the poor were negatively distinct and made to feel inadequate.

Throughout the nineteenth century social investigators were baffled by the question of how the poor managed to clothe themselves, given the inadequacy of their budgets even before clothing was taken into account. Steven King has argued that, at least until mid century, many of the poor relied on parish clothing provision and that it was characterised by relative generosity. But my evidence indicates that in the drive to reduce poor rates, which resulted in the new Poor Law of 1834, parish clothing became a specific target, albeit not fully met, and was replaced with a multiplicity of self-help charitable schemes, among which the most significant was the penny clothing society. Even where King believes parish provision to have been comparatively good he acknowledges that 'the total welfare package was rarely enough to guarantee subsistence' and he laments that little attention has been paid to 'the alternative avenues for making ends meet'.[13] My research shows that the poor scrimped, saved and went without food, patched and mended, cut down garments and remade them, set hierarchies of need, pawned, bought on credit, shared, borrowed and stole, made do with second-hand garments and took risks with inferior fabrics, pleaded and negotiated with parish officials, joined clothing societies and mother's meetings, bought from charity and jumble sales, hid themselves away and, in desperation, surrendered to the workhouse uniform. This was, without doubt, still an economy of makeshifts.

Clothing a poor family required constant and careful juggling of resources and strategies and the hope that need and opportunity would coincide. But even once acquired, possession was often tenuous, which raises questions, as yet unanswered, about ownership. To what extent, for example, can a person be said to 'own' something when it spends five days a week in the pawnshop? Did people still consider pledged clothing to be their own property, or was that feeling restored to them only on redemption? Such questions are particularly significant at a time when mass production and the proliferation of cheap goods meant that the type and quantity of things people owned became increasingly important criteria for establishing social status and a central facet of self-determination. Given the role of clothing in the formation of identity, did people experience a diminished sense of self when possession of their clothing rested on the ability to redeem it from the pawnshop?

The sartorial fate of the poor lay often in the hands of wealthier contemporaries, and the scale of the latter's philanthropic endeavours to clothe the former is testimony to their humanitarianism – and sometimes duty or guilt. But what surfaces repeatedly, even among the most well-meaning, is their utter incomprehension of the poor's circumstances, needs and desires. Many did not understand that the poor bought on credit simply because they lacked ready money, not because they were necessarily thriftless or harboured an inherent craving for showy dress that rendered the tallyman's patter irresistible; nor did they comprehend that if the poor appeared dishevelled and dirty it was not because they were oblivious to personal hygiene but because they lacked water or the money to heat it or to visit the public baths; nor that these same factors meant that bodily exposure might be a practical response to crowded living conditions, not incontrovertible evidence of evolutionary

---

[13] King, *Poverty and Welfare*, p. 258.

inferiority and moral degeneration. Lady Bell, who was so concerned about the living standards of the men employed at her husband's ironworks appears not to have made the very basic connection between their circumstances and the wages he paid them.

The gulf in understanding between rich and poor was manifested in a continual flow of evangelical literature which connected external appearance and inner purity and presented modest dress as a moral duty. It was expressed not only in the imposition of uniforms for domestic servants but in attempts to also restrict their leisure dress. It was articulated in the insistence that only plain sewing and the construction of plain garments be taught to working-class females. It was embodied in the rules of clothing societies and other paternalistic charitable initiatives which prohibited finery and permitted only the distribution of useful and necessary materials and garments, even when bought with the poor's own money. And it was actualised in the imposition of punitive uniforms in prisons and workhouses, the consciousness of their degrading effect acknowledged by their withdrawal in lunatic asylums. Even the jumble sale which, in the more liberal climate of the 1880s, dispensed with the sartorial restrictions of most other clothing charities, was a reversion to second-hand garments.

The poor used any means at their disposal to resist attempts to control their dress and some of the wealthy feared the obliteration of visual distinctions between the classes. Jose Harris claims that in the 1900s:

working people, especially young women, looked much more like their middle-class equivalents than they had done a generation before, and foreign observers noted that... the 'Sunday-best' clothes of many workers in Britain were identical with the everyday clothes of the middle class.[14]

But looking 'more like' something, or the best clothes of one class resembling the everyday wear of another, does not make them indistinguishable. 'On Sundays', said Robert Roberts of Salford in the 1900s, 'the artisan in his best suit looked like the artisan in his best suit: no one could ever mistake him for a member of the middle classes.' This, however, would not have concerned most of the 'workers' who had their own fashions, grounded in community pride and the practical realities of their own culture. And far from aiming to emulate elite dress, the goal for most of the poor was simply to pass unnoticed among their own class, since 'any day at all', continued Roberts, 'the poor looked poor'.[15]

[14] Harris, *Private Lives, Public Spirit*, p. 10.   [15] R. Roberts, *Classic Slum*, p. 39.

Bibliography

ARCHIVAL DOCUMENTS

BURNETT ARCHIVE OF WORKING CLASS AUTOBIOGRAPHIES (BAWCA), BRUNEL UNIVERSITY (ARRANGED BY CATALOGUE NUMBER)

1:93, Edward Brown, 'Untitled'.
1:141, Alice Maud Chase, 'The memoirs of Alice Maud Chase'.
1:181, Agnes Cowper, 'A backward glance on Merseyside'.
1:182, Daisy Cowper, 'De nobis'.
1:228, William Elliott, 'An octogenarian's personal life story'.
1:242, Stephen Forsdick, 'Untitled'.
1:250, Minnie Frisby, 'Memories'.
1:271, Arthur Frederick Goffin, 'A grey life'.
1:274, Jack Goring, 'Untitled'.
1:357, Anita Elizabeth Hughes, 'Untitled'.
1:361, Edward S. Humphries, 'Childhood. An autobiography of a boy from 1889–1906'.
1:371, Alfred Ireson, 'Reminiscences'.
1:421, Jack Lanigan, 'Thy kingdom did come'.
1:492, Frank Marling, 'Reminiscences'.
1:532, Dora Nicholls, 'My story'.
1:622, John Shinn, 'A sketch of my life and times'.
1:628, Susan Silvester, 'In a world that has gone'.
1:693, Joseph Terry, 'Recollections of my life'.
1:719, Mary Laura Triggle, 'Untitled'.
2:422, C. V. Horner, 'Up and downs. A lifetime spent in the Yorkshire Dales'.

DORSET HISTORY CENTRE (DHC)

PE/SH/CW/4/4/20, 'Notice for a rummage sale to pay for the repair of the tower pinnacles', Sherborne Parish, 1889.

EAST SUSSEX RECORD OFFICE (ESRO)

AMS 1189, Rotherfield Clothing Club Report 1867.
G/11/1a/8, Uckfield Union Minute Book.

G12/1a/1, West Firle Union Minute Book.
G12/20/2, General Ledger of West Firle Union.
PAR 342/7/1/5, *Forest Row Parish Magazine.*
PAR 403/26/1, Iford Clothing Club Accounts 1890–1931.
PAR 462/12/3, Vestry Book of the Parish of Rype in the County of Sussex, 1855–1874.
PAR 462/7/30/1, *Ripe Magazine*, December 1902.
PAR 462/25/5/1, Records of the Ripe Sunday School.
PAR 462/26/1, Account Book of Ripe Parish Clothing Club 1854–69.
PAR 465/7 Rotherfield Request Books 1810–35.
PAR 465/17/1, Rotherfield Clothing Club Book.
PAR 496/9/3/1, Rules of the Uckfield Clothing Society.
SPK P.6, Private correspondence of Lord Sheffield, 1811–19.

GREATER MANCHESTER COUNTY RECORD OFFICE (GMCRO)

M 346, Jews' School Ladies' Clothing Society Minute Book 1885–1937.

HEREFORDSHIRE RECORD OFFICE (HRO)

AC 16/64, Abbey Dore Clothing Club Accounts 1869–1909.
AN 91/122, *Eardisley Parish Magazine.*

LEWISHAM LOCAL HISTORY AND ARCHIVES CENTRE (LLHAC)

A58/18/F2/1, St. Margaret's Lee, District Visiting Society Minute Book, November 1899–December 1933.
A64/12/290, *St. Philip's, Sydenham* [parish magazine].
A78/18/J/1, *St. Margaret's, Lee, Parish Magazine.*
A83/21/91/2, *St. Mildred's, Lee, Parish Magazine and Parochial Record.*
A89/98/23, *Sydenham Churches of S. Bartholomew and S. Matthew, Parish Magazine.*
SPD/4/2–8, Churchwardens' and Overseers' Committee Minutes [St Paul's Deptford], 1785–1829.
SPD/4/15, Churchwardens' and Overseers' Committee Order Book [St Paul's Deptford], 1819–25.

LONDON METROPOLITAN ARCHIVES (LMA)

DRO 21/64, All Saints' Laleham Vestry Minute Book, 1803–1848.
DRO/056/028, *All Saints, South Acton, Church Monthly.*
P73/CAM/105, *Camden Parish Magazine.*
P79/MTW/42–43, *St. Matthew's, Upper Clapton, Service Paper.*
P83/MRK/109/42–3, Middlesex Needlework Guild.
P87/CTC/47, *Christ Church, Lancaster Gate, Parish Magazine.*
P87/CTC/60, *Christ Church, Lancaster Gate, Parochial Report*, 1900.

P89/ALS/149, *All Souls, Langham Place, Parish Magazine*.
P89/EMM/7, Emmanuel Church, Northwick Terrace, Maida Hill, District Visitors' Record of Relief Granted 1881–1892.
P92/TRI/75, *Holy Trinity, Southwark, Parish Magazine*.
P93/ALLI/15/1, *All Saints, Mile End New Town, Parish Magazine*.
P94/ALL/10, *All Saints, Aden Grove, Green Lanes, Stoke Newington, Parish Magazine*.
P95/ALL2/29, *All Saints, Clapham Park, Church Magazine*.
P95/PAU 1/25, *St Paul, Clapham* [parish magazine].

MANCHESTER ARCHIVES AND LOCAL STUDIES (MALS)

L108/1/23, *Emmanuel Parish Magazine*.
L135/1/11/1, *St. Clement Urmston Parish Magazine*.

SENATE HOUSE LIBRARY (SHL)

B.834, Hinton Clothing Club.

TOWER HAMLETS LOCAL HISTORY LIBRARY AND ARCHIVE (THLHLA)

TH8662/82, Protocol Book, Society of Ladies for Clothing the Children of Poor German Families, 1868–1883.
W/BGU/8/1/15, *The Annual Record for 1890*.
W/SMH/A/29/1/[3], *The Stepney Meeting Magazine*.

TRINITY COLLEGE LIBRARY CAMBRIDGE (TCLC)

GBR/0016/MUNB, Papers of A. J. Munby.

THE WOMEN'S LIBRARY (TWL)

5GFS/10/012, *Friendly Leaves*.

PARISH MAGAZINES (BRITISH LIBRARY)

The History of Pinner, Middlesex. [A scrapbook of cuttings from the *Pinner Parish Magazine*, 1887–1908, compiled by the Revd C. E. Grenside.]
Aldenham Parish Magazine.
The Alscot Magazine.
Evesham Parish Magazine.
Kinver Parish Magazine.
Loughton Parish Magazine.
Old Windsor Banner.
The Parish Magazine for Oswestry, Whittington, Moreton, Welsh Frankton, The Lodge, Trefonen and Other Neighbouring Parishes.

Bibliography 303

Pinner Parish Magazine.
S. James' [Euston] Parish Magazine.
S. Jude's Whitechapel [parish magazine].
St. Clement Danes Parish Magazine.
St. Jude's, S. Kensington [parish magazine].
St. Luke's, Camberwell Parish Magazine.
St Mary Newington Parish Magazine.
St. Paul's, Balsall Heath, Parish Magazine.

RULES AND REPORTS (BRITISH LIBRARY)

Annual Report of the Manesty-Lane Charity School March 14, 1821 (Liverpool, 1821).
Catholic Needlework Guild, *Twenty-Second Annual Report of the Portsmouth Diocesan Division* (Portsmouth, 1908).
The Fifth Annual Report of the Ladies' Benevolent Society, Liverpool (Liverpool, 1815).
Kettleburgh Penny Clothing Club [Rules] (Framlingham, 1837).
Rules for the Clothing Club at Stutton (1833).
Rules of the Ubbeston Provident Clothing Society (Halesworth, 1833).
Rules of the Ufford Penny Clothing Club (Woodbridge, 1834).
Rules of the Haveningham Provident Clothing Society (Halesworth, 1833).

PERIODICALS

The Cottager's Monthly Visitor.
The Family Economist.
The Graphic.
The Quarterly Magazine of the Independent Order of Odd-Fellows, Manchester Unity Friendly Society.

NEWSPAPERS

Birmingham Daily Post.
Blackburn Standard.
Bristol Mercury and Daily Post.
Daily Express.
Daily News.
Glasgow Herald.
Hampshire Advertiser.
Leeds Mercury.
Liverpool Mercury.
Sheffield and Rotherham Independent.
The Standard.
The Times.

PARLIAMENTARY PAPERS (ARRANGED CHRONOLOGICALLY)

A Bill To Amend so much of an Act, passed in the 8th & 9th year of King William the Third, as requires poor Persons receiving Alms to wear Badges. 1810 I.

Report from the Committee on Madhouses in England. 1814–15 IV.

First Report: Minutes of Evidence Taken Before the Select Committee Appointed to Consider of Provision Being Made for the Better Regulation of Madhouses, in England. 1816 IV.

Report from the Select Committee on the State of Gaols, & c. 1819 VII.

First Report. Minutes of Evidence Taken Before the Select Committee Appointed to Inquire into the Education of the Lower Orders of the Metropolis. 1816. 1816 IV.

A Bill for Consolidating and Amending the Laws Relating to the Building, Repairing, and Regulating of Certain Gaols, Bridewells, and Houses of Correction, in England and Wales. 1823 I.

Factories Inquiries Commission. First Report of the Central Board of His Majesty's Commissioners Appointed to Collect Information in the Manufacturing Districts, as to the Employment of Children in Factories, and as to the Propriety and Means of Curtailing the Hours of their Labour: with Minutes of Evidence, and Reports by District Commissioners. 1833 XX.

Report from the Select Committee of the House of Lords appointed to examine into the several Cases alluded to in certain Papers respecting the Operation of the Poor Law Amendment Act; and to report thereon... Part I. 1837–38 XIX.

Poor Law Amendment Act. Copies of Orders, &c. issued by the Poor Law Commissioners relating to the Poor Law Amendment Act; with an account of money expended for the relief and maintenance of the poor, &c. in England and Wales from 1834 to 1840 inclusive. 1841 XXI.

Children's Employment Commission. First Report of the Commissioners. Mines. 1842 XV.

Children's Employment Commission. Appendix to First Report of the Commissioners Mines. Part I. 1842 XVI.

Children's Employment Commission. Appendix to First Report of the Commissioners. Mines. Part II. 1842 XVII.

Seventh Report of the Inspectors Appointed Under the Provisions of the Act 5 & 6 Will. IV. c.38, to Visit the Different Prisons of Great Britain. I. Home District. 1842 XX.

Reports of Special Assistant Poor Law Commissioners on the Employment of Women and Children in Agriculture. 1843 XII.

A Bill (as amended by the Committee) for promoting the voluntary Establishment, in Boroughs and Parishes in England and Wales, of Public Baths and Washhouses. 1846 I.

Copies of correspondence between the Poor Law Commissioners and the Boards of Guardians of the Ledbury and Cricklade Unions, relative to supplying clothes for new-born infants on their quitting the workhouse;–also, of applications to the commissioners on providing clothes for infants born in the workhouse. 1846 XXXVI.

Fifteenth Report of the Inspectors Appointed, Under the Provisions of the Act 5 & 6 Will. IV. c.38, to Visit the Different Prisons of Great Britain. 1850 XXVIII.

Bibliography 305

Census of Great Britain, 1851. Population Tables. II. Ages, Civil Condition, Occupations, and Birth-Place of the People: with the Numbers and Ages of the Blind, the Deaf-and-Dumb, and the Inmates of Workhouses, Prisons, Lunatic Asylums, and Hospitals. 1852–53 LXXXVIII (I).

Education. Minute of the Committee of the Privy Council on Education Establishing A Revised Code of Regulations. 1861 XLVIII.

Commission on the Employment of Children, Young Persons, and Women in Agriculture (1867). Appendix Part I, To Second Report. 1868–69 XIII.

Lunacy. Copy of the Twenty-Fourth Report of the Commissioners in Lunacy to the Lord Chancellor. 1870 XXXIC.

Thirty-fourth Report of the Inspectors Appointed, under the Provisions of the Act 5 & 6 Will. IV. c.38, to Visit the Different Prisons of Great Britain. I. Southern District. 1870 XXXVII.

Education. 1871. Minute of the Right Honourable the Lords of the Committee of the Privy Council on Education Establishing a New Code of Regulations. 1871 LV.

Education Department. 1875. New Code of Regulations (As Modified by Minute of 5th April 1875) with an Appendix of New Articles and of All Articles Modified, by the Right Honourable the Lords of the Committee of the Privy Council on Education. 1875 LVIII.

Education Department. 1876. New Code of Regulations with an Appendix of New Articles and of All Articles Modified, by the Right Honourable the Lords of the Committee of the Privy Council on Education. 1876 LIX.

Elementary Education (Needlework). Copy of a Memorial on the Subject of Needlework in Elementary Schools from Managers and Teachers of Schools and Persons otherwise interested in the Education of Girls, presented to the Education Department in July 1877. 1877 LXVII.

School Savings Banks. Nominal Return of Schools in Receipt of Annual Grants which have Savings Banks attached to them for the use of the Children, stating whether they are Penny Banks, or whether they are in connection with the Post Office Savings Bank, and showing, in each Case, the Sums Deposited and Withdrawn, and the Number of Depositors, for the Year ending on the 31st day of August 1877. 1877 LXVII.

Education Department. 1879. New Code of Regulations with an Appendix of New Articles and of All Articles Modified, by the Right Honourable the Lords of the Committee of the Privy Council on Education. 1878–79 LVII.

Lunacy. Copy of the Thirty-Fourth Report of the Commissioners in Lunacy to the Lord Chancellor. 1880 XXIX.

Education Department. Minute of 6th March 1882, Establishing a New Code of Regulations, by the Right Honourable the Lords of the Committee of the Privy Council on Education. 1882 L.

Prison Rules Inquiry. Report of the Committee of Inquiry as to the Rules Concerning the Wearing of Prison Dress, &c., Together with Minutes of Evidence and Appendices. 1889 LXI.

Lunacy. Copy of the Forty-Fourth Report of the Commissioners in Lunacy to the Lord Chancellor. 1890 XXXC.

Royal Commission on the Aged Poor. Minutes of Evidence Taken Before the Royal Commission on the Aged Poor. Days 1 to 26. Vol. II. 1895 XIV.

Prison Act, 1898. Copy of Circular, Dated 25th April, 1899, Addressed to the Chairman of Each Bench of Magistrates Calling Attention to the Prison Act, 1898, and the Rules Made Under It. 1899 LXXIX.
Lunacy. Copy of the Fifty-Fourth Report of the Commissioners in Lunacy to the Lord Chancellor. 1900 XXXVII.
Report of the Commissioners of Prisons and the Directors of Convict Prisons, with Appendices. 1900 XLI.
Census of England and Wales. 1901. General Report with Appendices. 1904 CVIII.
Board of Education. 1912. Code of Regulations for Public Elementary Schools in England (Excluding Wales and Monmouthshire), with Schedules. 1912–13 LXV.

CENSUS RETURNS AND REPORTS (EXCLUDING PARLIAMENTARY PAPERS, ARRANGED CHRONOLOGICALLY)

Census Returns of England and Wales, 1851 (Kew: The National Archives of the UK: Public Record Office, 1851).
Census Returns of England and Wales, 1861 (Kew: The National Archives of the UK: Public Record Office, 1861).
Census of England and Wales, 1891, Area Houses and Population, Vol. I, Administrative and Ancient Counties (London: HMSO, 1893).
Index to the Population Tables for England and Wales in the County Volumes of the Census Report, 1901 (London: HMSO, 1903).

OTHER PUBLISHED PRIMARY SOURCES (INCLUDING MODERN REPRINTS)

A Lady, *The Lady's Economical Assistant. Or, the Art of Cutting Out, and Making, the Most Useful Articles of Wearing Apparel* (London, 1808).
A Lady [M. E. B.], *Method for Teaching Plain Needlework in Schools* (London, 1861).
A Lady, *The Workwoman's Guide Containing Instructions to the Inexperienced in Cutting Out and Completing Those Articles of Wearing Apparel, &c., Which are Usually Made at Home* (London: Simpkin, Marshall and Co.; Birmingham: Thomas Evans, 1838).
Allen, Mary S., *Lady in Blue* (London: Stanley Paul and Co., 1936).
Anon., *A Few Words on Pawnbroking* (London: Jackson and Keeson, 1866).
Anon., *An Account of the Last Days, Confessions, and Executions of the Mannings, for the Murder of Patrick O'Connor, at Bermondsey* (Leith: C. Drummond, 1849).
Anon., *Every Woman's Encyclopædia* (London: Amalgamated Press, 1910–11).
Anon. [Harriet Martineau], 'Female Industry', *The Edinburgh Review*, 222 (1859), 293–336.
Anon. [Edward Callow], *Five Years' Penal Servitude. By One Who Has Endured It* (London: Richard Bentley and Son, 1877).
Anon. [Harriet Martineau], *The Guide to Service; The Lady's Maid* (London, 1838).

Bibliography 307

Anon., *Hand-Book for Needlework Prize Associations Containing Schedules and Suggestions Adapted to the Various Classes and Districts in Great Britain and Ireland* (London: Griffith, Farran, Okeden & Welsh, 1884).
Anon., *Her Majesty's Prisons. Their Effects and Defects. By One Who Has Tried Them*, 2 vols (London: Sampson Low, Marston, Searle, and Rivington, 1881).
Anon., *Instructions for Cutting Out Apparel for the Poor. Principally Intended for the Assistance of the Patronesses of Sunday Schools, and other Charitable Institutions, but Useful in all Families* (London, 1789).
Anon. [John Weston], *Life in a Lunatic Asylum: an Autobiographical Sketch* (London, 1867).
Anon. [Peter Thompson], *London Wesleyan Mission, East. Record of Work for 1892–3, With Facts and Incidents* (London: J. & B. Dodsworth, 1893).
Anon., *The Management of Servants. A Practical Guide to the Routine of Domestic Service* (London: Warne and Co., 1880).
Anon., *The New Female Instructor. Or, Young Woman's Guide to Domestic Happiness; Being an Epitome of all the Acquirements Necessary to Form the Female Character, in Every Class of Life: With Examples of Illustrious Women, etc.* (London, 1824).
Anon., *Phœbe's Marriage. Or, The Perils of Dress* (London: Christian Knowledge Society, 1872).
Anon. [L. S. Floyer], *Plain Cutting Out for Standards V., VI., and VII., as Now Required by the Government Education Department, 1885, Adapted to the Principles of Elementary Geometry, Containing Also a Copy of What is Required in Other Subjects (Schedules I, II, III) and a Copy of the Instructions to Her Majesty's Inspectors* (London: Griffith, Farran, Okeden & Welsh, 1885).
Anon. [L. S. Floyer], *Plain Knitting and Mending in Six Standards Illustrated with Diagrams* (London, 1876).
Anon., *The Queen's Empire: A Pictorial and Descriptive Record* (London, Paris & Melbourne: Cassell and Company Ltd, 1897).
Anon. [Sarah Martin/George Mogridge], *Sarah Martin, The Prison-Visitor of Great Yarmouth. A Story of A Useful Life* (London: Religious Tract Society, 1872), pp. 55–6.
Anon. [Thomas Wright], *Some Habits and Customs of the Working Classes. By a Journeyman Engineer* (London, 1867).
Anon., *Startling Disclosures! Six Months of Hard Labour in the City Prison, Holloway, by One Who Was There, and Remand to Newgate* (London: Curtice and Co., 1878).
Anon., *Weldon's Home Dressmaker for Striped Materials* (London: Weldon and Co., 1888).
An Overseer [Sir George Nicholls], *Eight Letters on the Management of Our Poor, and the General Administration of the Poor Laws* (Newark, 1822).
Arch, Joseph, *From Ploughtail to Parliament: An Autobiography* (London: Cresset Library, 1986 [1898]).
Bailey, M. E., *School Needlework and Cutting Out: A Scheme of Instruction to Suit the New Government Code, Adopted by the Liverpool School Board* (Liverpool: George Gill & Co., 1875).

Balfour, Jabez Spencer, *My Prison Life* (London: Chapman and Hall, 1907).

Barlow, John, *The Probable Effects of Clothing Societies in Improving the Habits and Principles of the Poor* (London: C. J. G. and F. Rivington, 1828).

Becher, John Thomas, *The Anti-pauper System; Exemplifying the Positive and Practical Good, Realized by the Relievers and the Relieved, Under the Frugal, Beneficial, and Lawful, Administration of the Poor Laws, Prevailing at Southwell, and in the Neighbouring District* (London: W. Simpkin and R. Marshall, 1828).

Beck, S. William, *The Draper's Dictionary. A Manual of Textile Fabrics: Their History and Applications* (London: The Warehousemen and Drapers' Journal Office, 1844).

Beeton, Isabella, *The Book of Household Management* (London: Ward, Lock and Tyler, 1869 [1859–61]).

Bell, Lady, *At the Works: A Study of a Manufacturing Town* (London: Virago, 1985 [1907]).

Bidwell, George, *Forging His Chains. The Autobiography of George Bidwell* (London: H. C. Mott, 1888).

Booth, Charles, *Life and Labour of the People in London*, 17 vols (London: Macmillan, 1902–3).

Brierley, Ben, *Home Memories and Out of Work* (Bramhall: Reword, 2002 [1885–6]).

Brontë, Charlotte, *Shirley* (London: Penguin, 1985 [1849]).

———, *Jane Eyre* (London: Everyman/J. M. Dent, 1996 [1847]).

Bulwer-Lytton, Edward, *Paul Clifford*, 2 vols (New York, 1830).

Buxton, Thomas Fowell, *An Inquiry Whether Crime and Misery are Produced or Prevented, by our Present System of Prison Discipline* (London: J. and A. Arch, 1818).

Calder, F. L., and E. E. Mann, *A Teachers' Manual of Elementary Laundry Work*, 3rd edn (London: Longmans, Green and Co., 1894).

Capper, D., *Practical Results of the Workhouse System, as Adopted in the Parish of Great Missenden, Bucks*, 2nd edn (London: Hatchard and Son, 1834).

Carlyle, Thomas, *Sartor Resartus* (Oxford University Press, 1999 [1833–4]).

Caulfeild, S. F. A., and Blanche C. Saward, *The Dictionary of Needlework* (London: L. Upcott Gill, 1882).

Cecilia, Madame, Religious of St. Andrew's Convent, Streatham, *Girls Clubs and Mothers' Meetings* (London: Burns & Oates, 1911).

Clabburn, Pamela (ed.), *Working Class Costume from Sketches of Characters by William Johnstone White, 1818* (London: Costume Society, 1971).

Conlon, Denis J. (ed.), *The Collected Works of G. K. Chesterton VI* (San Francisco: Ignatius Press, 1991).

Conolly, John, *The Treatment of the Insane Without Mechanical Restraints* (London: Smith, Elder and Co., 1856).

———, *The Construction and Government of Lunatic Asylums and Hospitals for the Insane* (London: John Churchill, 1847).

———, *An Inquiry Concerning the Indications of Insanity, with Suggestions for the Better Protection and Care of the Insane* (London: John Taylor, 1830).

Copley, Esther, *Cottage Comforts, with Hints for Promoting Them, Gleaned from Experience* (London: Simpkin and Marshall, 1834 [1825]).

Cotterill, George, *A Pastoral Address to the Members of Clothing Clubs*, 3rd edn (London: Longman, Brown, Green and Co. and Norwich: J. Tippell, 1846).
Curtis, E. A., *Needlework. Schedule III. Exemplified and Illustrated. Intended for the Use of Young Teachers, and for the Upper Standards in Public Elementary Schools* (London: Griffith and Farran, 1879).
Cutts, Edward L., *Address to District Visitors* (London: Society for Promoting Christian Knowledge, 1873).
Day, Alice Catherine, *Glimpses of Rural Life in Sussex During the Last Hundred Years* (Oxford: The Countryman, 1927).
Dickens, Charles, *Sketches By Boz* (London: Penguin, 1995 [1839]).
Dodd, William, *A Narrative of the Experience and Sufferings of WD, Written by Himself* (London, 1841).
Dunn, James, *From Coal Mine Upwards, or Seventy Years of an Eventful Life* (London: W. Green, 1910).
Eden, Frederick Morton, *The State of the Poor: or, An History of the Labouring Classes in England, from the Conquest to the Present Period*, 3 vols (London, 1797).
Eliot, George, *Adam Bede* (Ware: Wordsworth Editions, 1997 [1859]).
Ellman, Edward Boys, *Recollections of a Sussex Parson* (London: Skeffington and Son, 1912).
Engels, Friedrich, *The Condition of the Working Class In England* (London: Penguin, 1987 [1845]).
Finch, E., *The Sampler. A System of Teaching Plain Needlework in Schools*, 2nd edn (London, 1855).
Fleming, Alice, 'Weekly payments: a humble tragedy', *Albemarle*, 1:2 (1892), 66–70.
Floyer, L. S., *Needle Drill, Position Drill, Knitting Pin Drill, To Which is Added 'Thimble Drill' as Required by Mundella's Code, Educational Department. Needlework Drill, 1881 'Girls' and Infants' Departments, Boys and Girls Below Standard I'* (London: Griffith and Farran, 1881).
Freeman, Flora Lucy, *Religious and Social Work Amongst Girls* (London, Skeffington & Son, 1901).
G., A. E., *Lancashire Needles and Thread. Or, the History of the Birtley Sewing Class* (London: 1864).
General Society for Promoting District Visiting, *The District Visitor's Manual. A Compendium of Practical Information and Facts, for the use of District Visitors* (London: J. W. Parker, 1840).
Gissing, George, *The Nether World* (Oxford University Press, 1999 [1889]).
Glennie, John D., *Hints from an Inspector of Schools. School Needlework Made Useful and School Reading Made Intelligent* (London, 1858).
Gordon, Helen, *The Prisoner. A Sketch* (Letchworth: Garden City Press, 1911).
Gosling, Harry, *Up and Down Stream* (London: Methuen and Co., 1927).
Gosse, Edmund, *Father and Son: A Study of Two Temperaments* (London: Penguin, 1989 [1907]).
Granville, J. Mortimer, *The Care and Cure of the Insane. Being the Reports of The Lancet Commission on Lunatic Asylums 1875–6–7 For Middlesex, the City of London and Surrey*, 2 vols (London: Hardwicke & Bogue, 1877).

Greenwood, James, *Unsentimental Journeys, or Byways of the Modern Babylon* (London, 1867).
Grey, Edwin, *Cottage Life in a Hertfordshire Village* (Harpenden: Harpenden and District Local History Society, 1977 [1935]).
Griffiths, Arthur, *Memorials of Millbank and Chapters in Prison History* (London, 1875).
Gurney, Joseph John, *Notes on a Visit Made to Some of the Prisons in Scotland and the North of England, in Company with Elizabeth Fry. With Some General Observations on the Subject of Prison Discipline* (London, 1819).
Halliday, Andrew, *A General View of the Present State of Lunatics, and Lunatic Asylums, in Great Britain and Ireland, and in Some Other Kingdoms* (London, 1828).
Heath, Francis George, *Peasant Life in the West of England* (London: Sampson Low & Co., 1880).
Holdenby, Christopher, *Folk of the Furrow* (London: Smith, Elder & Co., 1913).
Howell, M. J., *The Hand-Book of Millinery; Comprised in a Series of Lessons for the Formation of Bonnets, Capotes, Turbans, Caps, Bows, etc.: to which is Appended a Treatise on Taste and the Blending of Colours; also an essay on Corset Making* (London: Simpkin, Marshall & Co., 1847).
———, *The Hand-Book of Dress-Making: Including Correct Rules for the Pursuit of the Above Art, and Concisely Illustrating the Mode of Fitting at Sight* (London: Simpkin, Marshall and Co., 1845).
Hows, W. A. H., *A History of Pawnbroking, Past and Present* (London, 1847).
Hyde, Mrs, *How to Win Our Workers: A Short Account of the Leeds Sewing School for Factory Girls* (Cambridge, 1862).
Jack, Florence B., *The Art of Laundry Work Practically Demonstrated for use in Homes and Schools* (Edinburgh: T. C. and E. C. Jack and London: Whittaker & Co., 1898).
Jekyll, Gertrude, *Old West Surrey. Some Notes and Memories* (London: Longmans, Green and Co., 1904).
Jermy, Louise, *The Memories of a Working Woman* (Norwich: Goose and Son, 1934).
Joint Vestry, *Papers relating to the Parishes of St. Giles and St. George Bloomsbury. Abstract of the Contract for Maintaining the In-door Poor of the Parish of Greenwich* (London, 1826–51).
Jones, Thomas, *Clothing Societies Upon a Good Plan and Well Managed, Would, of All Institutions, Prove the Most Beneficial to the Poor, and Ought to be Established in All Parts of the Kingdom. A Specimen of One Tried for Years, is Here Exhibited, by the Rev. Thomas Jones, Curate of Creaton, Northamptonshire* (Northampton, c.1822).
Keats, Chatterton, *Without a Penny in the World. A Story of the 'Period.' A Christmas Annual* (London, 1870).
Kingsley, Charles, *The Water-Babies: A Fairy Tale for a Land-Baby* (London and Cambridge: Macmillan, 1863).
Kipling, Rudyard, *Something of Myself for my Friends Known and Unknown* (London: Macmillan, 1937).
Lanceley, William, *From Hall-Boy to House Steward* (London: E. Arnold, 1925).

Litchfield, F., *Three Years Results of the Farthinghoe Clothing Society With a Few Remarks on the Policy of Encouraging Provident Habits Among the Working Classes* (Northampton, 1832).
Llewelyn Davies, Margaret (ed.), *Life As We Have Known It by Co-operative Working Women* (London: Virago, 1977 [1931]).
———, *Maternity: Letters from Working Women* (London: Virago, 1984 [1915]).
Loane, M., *From Their Point of View* (London: E. Arnold, 1908).
———, *The Queen's Poor: Life as They Find it in Town and Country* (London: Middlesex University Press, 1998 [1905]).
Marr, T. R., *Housing Conditions in Manchester and Salford* (Manchester University Press, 1904).
Marshall, Sybil, *Fenland Chronicle* (London: Penguin, 1998 [1967]).
Maybrick, Florence Elizabeth, *Mrs. Maybrick's Own Story, My Fifteen Lost Years* (New York and London: Funk and Wagnalls Co., 1905).
Mayhew, Henry, *London Labour and the London Poor*, 4 vols (New York: Dover and London: Constable, 1968 [1861–2]).
Mayhew, Henry and John Binny, *The Criminal Prisons of London and Scenes of Prison Life* (London: Frank Cass, 1968 [1862]).
Meyer, Mrs Carl and Clementina Black, *Makers of Our Clothes: A Case for Trade Boards* (London: Duckworth and Co., 1909).
Miller, Herbert P., *The Scarcity of Domestic Servants; The Cause and Remedy. With a Short Outline of the Law Relating to Master and Domestic Servant* (London, 1876).
Mitchell (ed.), Geoffrey, *The Hard Way Up: The Autobiography of Hannah Mitchell. Suffragette and Rebel* (London: Virago, 1977).
Morrow, Alice, *Needlework and Knitting Drills for Infants with Music in Both Notations* (London: T. Nelson and Sons, 1900).
Moses, E. & Son, *The Growth of an Important Branch of British Industry. (The Ready-made Clothing System)* (London, 1860).
———, *The Universal Passport* (London, 1858).
———, *The Past, The Present, and the Future, A Public Address on the Opening of the New Establishment of E. Moses and Son* (London, 1846).
Murray, T. B., *The Children in St. Paul's. An Account of the Anniversary of the Assembled Charity Schools of London and Westminster, in the Cathedral Church of St. Paul* (London: SPCK, 1851).
N., W. B. [Lord William Beauchamp Nevill], *Penal Servitude* (London: Heinemann, 1903).
Paull, M. A., *The Romance of a Rag, and Other Tales* (London, 1876).
Pember Reeves, Maud, *Round About a Pound a Week* (London: Virago, 1979 [1913]).
Penn, Margaret, *Manchester Fourteen Miles* (London: Futura, 1982 [1947]).
Phillips, Watts, *The Wild Tribes of London* (London, 1855).
Potter, Beatrix, *The Tale of Benjamin Bunny* (London: Frederick Warne, 1904).
———, *The Tale of Peter Rabbit* (London: Frederick Warne, 1902).
Pyne, W. H., *The Costume of Great Britain* (London, 1808).
———, (ed.), *England, Scotland, and Ireland*, 4 vols (London, 1827).
Roberts, Robert, *A Ragged Schooling: Growing Up in the Classic Slum* (Manchester University Press, 1987 [1976]).

———, *The Classic Slum: Salford Life in the First Quarter of the Century* (Harmondsworth: Penguin, 1973 [1971]).
Rosevear, Elizabeth, *Manual of Needlework, Knitting and Cutting Out for Evening Continuation Schools* (London: Macmillan, 1894).
———, *A Text-Book of Needlework, Knitting and Cutting Out with Methods of Teaching* (London: Macmillan, 1893).
Rowntree, B. Seebohm, *Poverty: A Study of Town Life* (Bristol: Policy Press, 2000 [1901]).
Rowntree, B. Seebohm and May Kendall, *How the Labourer Lives: A Study of the Rural Labour Problem* (London: Thomas Nelson and Sons, 1913).
Russell, Charles E. B., *Manchester Boys: Sketches of Manchester Lads at Work and Play*, 2nd edn (Manchester University Press, 1913).
Sala, George Augustus, *Twice Round the Clock, or the Hours of the Day and Night in London* (London: Richard Marsh, 1862).
Samuel, Raphael, *East End Underworld: Chapters in the Life of Arthur Harding* (London: Routledge & Kegan Paul, 1981).
Schlesinger, Max, *Saunterings In and About London* (London, 1853).
Shaw, Charles, *When I Was a Child* (Firle: Caliban, 1977 [1903]).
Sims, George R., *How the Poor Live* (Gloucester: Dodo Press, 2009 [1883]).
———, (ed.), *Living London*, 3 vols (London, Paris, New York and Melbourne: Cassell and Company Ltd, 1906).
Smiles, Samuel, *Self-Help, With Illustrations of Character and Conduct* (London: John Murray, 1860).
Smith, Amy K., *Needlework for Student Teachers*, 4th edn (London: City of London Book Depôt, 1897).
Smith, Mary, *The Autobiography of Mary Smith Schoolmistress and Nonconformist. A Fragment of a Life with Letters from Jane Welsh Carlyle and Thomas Carlyle* (London: Bemrose and Sons, 1892).
Society for Bettering the Condition and Increasing the Comforts of the Poor, *Reports*, vol. III (1802).
Stacpoole, Florence, *Homely Hints for District Visitors* (London: National Health Society, 1897).
Stanley, Maude, 'Clubs for working girls', in The Baroness Burdett-Coutts (ed.), *Woman's Mission. A Series of Congress Papers on the Philanthropic Work of Women by Eminent Writers* (London: Sampson Low, Marston & Co., 1893), pp. 49–55.
———, *Clubs for Working Girls* (London: Macmillan, 1890).
T., H. P., *The Standard Needlework Book, A System of Graduated Instruction in Plain Needlework In Which Arithmetic is Brought to Bear Practically* (London, 1871).
Thale, Mary (ed.), *The Autobiography of Francis Place, 1771–1854* (London: Cambridge University Press, 1972).
Thompson, Flora, *Lark Rise to Candleford: A Trilogy* (London: Penguin, 1973 [1939–45]).
Thomson, John, *Victorian London: Street Life in Historic Photographs* (New York: Dover, 1994).
Tressell, Robert, *The Ragged Trousered Philanthropists* (Oxford University Press, 2005 [1914]).

Trimmer, Sarah, *Reflections Upon the Education of Children in Charity Schools. With the Outlines of a Plan of Appropriate Instruction for the Children of the Poor* (London, 1792).

———, *The Oeconomy of Charity* (London, 1787).

———, *The Servant's Friend; an Exemplary Tale Designed to Enforce the Religious Instructions Given at Sunday and Other Charity Schools: by Pointing Out the Practical Application of Them in a State of Service*, 7th edn (London, 1808 [1787]).

Trollope, Anthony, *The Way We Live Now* (London: Penguin, 1994 [1875]).

Trusler, John, *Trusler's Domestic Management, or the Art of Conducting a Family, with Economy, Frugality & Method* (Bath, 1819).

Tufnell, Edward Carleton, *On the Dwellings and General Economy of the Labouring Classes in Kent and Sussex* (London: W. Clowes & Sons, 1841).

Veblen, Thorstein, *The Theory of the Leisure Class* (New York: Dover Publications, 1994 [1899]).

W., A.C., *Rules for Young Women* (London and Oxford: SPCK, c.1873).

Walker, George, *The Costume of Yorkshire* (Firle: Caliban, 1978 [1814]).

White, William, *History, Gazetteer, and Directory, of Norfolk, and the City and County of the City of Norwich* (Sheffield, 1836).

Wise, Dorothy (ed.), *Diary of William Tayler, Footman. 1837* (London: The St. Marylebone Society, 1987).

Wilkinson, Robert, *The Law of Prisons in England And Wales, Being the Prison Act, 1865 (28 & 29 Vict. C.126) and The Prison Act, 1877 (40 & 41 Vict. C.21), With an Analysis of Acts; Notes; A Selection of Other Acts, and Portions of Acts Still in Force Relating to Prisons; and a Full Index* (London: Knight & Co., 1878).

Woodward, Kathleen, *Jipping Street* (London: Virago, 1983 [1928]).

Worth, Jennifer, *Shadows of the Workhouse* (London: Phoenix, 2009).

———, *Call the Midwife: A True Story of the East End in the 1950s* (London: Phoenix, 2012).

Young, Arthur, *General View of the Agriculture of the County of Sussex with Observations on the Means of its Improvement* (London, 1793).

SECONDARY SOURCES

Adburgham, Alison, *Shops and Shopping 1800–1914: Where and in What Manner the Well-Dressed Englishwoman Bought Her Clothes*, 2nd edn (London: Allen & Unwin, 1981).

Aldrich, Winifred, 'Tailors' cutting manuals and the growing provision of popular clothing 1770–1870', *Textile History*, 31:2 (2000), 163–210.

Alexander, David, *Retailing in England During the Industrial Revolution* (London: Athlone Press, 1970).

Alexander, Sally, *Becoming a Woman and Other Essays in 19th and 20th Century Feminist History* (New York University Press, 1995).

Al-Khalidi, Alia, 'Emergent technologies in menstrual paraphernalia in mid-nineteenth-century Britain', *Journal of Design History*, 14:4 (2001), 257–73.

Anderson, Anne, 'Victorian high society and social duty: the promotion of "recreative learning and voluntary teaching"', *History of Education*, 31:4 (2002), 311–34.
Anderson, Michael, *Family Structure in Nineteenth-Century Lancashire* (Cambridge University Press, 1971).
Andrews, Jonathan, 'The (un)dress of the mad poor in England, c.1650–1850. Part 2', *History of Psychiatry*, 18:2 (2007), 131–56.
───, 'The (un)dress of the mad poor in England, c.1650–1850. Part 1', *History of Psychiatry*, 18:1 (2007), 5–24.
Armstrong, Isobel, *Victorian Glassworlds: Glass Culture and the Imagination 1830–1880* (Oxford University Press, 2008).
Arnold, Janet, '*The Lady's Economical Assistant* of 1808', in Barbara Burman (ed.), *The Culture of Sewing: Gender, Consumption and Home Dressmaking* (Oxford: Berg, 1999), pp. 223–33.
Ash, Juliet, *Dress Behind Bars: Prison Clothing as Criminality* (London and New York: I. B. Tauris, 2009).
Ashenburg, Katherine, *Clean: An Unsanitised History of Washing* (London: Profile Books, 2008).
Atkinson, Diane, *Love and Dirt: The Marriage of Arthur Munby and Hannah Cullwick* (London: Macmillan, 2003).
Bamfield, Joshua, 'Consumer-owned community flour and bread societies in the eighteenth and early nineteenth centuries', in Nicholas Alexander and Gary Akehurst, *The Emergence of Modern Retailing, 1750–1950* (London: Frank Cass, 1999), pp. 16–36.
Barnes, C. J., *Sussex (East) Census – 1851 Index* (Hastings: C. J. Barnes, 1994).
Barrell, John, *The Dark Side of the Landscape: The Rural Poor in English Paintings 1730–1840* (Cambridge University Press, 1980).
Barthes, Roland, *The Fashion System*, trans. Matthew Ward and Richard Howard (Berkeley: University of California Press, 1990 [1967]).
Bartlett, Peter, 'The asylum and the Poor Law: the productive alliance', in Joseph Melling and Bill Forsythe (eds), *Insanity, Institutions and Society 1800–1914* (London and New York: Routledge, 1999), pp. 48–67.
Batchelor, Jennie and Cora Kaplan, 'Introduction', in Jennie Batchelor and Cora Kaplan (eds), *Women and Material Culture, 1660–1830* (Basingstoke: Palgrave Macmillan, 2007), pp. 1–8.
Bédarida, François, trans. A. S. Forster and Jeffrey Hodgkinson, *A Social History of England 1851–1990* (London: Routledge, 1991).
Belchem, John, *Popular Radicalism in Nineteenth-Century Britain* (Basingstoke: Macmillan, 1996).
Benson, John, *The Penny Capitalists: A Study of Nineteenth-century Working-Class Entrepreneurs* (Dublin: Gill & Macmillan, 1983).
Beveridge, Allan, 'Life in the asylum: patients' letters from Morningside, 1873–1908', *History of Psychiatry*, 9:36 (1998), 431–69.
Blaug, Mark, 'The Poor Law report reexamined', *The Journal of Economic History*, 24 (1964), 229–45.
───, 'The myth of the old Poor Law and the making of the New', *The Journal of Economic History*, 23:2 (1963), 151–84.

Bonner, Arnold, *British Co-operation: The History, Principles, and Organisation of the British Co-operative Movement* (Manchester: Co-operative Union, 1970).

Borowitz, Albert, *The Woman Who Murdered Black Satin: The Bermondsey Horror* (Columbus, OH: Ohio State University Press, 1981).

Bourke, Joanna, *Working-Class Cultures in Britain 1890–1960: Gender, Class and Ethnicity* (London: Routledge, 1994).

Bowlby, Rachel, *Just Looking: Consumer Culture in Dreiser, Gissing and Zola* (London: Methuen, 1985).

Breen, T. H., 'The meanings of things: interpreting the consumer economy in the eighteenth century', in John Brewer and Roy Porter (eds), *Consumption and the World of Goods* (London: Routledge, 1993), pp. 249–60.

Breward, Christopher, *The Hidden Consumer: Masculinities, Fashion and City Life 1860–1914* (Manchester University Press, 1999).

———, 'Patterns of respectability: publishing, home sewing and the dynamics of class and gender 1870–1914', in Barbara Burman (ed.), *The Culture of Sewing: Gender, Consumption and Home Dressmaking* (Oxford: Berg, 1999), pp. 21–31.

———, *The Culture of Fashion: A New History of Fashionable Dress* (Manchester University Press, 1995).

Briggs, Asa, *Victorian Things* (Stroud: Sutton, 2003).

———, *A Study of the Work of Seebohm Rowntree 1871–1954* (London: Longmans, 1961).

Brown, David, '"Persons of infamous character" or "an honest industrious and useful description of people"? The textile pedlars of Alstonfield and the role of peddling in industrialization', *Textile History*, 31:1 (2000), 1–26.

Buck, Anne, *Clothes and the Child: A Handbook of Children's Dress in England 1500–1900* (Bedford: Ruth Bean, 1996).

Burman, Barbara, 'Made at home by clever fingers: home dressmaking in Edwardian England', in Barbara Burman (ed.), *The Culture of Sewing: Gender, Consumption and Home Dressmaking* (Oxford: Berg, 1999), pp. 33–53.

Burman, Barbara and Jonathan White, 'Fanny's pockets: cotton, consumption and domestic economy, 1780–1850', in Jennie Batchelor and Cora Kaplan (eds), *Women and Material Culture, 1660–1830* (Basingstoke: Palgrave Macmillan, 2007), pp. 31–51.

Burnett, John, *Plenty and Want: A Social History of Diet in England from 1815 to the Present Day*, 3rd edn (Abingdon: Routledge, 1989).

———, *A Social History of Housing 1815–1970* (Newton Abbot: David & Charles, 1978).

———, *A History of the Cost of Living* (Harmondsworth: Penguin, 1969).

———, (ed.), *Destiny Obscure: Autobiographies of Childhood, Education and Family from the 1820s to the 1920s* (London: Routledge, 1994).

———, (ed.), *Useful Toil: Autobiographies of Working People from the 1820s to the 1920s* (London: Routledge, 1994).

Chapman, Stanley, 'The innovating entrepreneurs in the British ready-made clothing industry', *Textile History*, 24:1 (1993), 5–25.

Checkland, S. G. and E. O. A. (eds), *The Poor Law Report of 1834* (Harmondsworth: Penguin, 1974).

Cherry, Steven, *Mental Health Care in Modern England: The Norfolk Lunatic Asylum/St Andrew's Hospital c.1810–1998* (Woodbridge: Boydell Press, 2003).
Chinn, Carl, *Poverty Amidst Prosperity: The Urban Poor in England, 1834–1914* (Manchester University Press, 1995).
Clark, Anna, 'Wild workhouse girls and the Liberal imperial state in mid-nineteenth century Ireland', *Journal of Social History*, 39:2 (2005), 389–409.
———, *The Struggle for the Breeches: Gender and the Making of the British Working Class* (London: Rivers Oram, 1995).
Cockayne, Emily, *Hubbub: Filth, Noise and Stench in England 1600–1770* (New Haven and London: Yale University Press, 2007).
Coopey, Richard, Sean O'Connell and Dilwyn Porter, *Mail Order Retailing in Britain: A Business and Social History* (Oxford University Press, 2005).
Corbin, Alain, *The Foul and the Fragrant: Odor and the French Social Imagination* (Leamington Spa: Berg, 1986).
Cordery, Simon, *British Friendly Societies, 1750–1914* (Basingstoke: Palgrave Macmillan, 2003).
Craik, Jennifer, *Uniforms Exposed: From Conformity to Transgression* (Oxford: Berg, 2005).
Crane, Diana, *Fashion and Its Social Agendas: Class, Gender and Identity in Clothing* (Oxford University Press, 2000).
Crawford, Patricia, 'Attitudes to menstruation in seventeenth-century England', *Past and Present*, 91:1 (1981), 47–73.
Crompton, Frank, 'Needs and desires in the care of pauper lunatics: admissions to Worcester Asylum, 1852–72', in Pamela Dale and Joseph Melling (eds), *Mental Illness and Learning Disability Since 1850: Finding A Place for Mental Disorder in the United Kingdom* (London: Routledge, 2006), pp. 46–64.
Cunnington, C. Willett and Phillis, *Handbook of English Costume in the 19th Century*, 3rd edn (London: Faber, 1970).
———, *The History of Underclothes* (New York: Dover, 1992 [1951]).
Cunnington, Phillis, *Costume of Household Servants From the Middle Ages to 1900* (London: Adam & Charles Black, 1974).
Cunnington, Phillis and Catherine Lucas, *Charity Costumes of Children, Scholars, Almsfolk, Pensioners* (London: A. and C. Black, 1978).
———, *Occupational Costume in England From the 11th Century to 1914* (London: Adam & Charles Black, 1967).
Currie, R., A. Gilbert and L. Horsley, *Churches and Churchgoers: Patterns of Church Growth in the British Isles Since 1700* (Oxford University Press, 1977).
Daunton, M. J., *House and Home in the Victorian City: Working-Class Housing 1850–1914* (London: Edward Arnold, 1983).
Davidoff, Leonore, *Worlds Between: Historical Perspectives on Gender and Class* (Cambridge: Polity, 1995).
Davidson, Caroline, *A Woman's Work is Never Done: A History of Housework in the British Isles 1650–1950* (London: Chatto & Windus, 1986).
Davies, Andrew, *Leisure, Gender and Poverty: Working-Class Culture in Salford and Manchester, 1900–1939* (Buckingham: Open University Press, 1992).
Davin, Anna, *Growing Up Poor: Home, School and Street in London 1870–1914* (London: Rivers Oram Press, 1996).

Dawson, Graham, *Soldier Heroes: British Adventure, Empire and the Imagining of Masculinities* (London: Routledge, 1994).
Delap, Lucy, *Knowing Their Place: Domestic Service in Twentieth-century Britain* (Oxford University Press, 2011).
de Marly, Diana, *Working Dress: A History of Occupational Costume* (London: Batsford, 1986).
de Vries, Jan, *The Industrious Revolution: Consumer Behavior and the Household Economy, 1650 to the Present* (Cambridge University Press, 2008).
Dibbits, Hester C., 'Between society and family values: the linen cupboard in early-modern households', in Anton Schuurman and Pieter Spierenburg (eds), *Private Domain, Public Inquiry: Families and Life-Styles in the Netherlands and Europe, 1550 to the Present* (Hilversum: Verloren Publishers, 1996), pp. 125–45.
Digby, Anne, *Madness, Morality and Medicine: A Study of the York Retreat, 1796–1914* (Cambridge University Press, 1985).
———, 'Moral treatment at the Retreat, 1796–1846', in W. F. Bynum, Roy Porter and Michael Shepherd (eds), *The Anatomy of Madness: Essays in the History of Psychiatry*, 2 vols (London and New York: Tavistock Publications, 1985), vol. II, pp. 52–72.
———, *Pauper Palaces* (London: Routledge & Kegan Paul, 1978).
Dingle, A. E., 'Drink and working-class living standards in Britain, 1870–1914', *The Economic History Review*, 25:4 (1972), 608–22.
Dyhouse, Carol, *Girls Growing Up in Late-Victorian and Edwardian England* (London: Routledge & Kegan Paul, 1981).
English, Barbara, '*Lark Rise* and Juniper Hill: a Victorian community in literature and history', *Victorian Studies*, 29:1 (1985), 7–34.
Entwistle, Joanne, 'The dressed body', in Joanne Entwistle and Elizabeth Wilson (eds), *Body Dressing* (Oxford: Berg, 2001), pp. 33–58.
———, *The Fashioned Body: Fashion, Dress and Modern Social Theory* (Cambridge: Polity Press, 2000).
Evans, Eric J., *The Forging of the Modern State; Early Industrial Britain 1783–1870* (Harlow: Longman, 1983).
Ewart Evans, George, 'Dress and the rural historian', *Costume*, 8 (1974), 38–40.
Ewing, Elizabeth, *Everyday Dress 1650–1900* (London: Batsford, 1984).
———, *History of Children's Costume* (London: Batsford, 1977).
———, *Women in Uniform Through the Centuries* (London: Batsford, 1975).
Fields, Jill, *An Intimate Affair: Women, Lingerie, and Sexuality* (Berkeley and London: University of California Press, 2007).
Finn, Margot C., *The Character of Credit: Personal Debt in English Culture, 1740–1914* (Cambridge University Press, 2003).
———, 'Scotch drapers and the politics of modernity: gender, class and national identity in the Victorian tally trade', in Martin Daunton and Matthew Hilton (eds), *The Politics of Consumption: Material Culture and Citizenship in Europe and America* (Oxford: Berg, 2001), pp. 89–107.
Flanders, Judith, *The Victorian House: Domestic Life from Childbirth to Deathbed* (London: Harper Perennial, 2004).
Flugel, J. C., *The Psychology of Clothes* (London: Hogarth Press and Institute of Psychoanalysis, 1940 [1930]).

Fontaine, Laurence, *History of Pedlars in Europe*, trans. Vicki Whittaker (Cambridge: Polity, 1996).
Foster, Vanda, *A Visual History of Costume: The Nineteenth Century* (London: Batsford, 1992).
Foucault, Michel, *Discipline and Punish: The Birth of the Prison*, trans. Alan Sheridan (London: Penguin, 1991 [1975]).
———, *Madness and Civilization: A History of Insanity in the Age of Reason*, trans. Richard Howard (London and New York: Routledge, 2001 [1967]).
Fowler, Christina, 'Changes in provincial retail practice during the eighteenth century, with particular reference to central-southern England', in Nicholas Alexander and Gary Akehurst, *The Emergence of Modern Retailing, 1750–1950* (London: Frank Cass, 1999), pp. 37–54.
———, 'Robert Mansbridge, a rural tailor and his customers 1811–1815', *Textile History*, 28:1 (1997), 29–38.
Fussell, G. E., *The English Rural Labourer, His Home, Furniture, Clothing and Food from Tudor to Victorian Times* (London: Batchworth Press, 1949).
Gagnier, Regenia, *Subjectivities: A History of Self-Representation in Britain, 1832–1920* (Oxford University Press, 1991).
Gallagher, Catherine and Stephen Greenblatt, *Practicing New Historicism* (University of Chicago Press, 2001).
Garland, David, *Punishment and Welfare. A History of Penal Strategies* (Aldershot: Gower, 1985).
Gernsheim, Helmut and Alison Gernsheim, *The History of Photography: From the Camera Obscura to the Beginning of the Modern Era* (London: Thames & Hudson, 1969).
Ginsburg, Madeleine, 'Rags to riches: the second-hand clothes trade 1700–1978', *Costume*, 14 (1980), 121–35.
———, *Victorian Dress in Photographs* (London: Batsford, 1982).
Gittins, Diana, *Madness in its Place: Narratives of Severall's Hospital, 1913–1997* (London: Routledge, 1998).
Godfrey, Barry, 'Law, factory discipline and "theft": the impact of the factory on workplace appropriation in mid to late nineteenth century Yorkshire', *British Journal of Criminology*, 39:1 (1999), 56–71.
Godley, Andrew, 'Homeworking and the sewing machine in the British clothing industry 1850–1905', in Barbara Burman (ed.), *The Culture of Sewing: Gender, Consumption and Home Dressmaking* (Oxford: Berg, 1999), pp. 255–68.
———, 'Singer in Britain: the diffusion of sewing machine technology and its impact on the clothing industry in the United Kingdom, 1860–1905', *Textile History*, 27:1 (1996), 59–76.
———, 'The development of the UK clothing industry, 1850–1950: output and productivity growth', *Business History*, 37:4 (1995), 46–63.
Gorsky, Martin, 'The growth and distribution of English friendly societies in the early nineteenth century', *The Economic History Review*, 51 (1998), 489–511.
Gosden, P. H. J. H., *The Friendly Societies in England 1815–75* (Manchester University Press, 1961).
Green, Adrian, 'Heartless and unhomely? Dwellings of the poor in East Anglia and north-east England', in Joanne McEwan and Pamela Sharpe (eds), *Accommodating Poverty: The Housing and Living Arrangements of the English Poor, c.1600–1850* (Basingstoke: Palgrave Macmillan, 2011), pp. 69–101.

Green-Lewis, Jennifer, *Framing the Victorians: Photography and the Culture of Realism* (Ithaca, NY and London: Cornell University Press, 1996).
Hamilton, Peter and Roger Hargreaves, *The Beautiful and the Damned: The Creation of Identity in Nineteenth Century Photography* (Aldershot: Lund Humphries, 2001).
Hamlett, Jane and Lesley Hoskins, 'Comfort in small things? Clothing, control and agency in county lunatic asylums in nineteenth- and early twentieth-century England', *Journal of Victorian Culture*, 18:1 (2013), 93–114.
Hammond, J. L. and Barbara Hammond, *The Skilled Labourer 1760–1832* (London: Longmans, Green, and Co., 1919).
———, *The Town Labourer 1760–1832: The New Civilisation* (London: Longmans, Green, and Co., 1917).
———, *The Village Labourer 1760–1832: A Study in the Government of England Before the Reform Bill* (London: Longmans, Green, and Co., 1911).
Harris, Jose, *Private Lives, Public Spirit: Britain 1870–1914* (London: Penguin, 1994).
Harrison, Brian, *Peaceable Kingdom: Stability and Change in Modern Britain* (Oxford: Clarendon Press, 1982).
Harrison, J. F. C., *The Common People: A History from the Norman Conquest to the Present* (London: Fontana, 1984).
Hartwell, R. M., 'The consequences of the Industrial Revolution in England for the poor', in R. M. Hartwell (ed.), *The Long Debate on Poverty: Eight Essays on Industrialisation and 'The Condition of England'* (London: Institute of Economic Affairs, 1972), pp. 1–22.
Harvey, John, *Men in Black* (London: Reaktion, 1997).
Heeney, Brian, *The Women's Movement in the Church of England 1850–1930* (Oxford University Press, 1988).
Helland, Janice, *British and Irish Home Arts and Industries 1880–1914: Marketing Craft, Making Fashion* (Dublin: Irish Academic Press, 2007).
———, 'Embroidered spectacle: Celtic Revival as aristocratic display', in Betsey Taylor FitzSimon and James H. Marphy (eds), *The Irish Revival Reappraised* (Dublin: Four Courts Press, 2004), pp. 94–105.
———, 'Working bodies, Celtic textiles, and the Donegal Industrial Fund 1883–1890', *Textile*, 2:2 (2004), 134–55.
———, 'Rural women and urban extravagance in late nineteenth-century Britain', *Rural History*, 13:2 (2002), 179–97.
Henare, Amiria, 'Nga aho tipuna Maori: cloaks from New Zealand', in Susanne Küchler and Daniel Miller (eds), *Clothing as Material Culture* (Oxford: Berg, 2006), pp. 121–38.
Henderson, W. O., *The Lancashire Cotton Famine 1861–5* (Manchester University Press, 1969 [1934]).
Hennock, E. P. 'Poverty and social theory in England: the experience of the eighteen-eighties', *Social History*, 1:1 (1976), 67–91.
Higgs, Edward, 'Domestic service and household production', in Angela V. John (ed.), *Unequal Opportunities: Women's Employment in England 1800–1918* (Oxford: Basil Blackwell, 1986), pp. 125–50.
Higgs, Michelle, *Prison Life in Victorian England* (Stroud: Tempus, 2007).
Hiley, Michael, *Victorian Working Women: Portraits from Life* (London: Gordon Fraser, 1979).

Hilton, Boyd, *The Age of Atonement. The Influence of Evangelicalism on Social and Economic Thought, 1795–1865* (Oxford: Clarendon, 1988).

Hilton, George W., *The Truck System* (Westport, CT: Greenwood Press, 1975).

Himmelfarb, Gertrude, *Poverty and Compassion: The Moral Imagination of the Late Victorians* (New York: Knopf, 1981).

_____, *The Idea of Poverty: England in the Early Industrial Age* (London: Faber & Faber, 1985).

Hobsbawm, Eric, *The Age of Capital 1848–1875* (London: Weidenfeld & Nicolson, 1995).

Hobsbawm, E. J. and George Rudé, *Captain Swing* (London: Pimlico, 1993).

Hodson, Deborah, ' "The municipal store": adaptation and development in the retail markets of nineteenth-century urban Lancashire', in Nicholas Alexander and Gary Akehurst, *The Emergence of Modern Retailing, 1750–1950* (London: Frank Cass, 1999), pp. 94–114.

Hollander, Anne, *Seeing Through Clothes* (Berkeley, Los Angeles and London: University of California Press, 1993 [1978]).

Hopkins, Eric, *A Social History of the English Working Classes 1815–1945* (London: Edward Arnold, 1979).

Honeyman, Katrina, *Well Suited: A History of the Leeds Clothing Industry, 1850–1990* (Oxford University Press, 2000).

Horn, P., *Behind the Counter: Shop Lives from Market Stall to Supermarket* (Stroud: Sutton Publishing Ltd, 2006).

Hosgood, Christopher P., 'The "pigmies of commerce" and the working-class community: small shopkeepers in England, 1870–1914', *Journal of Social History*, 22:3 (1989), 439–60.

Howkins, Alun, *Reshaping Rural England, A Social History 1850–1925* (London: HarperCollins, 1991).

Hudson, Derek, *Munby, Man of Two Worlds: The Life and Diaries of Arthur J. Munby 1828–1910* (London: Abacus, 1974).

Humpherys, Anne, *Travels into the Poor Man's Country: The Work of Henry Mayhew* (Athens: University of Georgia Press, 1977).

Humphreys, Robert, *Sin, Organized Charity and the Poor Law in Victorian England* (Basingstoke: Macmillan, 1995).

Hunt, Alan, *Governance of the Consuming Passions: A History of Sumptuary Law* (Basingstoke: Macmillan, 1996).

Hunt, E. H., 'Industrialization and regional inequality: wages in Britain, 1760–1914', *Journal of Economic History*, 46:4 (1986), 935–66.

Hunt, Felicity, 'Divided aims: the educational implications of opposing ideologies in girls' secondary schooling, 1850–1940', in Felicity Hunt (ed.), *Lessons for Life: The Schooling of Girls and Women 1850–1950* (Oxford: Basil Blackwell, 1987), pp. 3–21.

Hunt, G., J. Mellor and J. Turner, 'Wretched, hatless and miserably clad: women and the inebriate reformatories from 1900–1913', *British Journal of Sociology*, 40:2 (1989), 244–70.

Ignatieff, Michael, *A Just Measure of Pain: The Penitentiary in the Industrial Revolution 1750–1850* (Harmondsworth: Penguin, 1989 [1978]).

Jeffrey, Julie Roy, ' "Stranger, buy ... lest our mission fail"; the complex culture of women's abolitionist fairs', *American Nineteenth Century History*, 4:1 (2003), 1–24.

John, Angela V., *By the Sweat of Their Brow: Women Workers at the Victorian Coal Mines* (London: Croom Helm, 1980).
Johnson, Paul, *Saving and Spending: The Working-Class Economy in Britain 1870–1939* (Oxford: Clarendon, 1985).
Jones, Mary Gwladys, *The Charity School Movement: A Study of Eighteenth-Century Puritanism in Action* (Cambridge University Press, 1938).
Jones, Peter, 'Clothing the poor in early-nineteenth-century England', *Textile History*, 37:1 (2006), 17–37.
Jones, Peter D., ' "I cannot keep my place without being deascent": pauper letters, parish clothing and pragmatism in the south of England, 1750–1830', *Rural History*, 20:1 (2009), 31–49.
Keep, Christopher, 'The cultural work of the type-writer girl', *Victorian Studies*, 40:3 (1997), 401–26.
Kidd, Alan J., *Manchester* (Edinburgh University Press, 2002).
——, 'Philanthropy and the "social history paradigm"', *Social History*, 21:2 (1996), 180–92.
Kidd, Alan J. and K. W. Roberts (eds), *City, Class and Culture: Studies of Social Policy and Cultural Production in Victorian Manchester* (Manchester University Press, 1985).
Kilgarriff, Michael, *Sing Us One of the Old Songs: A Guide to Popular Song 1860–1920* (Oxford University Press, 1998).
King, Peter, 'Pauper inventories and the material lives of the poor in the eighteenth and early nineteenth centuries', in Tim Hitchcock, Peter King and Pamela Sharpe (eds), *Chronicling Poverty: The Voices and Strategies of the English Poor, 1640–1840* (Basingstoke: Macmillan, 1997), pp. 155–91.
King, Steven, 'Reclothing the English poor, 1750–1840', *Textile History*, 33:1 (2002), 37–47.
——, *Poverty and Welfare in England 1700–1850* (Manchester University Press, 2000).
King, Steven and Christiana Payne, 'The dress of the poor', *Textile History*, 33:1 (2002), 3–8.
Kitteringham, Jennie, 'Country work girls in nineteenth-century England', in Raphael Samuel (ed.), *Village Life and Labour* (London: Routledge & Kegan Paul, 1975), pp. 73–138.
Koven, Seth, *Slumming: Sexual and Social Politics in Victorian London* (Princeton, NJ: Princeton University Press, 2004).
Lambertz, Jan, 'Sexual harassment in the nineteenth century English cotton industry', *History Workshop Journal*, 19 (1985), 29–61.
Lancaster, Bill, *The Department Store: A Social History* (London: Leicester University Press, 1995).
Lansdell, Avril, *The Clothes of the Cut: A History of Canal Costume* (London: British Waterways Board, 1976).
Lees, Lynn Hollen, *The Solidarities of Strangers: The English Poor Laws and the People, 1700–1948* (Cambridge University Press, 1998).
Lemire, Beverly, *The Business of Everyday Life: Gender, Practice and Social Politics in England, c.1600–1900* (Manchester University Press, 2005).
——, *Dress, Culture and Commerce: The English Clothing Trade Before the Factory, 1660–1800* (Basingstoke: Macmillan, 1997).

———, '"A good stock of cloaths": the changing market for cotton clothing in Britain, 1750–1800', *Textile History*, 22:2 (1991), 311–28.

———, 'Peddling fashion: salesmen, pawnbrokers, taylors, thieves and the second-hand clothes trade in England, c.1700–1800', *Textile History*, 22:1 (1991), 67–82.

———, *Fashion's Favourite: The Cotton Trade and the Consumer in Britain, 1660–1800* (Pasold Research Fund and Oxford University Press, 1991).

———, 'Developing consumerism and the ready-made clothing trade in Britain, 1750–1800', *Textile History*, 15:1 (1984), 21–44.

Levitt, Sarah, 'Cheap mass-produced men's clothing in the nineteenth and early twentieth centuries', *Textile History*, 22:2 (1991), 179–92.

———, *Victorians Unbuttoned: Registered Designs for Clothing, Their Makers and Wearers, 1839–1900* (London: Allen & Unwin, 1986).

Liddington, Jill, *The Life and Times of a Respectable Rebel: Selina Cooper (1864–1946)* (London: Virago, 1984).

Light, Alison, *Mrs Woolf and the Servants* (London: Penguin Fig Tree, 2007).

Lloyd, Sarah, 'Joys of the cottage: labourers' houses, hovels and huts in Britain and the British Colonies, 1770–1830', in Joanne McEwan and Pamela Sharpe (eds), *Accommodating Poverty: The Housing and Living Arrangements of the English Poor, c.1600–1850* (Basingstoke: Palgrave Macmillan, 2011), pp. 102–21.

Longmate, Norman, *The Workhouse: A Social History* (London: Pimlico, 2003).

MacArthur, Burke, *United Littles: The Story of the Needlework Guild of America* (New York: Coward-McCann, 1955).

Macfarlane, Alan and Gerry Martin, *Glass: A World History* (University of Chicago, 2002).

MacKinnon, Mary, 'English Poor Law policy and the crusade against outrelief', *The Journal of Economic History*, 47 (1987), 603–25.

Maidment, Brian, '101 things to do with a fantail hat: dustmen, dirt and dandyism, 1820–1860', *Textile History*, 33:1 (2002), 79–97.

Malcolmson, Patricia, *English Laundresses: A Social History 1850–1930* (Urbana and Chicago: University of Illinois Press, 1986).

Malcolmson, Robert W., *Popular Recreations in English Society 1700–1850* (Cambridge University Press, 1973).

Malcolmson, Robert and Stephanos Mastoris, *The English Pig, a History* (London: Hambledon Press, 1998).

Martin, Jane, *Women and the Politics of Schooling in Victorian and Edwardian England* (London: Leicester University Press, 1999).

Maslin, George, 'The Deptford Ragged School', *Lewisham History Journal*, 4 (1996), 1–14.

Mason, Michael, *The Making of Victorian Sexuality* (Oxford University Press, 1994).

Mauss, Marcel, *The Gift: The Form and Reason for Exchange in Archaic Societies*, trans. W. D. Halls (London: Routledge, 1990 [1923–4]).

May, Trevor, *The Victorian Railway Worker* (Princes Risborough: Shire, 2003).

Maynard, Margaret, *Fashioned From Penury: Dress as Cultural Practice in Colonial Australia* (Oakleigh, Vic. and New York: Cambridge University Press, 1994).

McBride, Theresa M., *The Domestic Revolution: The Modernisation of Household Service in England and France, 1820–1920* (London: Croom Helm, 1976).
McConville, Seán, *English Local Prisons 1860–1900: Next Only to Death* (London: Routledge, 1995).
McDermid, Jane, 'The making of a "domestic" life: memories of a working woman', *Labour History Review*, 73:3 (2008), 253–68.
McKendrick, Neil, 'The commercialization of fashion', in Neil McKendrick, John Brewer and J. H. Plumb (eds), *The Birth of a Consumer Society: The Commercialization of Eighteenth-century England* (London: Europa, 1982), pp. 34–99.
McLeod, Hugh, *Secularisation in Western Europe, 1848–1914* (Basingstoke: Macmillan, 2000).
———, *Religion and the People of Western Europe 1789–1989* (Oxford University Press, 1997).
Meacham, Standish, *A Life Apart: The English Working Class 1890–1914* (London: Thames & Hudson, 1977).
Midgley, Clare, 'Slave sugar boycotts, female activism and the domestic base of British anti-slavery culture', *Slavery and Abolition*, 17:3 (1996), 137–62.
Miller, Daniel, *Stuff* (Cambridge: Polity Press, 2010).
———, 'Introduction', in Susanne Küchler and Daniel Miller (eds), *Clothing as Material Culture* (Oxford: Berg, 2006), pp. 1–19.
Morgan, Prys, 'From a death to a view: the hunt for the Welsh past in the Romantic period', in Eric Hobsbawm and Terence Ranger (eds), *The Invention of Tradition* (Cambridge University Press, 2002), pp. 43–100.
Mort, Frank, *Dangerous Sexualities: Medico-moral Politics in England Since 1830* (London: Routledge, 2000).
Muldrew, Craig and Steven King, 'Cash, wages and the economy of makeshifts in England, 1650–1800', in Peter Scholliers and Leonard Schwarz (eds), *Experiencing Wages: Social and Cultural Aspects of Wage Forms in Europe since 1500* (New York and Oxford: Berghahn, 2003), pp. 155–180.
Murphy, Elaine, 'Workhouse care of the insane, 1845–90', in Pamela Dale and Joseph Melling (eds), *Mental Illness and Learning Disability Since 1850: Finding A Place for Mental Disorder in the United Kingdom* (London: Routledge, 2006), pp. 24–45.
Nead, Lynda, *Victorian Babylon: People, Streets and Images in Nineteenth-Century London* (New Haven and London: Yale University Press, 2000).
Neal, Lawrence E., *Retailing and the Public* (London: Allen & Unwin, 1932).
Nelson, Brian, 'Introduction', in Émile Zola, *The Ladies' Paradise* (Oxford University Press, 1998).
Nevett, T. R., *Advertising in Britain: A History* (London: Heinemann, 1982).
Nunn, Joan, *Fashion in Costume 1200–2000* (London: Herbert, 2000).
Obelkevich, James, 'Religion', in F. M. L. Thompson, *The Cambridge Social History of Britain 1750–1950*, 3 vols (Cambridge University Press, 1993), vol. III, pp. 311–56.
O'Connell, Sean, *Credit and Community: Working-Class Debt in the UK Since 1880* (Oxford University Press, 2009).
Oddy, Nicholas, 'A beautiful ornament in the parlour or boudoir: the domestication of the sewing machine', in Barbara Burman (ed.), *The Culture of*

Sewing: Gender, Consumption and Home Dressmaking (Oxford: Berg, 1999), pp. 285–301.

Parker, Rozsika, *The Subversive Stitch: Embroidery and the Making of the Feminine* (London: The Women's Press, 1984).

Parsons, Gerald (ed.), *Religion in Victorian Britain*, 4 vols (Manchester University Press, 1988).

Pelling, Henry, *A History of British Trade Unionism* (Middlesex: Penguin, 1963).

Perrot, Philippe, *Fashioning the Bourgeoisie: A History of Clothing in the Nineteenth Century* (Princeton, NJ: Princeton University Press, 1994).

Philips, David, 'Crime, law and punishment in the Industrial Revolution', in Patrick O'Brien and Roland Quinault (eds), *The Industrial Revolution and British Society* (Cambridge University Press, 1993), pp. 156–82.

Pickering, Paul, 'Class without words: symbolic communication in the Chartist movement', *Past and Present*, 112 (1986), 144–62.

Pinchbeck, Ivy, *Women Workers and the Industrial Revolution 1750–1850* (London: Virago, 1981 [1930]).

Pope, Dudley, *Life in Nelson's Navy* (London: Allen & Unwin, 1981).

Porter, Roy, *A Social History of Madness: Stories of the Insane* (London: Weidenfeld & Nicolson, 1987).

Priestley, Philip, *Victorian Prison Lives: English Prison Biography, 1830–1814* (London: Pimlico, 1999).

Prochaska, F., 'A mother's country: mothers' meetings and family welfare in Britain, 1850–1950', *History*, 74:242 (1989), 379–99.

Prochaska, F. K., *Women and Philanthropy in Nineteenth-Century England* (Oxford: Clarendon Press, 1980).

Putnam, Tim, 'The sewing machine comes home', in Barbara Burman (ed.), *The Culture of Sewing: Gender, Consumption and Home Dressmaking* (Oxford: Berg, 1999), pp. 269–83.

Purvis, June, *Hard Lessons: The Lives and Education of Working-Class Women in Nineteenth-century England* (London: Polity Press, 1989).

Rappaport, Erika Diane, *Shopping for Pleasure: Women in the Making of London's West End* (Princeton, NJ and Woodstock, UK: Princeton University Press, 2000).

Reay, Barry, *Rural Englands: Labouring Lives in the Nineteenth Century* (Basingstoke: Palgrave Macmillan, 2004).

———, *Microhistories: Demography, Society and Culture in Rural England, 1800–1930* (Cambridge University Press, 2002).

———, *Watching Hannah: Sexuality, Horror and Bodily De-formation in Victorian England* (London: Reaktion, 2002).

Reid, Fred, *Keir Hardie: The Making of a Socialist* (London: Croom Helm, 1978).

Ribeiro, Aileen, *Dress and Morality* (London: Batsford, 1986).

———, *Fashion in the French Revolution* (New York: Holmes and Meier, 1988).

Richardson, Ruth, *Death, Dissection and the Destitute*, 2nd edn (London: Phoenix Press, 2001).

Richmond, Vivienne, 'Rubbish or riches? Church jumble sale purchases in late-Victorian England', *Journal of Historical Research in Marketing*, 2:3 (2010), 327–41.

———, 'The English Church jumble sale: parochial charity in the modern age', in Ilja Van Damme and Jon Stobart (eds), *Modernity and the Second-Hand Trade: European Consumption Cultures and Practices 1700–1900* (Basingstoke: Palgrave Macmillan, 2010), pp. 242–58.

———, '"Indiscriminate liberality subverts the morals and depraves the habits of the poor": A contribution to the debate on the Poor Law, parish clothing relief and clothing societies in early nineteenth-century England', *Textile History*, 40:1 (2009), 51–69.

———, 'Stitching the self: Eliza Kenniff's drawers and the materialization of identity in late-nineteenth-century London', in Maureen Daly Goggin and Beth Fowkes Tobin (eds), *Women and Things: Gendered Material Practices, 1750–1950* (Farnham: Ashgate, 2009), pp. 43–54.

———, 'Report back: "The dress of the poor 1750–1900"', *History Workshop Journal*, 49 (2000), 271–3.

Riello, Giorgio, 'Fabricating the domestic: the material culture of textiles and the social life of the home in early modern Europe', in Beverly Lemire (ed.), *The Force of Fashion in Politics and Society: Global Perspectives from Early Modern to Contemporary Times* (Farnham: Ashgate, 2010), pp. 41–65.

Roberts, Elizabeth, *A Woman's Place: An Oral History of Working-Class Women 1890–1940* (Oxford: Basil Blackwell, 1985).

Roche, Daniel, *The Culture of Clothing: Dress and Fashion in the 'Ancien Régime'*, trans. Jean Birrell (Cambridge University Press, 1996).

Roper, Michael, 'Slipping out of view: subjectivity and emotion in gender history', *History Workshop Journal*, 59 (2005), 57–72.

Rose, Clare, *Making, Selling and Wearing Boys' Clothes in Late-Victorian England* (Farnham: Ashgate, 2010).

———, *Children's Clothes Since 1750* (London: Batsford, 1989).

Rose, Clare and Vivienne Richmond (eds), *Clothing, Society and Culture in Nineteenth-Century England*, 3 vols (London: Pickering & Chatto, 2011).

Rose, Michael E., 'The disappearing pauper: Victorian attitudes to the relief of the poor', in Eric M. Sigsworth (ed.), *In Search of Victorian Values: Aspects of Nineteenth-century Thought and Society* (Manchester University Press, 1988), pp. 56–72.

———, *The Relief of Poverty 1834–1914* (Basingstoke: Macmillan, 1972).

Ross, Ellen, *Love and Toil: Motherhood in Outcast London, 1870–1918* (Oxford University Press, 1993).

———, 'Survival networks: women's neighbourhood sharing in London before World War I', *History Workshop Journal*, 15:1 (1983), 4–28.

Rublack, Ulinka, *Dressing Up: Cultural Identity in Renaissance Europe* (Oxford University Press, 2010).

Rule, John, *The Labouring Classes in Early Industrial England 1750–1850* (Harlow: Longman, 1986).

Samuel, Raphael, 'Mineral workers', in Raphael Samuel (ed.), *Miners, Quarrymen and Saltworkers* (London: Routledge & Kegan Paul, 1977), pp. 1–97.

Sayer, Karen, '"A sufficiency of clothing": dress and domesticity in Victorian Britain', *Textile History*, 33:1 (2002), 112–22.

Schwartz, Laura, *A Serious Endeavour: Gender, Education and Community at St Hugh's, 1886–2011* (London: Profile Books, 2011).
Scull, Andrew, *The Most Solitary of Afflictions: Madness and Society in Britain 1700–1900* (New Haven: Yale University Press, 1993).
———, *Museums of Madness: The Social Organisation of Insanity in Nineteenth-Century England* (London: Allen Lane, 1979).
Sharpe, Pamela, ' "Cheapness and economy": manufacturing and retailing ready-made clothing in London and Essex 1830–50', *Textile History*, 26:2 (1995), 203–13.
Shesgreen, Sean, *Images of the Outcast: The Urban Poor in the Cries of London* (Manchester University Press, 2002).
Showalter, Elaine, *The Female Malady: Women, Madness and English Culture, 1830–1980* (London: Virago, 1987).
Showalter, Elaine and English, 'Victorian women and menstruation', *Victorian Studies*, 14:1 (1970), 83–9.
Shuttleworth, Sally, 'Female circulation: medical discourse and popular advertising in the mid-Victorian era', in Mary Jacobus, Evelyn Fox Keller and Sally Shuttleworth (eds), *Body/Politics: Women and the Discourses of Science* (New York and London: Routledge, 1990), pp. 47–68.
Smiles, Sam, 'Defying comprehension: resistance to uniform appearance in depicting the poor, 1770s to 1830s', *Textile History*, 33:1 (2002), 22–36.
Smith, Leonard D., ' "Your very thankful inmate": discovering the patients of an early county lunatic asylum', *Social History of Medicine*, 21:2 (2008), 237–52.
———, *'Cure, Comfort, and Safe Custody': Public Lunatic Asylums in Early Nineteenth Century England* (London: Leicester University Press, 1999).
Smith, Virginia, *Clean: A History of Personal Hygiene and Purity* (Oxford University Press, 2007).
Snell, K. D. M., *Parish and Belonging: Community, Identity and Welfare in England and Wales, 1700–1950* (Cambridge University Press, 2009).
———, 'The Sunday school movement in England and Wales: child labour, denominational control and working-class culture', *Past & Present*, 164 (1999), 122–68.
———, *Annals of the Labouring Poor: Social Change and Agrarian England 1660–1900* (Cambridge University Press, 1985).
Spanabel Emery, Joy, 'Dreams on paper: a story of the commercial pattern industry', in Barbara Burman (ed.), *The Culture of Sewing: Gender, Consumption and Home Dressmaking* (Oxford: Berg, 1999), pp. 235–53.
Spufford, Margaret, 'The cost of apparel in seventeenth-century England, and the accuracy of Gregory King', *The Economic History Review*, New Series, 53:4 (2000), 677–705.
———, *The Great Reclothing of Rural England: Petty Chapmen and Their Wares in the Seventeenth Century* (London: Hambledon Press, 1984).
———, *Small Books and Pleasant Histories: Popular Fiction and its Readership in Seventeenth-century England* (Athens, GA: University of Georgia Press, 1981).
Spurrier, Lisa, 'Absconding with the clothing club money', *The Berkshire Echo, The Newsletter of Berkshire Record Office*, No. 22 (January 2003).

Stanley, Liz (ed.), *The Diaries of Hannah Cullwick, Victorian Maidservant* (London: Virago, 1984).
Stedman Jones, Gareth, *Outcast London: A Study in the Relationship Between Classes in Victorian Society*, new edn (London: Penguin, 1984).
Steedman, Carolyn, *Labours Lost: Domestic Service and the Making of Modern England* (Cambridge University Press, 2009).
_____, *Master and Servant: Love and Labour in the English Industrial Age* (Cambridge University Press, 2007).
_____, 'Englishness, clothes and little things', in Christopher Breward, Becky Conekin and Caroline Cox (eds), *The Englishness of English Dress* (Oxford: Berg, 2002), pp. 29–44.
_____, *Dust* (Manchester University Press, 2001).
_____, *The Radical Soldier's Tale* (London: Routledge, 1988).
Steele, Jess, *Turning the Tide: The History of Everyday Deptford* (London: Deptford Forum, 1993).
_____, (ed.), *The Streets of London: The Booth Notebooks – South East* (London: Deptford Forum, 1997).
Steele, Valerie, *Fashion and Eroticism: Ideals of Feminine Beauty from the Victorian Era to the Jazz Age* (Oxford University Press, 1985).
Strange, Julie-Marie, '"I believe it to be a case depending on menstruation": madness and menstrual taboo in British medical practice, c.1840–1930', in Andrew Shail and Gillian Howie (eds), *Menstruation: A Cultural History* (Basingstoke: Palgrave Macmillan, 2005), pp. 102–16.
Stuart, Dorothy Margaret, *The English Abigail* (London: Macmillan, 1946).
Styles, John, *The Dress of the People: Everyday Fashion in Eighteenth-Century England* (New Haven and London: Yale University Press, 2007).
_____, 'Involuntary consumers? Servants and their clothes in eighteenth-century England', *Textile History*, 33:1 (2002), 9–21.
_____, 'Dress in history: reflections on a contested terrain', *Fashion Theory*, 2:4 (1998), 383–9.
_____, 'Clothing the north: the supply of non-elite clothing in the eighteenth-century north of England', *Textile History*, 25:2 (1994), 139–66.
_____, 'Manufacturing, consumption and design in eighteenth-century England', in John Brewer and Roy Porter (eds), *Consumption and the World of Goods* (London: Routledge, 1993), pp. 527–54.
Summers, Anne, 'A home from home – women's philanthropic work in the nineteenth century', in Sandra Burman (ed.), *Fit Work for Women* (London: Croom Helm, 1979), pp. 33–63.
Summers, Leigh, *Bound to Please: A History of the Victorian Corset* (Oxford: Berg, 2001).
Summerscale, Kate, *The Suspicions of Mr Whicher: or The Murder at Road Hill House* (London: Bloomsbury, 2008).
Suzuki, Akihito, 'Lunacy and labouring men: narratives of male vulnerability in mid-Victorian London', in Roberta Bivins and John V. Pickstone (eds), *Medicine, Madness and Social History: Essays in Honour of Roy Porter* (Basingstoke: Palgrave Macmillan, 2007), pp. 118–28.
_____, 'The politics and ideology of non-restraint: the case of the Hanwell Asylum', *Medical History*, 39:1 (1995), 1–17.

Tagg, John, *The Burden of Representation: Essays on Photographies and Histories* (Basingstoke: Macmillan, 1988).

Tarlo, Emma, *Clothing Matters: Dress and Identity in India* (London: Hurst & Company, 1996).

Taylor, Alice, ' "Fashion has extended her influence to the cause of humanity": the transatlantic female economy of the Boston Antislavery Bazaar', in Beverly Lemire (ed.), *The Force of Fashion in Politics and Society: Global Perspectives from Early Modern to Contemporary Times* (Farnham: Ashgate, 2010), pp. 115–42.

Taylor, Lou, *The Study of Dress History* (Manchester University Press, 2002).

———, *Mourning Dress: A Costume and Social History* (London: Allen & Unwin, 1983).

Tebbutt, Melanie, *Making Ends Meet: Pawnbroking and Working-Class Credit* (Leicester University Press, 1983).

Thane, Pat, *Old Age In English History: Past Experiences, Present Issues* (Oxford University Press, 2000).

Thompson, Paul, *The Edwardians: The Remaking of British Society*, 2nd edn (London: Routledge, 1992).

Thorsheim, Peter, *Inventing Pollution: Coal, Smoke, and Culture in Britain Since 1800* (Athens, OH: Ohio University Press, 2006).

Tobin, Shelley, *Inside Out: A Brief History of Underwear* (London: The National Trust, 2001).

Todd, Selina, *Young Women, Work, and Family in England 1918–1950* (Oxford University Press, 2005).

Tomkins, Alannah and Steven King, 'Introduction', in Steven King and Alannah Tomkins (eds), *The Poor in England 1700–1850: An Economy of Makeshifts* (Manchester University Press, 2003), pp. 1–38.

Tozer, Jane and Sarah Levitt, *Fabric of Society: A Century of People and their Clothes 1770–1870* (Carno, Wales: Laura Ashley, 1983).

Treble, James. H., *Urban Poverty in Britain 1830–1914* (London: Batsford, 1979).

Trevor-Roper, Hugh, 'The invention of tradition: the Highland tradition of Scotland', in Eric Hobsbawm and Terence Ranger (eds), *The Invention of Tradition* (Cambridge University Press, 2002), pp. 15–41.

Turnbull, Annemarie, 'Learning her womanly work: the elementary school curriculum, 1870–1914', in Felicity Hunt (ed.), *Lessons for Life: The Schooling of Girls and Women 1850–1950* (Oxford: Basil Blackwell, 1987), pp. 83–100.

Ugolini, Laura, *Men and Menswear: Sartorial Consumption in Britain 1880–1939* (Aldershot: Ashgate, 2007).

Vickery, Amanda, *Behind Closed Doors: At Home in Georgian England* (New Haven and London: Yale University Press, 2009).

———, *The Gentleman's Daughter: Women's Lives in Georgian England* (New Haven and London: Yale University Press, 1998).

Vigarello, Georges, *Concepts of Cleanliness: Changing Attitudes in France Since the Middle Ages*, trans. Jean Birrell (Cambridge University Press, 1988).

Vigeon, Evelyn, 'Clogs or wooden soled shoes', *Costume*, 11 (1977), 1–27.

Vincent, David, *Bread, Knowledge and Freedom: A Study of Nineteenth-Century Working Class Autobiography* (London: Europa, 1981).

Vostral, Sharra L., *Under Wraps: A History of Menstrual Hygiene Technology* (Plymouth: Lexington Books, 2008).
Walkowitz, Judith, *City of Dreadful Delight: Narratives of Sexual Danger in Late-Victorian London* (London: Virago, 1992).
Weatherill, Lorna, *Consumer Behaviour and Material Culture in Britain 1660–1760*, 2nd edn (London: Routledge, 1996).
Whitlock, Tammy C., *Crime, Gender, and Consumer Culture in Nineteenth-Century England* (Aldershot: Ashgate, 2005).
Williams-Mitchell, Christobel, *Dressed for the Job: The Story of Occupational Costume* (Poole: Blandford, 1982).
Wilson, Elizabeth, *Adorned in Dreams: Fashion and Modernity*, revd edn (London: I. B. Tauris, 2003).
———, *The Sphinx in the City. Urban Life, the Control of Disorder, and Women* (London: Virago, 1991).
Wohl, Anthony S., *Endangered Lives: Public Health in Victorian Britain* (London: Dent, 1983).
Woods, Robert, *The Population of Britain in the Nineteenth Century* (Cambridge University Press, 1995).
Worth, Rachel, 'Rural working-class dress, 1850–1900: a peculiarly English tradition?', in Christopher Breward, Becky Conekin and Caroline Cox (eds), *The Englishness of English Dress* (Oxford: Berg, 2002), pp. 97–112.
———, 'Rural laboring dress, 1850–1900: some problems of representation', *Fashion Theory*, 3:3 (1999), 323–42.
Wright, David, 'Getting out of the asylum: understanding the confinement of the insane in the nineteenth century', *Social History of Medicine*, 10:1 (1997), 137–55.
Wright, Simon, 'The Streatfeild family and The Rocks estate', *Hindsight*, 6 (2000), 46–61.
Wynter, Rebecca, 'Good in all respects': appearance and dress at Staffordshire County Lunatic Asylum, 1818–54', *History of Psychiatry*, 22:1 (2011), 40–57.
Yeo, Stephen, *Religion and Voluntary Organisations in Crisis* (London: Croom Helm, 1976).
Zimmeck, Meta, 'Jobs for the girls: the expansion of clerical work for women, 1850–1914', in Angela V. John, *Unequal Opportunities: Women's Employment in England 1800–1918* (Oxford: Basil Blackwell, 1986), pp. 152–77.

UNPUBLISHED THESES

Pinches, Sylvia Margaret, 'Charities in Warwickshire in the eighteenth and nineteenth centuries', PhD, University of Leicester (2001).
Reader, Nicola Sian, 'Female friendly societies in industrialising England, 1780–1850', PhD, University of Leeds (2005).
Toplis, Alison E. M., 'The non-elite consumer and "wearing apparel" in Herefordshire and Worcestershire, 1800–1850', PhD, University of Wolverhampton (2008).

AUDIO CD

Pulp, 'Underwear', *Different Class* (Universal/Island, 1999).

WEBSITES AND ELECTRONIC RESOURCES

'Almshouses' [Exeter], *GENUKI*, genuki.cs.ncl.ac.uk/DEV/Exeter/ExeterHist 1850/.
A. McFarlane-Melloy, email to V. Richmond, 25 April 2004.
'Birmingham Daily Post', *19th Century British Library Newspapers*, 0-find. galegroup.com.catalogue.ulrls.lon.ac.uk/.
'Education in Langford and Little Faringdon', *Berkshire Family Historian*, www.berksfhs.org.uk/journal/Jun2000/Jun2000EducationLangfordAnd LittleFaringdon.htm.
'History of the School', *Watford Grammar School for Boys*, www.watfordboys.org.
Kingsford, Peter, *Victorian Lives in North Mymms*, Chapter 4, www.brookmans .com/history/kingsford4/ch4.shtml.
'Lily Burnand': freepages.genealogy.rootsweb.ancestry.com/~jgar/lily burnand music hall artist.htm.
M. H. Rackstraw's Great Winter Sale (Letterpress works, 1895), Oxford, Bodeleian Library, John Johnson Collection of Printed Ephemera, Bazaars and Sales 1 (71), in *The John Johnson Collection: An Archive of Printed Ephemera*, johnjohnson.chadwyck.com.
Oxford Dictionary of National Biography, Oxford University Press, 2004, www .oxforddnb.com.
Roberts, Andrew, '5: The Lunacy Commission', *The Lunacy Commission, A Study of its Origin, Emergence and Character*, studymore.org.uk/5s.htm.
'Rotherfield', *The Weald of Kent, Surrey and Sussex*, www.thesussexweald.org.
'Two Little Girls in Blue', *Folksongs Around the World*: ingeb.org/songs/twolittg .html.
'Upminster: Introduction and manors', *A History of the County of Essex: Volume 7* (1978), www.british-history.ac.uk.

Index

accessories
  canal men, 29–30
  costers, buttons, kerchiefs, 29–30
  groups distinguished by, 29–30
  pocket handkerchief, 30
Adam Bede (Eliot), 176–7
adult and post-school instruction, needlework, 105–7
agricultural labourers, nineteenth century, 55
agricultural overpopulation, 187
alcohol consumption, increase, 66–7
Alexander, David, 73
Alexander, Sally, 15
The Alscot Magazine, 236
Anatomy Act, 207
ancestors
  cloaks, heirlooms, 171–2
Anderson, Michael, 61–2
Andrews, Jonathan, 246–7
Anglican clergy, 194
Anglican evangelicalism, philanthropy, 193
annual clothing budget, 63
apron
  artisans, butchers, grocers, potters, 30–1
  kerchief used as, 29–30
  leather, trades, 21–2, 30–1
  pinafore replaced by, 25–6
  used to carry things, 30–1
  white, 123–5
Armstrong, Isobel, 136
Arnold, Janet, 214
Ash, Juliet, 265
Ashenburg, Katherine, 142
asylums. *See* Lunatic asylums
autobiographies
  identity, 18
  memories of clothing, 16

badging
  abolition, 189
  legal repeal ignored, 189
  parish paupers, 189
  prison, 282
Barrell, John, 12
Barthes, Roland, 7
Barthes theory of clothes, 297
Baths and Washhouses Act, 139–41
bazaars, 226–7
  Boston Antislavery Bazaar, 227
  women, business experience, 227
Bédarida, François, 8–9
Bell, Lady, 11, 69, 88, 119
Benson, John, 54, 85
The Bitter Cry of Outcast London (Mearns), 223
Blackburn Standard, 106
blanket distribution, 212
Blaug, Mark, 187
Bluecoat schools
  charity uniform stigma, humiliation, 246
  clothing provision, antiquated uniforms, 243
  Girls' uniforms, 244–6
  Select Committee 1816, 243
bonnet
  mussel gatherers, poke bonnet, 27–8
  pit-brow workers, 28
  sun, cotton, field-workers, 24
  sun bonnets, rural, 2–3, 13, 20
  women field-workers, 24
Booth, Charles, 8–11, 223, 224–5
Booth, William, 223
boots
  cast-off, 91
  children's, pawned, 85
  mending, 153–4
Boston Antislavery Bazaar, 227
Bourke, Joanna, 153–4
breeches
  drawers, 34
  trousers, 34
Breen, T. H., 5
Breward, Christopher, 6, 39–40, 181–2

331

332   Index

Brierley, Ben, 23
Bristol Mercury, 275
Brontë, Charlotte, 196
Brown, Edward, 126
budget
  annual cost of clothing, 63
  boots, 64
  colliers, 56
  commercial credit systems, 86–7
  earnings shortfall, 52–3
  example, family budget, 55
  family, 52–3
  financial management, 59–60
  food *vs* clothing, 63
  inconsistent income, 61
  individual skill, 58–9
  life cycle points, 53
  Michaelmas money, 54
  pigs, source of income, 54
  poverty line, 63
  prioritisation, 59
  replacement garments, 61
  role of men, 62–3
  role of women, 60–1
  Rowntree's model, 9–11
  rural areas, 54
  sickness, 53–4
  single men and women, 59–60
  smoking, drinking, 62–3
  sources of income, 56–7
  standard of living, 56
  strained by credit, 91–2
  tallymen, pedlars, 91–2
  textile workers, 56
  truck system, 57
  women, psychological effects, 71
Burke, Edmund, 8–9
Burman, Barbara, 152–3
Burnett, John, 8–9

Calder, F. L., 114
calico, cotton fabric, 67–8
charity
  clothing, 18
  deserving, 217–18
  evangelicalism, 18
  jumble sales, 18
  Needlework Guilds, 18
  school uniforms, 243, 246
  self-help, 217–18
charity schools
  eighteenth century, 242–3
  uniform, blue dye, cheapest, 246–7
  uniforms, 18–19, 246
  workhouses, 242–3

Chesterton, G. K., 225
children
  absence from Sunday school, 133
  of agricultural workers, 121
  appearance, school, performance, 64–5
  barefoot, 65, 164–5
  boots, pawned, 85
  cast-offs, 65–6
  charity schools, 242–3
  cleanliness, 141
  clothing theft, 81–2
  dressed like miniature adults, 24–5
  employed in factories, mines, 93–4
  employment, 133, 141
  flammable clothing, 70–1
  girls' clubs, 108
  lack of shoes, missing school, 61
  leaving school, minimum age, 107–8
  needle-threading drill, 102–4
  parades, 78
  stigma of dress, 275
  Sunday, 141
  wages, family budget, 61–2
  wealthy, 216
Children's Employment Commission 1842, 55
Chinn, Carl, 11, 122–3
Christian Socialism, 18
  religious liberalism, 237–8
Christmas
  clothes sale, 219–20
  depositors, 206
  extra money, 52, 257
  gift, uniform, 257
  gifts for the poor, 220
  overtime, 55
  tradesmen, 206
church
  charity, congregational debt, 224–5
  Church of England, 106
  churchwardens, 212
  clothing societies, clergy, 212
  declining attendance, 224, 225
  educational supremacy, 224
  financial challenges, 224
  garment sales, 220–1
  maternity box, 218
  paupers, attending church, 189
  raising funds, 224–5
  shame, cleanliness, 106
Church of England, 106
Clabburn, Pamela, 5
Clark, Anna, 62–3, 95
class
  cloth cap, class symbol, 33

Index

differences, 38–9
division, the 'Great Unwashed', 142
dress, identity, 6
  'finery', 109
  gender, 14
  human beings, 11
  imitation of elite dress, 21
  rejection of modernity, 20
  symbol, 33
cleanliness
  development of germ theory, 142–3
  education, 137
  eighteenth century, 135–6
  'hygiene police', 136–7
  immersion in water 'dangerous', 135–6
  nineteenth century, 136
  privacy, 144–5
  public baths, 139–41
  underclothes, 150–1
  visible, invisible, linked, 136
  washing with water, 135–6
  water, availability, 138–9
cloaks
  ancestors, 171–2
  baptism, 171–2
  childhood, 171, 172
  children, wealthy, 216
  country attire, 23
  funeral procession, 23
  Maori, ritual use, 171, 172
clothes storage, 156–60
  chest of drawers, baskets, boxes, 158
  folded, creased appearance, 156
clothing
  advancement, 3
  annual cost, 63
  annual replacements, 64
  boots, expense, 64–5
  budget, 17
  budget, food vs, 63
  cash value of, 3
  charity, 18
  credit, role of, 17
  culture of recycling, 13
  degradation, 3
  difficulty obtaining clothing, 79–80
  eighteenth century, theft, 80–1
  funeral clothes, 86
  homeless, 3–4
  identity, 3, 161–2
  importance surpasses bodily comfort, 296–7
  issued to prisoners, 277
  low price, availability, 7
  mass production, 36, 41, 293–4
  nineteenth century, theft, 80–1
  opportunities, 3
  parades, 78
  parents, children, social status, 78–9
  pawnshops, 3
  poor family strategies, credit, pawning, 17
  priorities, 17
  prizes at events, 79–80
  production, 72
  question of ownership, 298
  ready-made, 2–3, 40, 41, 293–4
  replacement garments, 61
  respectability, 3, 159
  second-hand garments, 75–6
  self-determination, 161
  self-perception, 297
  shelter vs, 3–4
  textile trades, theft, 80–1
  used-clothes dealers, 75–6
  views of the poor on, 15–16
clothing charities
  local, 213–18
  middle, upper-class women, purpose, meaning, 221
  parochial, interrelated organisations, 220
clothing production
  elementary schools, 17
  home-made clothing, 17
  practical importance of, 17
clothing societies
  class relations, 201–5
  at close of century, 208–11
  contact between classes, 194
  earliest society, 194–5
  fines, late payment, 209
  inferior quality clothing, 209–10
  moral regulation, 199–200
  new trade practices, 208
  northern poor, 208
  regulations, 199–201
  rural pedlar, 208
  scarcity of northern, 205–8
  self-respect, reliance, 194
  spread of, 193–9
  subscriptions, gratuity, 209
  weekly deposits by the poor, 194
The Club of Queer Trades (Chesterton), 225
clubs
  blanket, 231
  boot, 231
  burial, 129
  clothing, 195–6, 198, 202–4
  clothing, member payments, 84
  coal, 197, 198

334 Index

clubs (cont.)
  footwear, 197
  girls', 108
  Manchester Lads, 138
  watch, 209
colliers, 55
  pit-head baths, 55, 140
  religious instruction, 208
  wages, 56
communal celebrations, role of dress, 16
Conolly, John, 270–1
Cooper, Selina, suffragette, 115
Coopey, Richard, 87
Corbin, Alain, 136–7, 142
corsetry, 127
costers
  buttons, 29
  heavy boots, 32
  kerchief, 30
Costume of Yorkshire (Walker), 22
The Cottager's Monthly Visitor, 7
cotton, 36–40
  ascendancy over wool, linen, 2–3
  calico, 67–8
  cambric, 36–40
  fabric, varieties, 37–8
  factory, 149
  famine, 106
  flannelette, 70–1
  fustian, 39
  health and, 69
  mass production, 36–40, 293–4
  plebeian underclothes, 36–40
  reduced price, 293
  rise of, eighteenth, early nineteenth century, 5–6
cotton famine, 106
cotton-factory workers, nineteenth century, 55
Craik, Jennifer, 242–3, 247
credit
  burial expenses, 90–1
  check trading, 83–4
  credit rotation, 84
  credit-worthiness, 86–7
  debt limits, 86
  low wages, 86–7
  mail-order, 86–7
  nineteenth century, 72
  pawning, 82–3
  pedlars, 83
  purchase of fabric, 91–2
  shopkeepers, 82–3, 86
  tallymen, 83
  unemployment, 86–7
  used to ensure respectability, 90–1
  weekly deposits, 84
  working-class credit, 87
  working-classes, extravagance, 90–1
credit, women
  budget management, 83–4
  family treasurers, 90
  household accounting, 60–1
'Crooked lives, and how they come so', 90
cross-dressing, 29
Crystal Palace, 177, 244–6
Cullwick, Hannah, 14, 98, 244–6
Cunnington, Phillis, 34, 253
Cunnington, Willett, 34, 253

Daily Express, 240
Daily News, 257
Davidoff, Leonore, 248
Davin, Anna, 15–16, 25, 35, 144
Davis, S., 116
de Marly, Diana, 22
death
  burial clubs, 129
  burial expenses, credit, 90–1
  burial society, Anatomy Act, 207
  mourning dress, 130
  pauper burial, 129
Destiny Obscure (Burnett), 161
Dickens, Charles, 212, 214
Dictionary of Needlework (Caulfield), 70
Digby, Anne, 203, 266–7
Dingle, A. E., 66–7
domestic servants
  box, storage, 157
  cast-off clothes, gifts, 252
  dress restriction, 250–1
  dressy, suspicious, 249–50
  employers' manuals, 249–50
  how to manage, 252
  ladies' maids, wages, 253
  numbers, males, females, 21
  off-duty dress restrictions, 257
  profession disadvantages, 258–9
  sartorial assimilation, 45
  Servant Question, 258
  stays, corset, 23
  uniforms, 18–19, 254–5
Dorcas society, 216
drawers
  children, 34–6
  inmates, 34–6
  nineteenth century, 33, 34–6
  women, 34–6
dress
  clothes of the poor, 12–13

Index 335

cultural context, 5
displacement of traditional, 23
economic context, 5
history of, 4
identity, 4
non-elite, 4–7
ostracism, role of, 16
recycled clothing of the poor, 11–12
sources of data, 14
working-class, 20–1
Dress Behind Bars (Ash), 265
dressmakers, reasons for choosing profession, 258–9
dustmen, breeches, distinctive costume, 23

education
  children, school, lack of shoes, 61
  cleanliness, 137
  Education Act, 1870, 224
  girls, mathematics and science, 114
  grant-aided schools, 99–100
  income from sewing students, 99
  needlework, status of, 99–100
  needlework in schools, 97
  state grants, 98–9
  structured courses, 98–9
  tuition, 98–9
  utilitarian skills, needlework, 101
effeminacy
  socially superior dress, 50
  umbrellas, 50
eighteenth century
  charity schools, 242–3
  cleanliness, 135–6
  clothing theft, 80–1
  emulation, 45–6
  itinerant trade, 83
  main retail market, 76
  Old Clothes Exchange, 75–6
  pedlars, 82–3
  plebeian fashions, 5
  regional dress, 26
  second-hand garments, 75–6
  trousers *vs* breeches, 22
  white linen, 135–6
  women, household accounting, 60–1
eighteenth century, late
  typical dress, non-elite men, 21–2
  typical dress, non-elite women, 22–3
elderly
  paupers, leniency, Poor Law, 288–9
  permission to wear own clothes, 272–8
  poverty, stigma of dress, 275

Royal Commission on the Aged Poor, 275–6
  workhouses, 275
elementary schools
  clothing production, 17
  curricula, domestic skills, 104
  grant-aided schools, 99–100
  laundry, 154
  needlework, 99–100
  student teacher ratio, needlework, 112–13
Eliot, George, 176–7
emigrants, voyage, 134
employer-servant relationship, 248
employment
  servants, alternative opportunities, 248
  women, declining church attendance, 225
  women and children, 133
  working-class women, staff retention, 258
emulation
  budgetary constraints, 48–9
  elite dress styles, 46, 48–9
  exemplary conduct, 199–200
  of lower-class by upper-class, 45–6
  masculinity, 167
  nineteenth century, 45–6
  novelty *vs*, 48
  peer equality, 258
  peers, 199–200
  social and economic improvement, 45–6
  theory, negated, 46
  wool suit, worn by working-class, 45
Engels, Friedrich, 39, 68, 80, 118, 135–6
England, Scotland, & Ireland (Pyne), 26
English slums, 136–7
English sumptuary legislation, class separation, 6
Entwistle, Joanne, 132
Essay on Corsetry (Howell), 111
eugenists
  domesticity, maternity, 104
  women, 104
evangelical attitudes, clothing, 144–5
evangelicalism, charity, 18
Every Woman's Encyclopaedia, 157, 181
Excise Tax on glass, 182
Eyles, Leonora, 64
Eyre, Jane, 266

fabric
  calico, 67–8
  class differences, 38–9
  colourful, 250–1

fabric (cont.)
  cotton, health and, 69
  cotton, washable, 67–8
  fashionable types of, 253
  flammable, 295
  flannel, 67–8
  flannel, health benefits, 68
  flannelette, 67–8
  fustian, social hierarchy, 39
  leather, replacement of, 67–8
  linen, 67–8
  non-washable, 153
  pedlars, 293
  political connotations of, 39
  silk, 56
  stains, 153
  velvet, social hierarchy, 39
  wool, infants, 69
  wool-trade vigilantes, 67–8
Factories Inquiries Commission 1833, 55
factory work, moral effect of, 149
factory workers
  children employed in, 93–4
  girls, 258–9
  sewing school for, 107
  standard of living, 56
Family Economist, 257
farmer employers, 202
femininity
  feminist historians, 120
  model of, 165–6
  needlework, 17
  sewing, 94
  working-class, 99–100
feminist history. See also Women
  controllability of women, 7
  identity, 4
  women's domestic role, 120
Finn, Margot, 84–5
fishwomen, French, 126–7
flammable clothing, 70–1
flannel, 68–9
flannelette, 70–1
Flugel, J. C., 39–40
Fontaine, Laurence, 26, 82–3, 88
food *vs* clothing, 63
Foster, Vanda, 27
Foucault, Michel, 12, 247, 272
Fowler, Christina, 77–8
Freeman, Flora, 108
Frisby, Minnie, 35, 257
funeral
  burial clubs, 129
  burial expenses, credit, 90–1
  burial society, Anatomy Act, 207

cloaks, 23
clothes, 86
  mourning dress, 130
  pauper burial, 129
Fussell, G. E., 5
fustian, 39

Gagnier, Reginia, 168, 174
George VI, 1–2
Ginsburg, Madeleine, 13, 32, 225–6, 230–1
Gittins, Diana, 272
The Glasgow Herald, 70
glass
  camera lens, 177
  fascination with, 177
  looking glass, 176–7
  manufacture, 161–2
  plate-glass window, 161–2
Glennie, John D., 98
Godley, Andrew, 115
Goffin, Arthur, 121
grants
  arithmetic, 100
  needlework, 98
  reading, 100
Granville, J. Mortimer, 268–9
Graphic, 236
Green-Lewis, Jennifer, 182
Greenwood, James, 24
Grey, Edwin, 78

handkerchief, 22, 30, 33–4
Hardie, Keir, 33
Harris, Jose, 60–1
Harte, Negley, 5
Hartwell, Max, 11
hats
  bowler, 33
  cloth cap, class symbol, 33
  glazed oilcase hat, 80
  hat pins, danger to patients, 270
  hatless, social significance, 125
  ostrich feather, 170
  prizes, 80
  silk hats, 240
  straw hat, 244
  tall silk hat, 33
  wedding present, 170
Helland, Janice, 223, 229
Henare, Amiria, 171–2
Hiley, Michael, 126–7
Hilton, George, 57
Himmelfarb, Gertrude, 8–9
Hints from an Inspector of Schools (Glennie), 98

Index

historians
  drawers, nineteenth-century, 34
  non-elite dress, 4–5
Holdenby, Christopher, 24
Home Arts and Industry Association, 108–9
homeless clothing, 3–4
Homely Hints for District Visitors (Stacpoole), 69
home-made clothing
  underclothes, 94
  women and children, 94
Honeyman, Katrina, 45–6
Household Management (Beeton), 253
Howard, John, 278
Howell, M. J., 111

identity
  autobiographies, 18, 163–4
  class, 6
  clothes, 3
  collective, 23
  creation, 18
  expression of, 161
  garments, 23
  history of dress, 4
  needlework, crucial element of, 119
  provider, recipient of clothing, 296–7
  self-confidence, 184
  self-perception, 161–2
immorality, sanitary code, 181–2
In Darkest England and the Way Out (Booth), 223
industrial proletariat, 68
industrial workers, nineteenth century, 55
industrialisation
  changes in non-elite dress, 6
  displacement of traditional dress, 23
  expenses of workers, 70–1
  nineteenth century, 75–6
  proletarian dress, 21
  wages, 70–1
inflation, 187
institutional uniforms *vs.* rural dress, 2–3
Instructions for Cutting Out Apparel for the Poor, 111, 194, 214–15
Items for maternity boxes, ladies' infants, 215

Jermy, Louise, 168–76
Jipping Street (Woodward), 174–5
Jones, Peter, 6
judgement about the poor, 181–2
jumble sales
  anti-slavery bazaars, transatlantic exchange, 230–41
  appearance of, 223–4
  charity, 18
  ideology of self-help, 230–1
  no capital expenditure, 233–4
  organised by women, 234–5
  profitable for church, 233–4
  rubbish into useful things, 238

Kidd, Alan, 205
King, Peter, 158
King, Steven, 6, 9, 56–7, 186–7, 275
Kingsley, Charles, 179–81
knickerbockers, petticoats replaced, 25
knitting, needlework standardisation, 100–1

Lady Bell, 11, 57–8, 60–1, 64–5, 119, 130, 134
The Lady's Economical Assistant, 99, 214–15
Lancet (Granville), 268–9
late-Victorian period, sailor suit, 25
laundry, 152–3
Leeds Mercury, 258
Lemire, Beverly, 3, 43–4, 60–1, 75–6, 80–1
Levitt, Sarah, 27, 36–40
Loane, Martha, 118
London
  fairs, 226–7
  fashion, 44–5
London Labour and the London Poor (Mayhew), 8
Lunacy Commissioners, 265
lunatic asylums, 266–72
  deficiencies, clothing, nakedness, 266
  Granville's method, 268–9
  Inspectors' reports, 270–1
  Lunatics Asylums and Pauper Lunatics Act 1845, 268
  military, prison, influence, 263–4
  moral therapy, 266–7
  nakedness, 265
  privately owned, exceptions, 266
  reward for self-control, 268–9
  Sunday dress, 265
  uniforms, 18–19, 265
  uniforms, opposition to, 268–9
  womens' dress, 269–70
lunatic asylums, workhouses, prisons, 265
  classifications, class separation, 264–5
  clothing, social integration *vs* punishment, 291–2
  military, prison, influence, 263–4
  pauper lunatic asylums, link to workhouses, 262–3

lunatic asylums, workhouses, prisons (*cont.*)
  population growth, male dominated, 261–2
  reform programme, work, clothing production, 286–7
  transformation, reform, role of clothing, 261
  uniforms, punitive purpose, 261

Management of Servants, 254–5
Maori, 171
Martineau, Harriet, 34
masculinity
  consumption, 6
  effeminacy, 118
  emasculating institutional dress, 270–1
  institutional dress, emasculating, 270–1
  men dressed as women, 29
  ritual of 'breeching', 24–5
  sewing, 117
  socially superior dress, 50
  umbrellas, 50
  waterman, 167
mass consumption, 19
mass production
  boys' clothing, 25
  cotton, 36–40, 293–4
Maternity Society, 218
Mayhew, Henry, 29–30, 75–6, 81–2, 110–11, 258
Maynard, Margaret, 134, 145–6, 285–6
McLeod, Hugh, 224, 225
Meacham, Standish, 121
Mearns, Andrew, 223
menstruation
  pessaries, pads, 151
  problematic, taboo, 152
  sanitary towels, 150
  technologies, nineteenth-century, 150–1
Miller, Daniel, 2, 296
Miller, Herbert, 258–9
milliners
  appearance of, 43
  payment, 78–9
  reasons for choosing profession, 258–9
  wages, 43
miners
  female, 93
  standard of living, 56
  Sunday school, 133
  truck shops, 57
mirrors
  nineteenth-century, 136

sense of individualism, 177
small *vs* large, 176–7, 181
Mitchell, Hannah, 157
Morning Chronicle, 53–4
Moses and Son, 40, 75–6
The Most Solitary of Afflictions (Scull), 265
mothers, unmarried, 289
mothers' meetings, 218–23
  patronising attitude, 219
Munby, Arthur, 20–1, 23, 57–8, 73, 123, 244–6
Murphy, Elaine, 262
museum collections, 13
mussel gatherers, women, masculine dress, 27–8

nakedness, 149–50
  asylums, 265
  evangelical attitudes, 144–5
  working-class attitude, unremarkable, 149–50
  in workplaces, hot mills, 144–5
National Penitentiary at Millbank, 279
needlework
  basic garments, 96
  female inmates, 97
  girls' clubs, 108
  grants, 101
  informal learning, 97
  instruction, 119
  learned as domestic servant, 97
  men, 117
  patterns, 111
  professional tailors, 117
  separate subject of education, 101
  sewing, mending, 96
  simple garments, 101
  skills, 110–11
  tuition for boys, 118
  women, budget contribution, 95–6
Needlework Guilds, 225–30
  appearance of, 223–4
  aristocratic women's involvement, 229
  countries located in, 225–6
  effects of, 223–4
  efficient, reaction against bazaars, 226
  ideology of self-help, 230–1
  non-denominational, 225–6
  orphanages, 225–6
  systematic clothing distribution, 225–6
Needlework Prize Associations, 101–2, 105–6
new clothing, status, 19
New Code of Regulations, 100–1
New Historicism, 14

Index

New Poor Law, 129
new *vs* second-hand clothing, 17
Nicholls, George, 273
nineteenth century
  agricultural labourers, 55
  alternative forms of credit, 88
  changes in the workplace, 109–10
  cleanliness, 136
  clothing theft, 80–1
  colliers, 55
  cooperatives, 91
  cotton-factory workers, 55
  credit, 72
  debate over girls and mathematics, 114
  debt crisis, 88
  drawers, standard wear, 34–6
  elite spaces, 136
  emulation, 45–6
  era of public glass, 182
  evangelicalism, 15
  fabric, class differences, 38–9
  improved retailing methods, 91
  industrial workers, 55
  industrialised production, 75–6
  living standards, 72
  lower orders, 8–9
  mass consumption, 19
  pawning, 72
  philanthropy, 15
  poor, occupational dress, 5
  sartorial change, 2–3
  sewing machines, 116
  women, household accounting, 60–1
  working-class dress, 50–1
  working-class housing, 109–10
nineteenth century, early
  main retail market, 76
  retailing opportunities, 83
  urban itinerant trade, 83
nineteenth century, late
  childbirth, conditions, 214
  lack of education, appearance, 3
  mirrors, 185
  photography, 185
  unreasonable employer demands, 181–2
  working-class budgets, 32
non-elite dress
  history, 4–7
  men, late eighteenth century, 21–2
  nineteenth-century historians, 4–5

occupational clothing, 27
  agricultural labourer, 57–8
  clerks, 57–8
  factory employee, 57–8

nineteenth-century poor, 5
office workers, 57–8
shop assistants, 57–8
uniforms, 42–3
Oeconomy of Charity (Trimmer), 251
orphanages, Needlework Guilds, 225–6
ostracism, role of dress, 16
outdoor clothing relief
  abolition, 18
  local opposition, 189–90
Oxford English Dictionary, 230–1

parish, role of, Poor Law, 6
parish clothing, 18
Parliamentary Inquiry 1833, 93–4
Paull, M. A., 66
Pauper Lunatics Act, 268
paupers
  branding, Poor Law, 288–9
  burial, 129
  elderly, asylum uniforms questioned, 261
  elderly, workhouse population, 275
pawnbrokers
  clothes storage, 157
  clothing, 3
  clothing theft, 82
  debt, 86
  domestic budget management, 84–5
  evangelical beliefs, 89
  Factories Inquiries Commission, 89
  illness, pawning, 89
  independence *vs* parish relief and charity, 89
  nineteenth century, 84–5
  rural counties, 84–5
  sailors, 84–5
  stamped clothing, 228
  stolen goods, 82
  stolen property, 85
  unlicensed trade, 85
pawning
  alternative forms of credit, 88
  children's clothes, 85
  credit and, 72
  pledges, 82, 89, 298
  shortage of coinage, 88
  Sunday clothes, 85, 86, 157
  used to ensure respectabliity, 90–1
Payne, Christina, 9
peer pressure, social aspiration, 50
Pember Reeves, Maud, 52–3, 63, 70–1, 88, 114–15
penny clothing society, 297–8

petticoats
  breeches, 27–8, 46
  children, 25
  expensive, 123–5
  factory injuries, 113
  mussel gatherers, 25, 27–8
  recycling old garments, 69
  replaced by shorts, knickerbockers, 25
philanthropy
  Anglican evangelicalism, 15, 193
  'Crusade' against outdoor relief, 198
  needlework, 212
  women, 212
Phoebe's Marriage, or, The Perils of Dress, 89
photograph, 182
pit-brow workers, distinctive dress, 27
the poor
  clothing, culture of recycling, 13
  clothing, makeshift economy, 297–8
  dress goal, to pass unnoticed, 299
  sartorial judgement about, 181–2
  shame of dirtiness, 180
  their own voices, 15–16
  utter incomprehension of, 298–9
  view on clothing, 15–16
Poor House (Nicholls), 273
Poor Law
  Amendment Act 1834, 186–7, 190–1
  baby clothes refused, workhouse, 192–3
  burial, 129
  charity, clothing provision, 288–9
  clothing, 186–7
  clothing clubs, proliferation, 194–5
  coffins and grave clothes, 129
  concepts of poverty, 288–9
  elderly, 288–9
  indoor relief, assistance, 186–7
  Ledbury Guardians, 192–3
  lunatic asylum, 263–4
  New, 129
  outdoor clothing relief, Commissioner opposition, 210
  outdoor relief restrictions, 195–6
  Parliamentary Reports, 189
  Parliamentary Select Committee on the Operation of, 189
  pauper branding, 288–9
  penny clothing societies, 297–8
  poverty man-made problem, 288–9
  poverty *vs* indigence, 8–9
  role of parish, 6
  social stratification, 6
  uniforms, 261
  unmarried mothers, 289
  Victorian society, 210–11
Poor Law Unions, 289
population, England, Wales, 21
Portfolio of Monthly Fashions (Howell), 111
Potter, Beatrix, 30
potters
  attire, 31
  children, employment, 133
  hierarchy, 131
  women, 133
poverty
  alternating cycles, 9–11
  bespoke services, 78
  clothing theft, 81–2
  cost of living, 52–3
  craftwork, 108–9
  dangers of, 223
  debt, 86
  definition of, 8–9
  deprivation, 11
  deserving help, 217–18
  difficulty obtaining clothing, 79–80
  early nineteenth century, 9
  flammable clothing, 70–1
  food *vs* clothing, 63
  funeral clothes, 86
  Hartwell's model, 11
  highest risk, 9–11
  human creation, rather than divine, 295
  indigence, distinction, 8–9
  indigence, *vs*, 8–9
  inflation, 187
  life cycle points, 53
  material realities of, 181–2
  mirrors, 185
  pauper burial, 129
  perceived as problem, 223
  photography, self-image, 185
  physical needs, 9–11
  poor quality garments, 91
  psychological effects, women, 71
  Rag Fair, 76
  Rowntree's model, 9–11
  rural, 56
  rural areas, 54
  sharing resources, 80
  skilled artisans, 56
  social status, clothing, 78–9
  standard of living, 56
  stolen goods, property, 82, 85
  subsistence, normative, relative, 11
  temporary clothes, 86
  vestimentary vicious circle, 296
  women, psychological effects, 71
Preston Plug Plot Riots, 30

Index

prison, 278–83
  badge, 283
  clothing, used as resistance, 285–6
  clothing issued to prisoners, 277
  dress as punishment, 287–8, 289
  fetters, straitjackets, refractory prisoners, 290
  institutional blueprint, badging, 282
  reform, 278
  rules, men, women, 283
  uniforms, 18–19
  uniforms, Prison Act 1877, 281
  uniforms, introduction, 279
  withholding clothing as punishment, 291
  women, scandals, 285–6
Prison Act, 281
privacy, the poor, 144
Prochaska, Frank, 226–7
proletarian dress, industrialisation, 21
public baths, 139–41
Pyne, W. H., 26, 82–3

Queen Anne period, 244
Queen Victoria, 47
Queen's Theatre, Long Acre, 256

ready-made clothing, 40
  available to the masses, 50–1
  bespoke suits, 74–5
  cotton, 2–3
  marketing strategies, 74–5
  provincial clothing factories, 74
  rural areas, 74
  shops, 74
Reay, Barry, 60–1, 83–4
regional dress, variation, 27
relief, poor, 275–6
respectability, responsibility, 121
  absence of certain garments, 125
  appearance, 122
  apron, white, 123–5
  cleanliness, 17–18, 122
  clothing, fundamental pillar, 121
  family enterprise, 121–2
  the 'Great Unwashed', 142
  lack of garments, 17–18
  manual labourers, 122
  role of clothing, 6
  Sunday best, 17–18, 130–1
  white collar, 122
retail
  bespoke customers, 77–8
  bread and flour societies, 73
  clothing trade, 73
  co-operative societies, 74
  department store, 73
  direct selling, 74–5
  dressmakers, 77–8
  eighteenth century, 75–6
  fairs, 72–3
  industrialised production, 75–6
  instalment system, 83
  mail-order, 74–5, 84
  market facilities, 72–3
  marketing strategies, 74–5
  markets, northern working-class, 73
  new clothing, 17
  new opportunities, 77–8
  nineteenth century, 72
  nineteenth century, early, 83
  Old Clothes Exchange, 75–6
  pedlars, 82–3
  purchase clubs, 84
  Rag Fair, 76
  ready-made clothing, availability, 78
  sales strategies, 72–3
  second-hand garments, 75–6
  selling on credit, 84
  shipping second-hand garments, 75–6
  tailors, 77–8
  unlicensed trade, 85
  used-clothes dealers, 75–6
  village shops, 73
  wholesale, 72–3
  wholesale bespoke production, 74–5
  working-class clothing, 73
Riello, Giorgio, 109–10
riots
  Poor Law, 210
  Preston Plug Plot Riots, 30
  social crisis, 223
  Swing riots, 202
Roberts, Robert, 59–60, 69, 153
Rochdale Friendly Co-operative Society, 74
Roche, Daniel, 24–5, 136, 278–83
The Romance of a Rag (Paull), 66
Rose, Clare, 6, 16, 19, 25, 59, 91, 122–3
Rosevear, Elizabeth, 104
Ross, Ellen, 62–3, 64–5, 80
Rowntree, Seebohm, 8–11, 64, 114–15
  life cycle points, 53
Rowntree's model, 9–11
Royal Commission on the Aged Poor, 275–6
Rublack, Ulinka, 3
Rule, John, 56
rural dress, middle-class nostalgia, 6

Russell, Charles, 3

sailors
  autobiography, 163-4
  pawnbrokers, 84-5
  sewing, 117
  uniform, 167
The Sampler, 98-9
sartorial underclass, 294
satin
  fashionable ladies, 253
  wedding dress, 47-8
The Scarcity of Domestic Servants (Miller), 258-9
School Board of London, 105-6
school(s)
  adult needlework classes, 105-6
  Bluecoat, 243
  curricula, 104
  evening classes, adult, 105-6
  funded by relief committees, 106
  girls, mathematics and science, 114
  income from sewing students, 99
  needlework taught in, 97
  revised Education Codes, 102-4
  sewing schools, 106
  uniforms, 247
  uniforms, psychological effect, 18-19
  universal elementary education, 98
  utilitarian skills, 101
Scott, Fred, 56
Scull, Andrew, 265
self
  adornment, peer-equality, 258, 260
  awareness, full-length mirror, photography, 18, 177, 182
  confidence, 184
  control, 268-9
  definition, clothing means to, 19
  discipline, 101-2
  help, independent, 207
  inner, social, subdued by uniforms, 242
  perception, new-forms, 177
  respect, reliance, 194
  sartorial perception of, 161-2
  self-help schemes, clothing society, 194
self-determination, cultural importance, 18
servant docility, 247
servants, decoration, peer respect, 258-9
sewing classes, social divide, 107
sharing clothes to pawn, 80
Shaw, Charles, 121
Sims, George, 137
Smith, Adam, 11
Smith, Virginia, 142-3

smock, urban, rural use, 24
Snell, Keith, 15-16
social crisis, 1880s, 223
social status, clothing, 78-9
social stratification, providential, 6
societies
  Bible, circulation, 212
  burial society, Anatomy Act, 207
  soup distribution, 212
Spufford, Margaret, 4-5, 26, 67-8
Stacpoole, Florence, 69
standard of living, skilled artisans, 56
Startling Disclosures!, 284
status, new clothing, 19
stays, 127
Steedman, Carolyn, 127
Steele, Valerie, 126
Stepney Meeting Magazine, 90
stockings, 125-6
Styles, John, 4, 5, 26, 38-9, 52-3, 68
Summerscale, Kate, 249-50
Sunday
  Charity Sunday, 78, 121
  clothes, pawning, 85, 86, 157
  clothes, working-class, 131
  crinoline dresses, 127
  parades, 78
  pawned, Sunday suit, 66-7
  Rag Fair, 76
  'Sunday best', lack of, 134
  worn only on Sunday, holidays, 131-2
Sunday school
  Anglican, 132
  appearance in, 132
  children, absence from, 133
  modesty and obedience, 251
  needlework prohibited by Sabbath, 98
  workhouse clothes, 132
Suzuki, Akihito, 61, 263-4, 272
Swing riots, 202

Taylor, Alice, 234-5
Taylor, Lou, 4
Teachers' Manual of Elementary Laundry Work (Calder), 114
Terry, Joseph, 162-7
The Times, 192-3, 226-7
Toplis, Alison, 6, 78, 82
Tozer, Jane, 27
Trimmer, Sarah, 250-1
trousers, masculine dress, women, 28
truck system, 57

Index 343

Trusler's Domestic Management, 249–50, 252
Tudor dress, 243
Tufnell, Edward, 52–3

Ugolini, Laura, 6, 74–5
underclass, sartorial, 19
underclothing
  clean, 136
  cotton, 38
  linen, 38
  pessaries, pads, 151
  towels, 150
  utilitarian, 225–6
  Victorian charity clothing, 226
'Underwear' (Cocker), 1
uniforms
  asylums, 265, 268
  blue, cheap dye, 246–7
  Bluecoat schools, girls, 244–6
  charity, stigma, humiliation, 246
  charity schools, psychological effect, 18–19
  domestic servants, 18–19
  individuality vs, 242
  inmates, 18–19
  limitations on freedom, 18–19
  lunatic asylums, 18–19
  occupational clothing, 27, 42
  out of date, 244
  Poor Law, 261
  prison, 18–19, 265
  psychological effect, 18–19
  school, 247
  subservience, 18–19
  workhouses, 18–19, 265, 276–8
urbanisation
  changes in non-elite dress, 6
  crowded homes, disease, 136
  industrialisation, 50–1
  mass production, 293–4
  rise in living standards, 293–4

Veblen, Thorstein, 131
vestimentary vicious circle, 296
Vickery, Amanda, 157
Victorian society, Poor Law, 210–11
Victorian women, 126
Vigarello, Georges, 136
Vincent, David, 162, 176

wages, truck system, 57
waistcoats, 149
Walker, George, 22, 26
Walkowitz, Judith, 225, 235–6

wardrobes, 157
  pre-marriage, 60
The Water Babies (Kingsley), 179–81
water supply, 138–9
waterman, masculinity, 167
Weatherill, Lorna, 11–13
wedding
  blue, 48
  bridegroom, 47
  bridesmaids, 47, 48
  clothes reused, 48
  dressmaker, 47
  elite fashion, 47
  grey, 47
  white weddings, 47–8
Weldon's Home Dressmaker for Striped Materials, 113
welfare professionals, 225–6
wesht, 134
white collar, 30–1
  respectability, 122–3
Wigan pit-brow girls, 123, 127
Without a Penny in the World, A Story of the 'Period' (Keats), 116
Wohl, Anthony, 142
The Woman Who Murdered Black Satin (Borowitz), 252–3
women
  anti-slavery campaign, 229–30
  budget managers, resource management, 295
  corsetry, 127
  domestic role, 120
  employed in agriculture, 93–4
  employed in mines, 93–4
  fair wage, 95
  feminist historians, 120
  field-workers, 24
  industrial employment, 95
  masculine dress, mussel gatherers, 27–8
  menstruation, 150–1
  middle-class, leisure time, activities, 225
  needlework, budget contribution, 95–6
  political voice, philanthropy and, 229–30
  poverty, psychological effects, 71
  productive leisure time, needlework, 104
  rights, 152
  shopping, 235–6
  single, pre-marriage wardrobe, 60
  suffragette, 152
  Victorian, 126
  weavers, income, 95
Women's Co-operative Guild, 219

Woodward, Kathleen, 174–5
wool
  colds, rheumatism, 69
  flannel, 68–9
  infants, 69
  shrinkage, 70
  stockings, 69
  underwear, 70
Worcestershire Chronicle, 192–3
workhouses, 272–8
  depersonalising uniform dress, 276–8
  designated lunatics in, 262
  dress, sartorial humiliation, exclusion, 132
  moral reform, rough clothes, 274
  special wards, 262
  test of destitution, 191
  uniforms, 18–19, 265
  workhouse clothing, humiliation, 274–5
  yellow, colour of disgrace, 289

working-class
  exclusion of women from workforce, 95
  femininity, 99–100
  men, fustian, 38–9
  purchasing power, 84
  respectability, 95
  women, utilitarian domesticity, 105–6
working-class dress, 20–1
  budgets, boots, 32
  changes with urbanisation, industrialisation, 17, 21
  cotton, 17
  elite imitation, repeated claim, 21
  girls, clothing changes, adulthood, 25–6
  Sunday clothes, 131
  surplus clothing, 131
workmates, 295
Workwoman's Guide, 110, 214–15
Worth, Rachel, 6, 13

yellow, colour of disgrace, 289
Young, Arthur, 52–3

Printed in Great Britain
by Amazon